Snow Drop

Volume Ten
by Choi Kyung-ah

English Adaptation
by Sarah Dyer

OWAC

D0111137

JAN 2012

HAMBURG // LONDON // LOS ANGELES // TOKYO

Snow Drop Vol. 10
created by Choi Kyung-ah

Translation - Jennifer Hahm
English Adaptation - Sarah Dyer
Retouch and Lettering - Benchcomix
Production Artist - Irene Woori Choi
Cover Design - Thea Willis

Editor - Julie Taylor
Digital Imaging Manager - Chris Buford
Production Managers - Jennifer Miller and Mutsumi Miyazaki
Managing Editor - Jill Freshney
VP of Production - Ron Klamert
Publisher and E.I.C. - Mike Kiley
President and C.O.O. - John Parker
C.E.O. - Stuart Levy

A **TOKYOPOP** Manga

TOKYOPOP Inc.
5900 Wilshire Blvd. Suite 2000
Los Angeles, CA 90036

E-mail: info@TOKYOPOP.com
Come visit us online at www.TOKYOPOP.com

ISBN: 1-59532-046-6

First TOKYOPOP printing: August 2005
10 9 8 7 6 5 4 3 2 1
Printed in the USA

Previously in

Snow Drop

Two years have passed, and
So-Na convinces Hwi-Rim to go
to Hollywood with her to find
Hae-Gi once and for all. Will
their love stand the test of time?
Can So-Na forget the promise
she made to Hae-Gi's mother--
and be true to her heart?

C·O·N·T·E·N·T·S

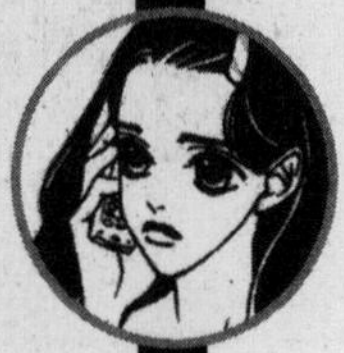

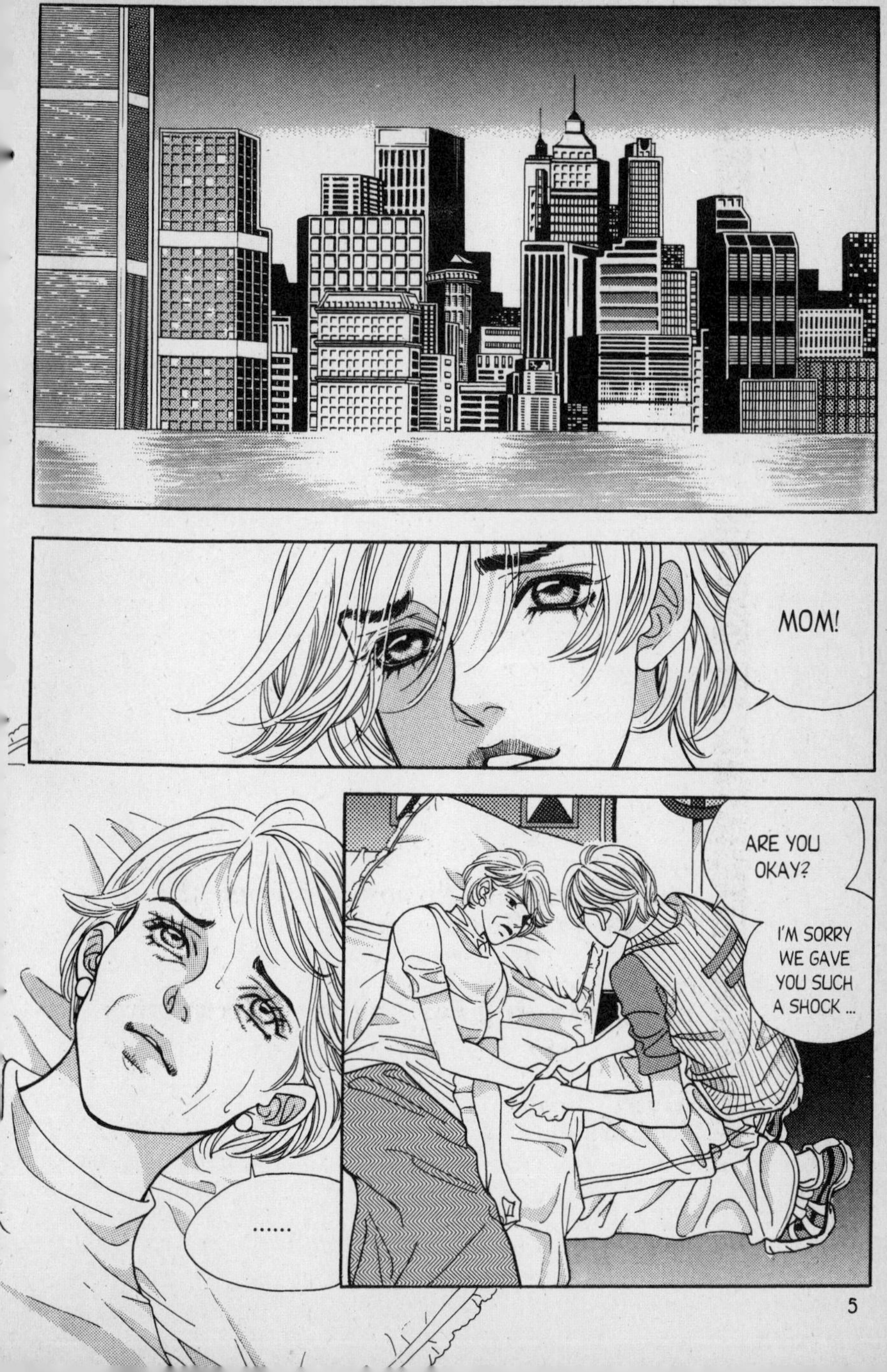
MOM!
......
ARE YOU OKAY?
I'M SORRY WE GAVE YOU SUCH A SHOCK ...

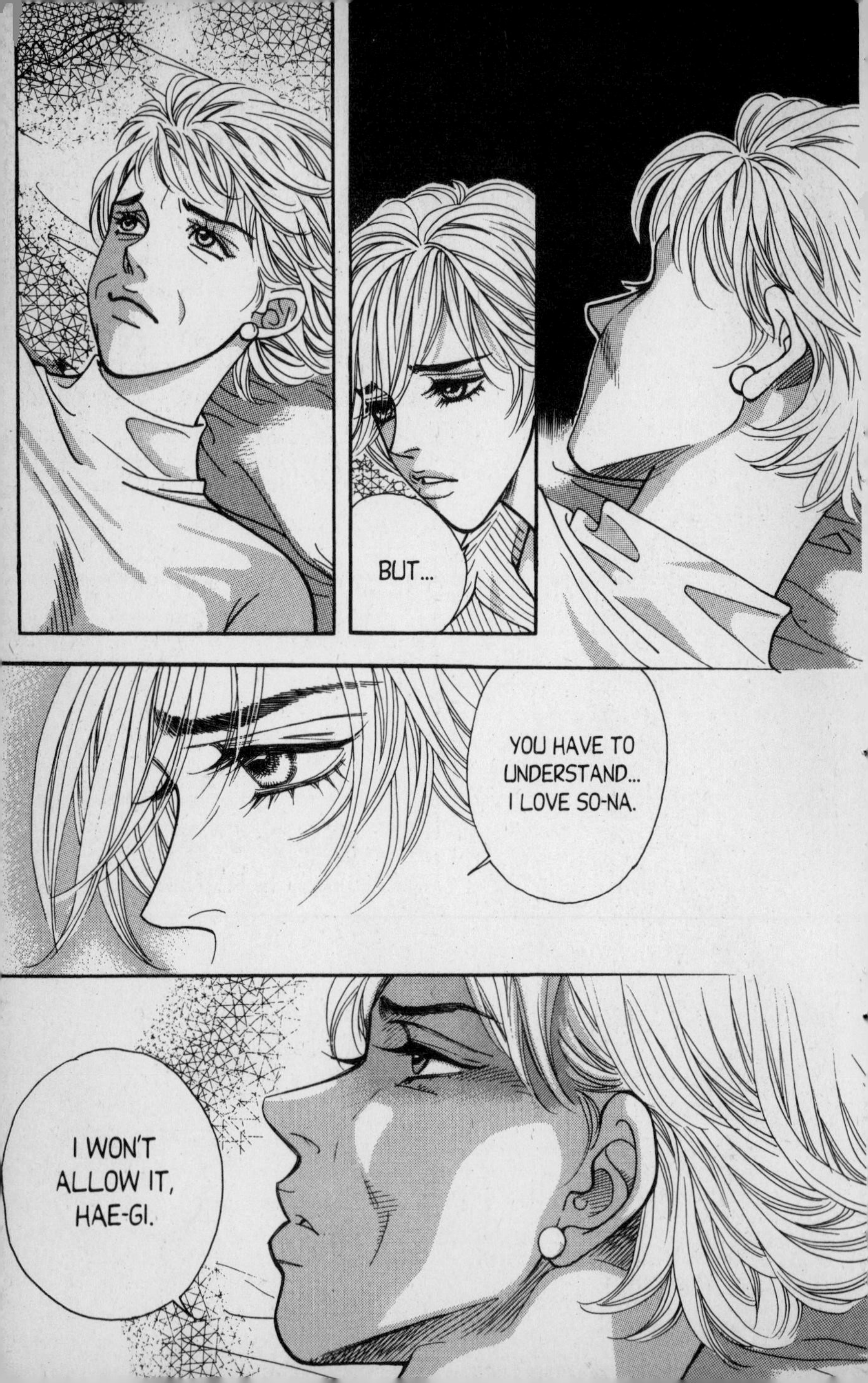
BUT...
YOU HAVE TO UNDERSTAND... I LOVE SO-NA.
I WON'T ALLOW IT, HAE-GI.

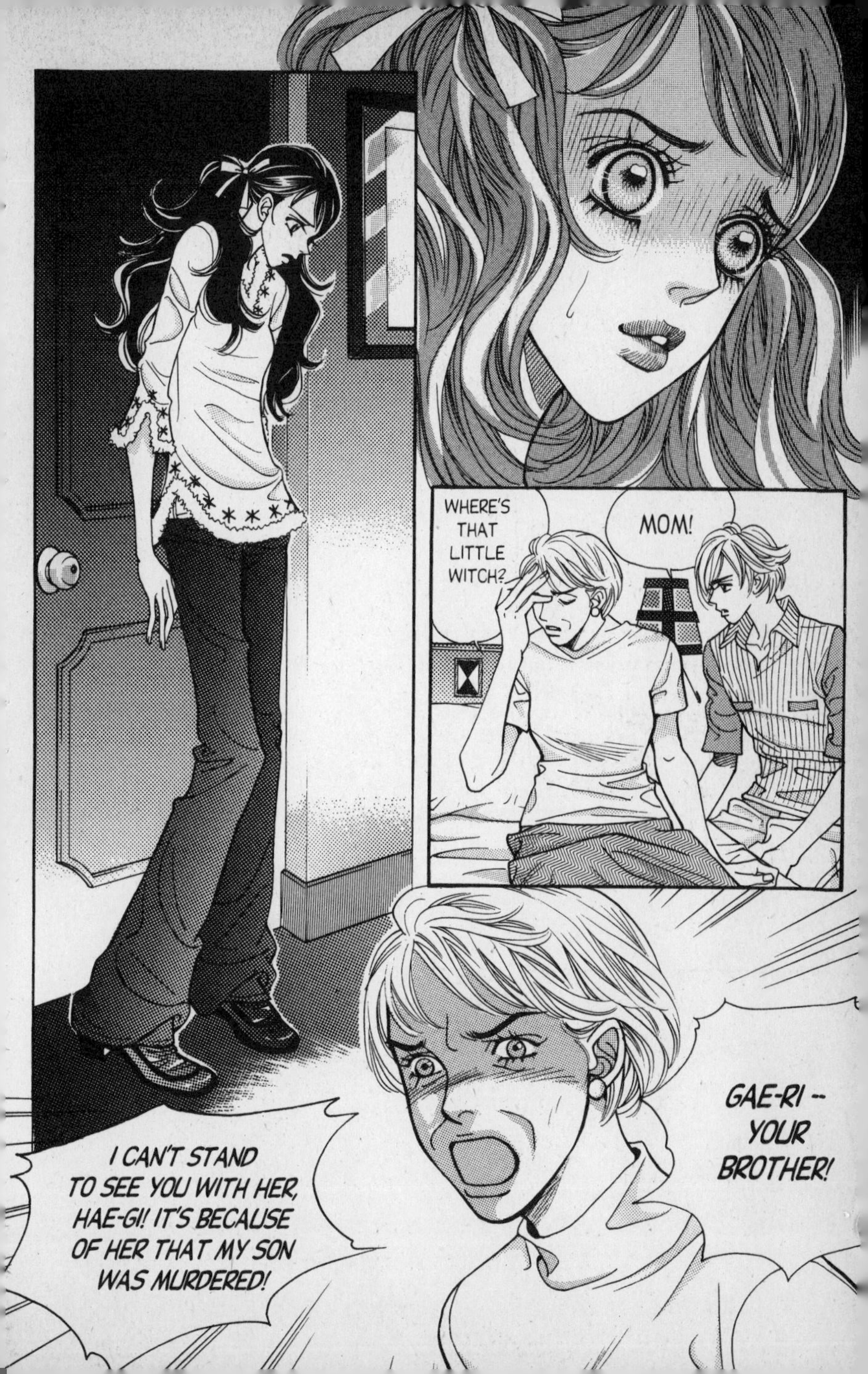
WHERE'S THAT LITTLE WITCH?
MOM!
I CAN'T STAND TO SEE YOU WITH HER, HAE-GI! IT'S BECAUSE OF HER THAT MY SON WAS MURDERED!
GAE-RI -- YOUR BROTHER!

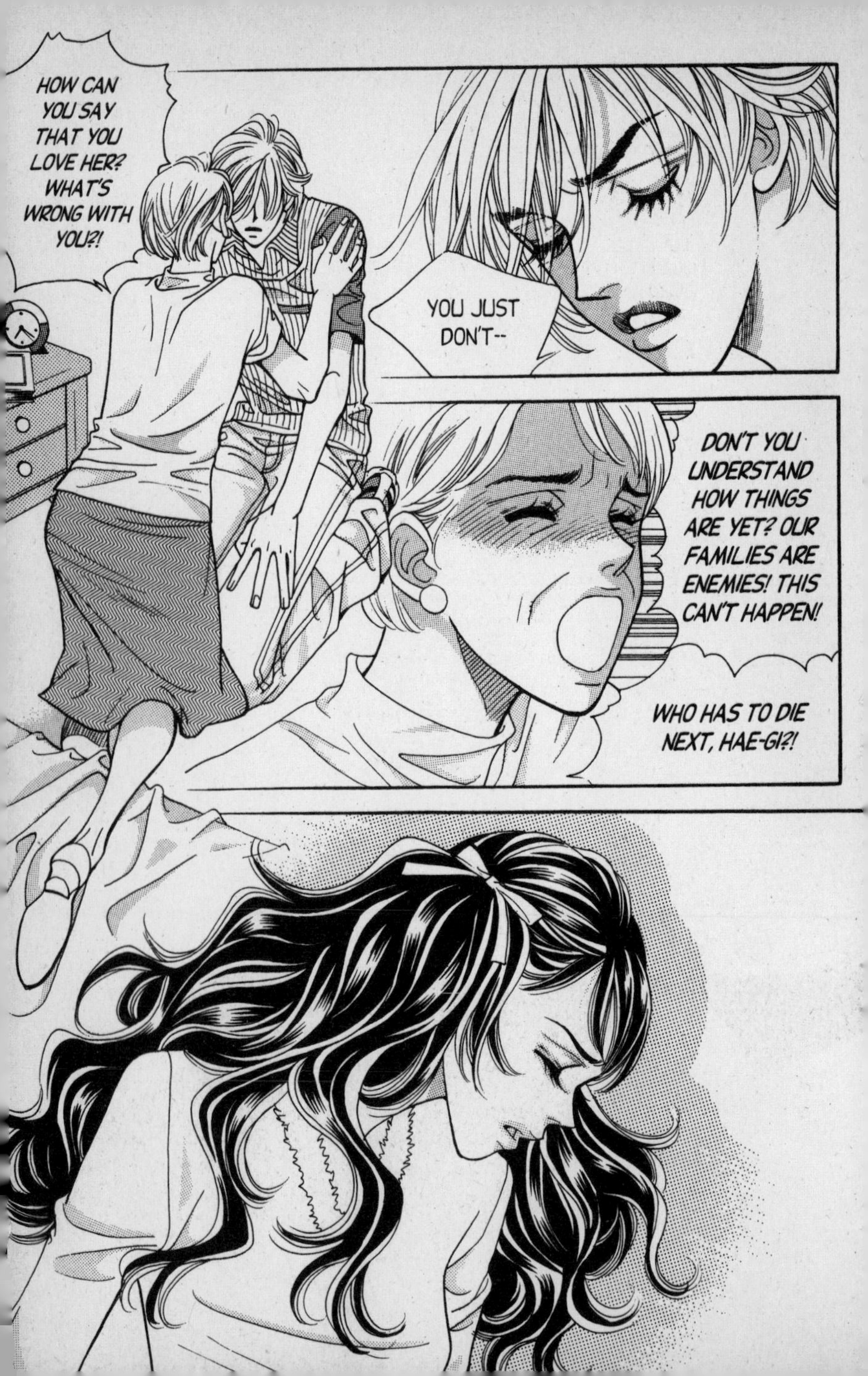
HOW CAN YOU SAY THAT YOU LOVE HER? WHAT'S WRONG WITH YOU?!
YOU JUST DON'T--
DON'T YOU UNDERSTAND HOW THINGS ARE YET? OUR FAMILIES ARE ENEMIES! THIS CAN'T HAPPEN!
WHO HAS TO DIE NEXT, HAE-GI?!

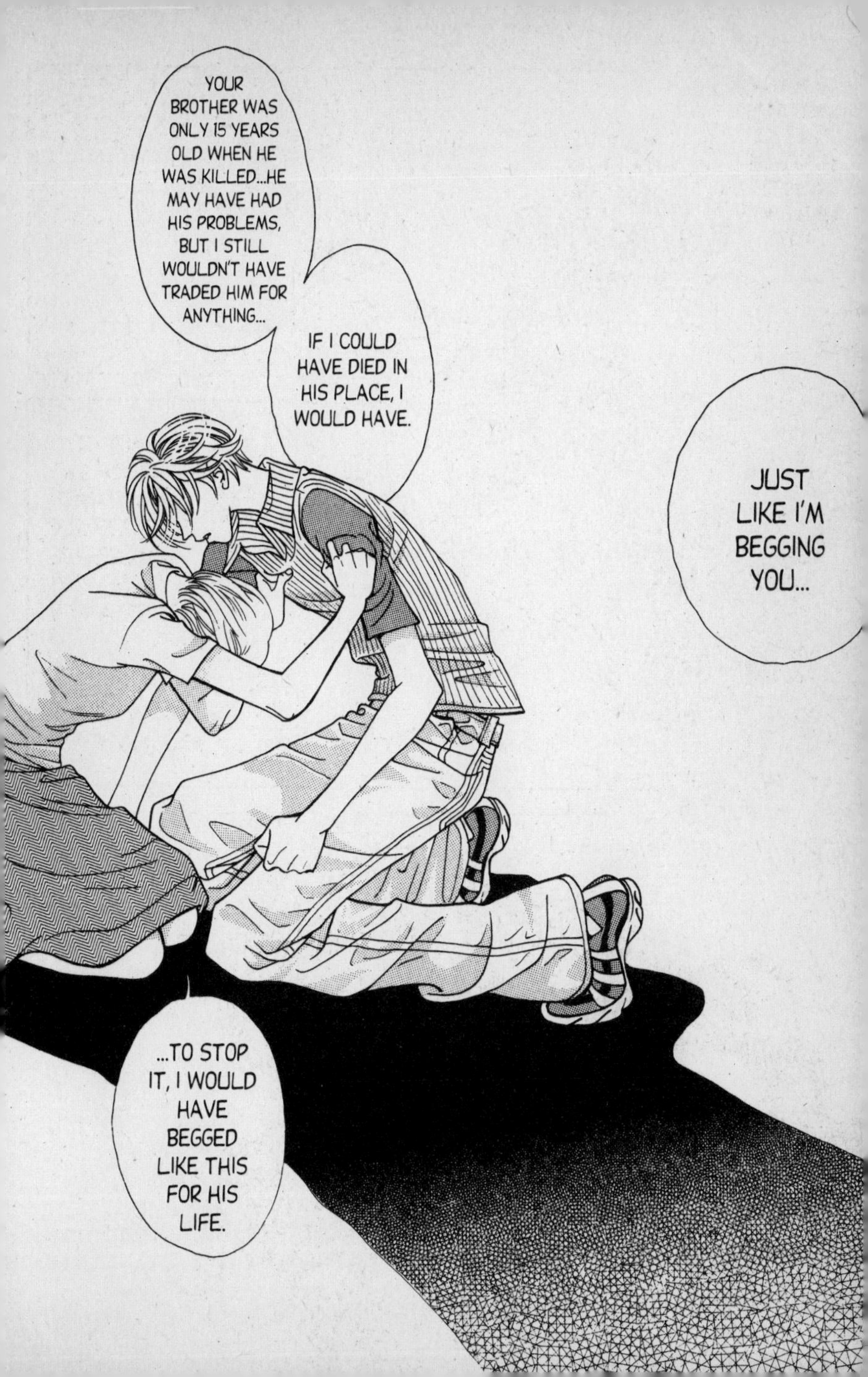
YOUR BROTHER WAS ONLY 15 YEARS OLD WHEN HE WAS KILLED...HE MAY HAVE HAD HIS PROBLEMS, BUT I STILL WOULDN'T HAVE TRADED HIM FOR ANYTHING...
IF I COULD HAVE DIED IN HIS PLACE, I WOULD HAVE.
JUST LIKE I'M BEGGING YOU...
...TO STOP IT, I WOULD HAVE BEGGED LIKE THIS FOR HIS LIFE.

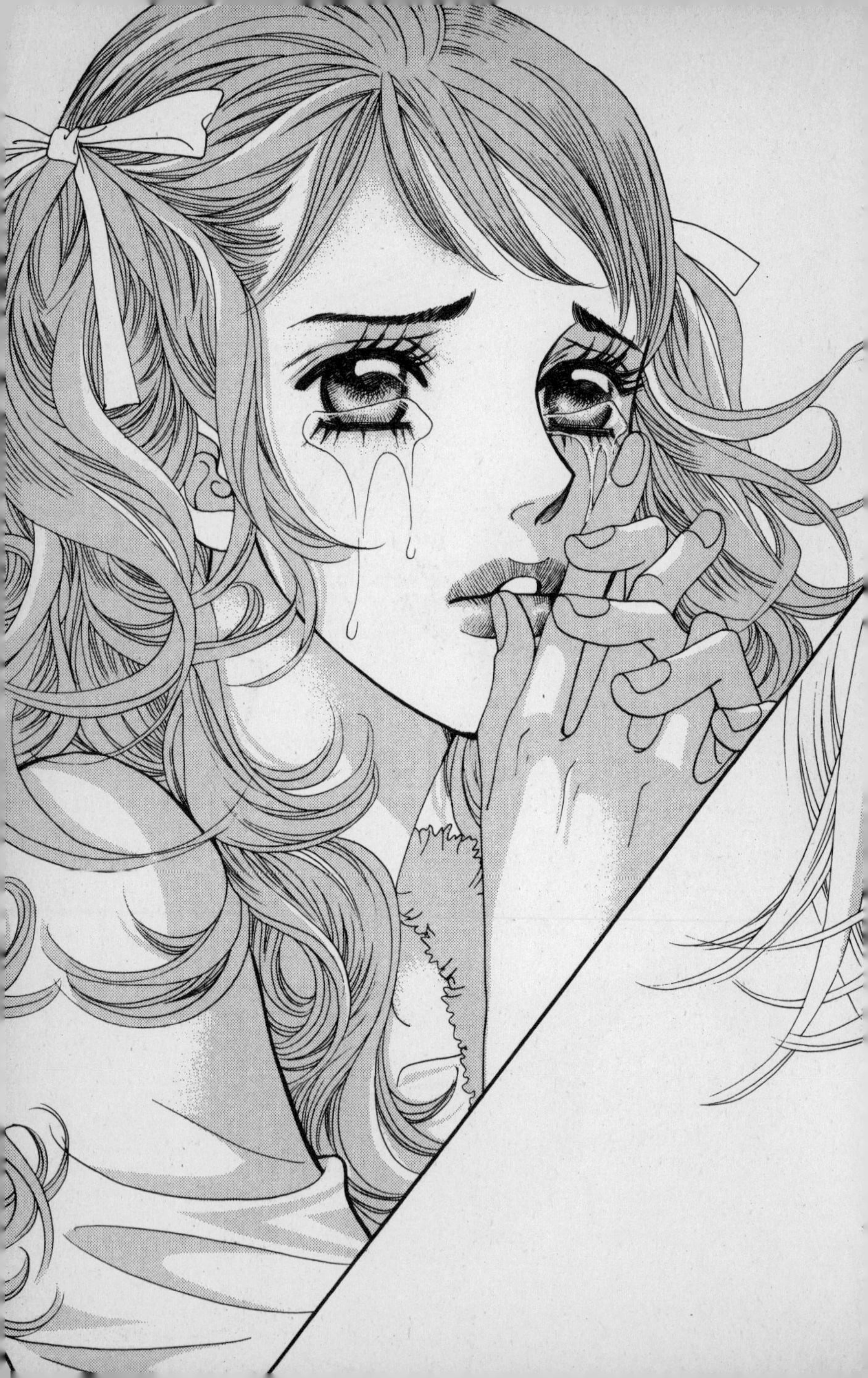

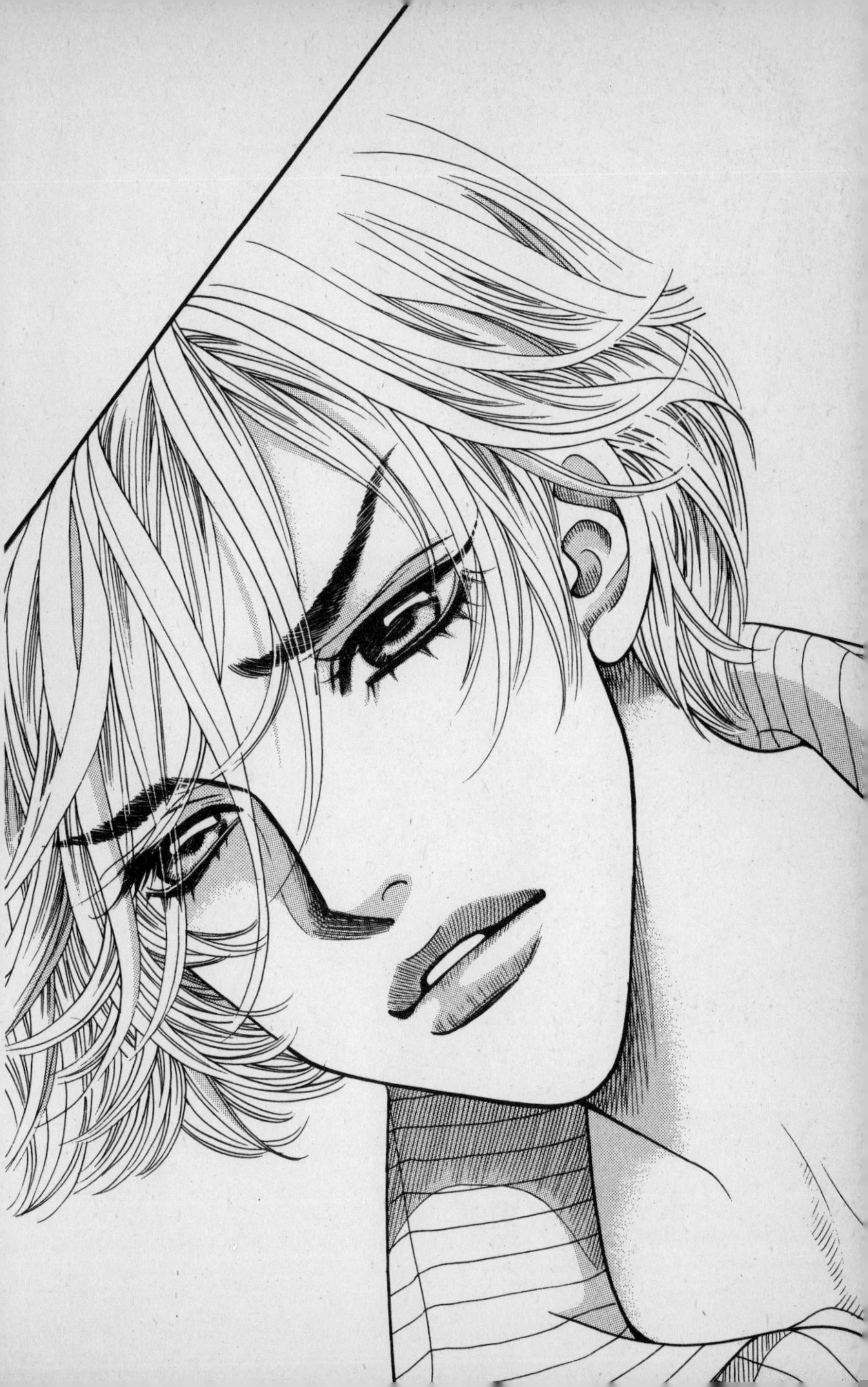

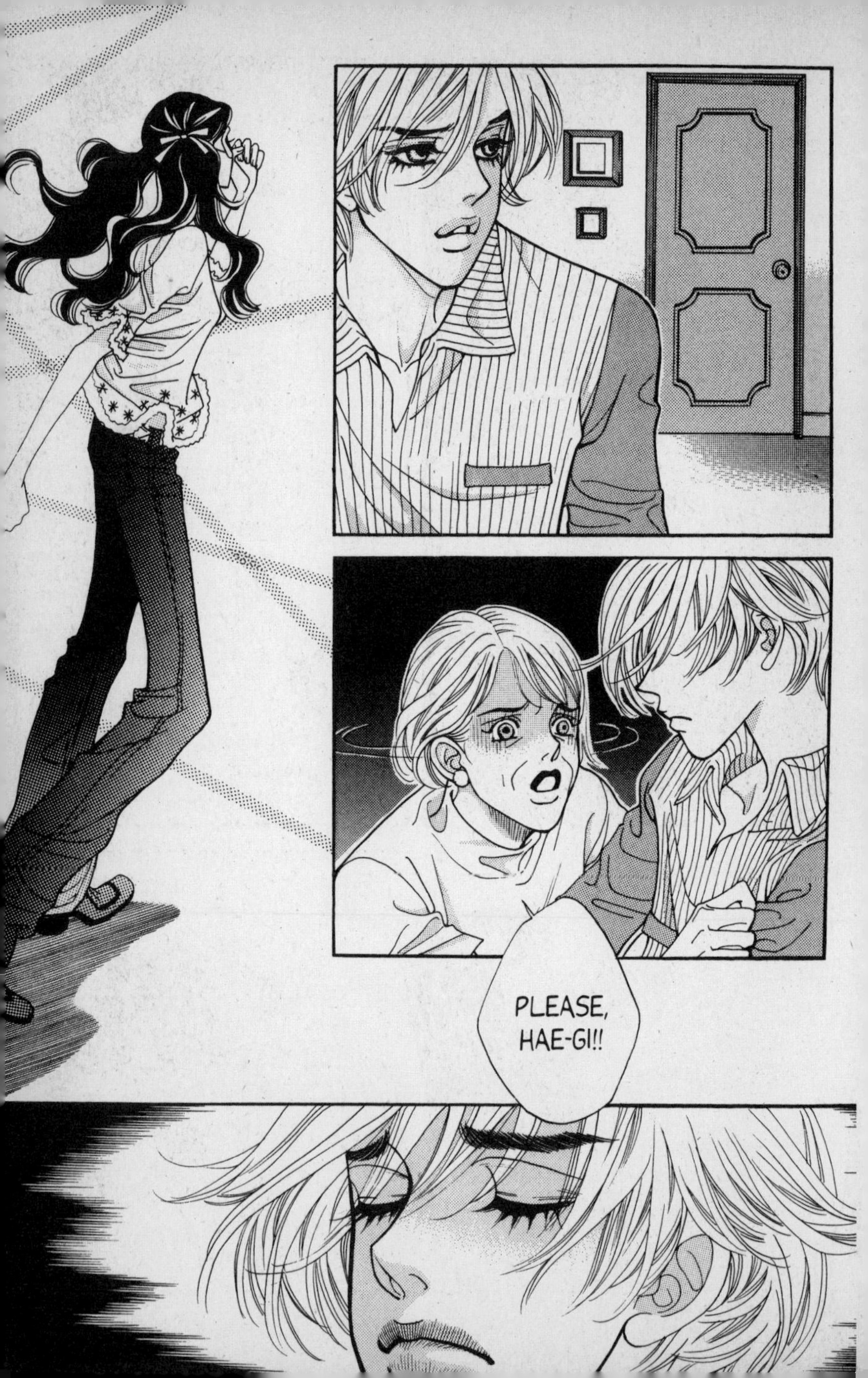
PLEASE, HAE-GI!!

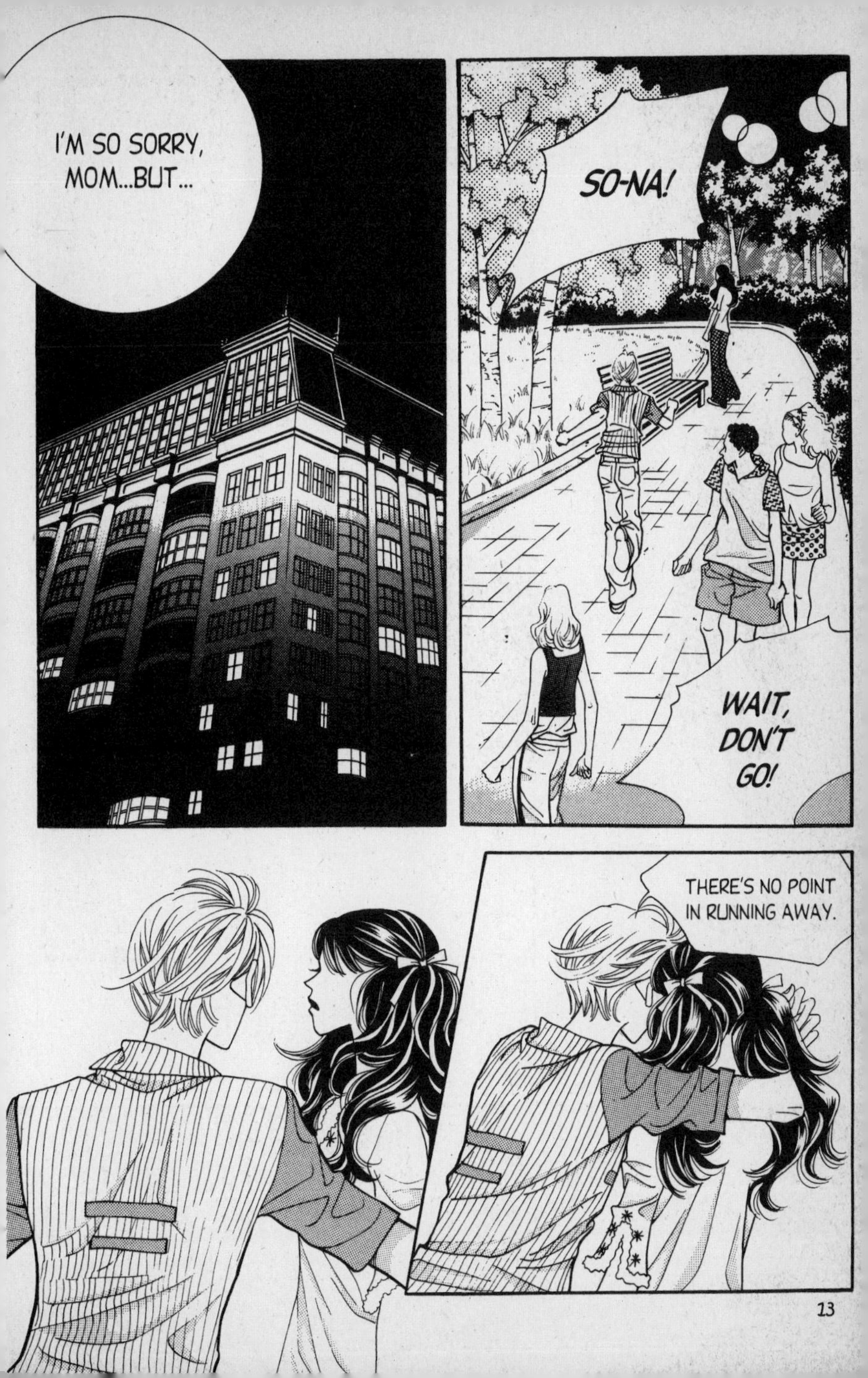
I'M SO SORRY, MOM...BUT...
SO-NA!
WAIT, DON'T GO!
THERE'S NO POINT IN RUNNING AWAY.

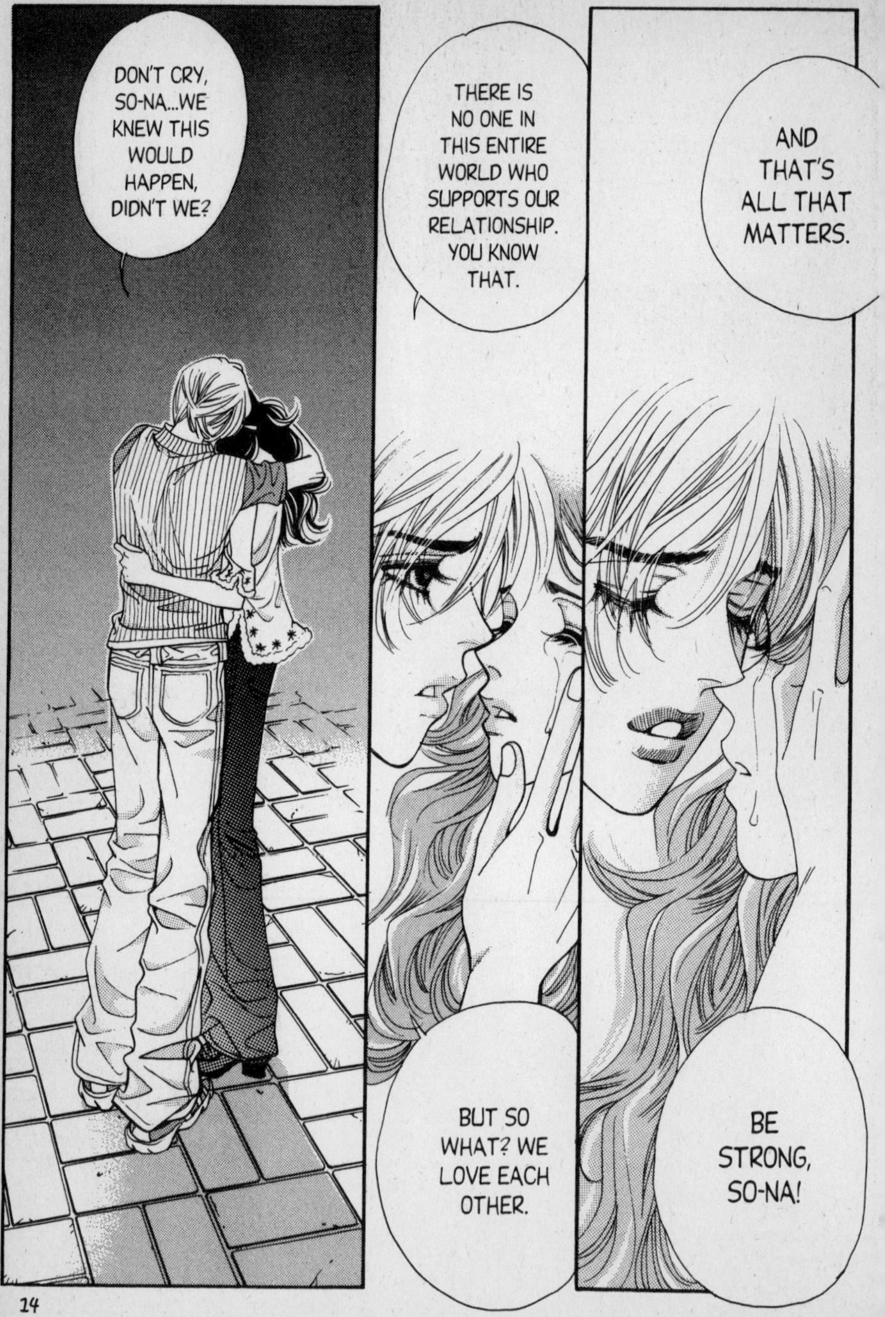
DON'T CRY, SO-NA...WE KNEW THIS WOULD HAPPEN, DIDN'T WE?
THERE IS NO ONE IN THIS ENTIRE WORLD WHO SUPPORTS OUR RELATIONSHIP. YOU KNOW THAT.
AND THAT'S ALL THAT MATTERS.
BUT SO WHAT? WE LOVE EACH OTHER.
BE STRONG, SO-NA!

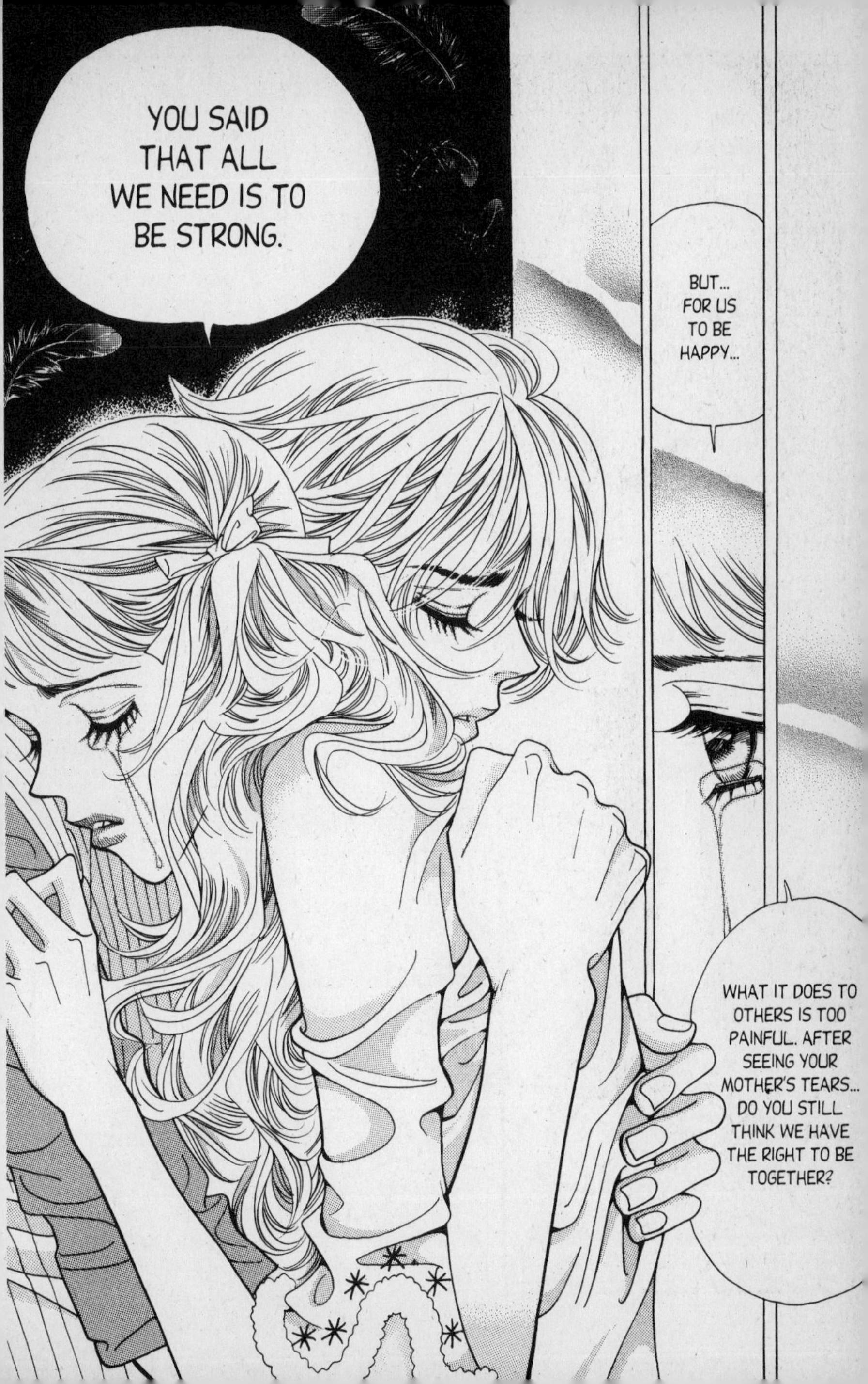
YOU SAID THAT ALL WE NEED IS TO BE STRONG.
BUT... FOR US TO BE HAPPY...
WHAT IT DOES TO OTHERS IS TOO PAINFUL. AFTER SEEING YOUR MOTHER'S TEARS... DO YOU STILL THINK WE HAVE THE RIGHT TO BE TOGETHER?

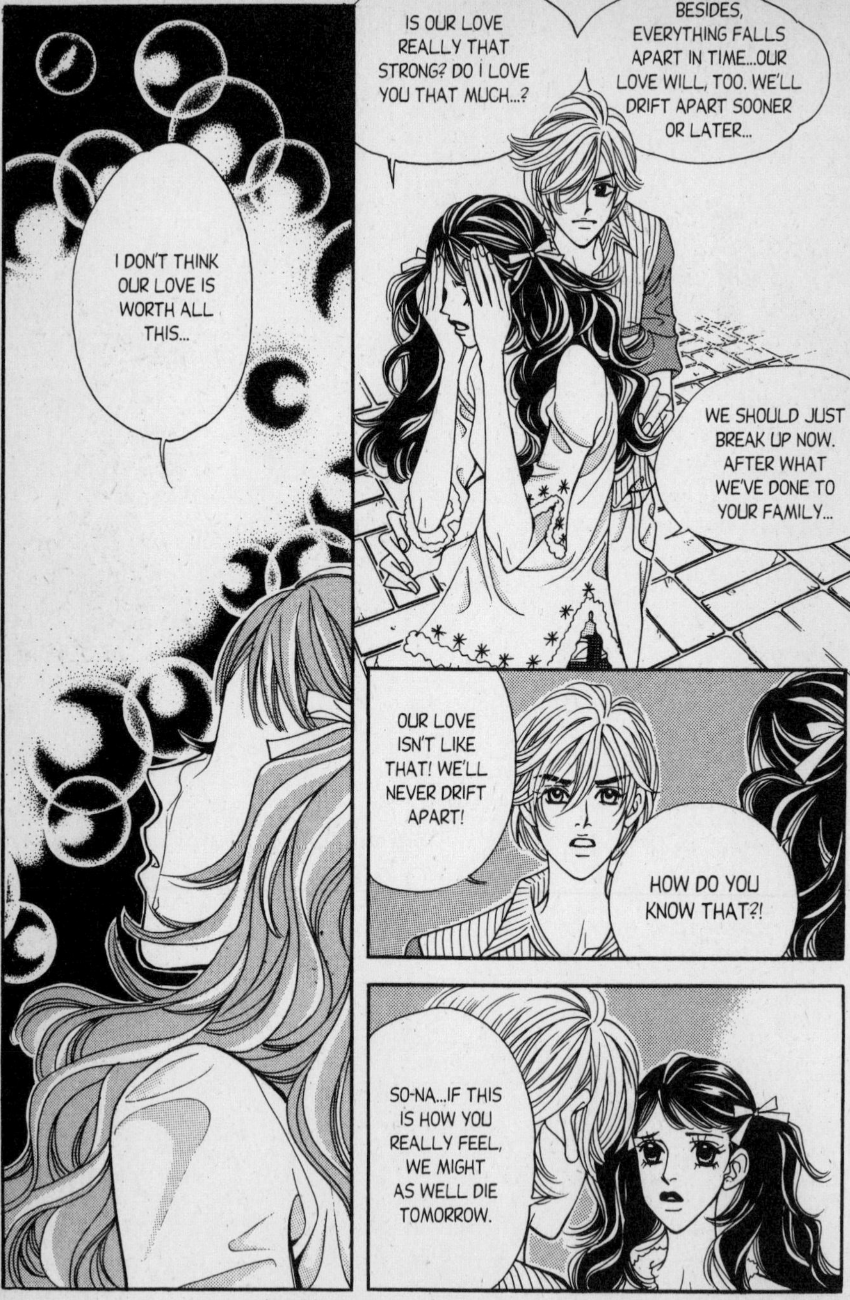
I DON'T THINK OUR LOVE IS WORTH ALL THIS...
IS OUR LOVE REALLY THAT STRONG? DO I LOVE YOU THAT MUCH...?
BESIDES, EVERYTHING FALLS APART IN TIME...OUR LOVE WILL, TOO. WE'LL DRIFT APART SOONER OR LATER...
WE SHOULD JUST BREAK UP NOW. AFTER WHAT WE'VE DONE TO YOUR FAMILY...
OUR LOVE ISN'T LIKE THAT! WE'LL NEVER DRIFT APART!
HOW DO YOU KNOW THAT?!
SO-NA...IF THIS IS HOW YOU REALLY FEEL, WE MIGHT AS WELL DIE TOMORROW.

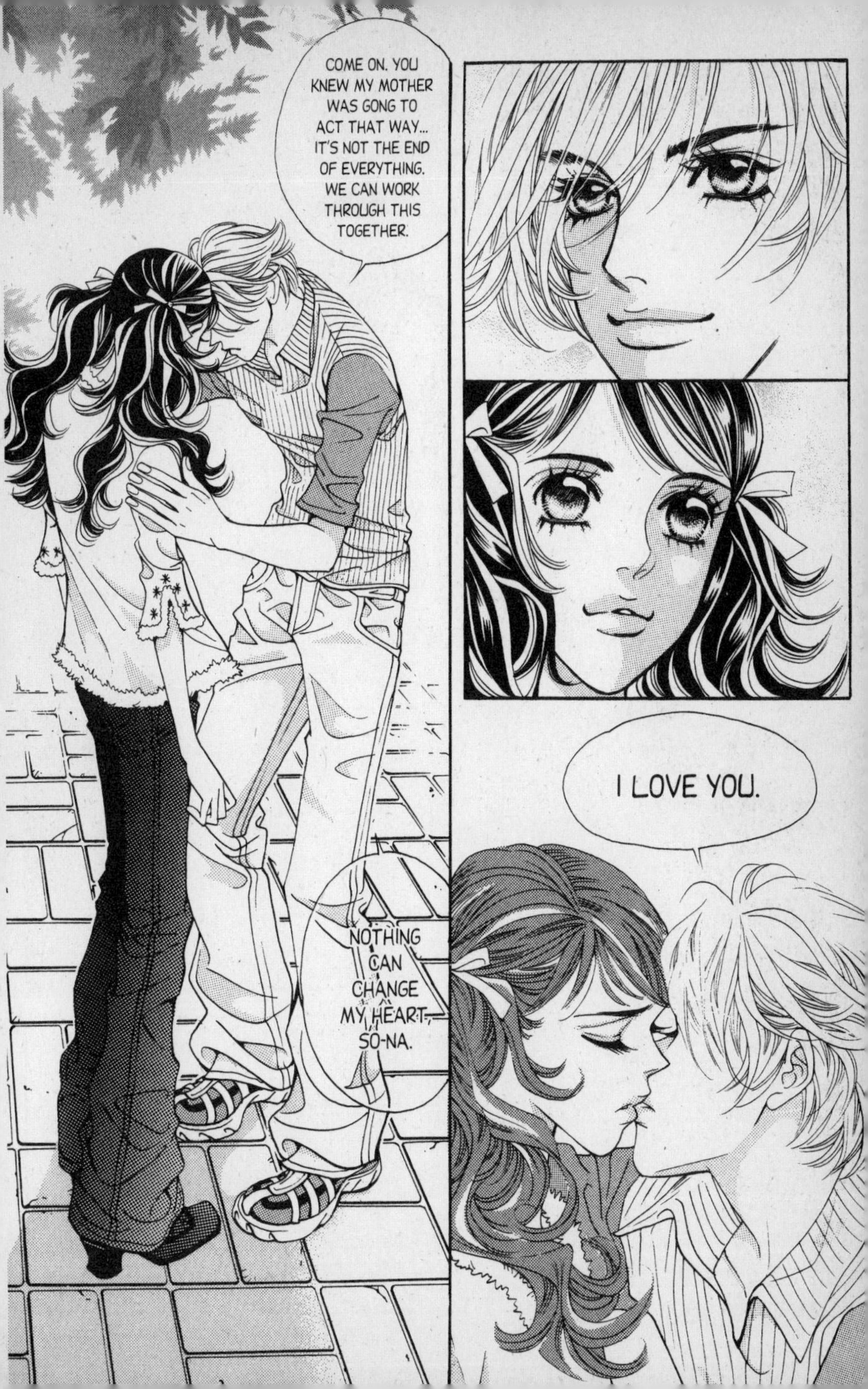
COME ON. YOU KNEW MY MOTHER WAS GONG TO ACT THAT WAY... IT'S NOT THE END OF EVERYTHING. WE CAN WORK THROUGH THIS TOGETHER.
NOTHING CAN CHANGE MY HEART, SO-NA.
I LOVE YOU.

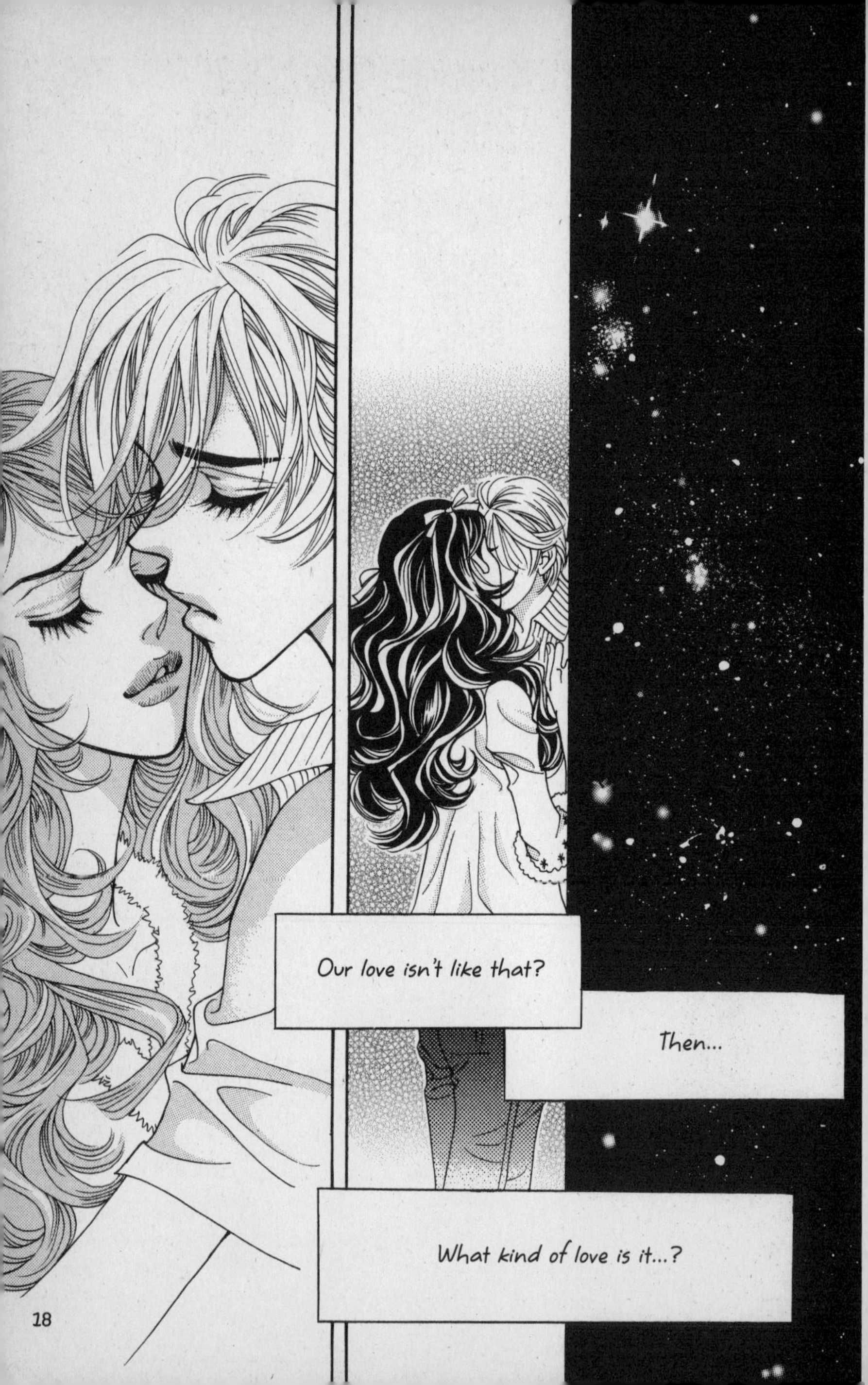
Our love isn't like that?
Then...
What kind of love is it...?

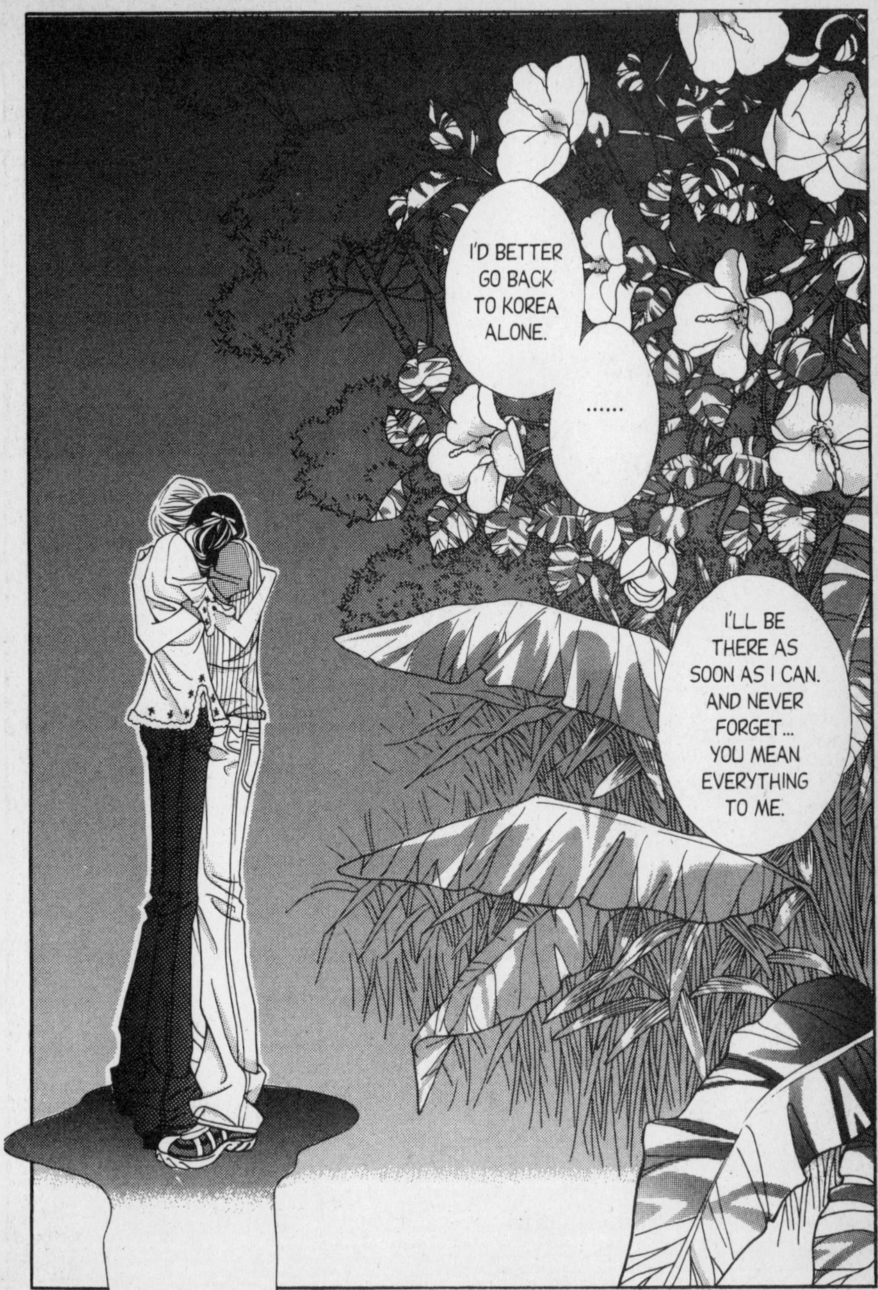
I'D BETTER GO BACK TO KOREA ALONE.
......
I'LL BE THERE AS SOON AS I CAN. AND NEVER FORGET... YOU MEAN EVERYTHING TO ME.

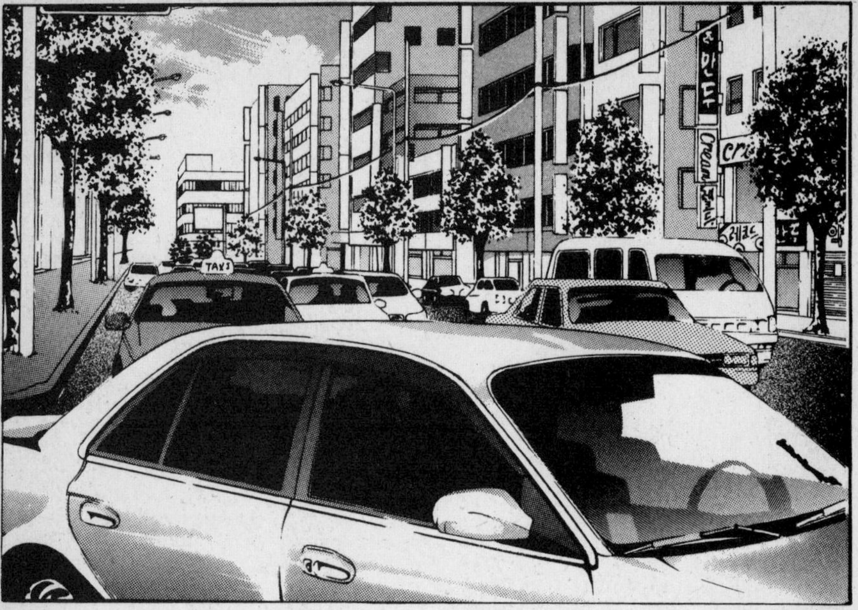
TAXI

Part 35 : Adam and Eve thrown out of the Garden of Eden

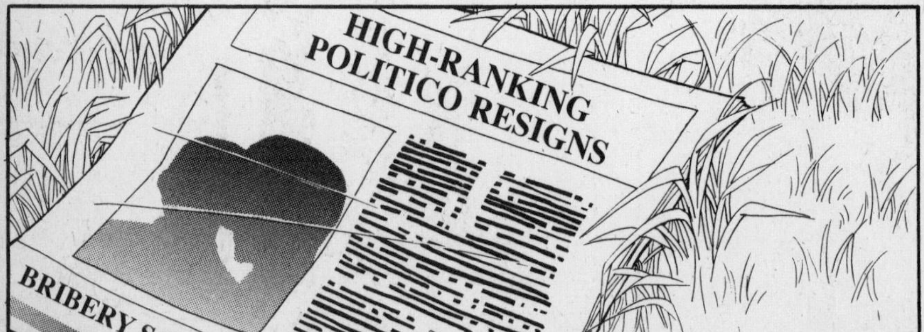
HIGH-RANKING POLITICO RESIGNS
BRIBERY SCANDAL!

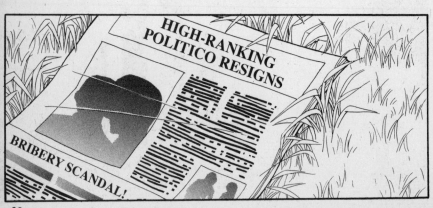

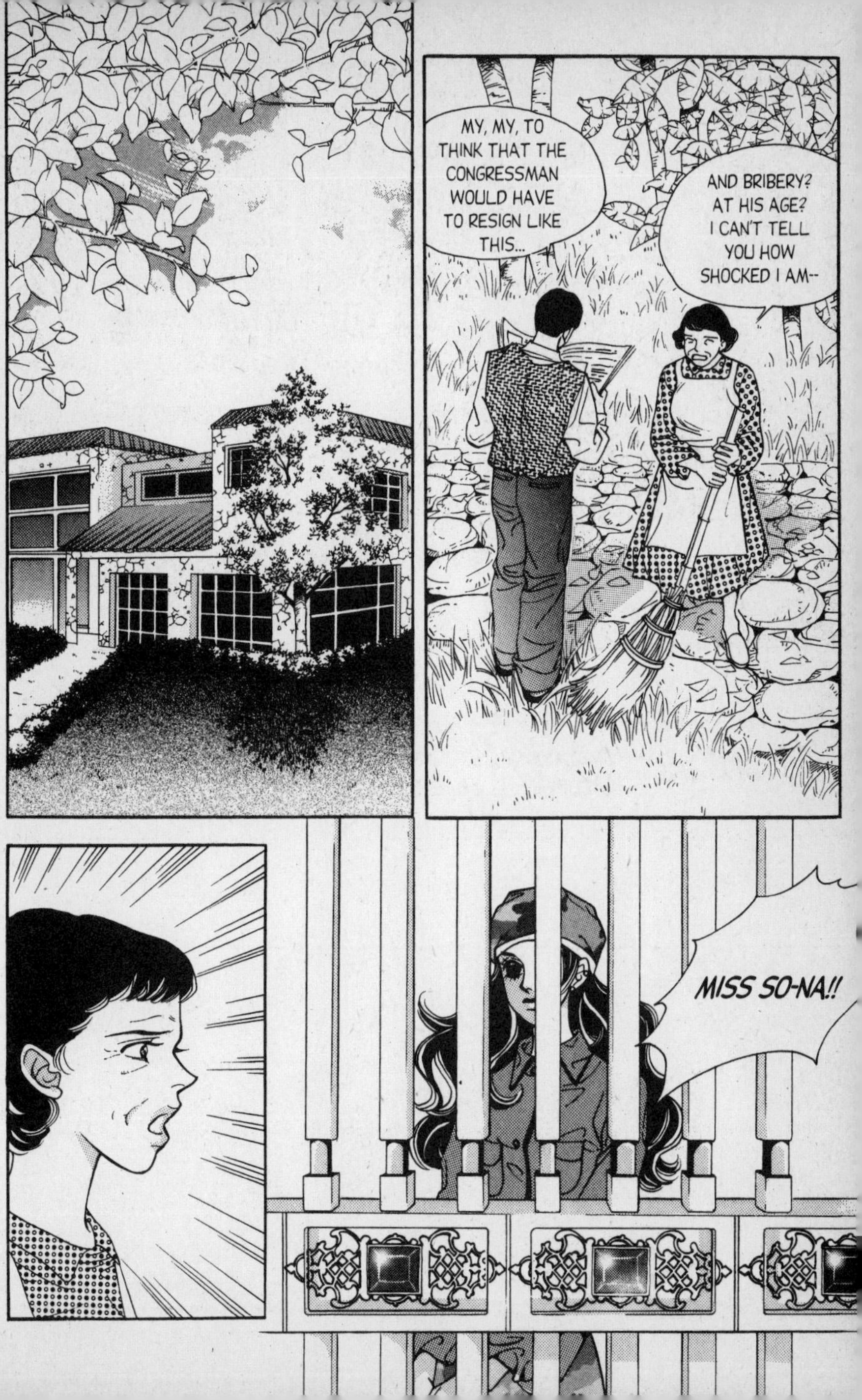
MY, MY, TO THINK THAT THE CONGRESSMAN WOULD HAVE TO RESIGN LIKE THIS...
AND BRIBERY? AT HIS AGE? I CAN'T TELL YOU HOW SHOCKED I AM--
MISS SO-NA!!

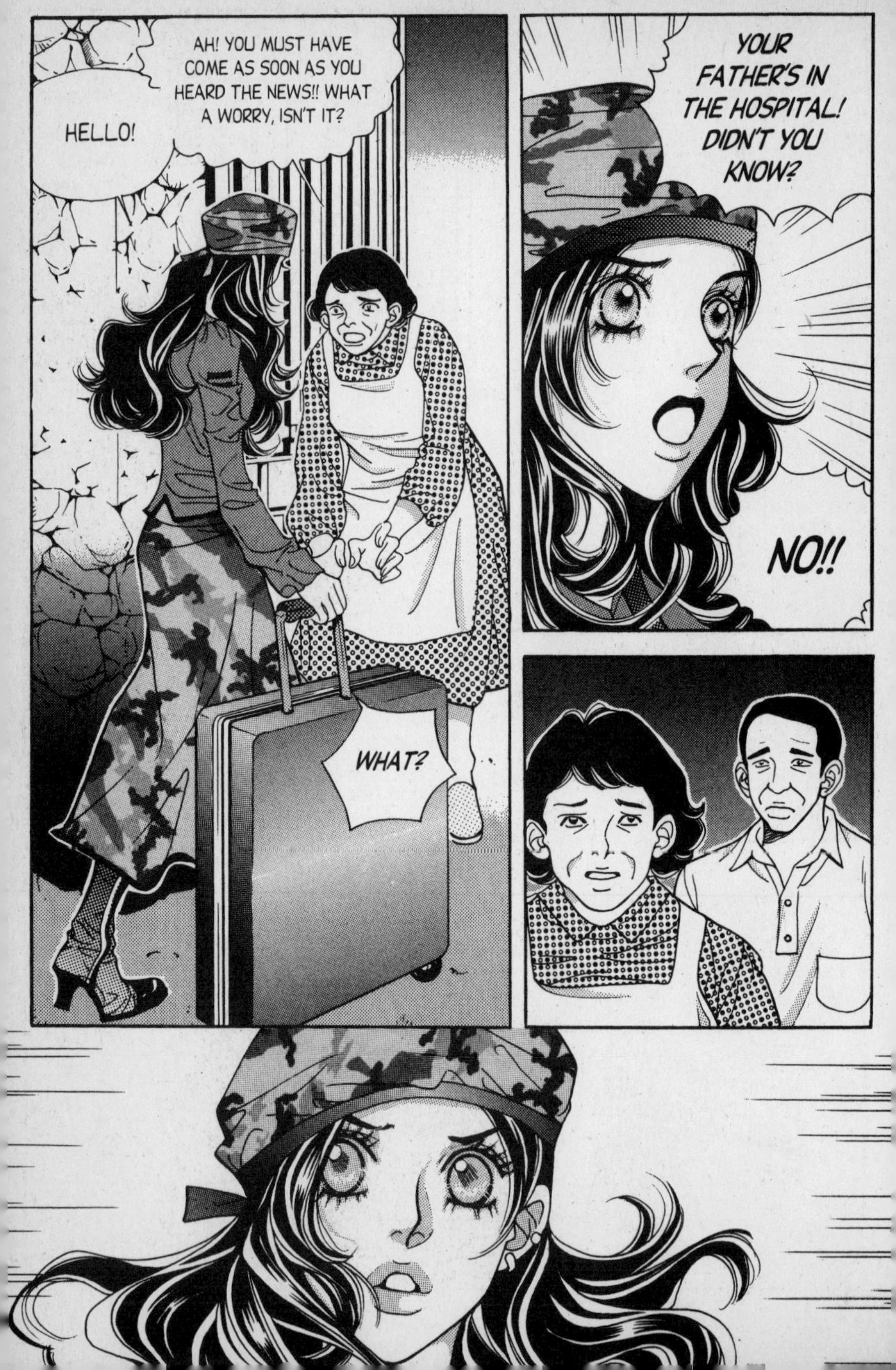
HELLO!
AH! YOU MUST HAVE COME AS SOON AS YOU HEARD THE NEWS!! WHAT A WORRY, ISN'T IT?
WHAT?
YOUR FATHER'S IN THE HOSPITAL! DIDN'T YOU KNOW?
NO!!

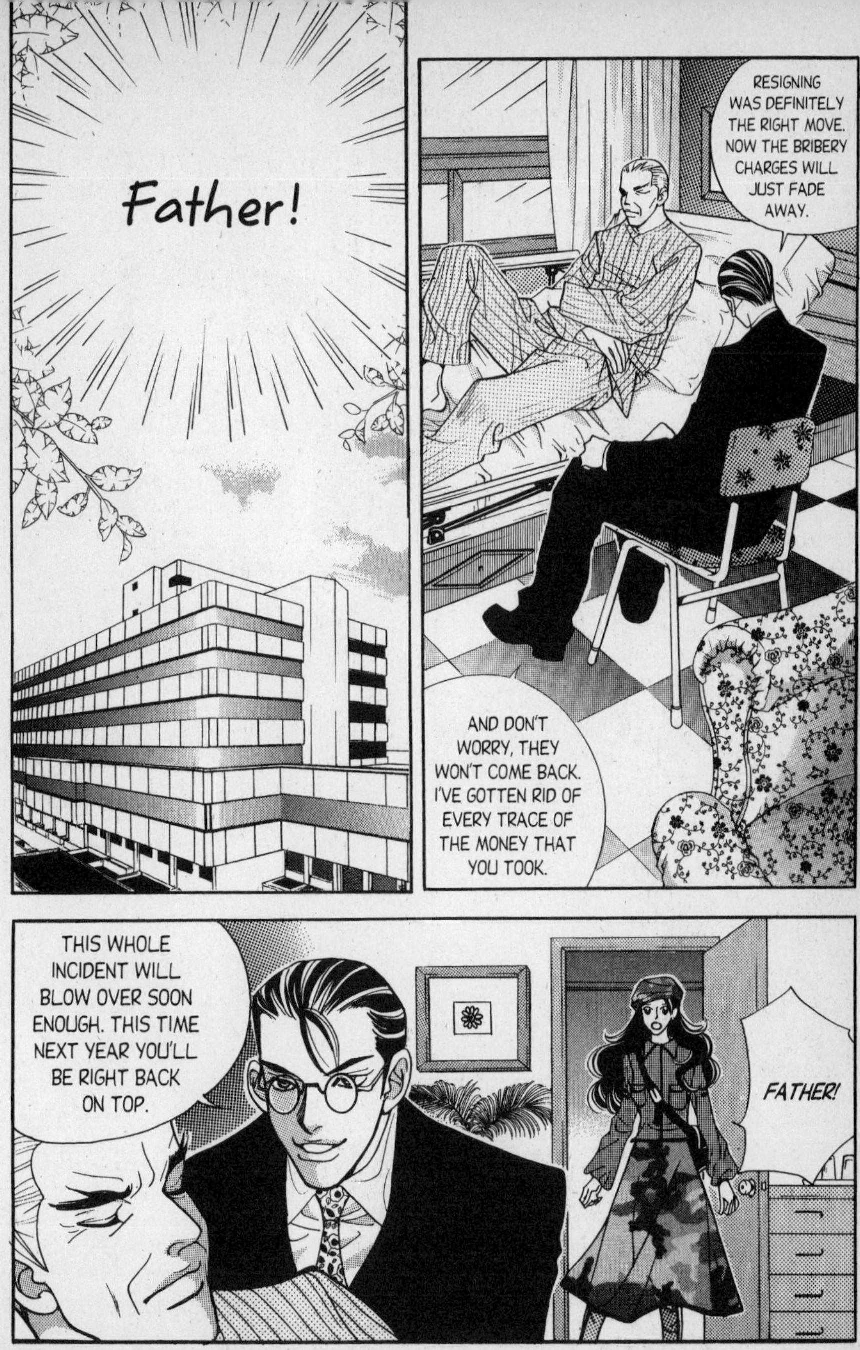
Father!
RESIGNING WAS DEFINITELY THE RIGHT MOVE. NOW THE BRIBERY CHARGES WILL JUST FADE AWAY.
AND DON'T WORRY, THEY WON'T COME BACK. I'VE GOTTEN RID OF EVERY TRACE OF THE MONEY THAT YOU TOOK.
THIS WHOLE INCIDENT WILL BLOW OVER SOON ENOUGH. THIS TIME NEXT YEAR YOU'LL BE RIGHT BACK ON TOP.
FATHER!

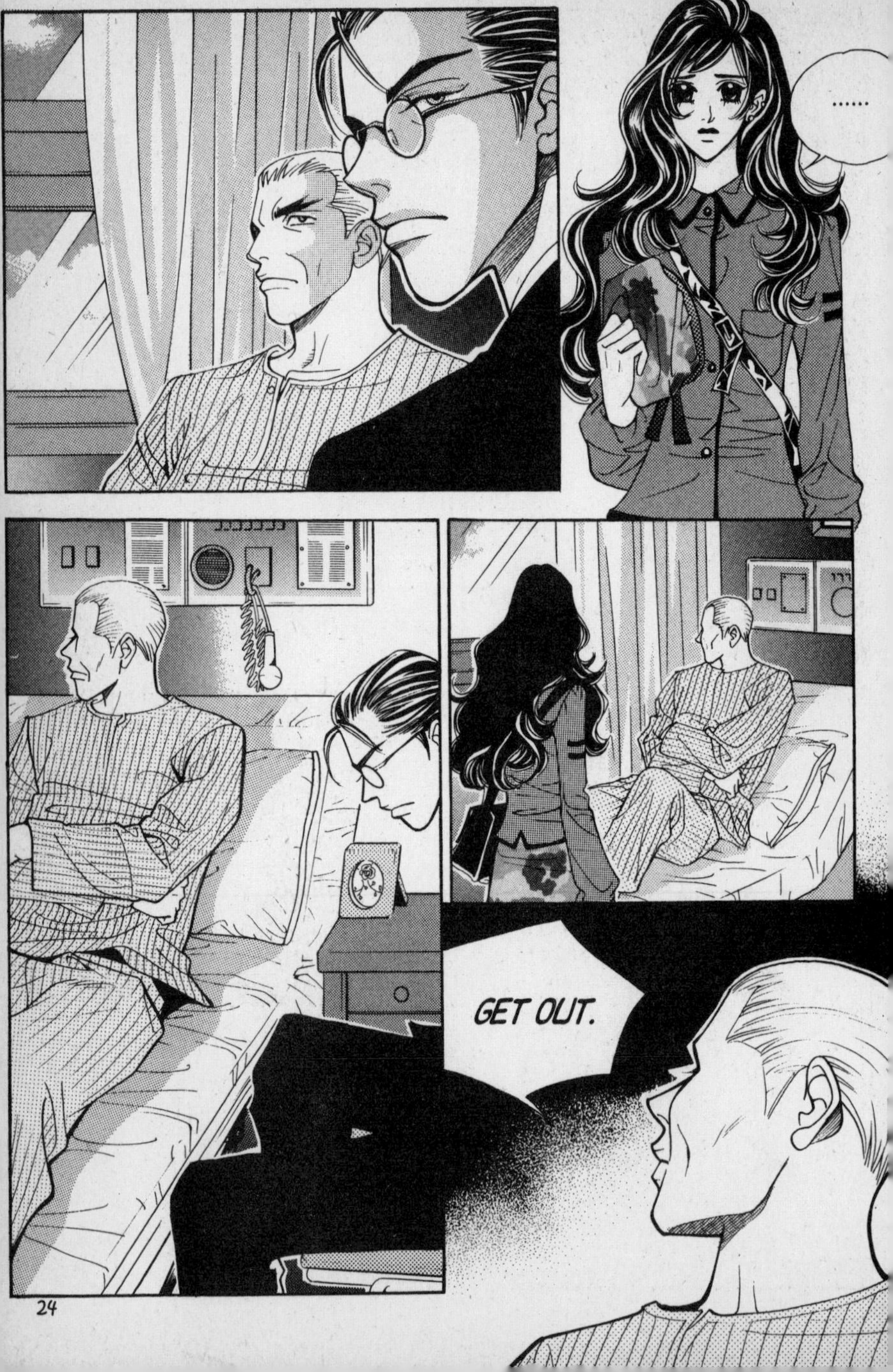
......
GET OUT.

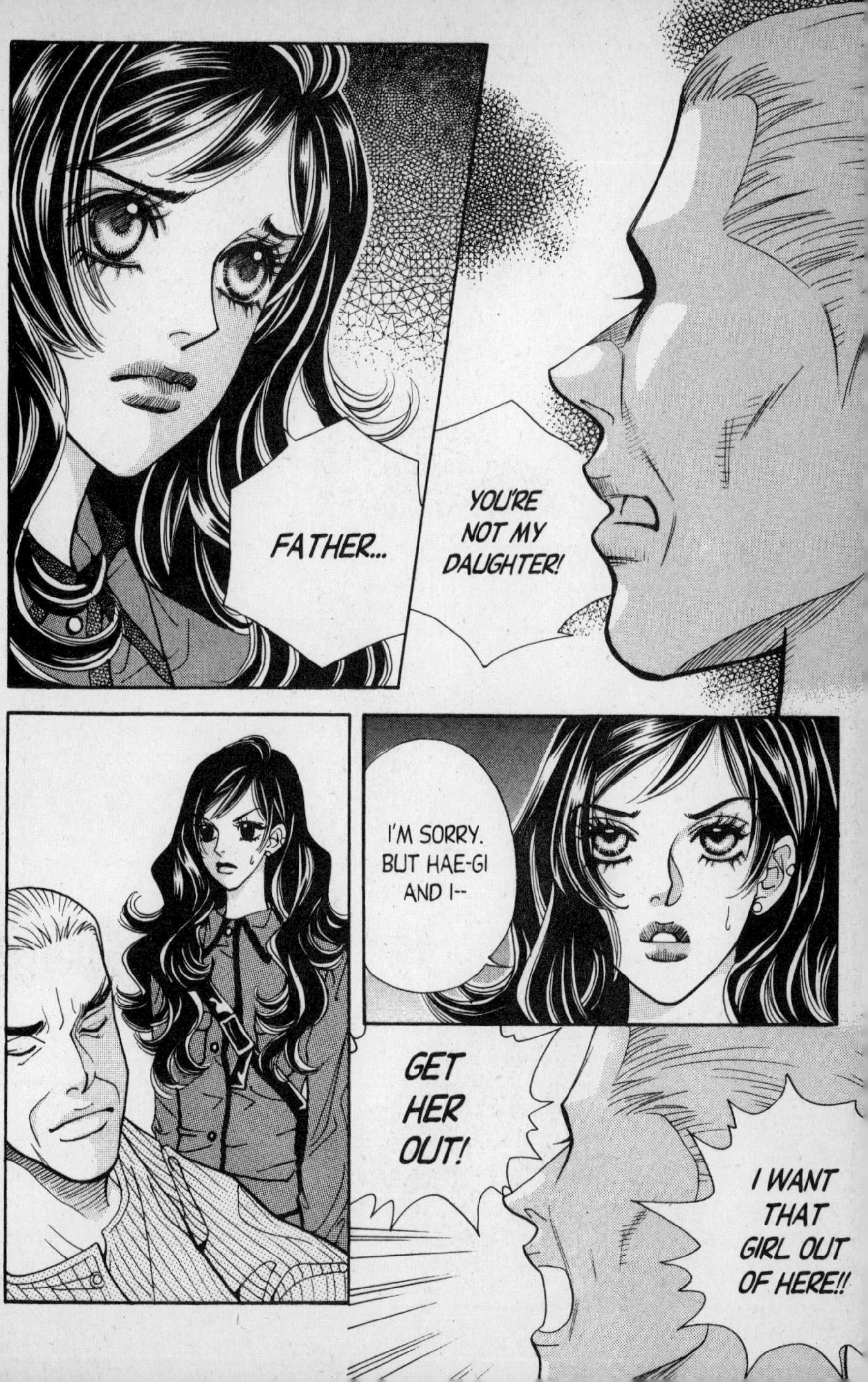
FATHER...
YOU'RE NOT MY DAUGHTER!
I'M SORRY. BUT HAE-GI AND I--
GET HER OUT!
I WANT THAT GIRL OUT OF HERE!!

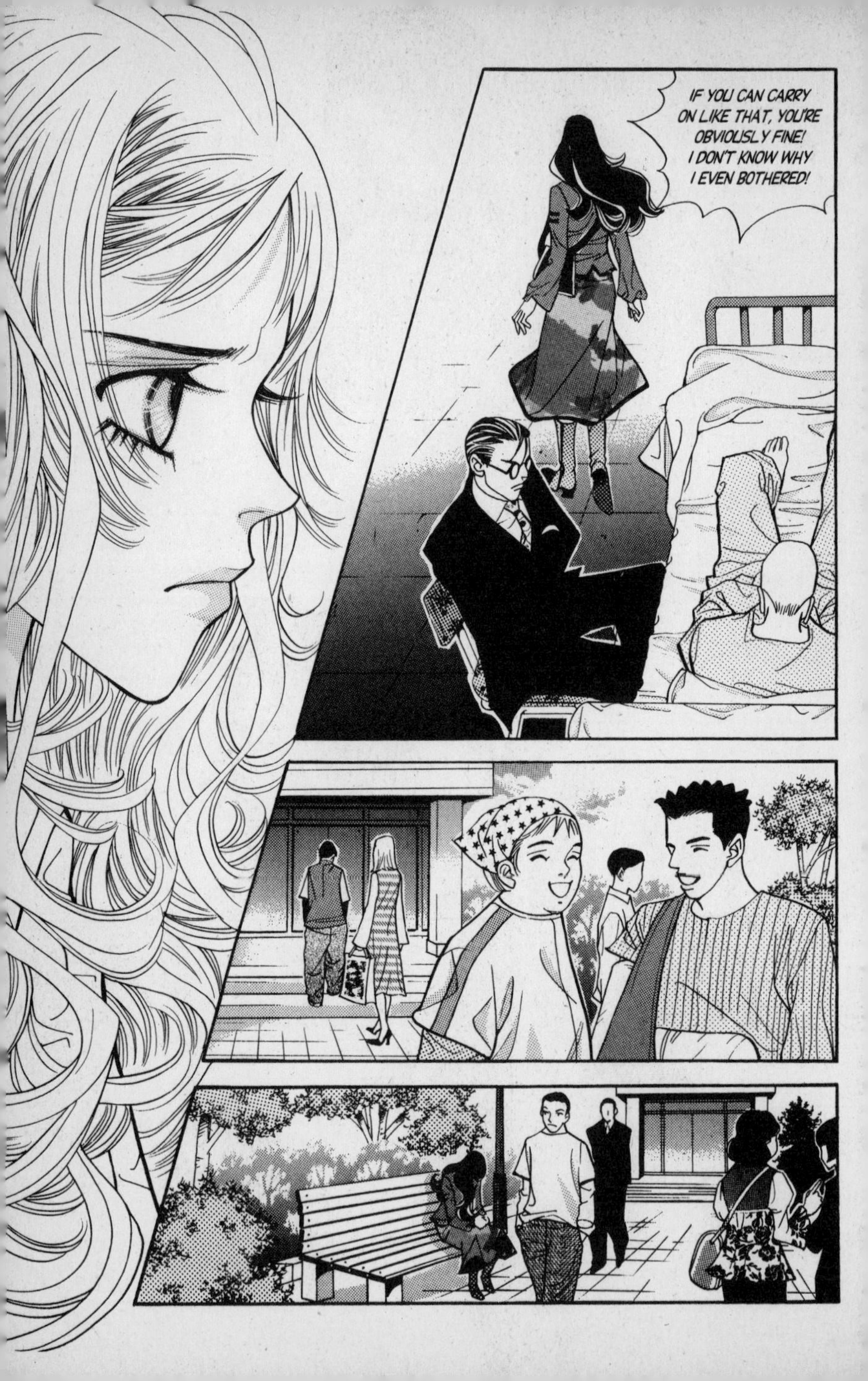
IF YOU CAN CARRY ON LIKE THAT, YOU'RE OBVIOUSLY FINE! I DON'T KNOW WHY I EVEN BOTHERED!

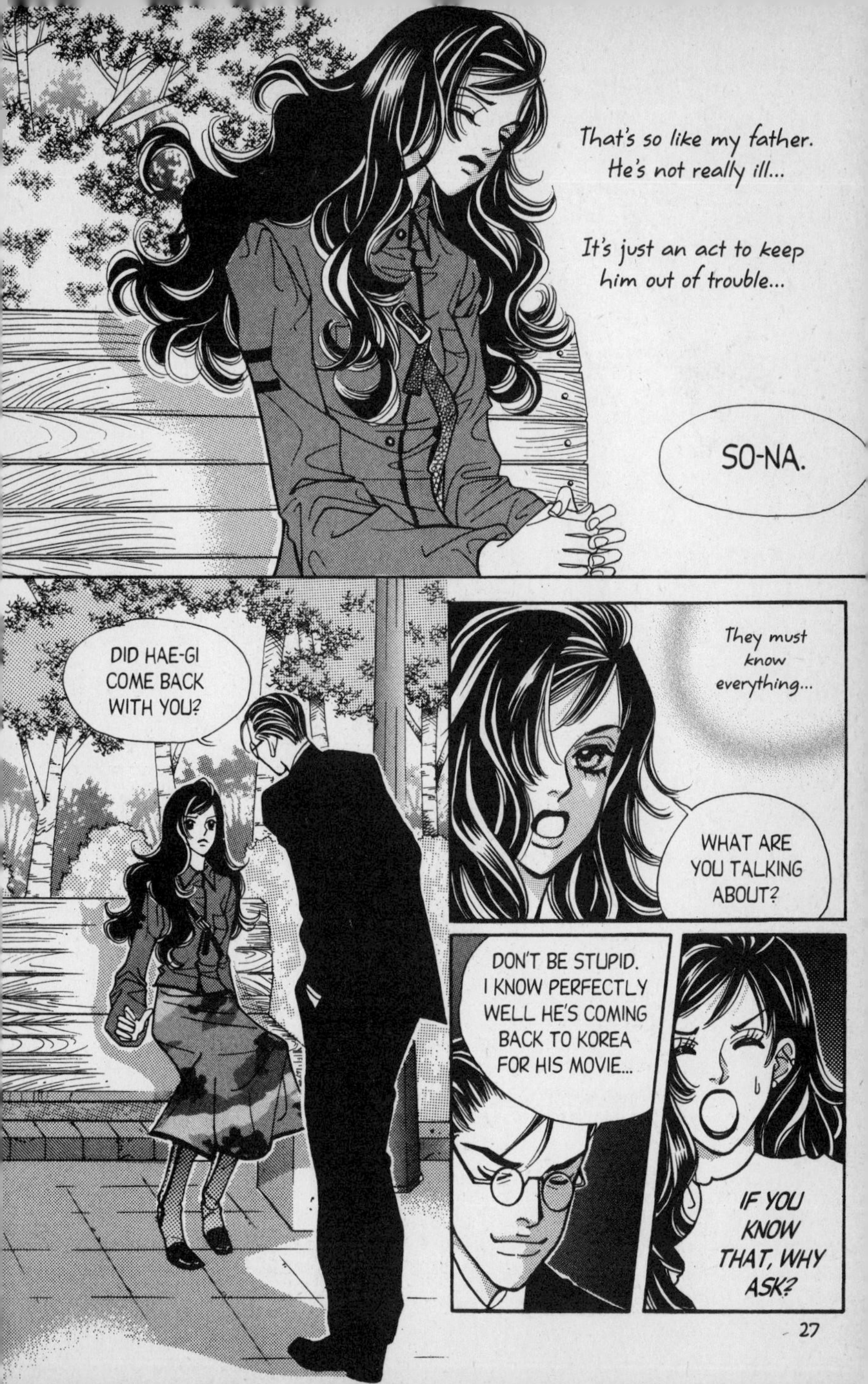
That's so like my father. He's not really ill...
It's just an act to keep him out of trouble...
SO-NA.
DID HAE-GI COME BACK WITH YOU?
They must know everything...
WHAT ARE YOU TALKING ABOUT?
DON'T BE STUPID. I KNOW PERFECTLY WELL HE'S COMING BACK TO KOREA FOR HIS MOVIE...
IF YOU KNOW THAT, WHY ASK?

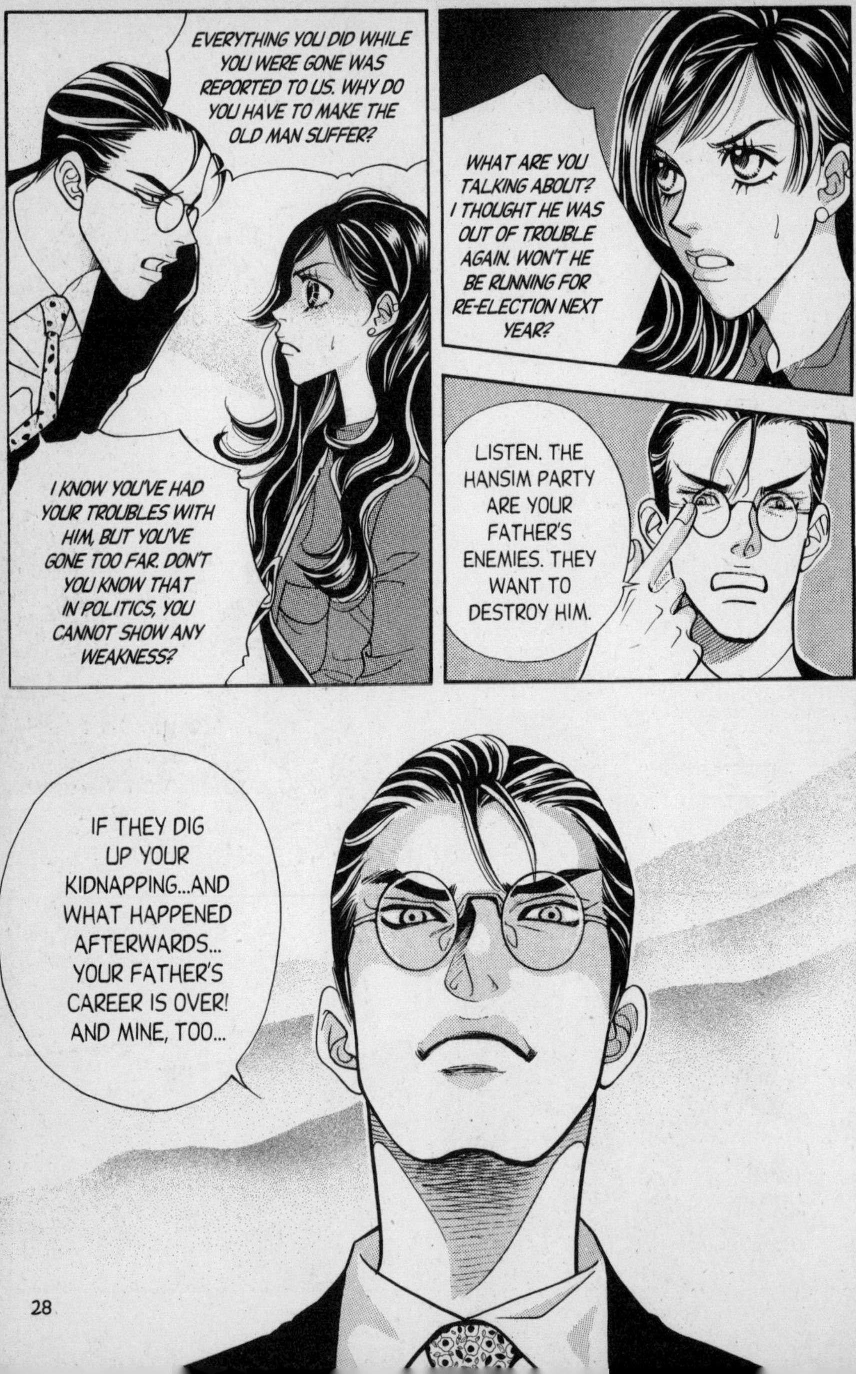
EVERYTHING YOU DID WHILE YOU WERE GONE WAS REPORTED TO US. WHY DO YOU HAVE TO MAKE THE OLD MAN SUFFER?
I KNOW YOU'VE HAD YOUR TROUBLES WITH HIM, BUT YOU'VE GONE TOO FAR. DON'T YOU KNOW THAT IN POLITICS, YOU CANNOT SHOW ANY WEAKNESS?
WHAT ARE YOU TALKING ABOUT? I THOUGHT HE WAS OUT OF TROUBLE AGAIN. WON'T HE BE RUNNING FOR RE-ELECTION NEXT YEAR?
LISTEN. THE HANSIM PARTY ARE YOUR FATHER'S ENEMIES. THEY WANT TO DESTROY HIM.
IF THEY DIG UP YOUR KIDNAPPING...AND WHAT HAPPENED AFTERWARDS... YOUR FATHER'S CAREER IS OVER! AND MINE, TOO...

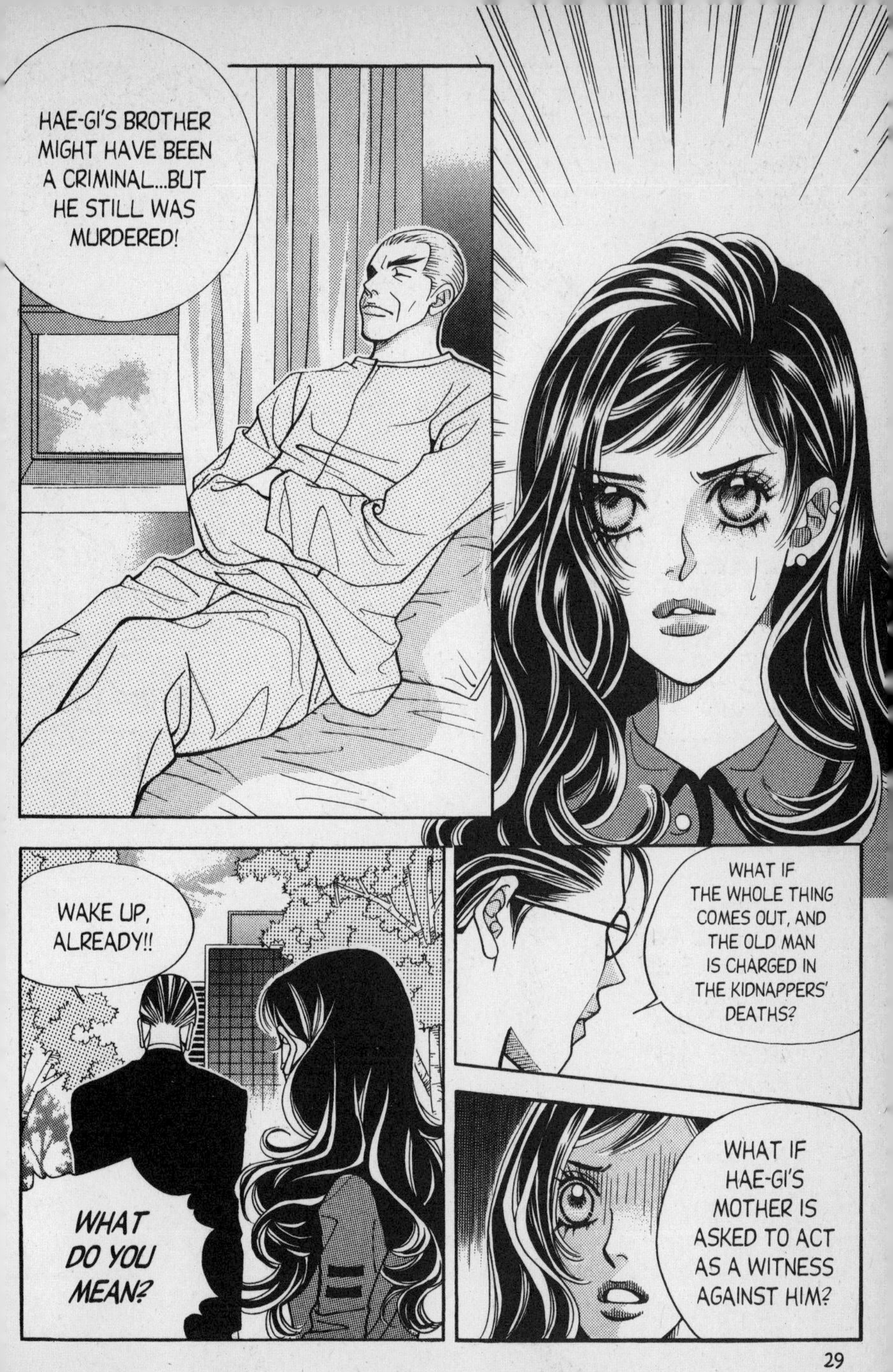
HAE-GI'S BROTHER MIGHT HAVE BEEN A CRIMINAL...BUT HE STILL WAS MURDERED!
WAKE UP, ALREADY!!
WHAT DO YOU MEAN?
WHAT IF THE WHOLE THING COMES OUT, AND THE OLD MAN IS CHARGED IN THE KIDNAPPERS' DEATHS?
WHAT IF HAE-GI'S MOTHER IS ASKED TO ACT AS A WITNESS AGAINST HIM?

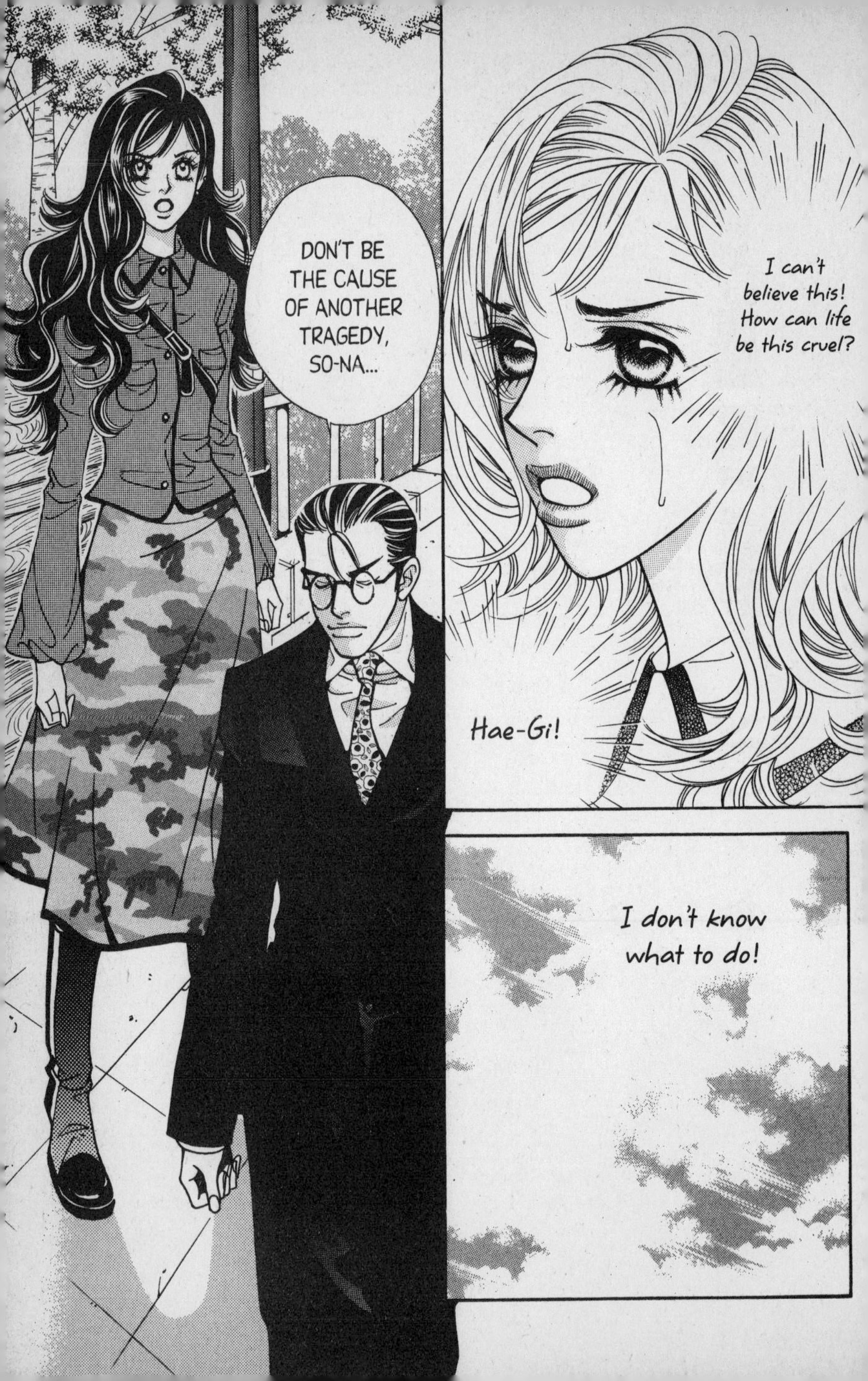
DON'T BE THE CAUSE OF ANOTHER TRAGEDY, SO-NA...
I can't believe this! How can life be this cruel?
Hae-Gi!
I don't know what to do!

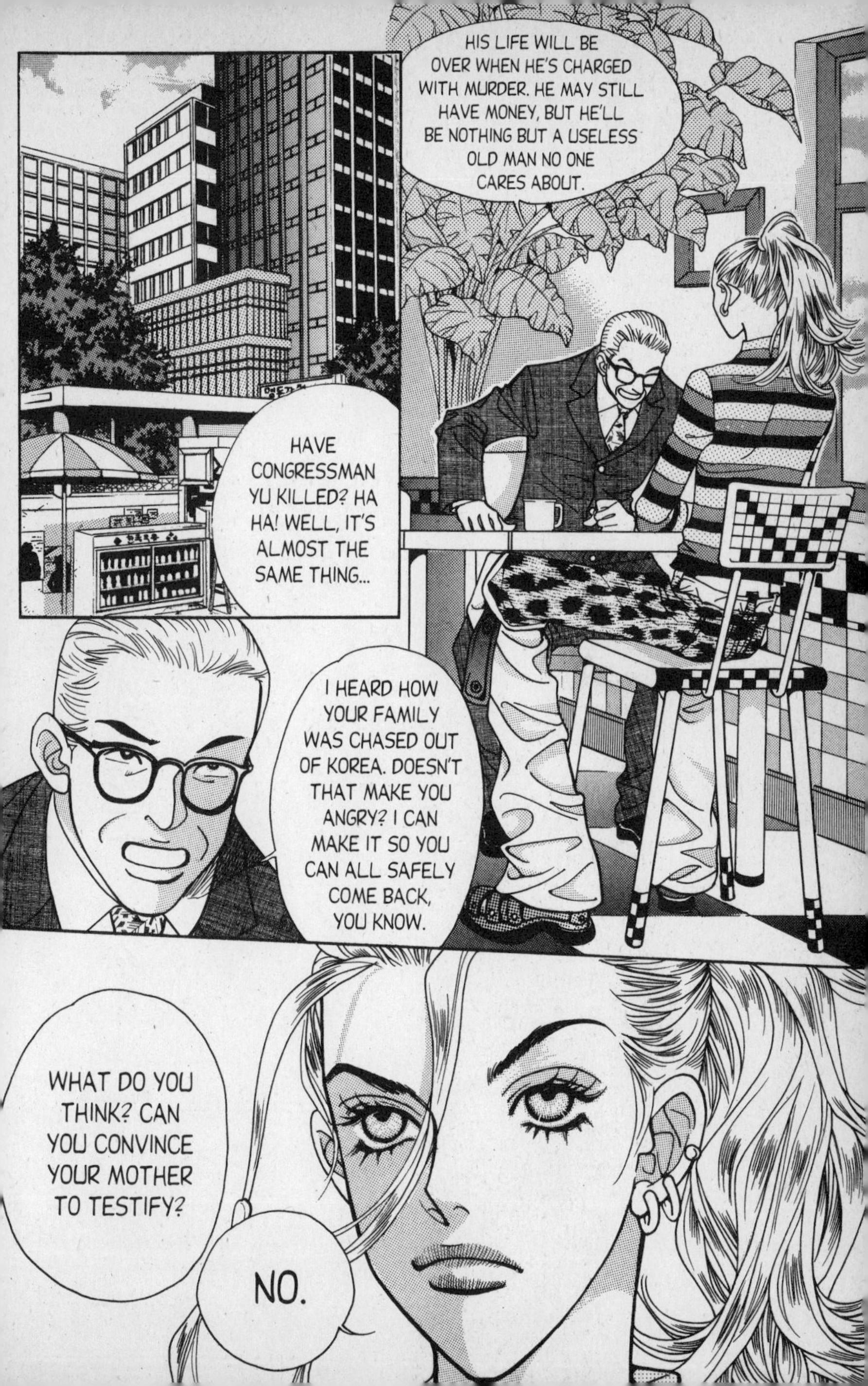
HAVE CONGRESSMAN YU KILLED? HA HA! WELL, IT'S ALMOST THE SAME THING...
HIS LIFE WILL BE OVER WHEN HE'S CHARGED WITH MURDER. HE MAY STILL HAVE MONEY, BUT HE'LL BE NOTHING BUT A USELESS OLD MAN NO ONE CARES ABOUT.
I HEARD HOW YOUR FAMILY WAS CHASED OUT OF KOREA. DOESN'T THAT MAKE YOU ANGRY? I CAN MAKE IT SO YOU CAN ALL SAFELY COME BACK, YOU KNOW.
WHAT DO YOU THINK? CAN YOU CONVINCE YOUR MOTHER TO TESTIFY?
NO.

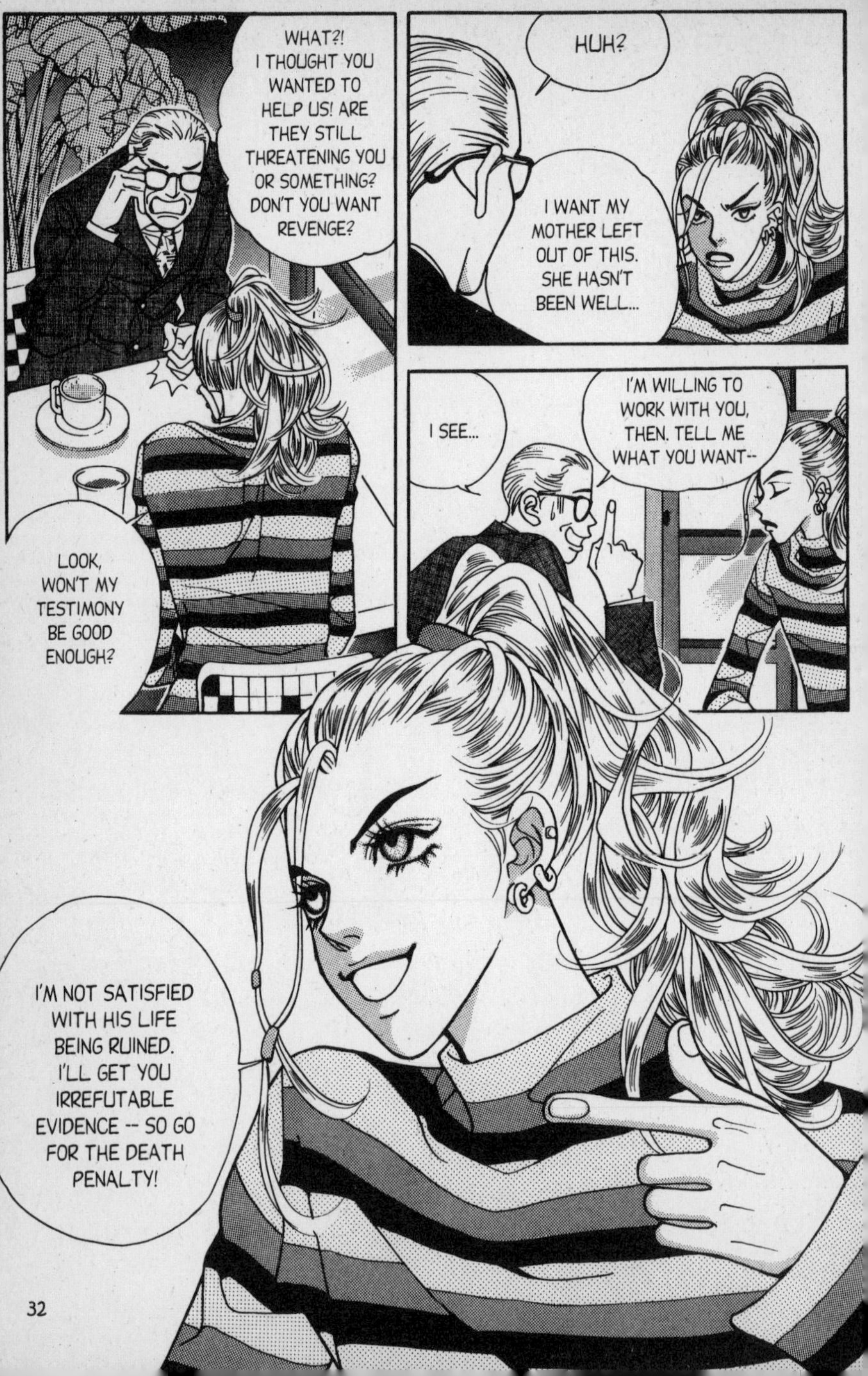
WHAT?! I THOUGHT YOU WANTED TO HELP US! ARE THEY STILL THREATENING YOU OR SOMETHING? DON'T YOU WANT REVENGE?
LOOK, WON'T MY TESTIMONY BE GOOD ENOUGH?
HUH?
I WANT MY MOTHER LEFT OUT OF THIS. SHE HASN'T BEEN WELL...
I SEE...
I'M WILLING TO WORK WITH YOU, THEN. TELL ME WHAT YOU WANT--
I'M NOT SATISFIED WITH HIS LIFE BEING RUINED. I'LL GET YOU IRREFUTABLE EVIDENCE -- SO GO FOR THE DEATH PENALTY!

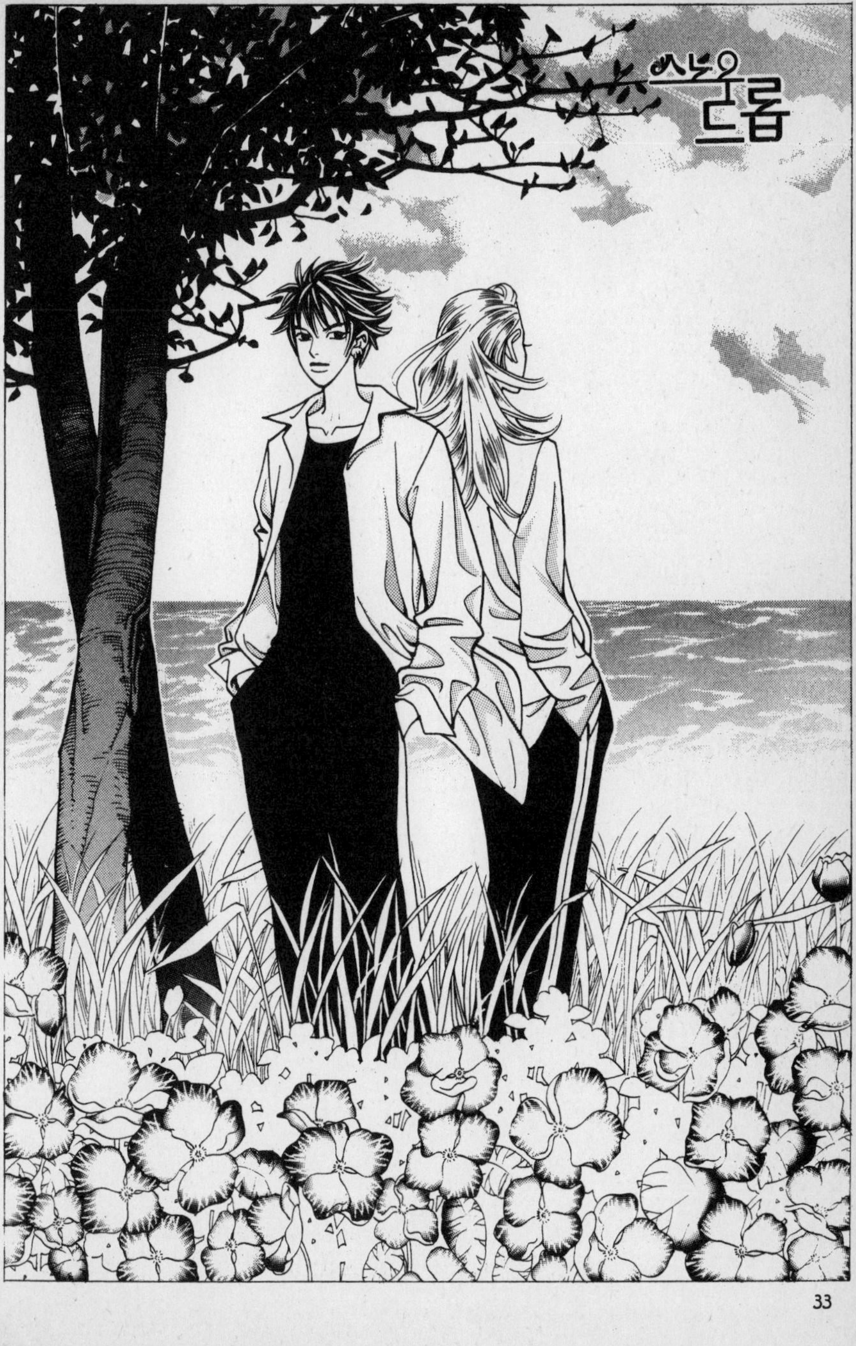
스노우 드롭

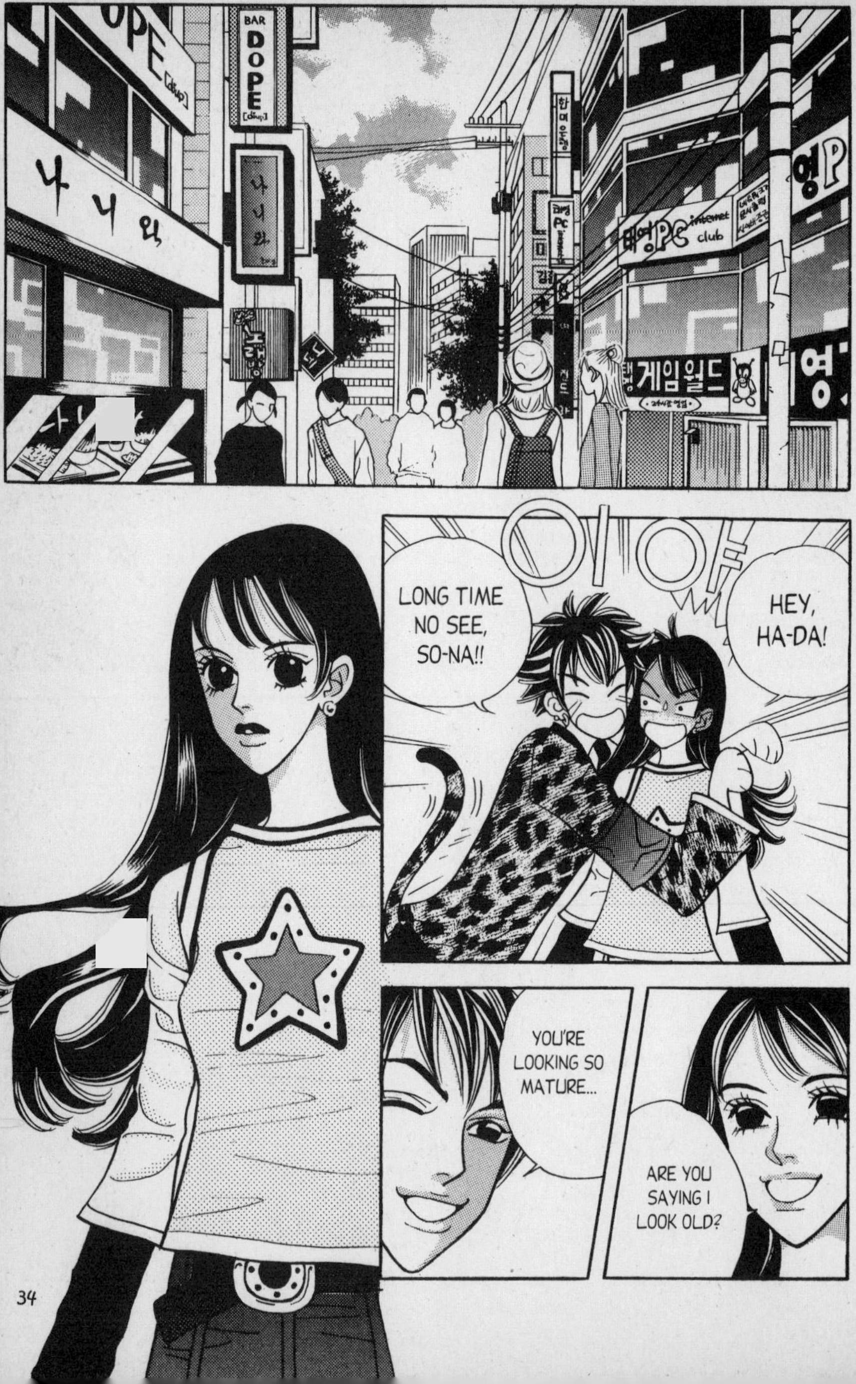
이야
LONG TIME NO SEE, SO-NA!!
HEY, HA-DA!
YOU'RE LOOKING SO MATURE...
ARE YOU SAYING I LOOK OLD?

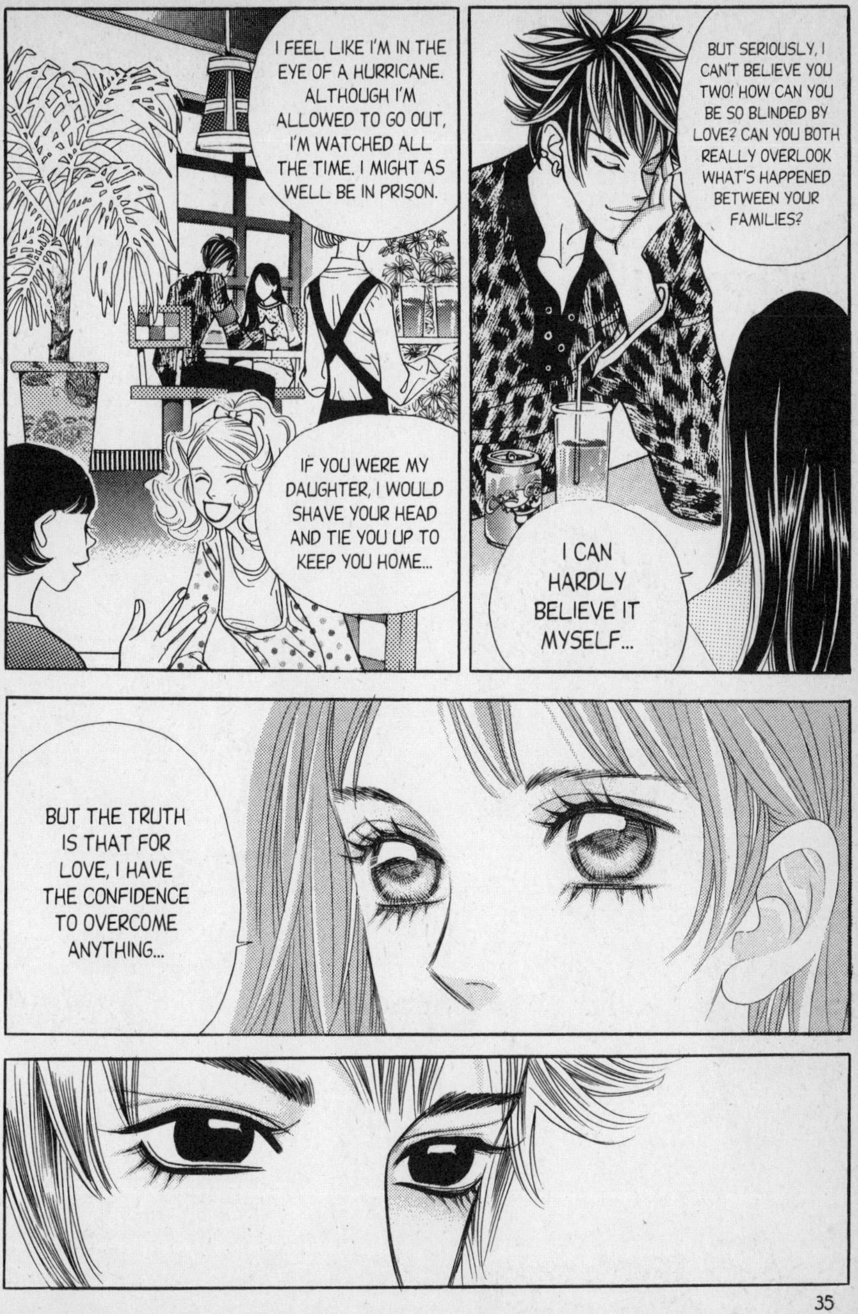
I FEEL LIKE I'M IN THE EYE OF A HURRICANE. ALTHOUGH I'M ALLOWED TO GO OUT, I'M WATCHED ALL THE TIME. I MIGHT AS WELL BE IN PRISON.
IF YOU WERE MY DAUGHTER, I WOULD SHAVE YOUR HEAD AND TIE YOU UP TO KEEP YOU HOME...
BUT SERIOUSLY, I CAN'T BELIEVE YOU TWO! HOW CAN YOU BE SO BLINDED BY LOVE? CAN YOU BOTH REALLY OVERLOOK WHAT'S HAPPENED BETWEEN YOUR FAMILIES?
I CAN HARDLY BELIEVE IT MYSELF...
BUT THE TRUTH IS THAT FOR LOVE, I HAVE THE CONFIDENCE TO OVERCOME ANYTHING...

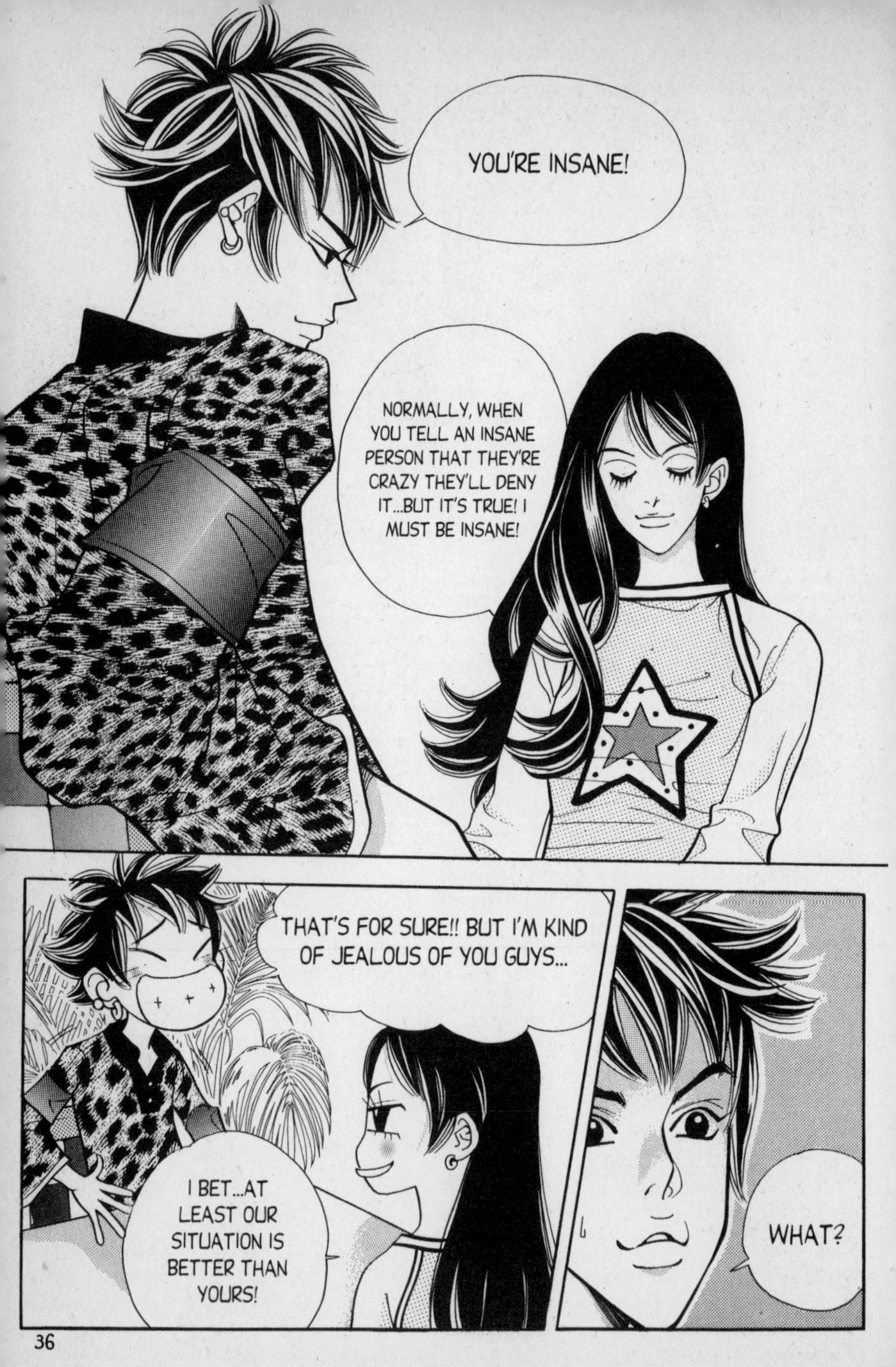
YOU'RE INSANE!
NORMALLY, WHEN YOU TELL AN INSANE PERSON THAT THEY'RE CRAZY THEY'LL DENY IT...BUT IT'S TRUE! I MUST BE INSANE!
THAT'S FOR SURE!! BUT I'M KIND OF JEALOUS OF YOU GUYS...
I BET...AT LEAST OUR SITUATION IS BETTER THAN YOURS!
WHAT?

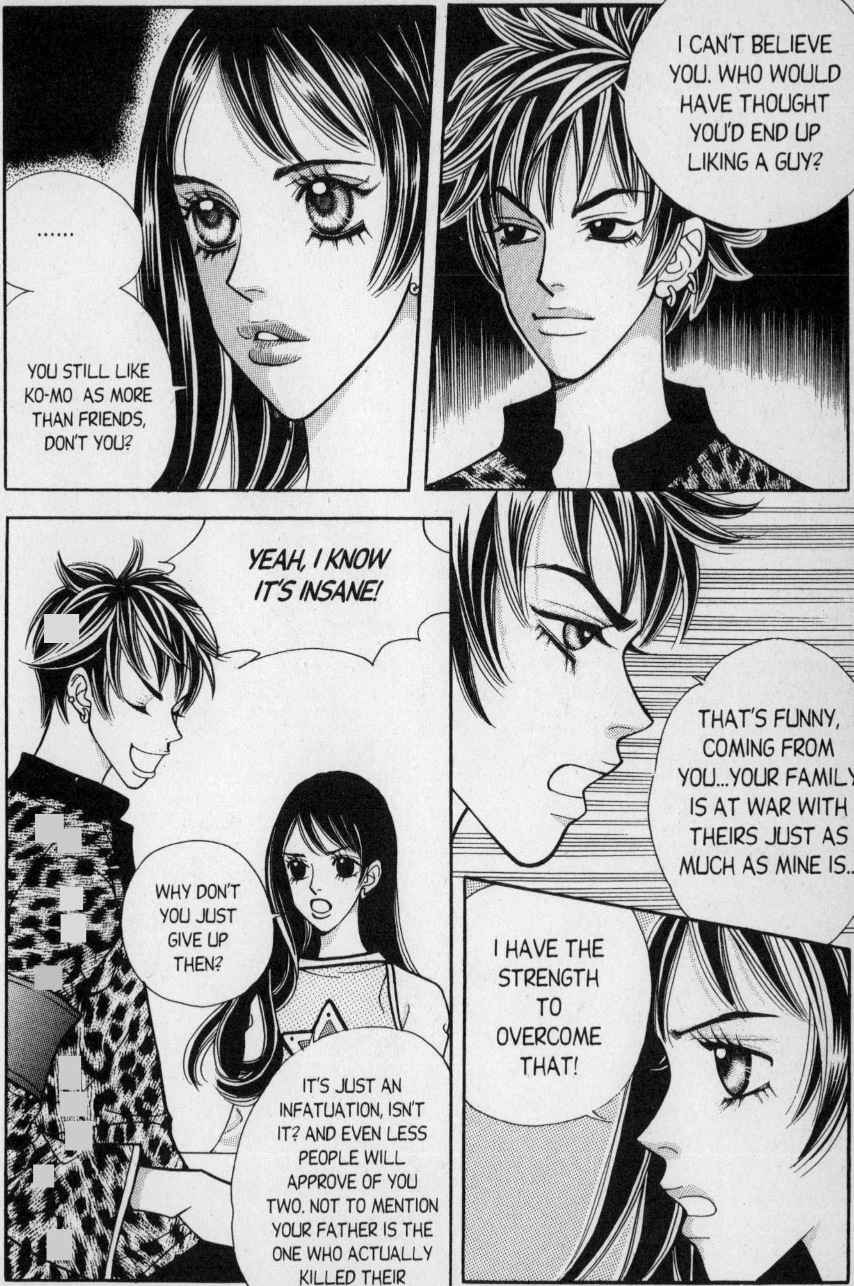
......
YOU STILL LIKE KO-MO AS MORE THAN FRIENDS, DON'T YOU?
I CAN'T BELIEVE YOU. WHO WOULD HAVE THOUGHT YOU'D END UP LIKING A GUY?
YEAH, I KNOW IT'S INSANE!
WHY DON'T YOU JUST GIVE UP THEN?
IT'S JUST AN INFATUATION, ISN'T IT? AND EVEN LESS PEOPLE WILL APPROVE OF YOU TWO. NOT TO MENTION YOUR FATHER IS THE ONE WHO ACTUALLY KILLED THEIR BROTHER...
THAT'S FUNNY, COMING FROM YOU...YOUR FAMILY IS AT WAR WITH THEIRS JUST AS MUCH AS MINE IS...
I HAVE THE STRENGTH TO OVERCOME THAT!

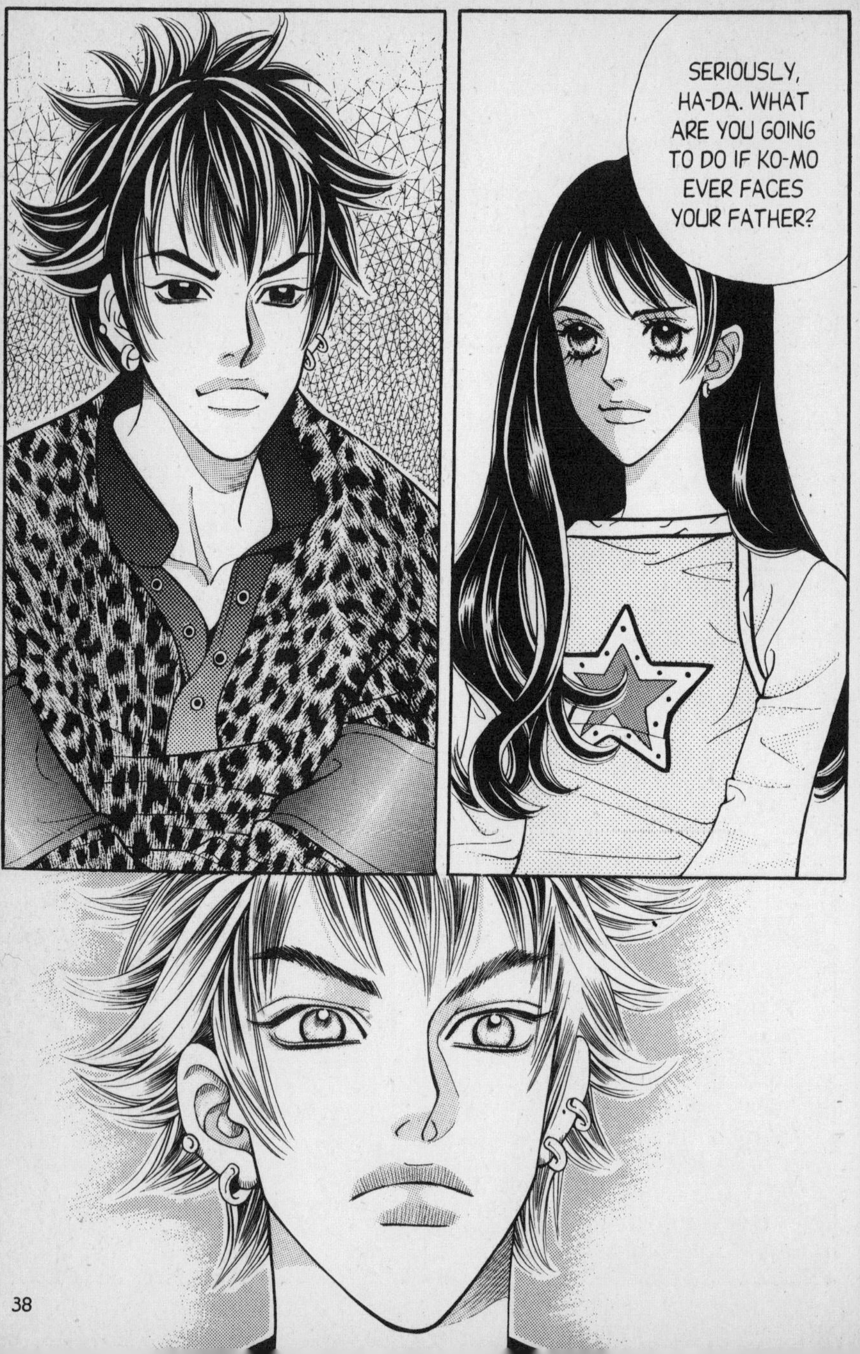
SERIOUSLY, HA-DA. WHAT ARE YOU GOING TO DO IF KO-MO EVER FACES YOUR FATHER?

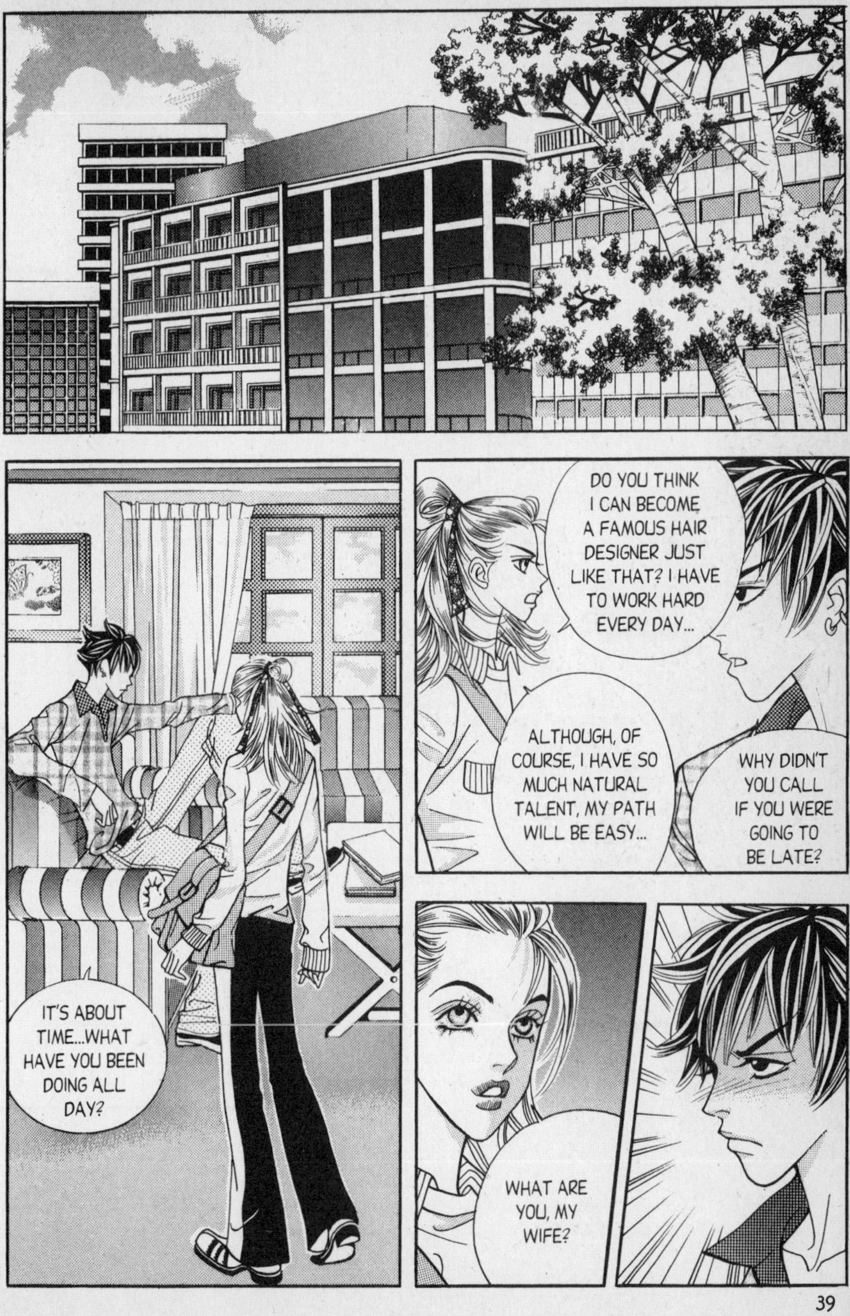
IT'S ABOUT TIME...WHAT HAVE YOU BEEN DOING ALL DAY?
DO YOU THINK I CAN BECOME A FAMOUS HAIR DESIGNER JUST LIKE THAT? I HAVE TO WORK HARD EVERY DAY...
ALTHOUGH, OF COURSE, I HAVE SO MUCH NATURAL TALENT, MY PATH WILL BE EASY...
WHY DIDN'T YOU CALL IF YOU WERE GOING TO BE LATE?
WHAT ARE YOU, MY WIFE?

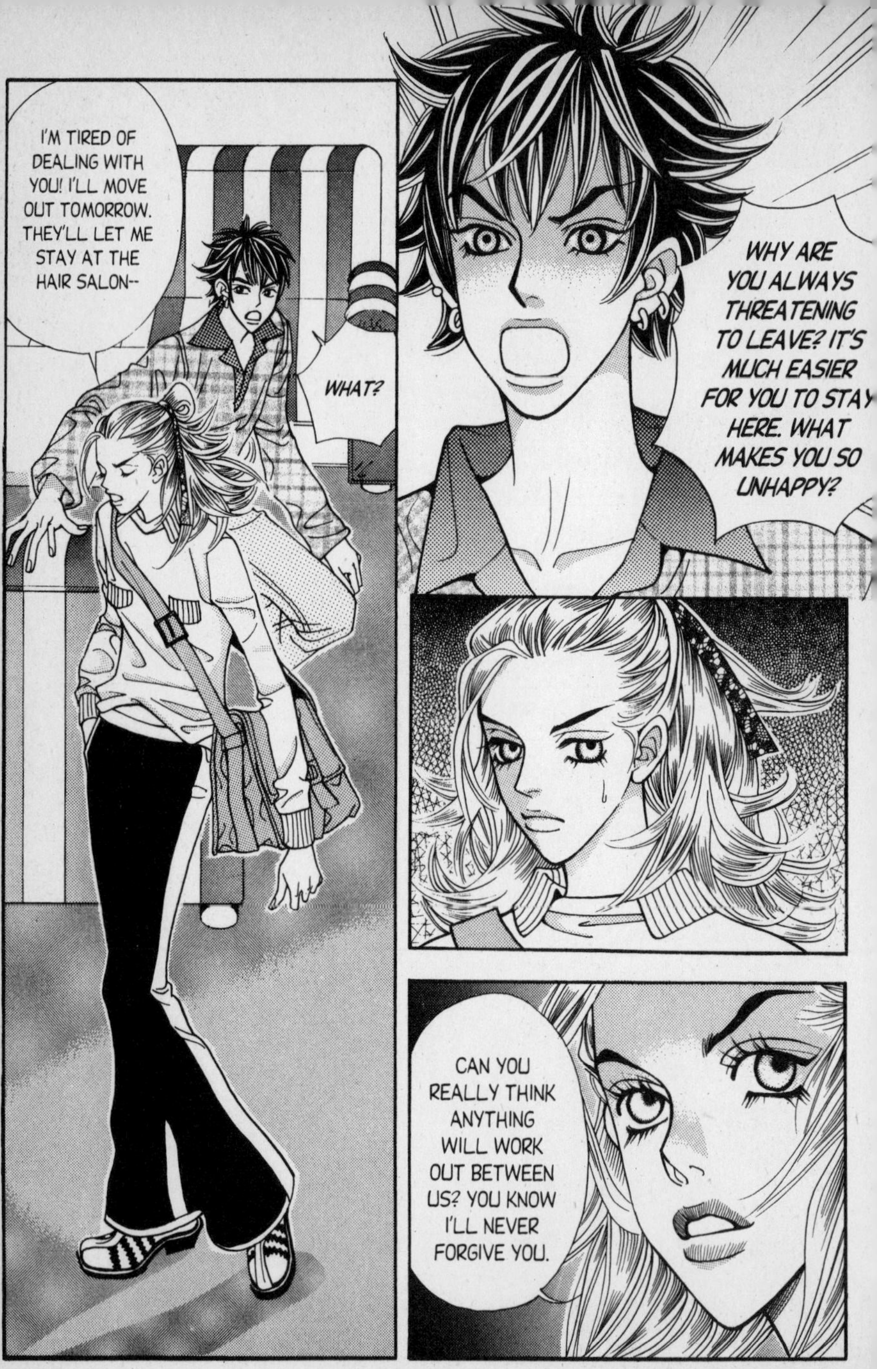
I'M TIRED OF DEALING WITH YOU! I'LL MOVE OUT TOMORROW. THEY'LL LET ME STAY AT THE HAIR SALON--
WHAT?
WHY ARE YOU ALWAYS THREATENING TO LEAVE? IT'S MUCH EASIER FOR YOU TO STAY HERE. WHAT MAKES YOU SO UNHAPPY?
CAN YOU REALLY THINK ANYTHING WILL WORK OUT BETWEEN US? YOU KNOW I'LL NEVER FORGIVE YOU.

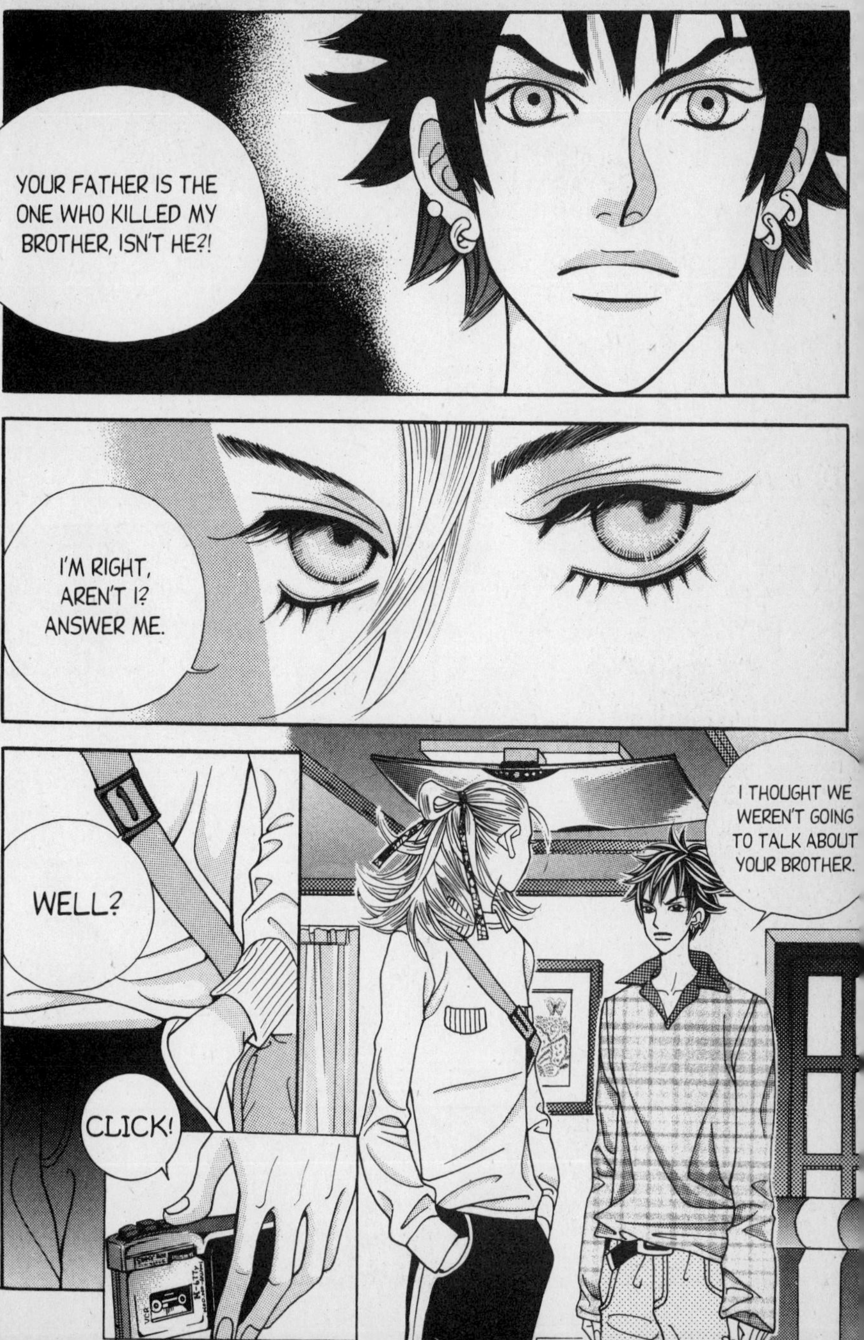
YOUR FATHER IS THE ONE WHO KILLED MY BROTHER, ISN'T HE?!
I'M RIGHT, AREN'T I? ANSWER ME.
WELL?
CLICK!
I THOUGHT WE WEREN'T GOING TO TALK ABOUT YOUR BROTHER.

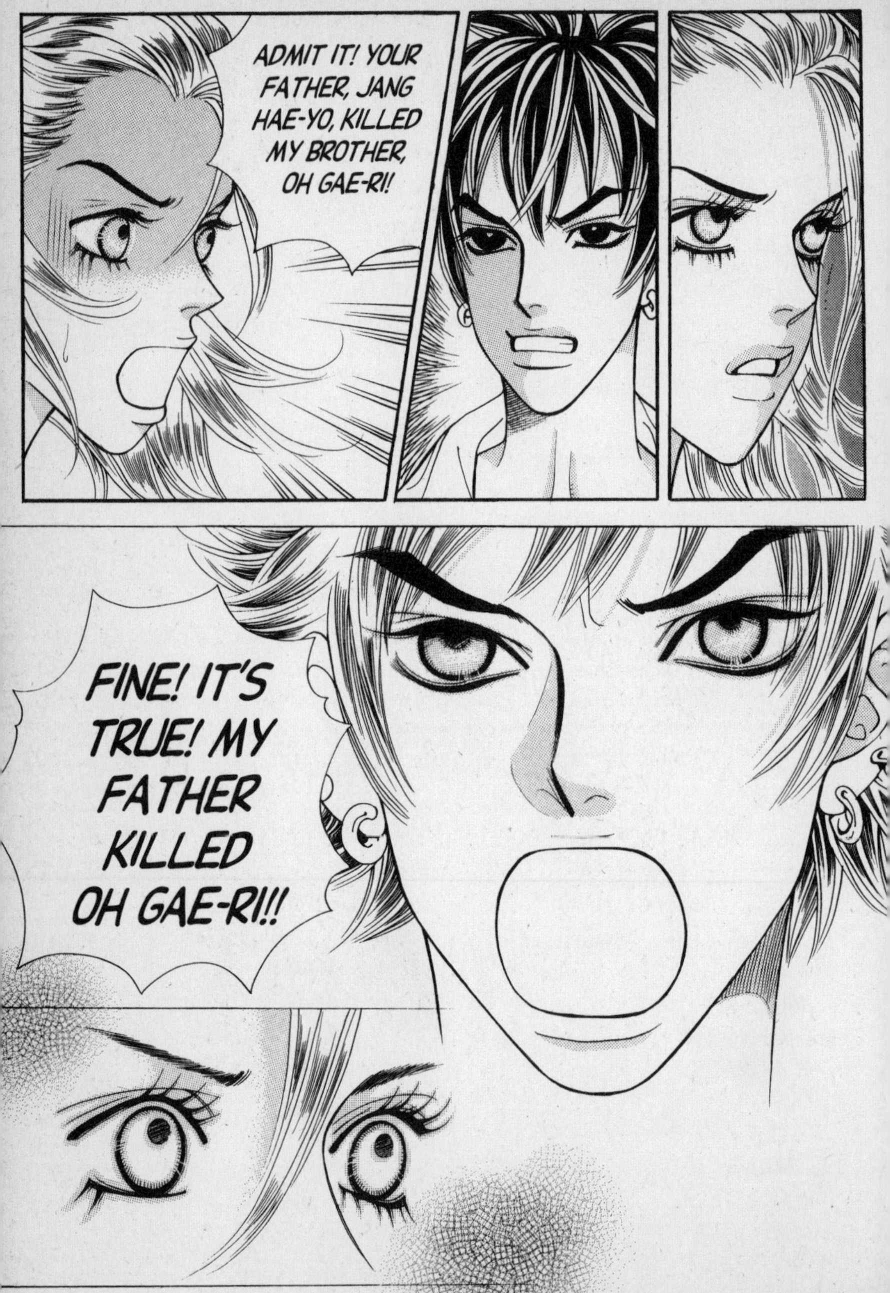
ADMIT IT! YOUR FATHER, JANG HAE-YO, KILLED MY BROTHER, OH GAE-RI!
FINE! IT'S TRUE! MY FATHER KILLED OH GAE-RI!!

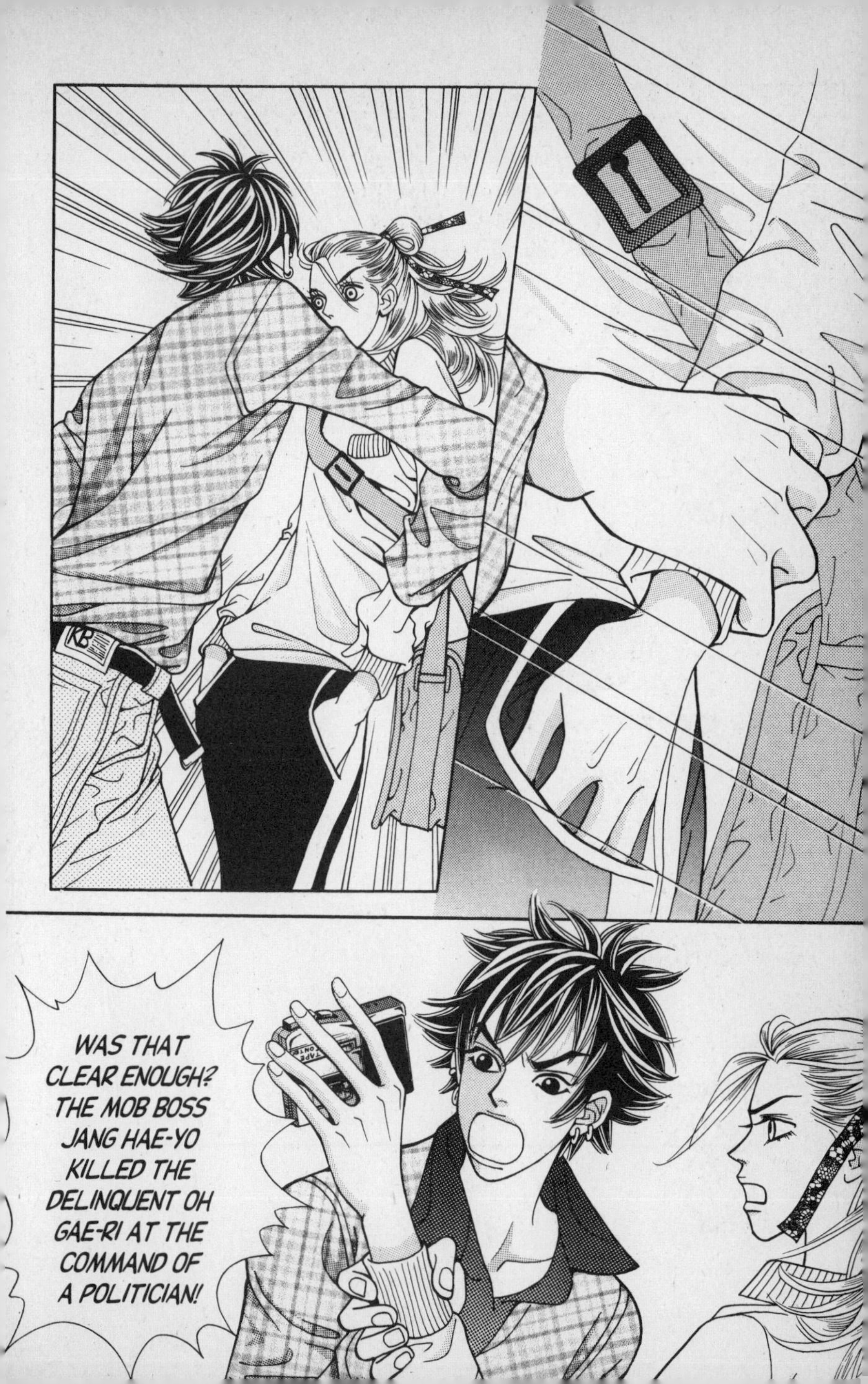
WAS THAT CLEAR ENOUGH? THE MOB BOSS JANG HAE-YO KILLED THE DELINQUENT OH GAE-RI AT THE COMMAND OF A POLITICIAN!

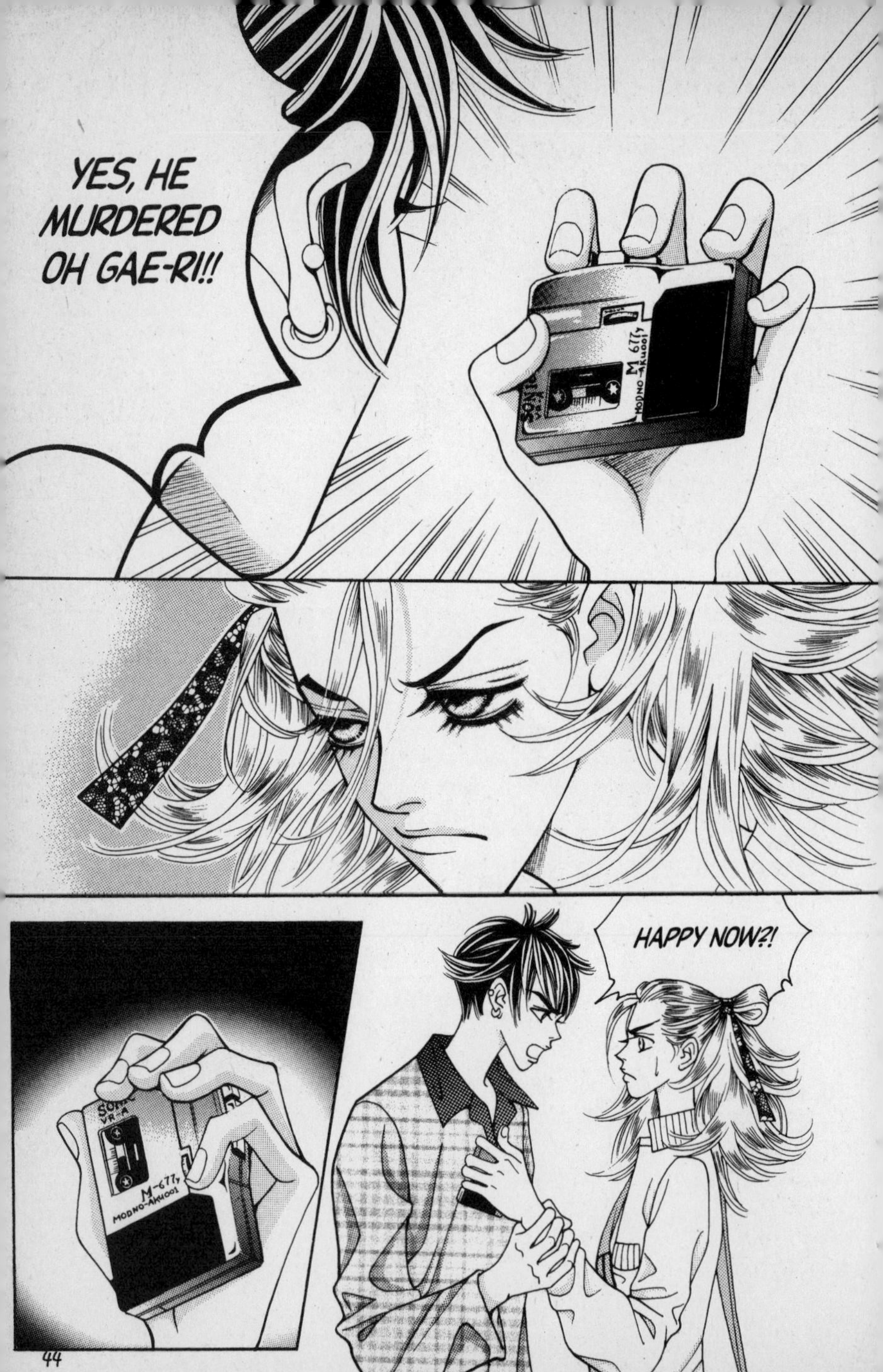
YES, HE MURDERED OH GAE-RI!!
HAPPY NOW?!

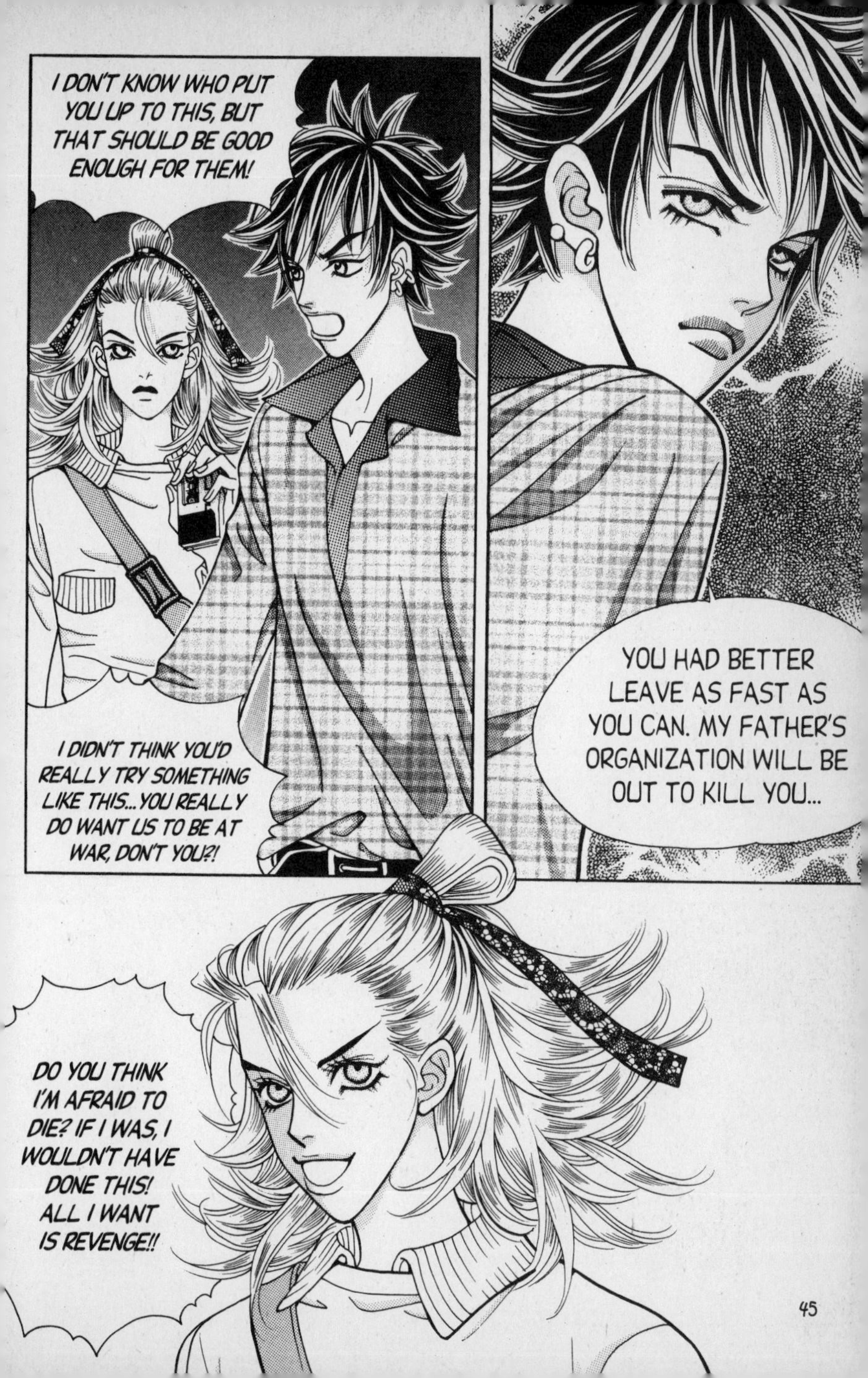
I DON'T KNOW WHO PUT YOU UP TO THIS, BUT THAT SHOULD BE GOOD ENOUGH FOR THEM!
I DIDN'T THINK YOU'D REALLY TRY SOMETHING LIKE THIS...YOU REALLY DO WANT US TO BE AT WAR, DON'T YOU?!
YOU HAD BETTER LEAVE AS FAST AS YOU CAN. MY FATHER'S ORGANIZATION WILL BE OUT TO KILL YOU...
DO YOU THINK I'M AFRAID TO DIE? IF I WAS, I WOULDN'T HAVE DONE THIS! ALL I WANT IS REVENGE!!

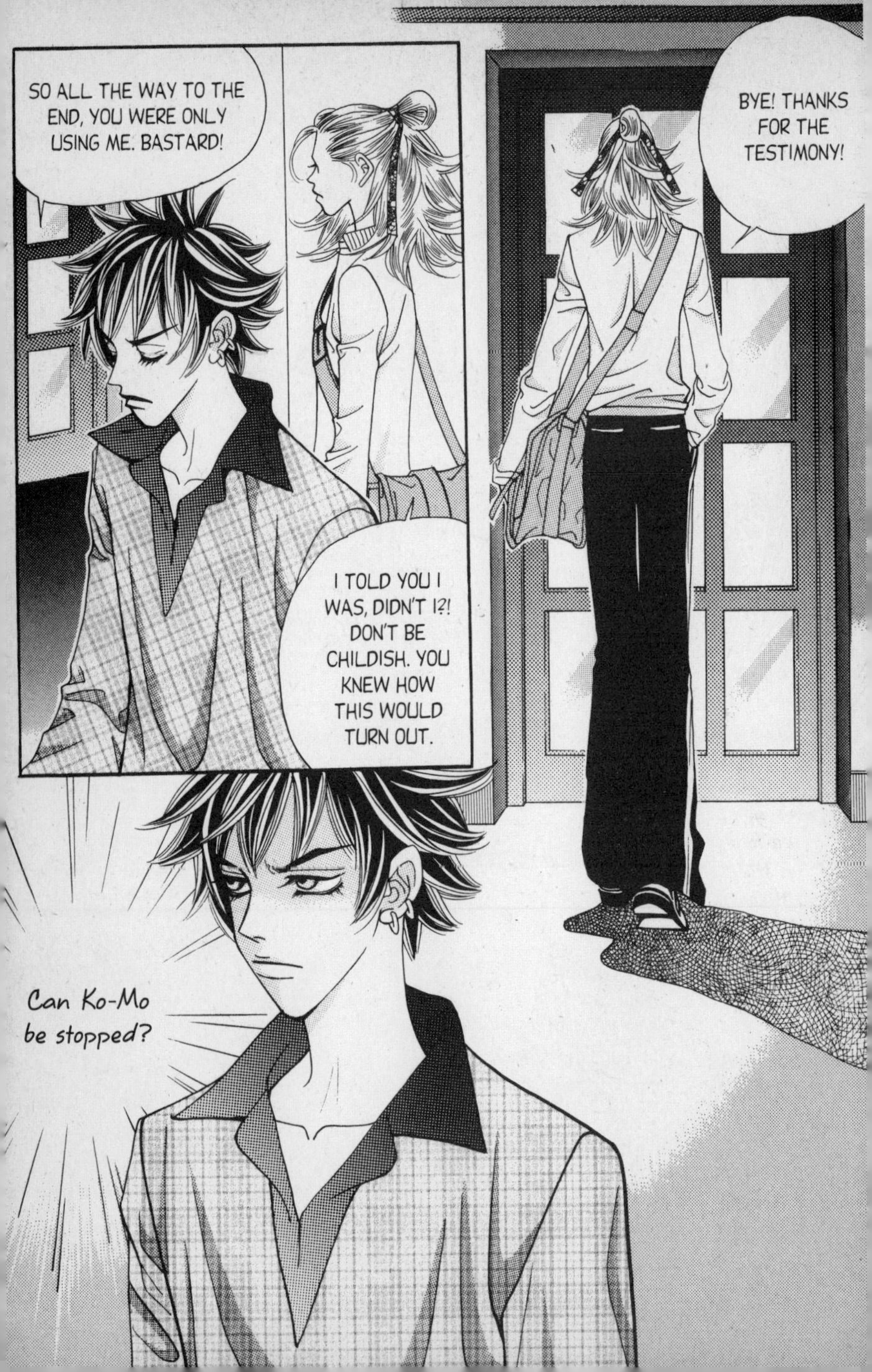
SO ALL THE WAY TO THE END, YOU WERE ONLY USING ME. BASTARD!
I TOLD YOU I WAS, DIDN'T I?! DON'T BE CHILDISH. YOU KNEW HOW THIS WOULD TURN OUT.
BYE! THANKS FOR THE TESTIMONY!
Can Ko-Mo be stopped?

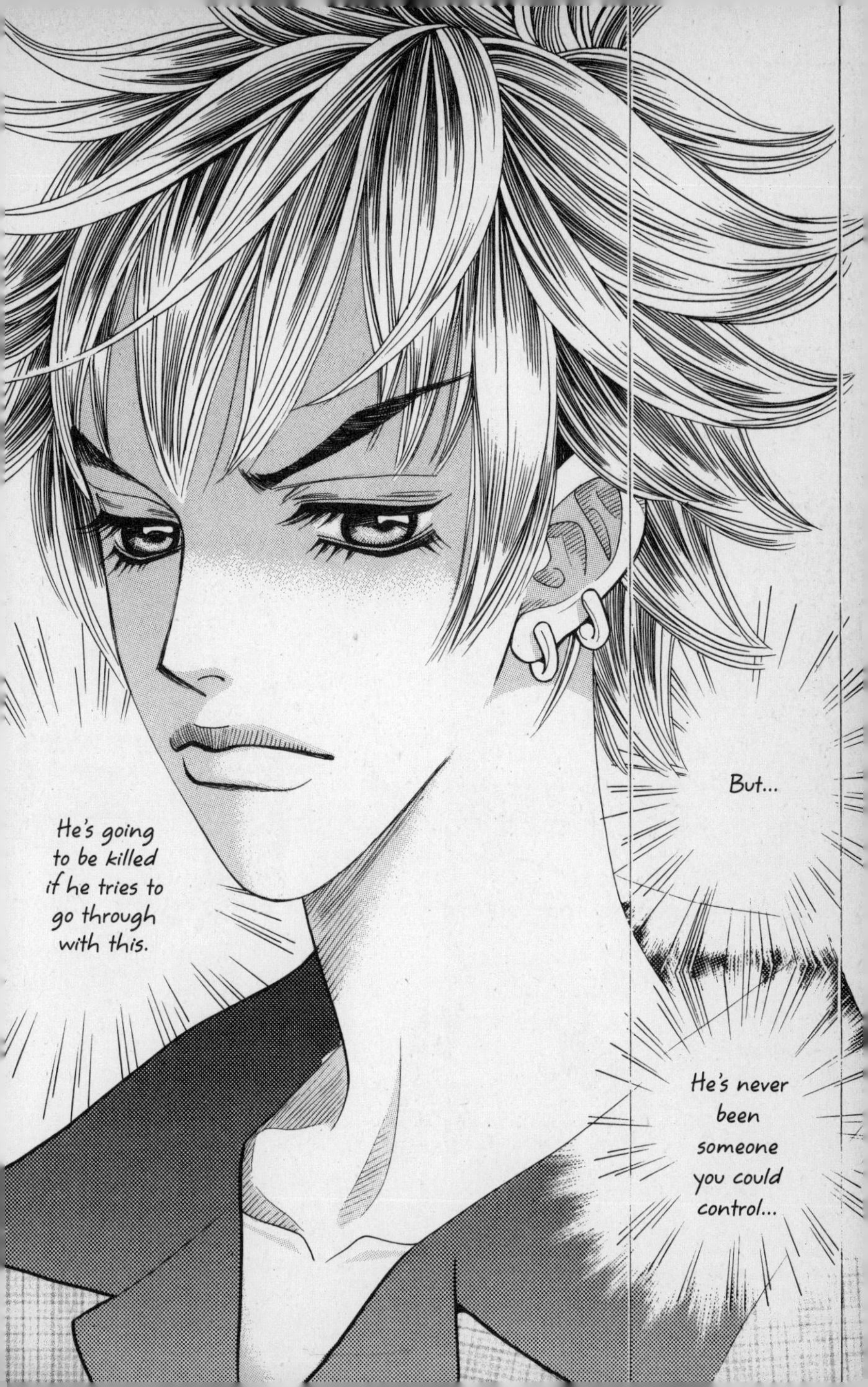
He's going to be killed if he tries to go through with this.
But...
He's never been someone you could control...

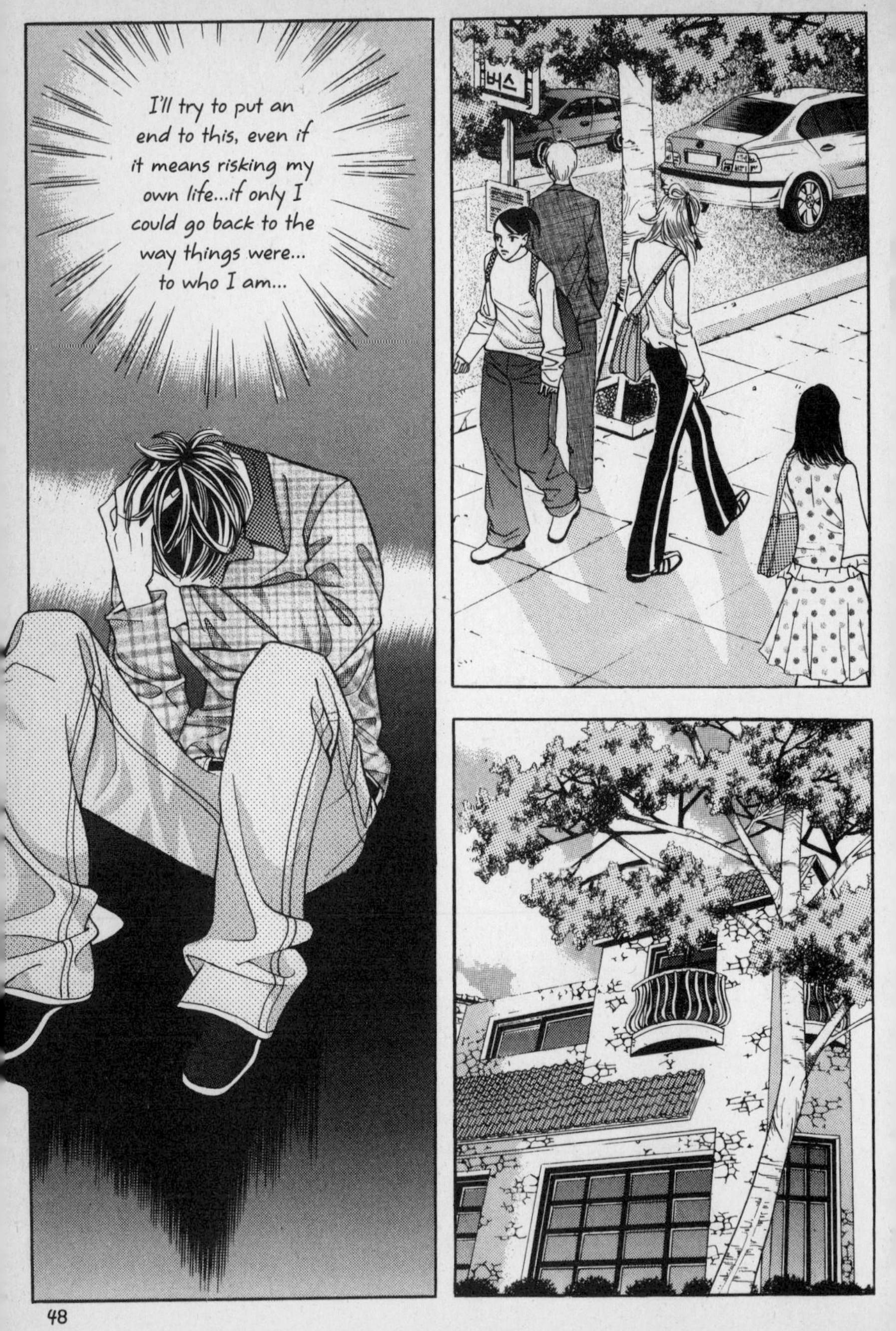
I'll try to put an end to this, even if it means risking my own life...if only I could go back to the way things were... to who I am...
버스

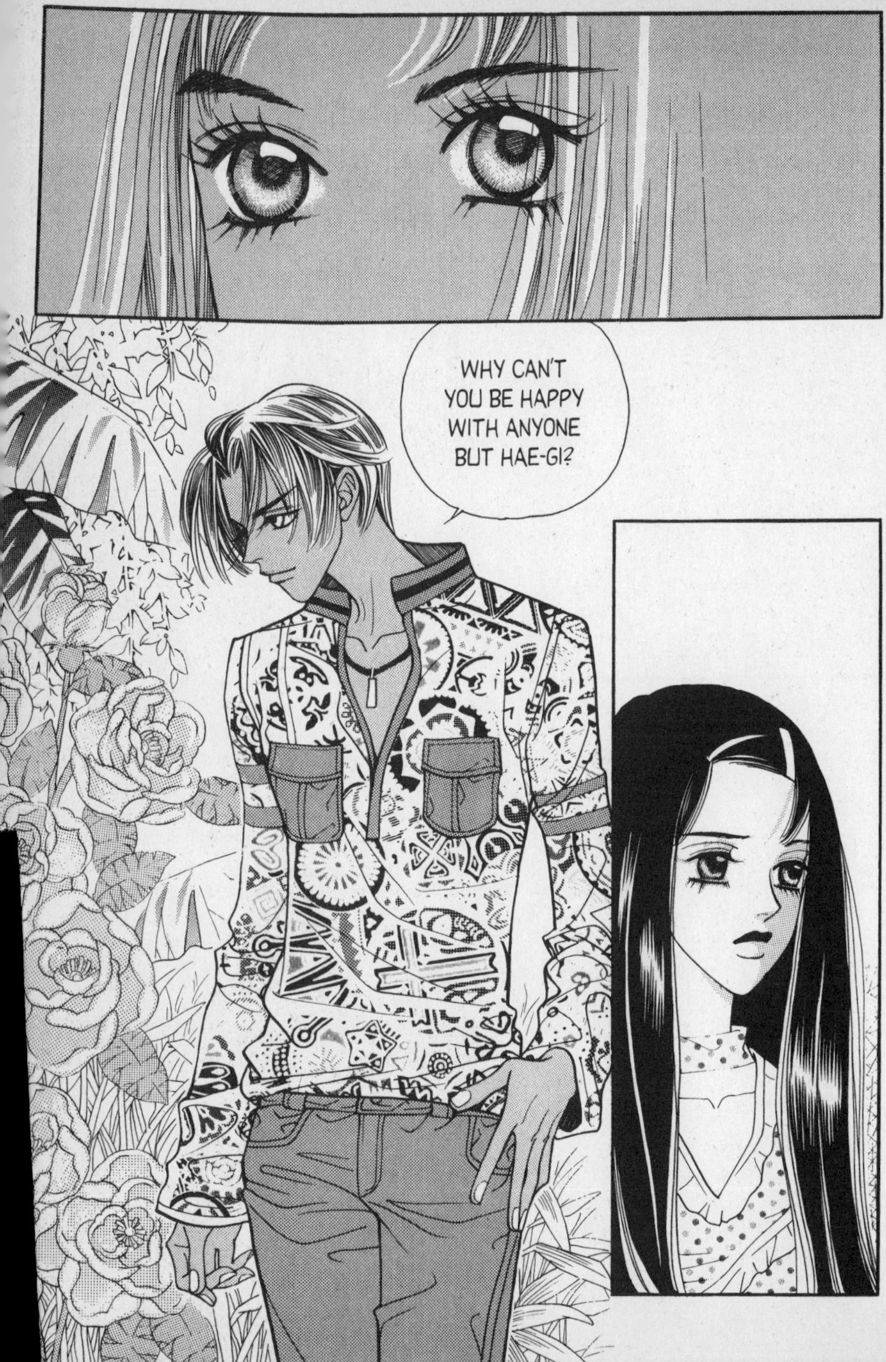
WHY CAN'T YOU BE HAPPY WITH ANYONE BUT HAE-GI?

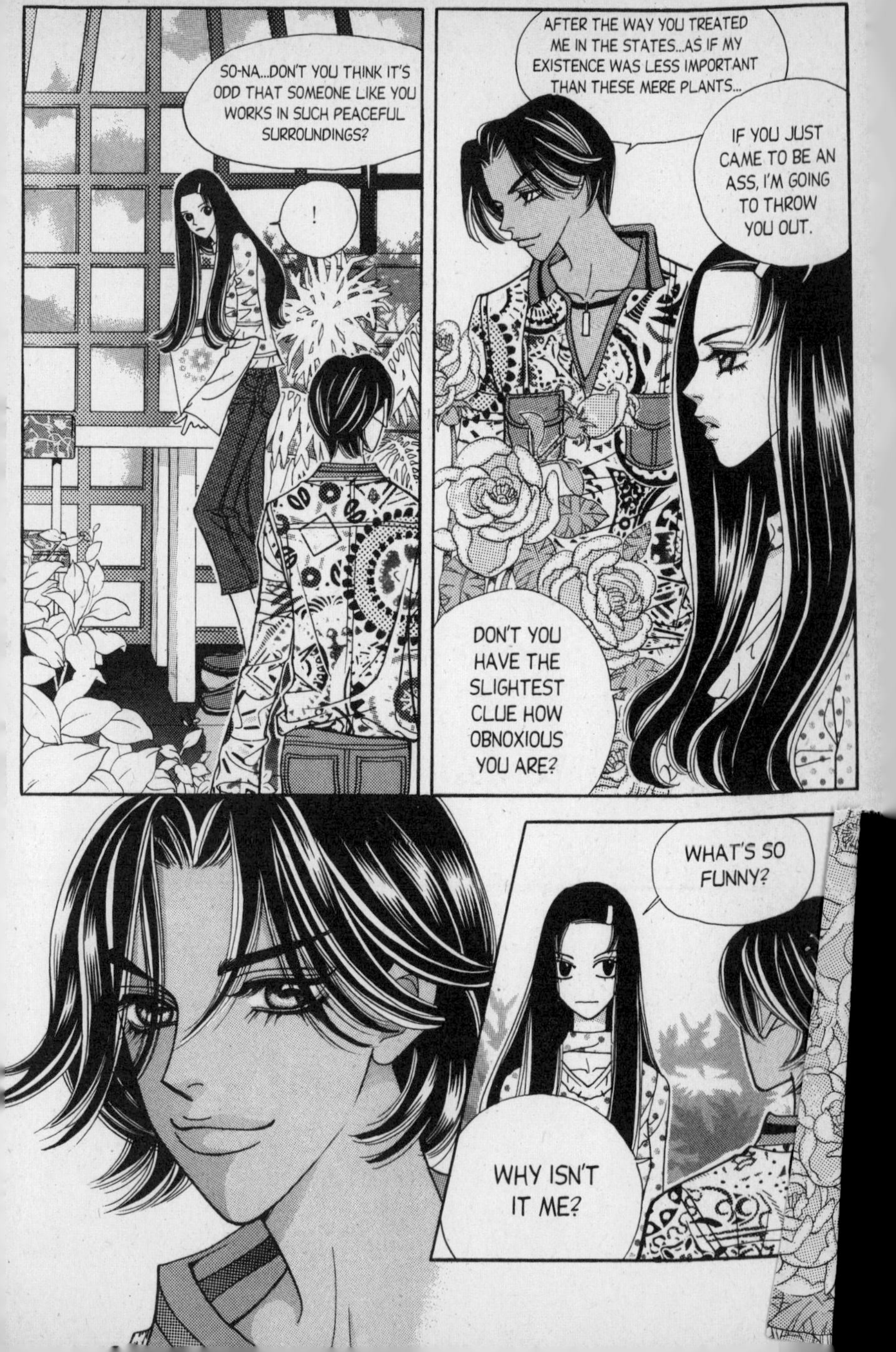
SO-NA...DON'T YOU THINK IT'S ODD THAT SOMEONE LIKE YOU WORKS IN SUCH PEACEFUL SURROUNDINGS?
!
AFTER THE WAY YOU TREATED ME IN THE STATES...AS IF MY EXISTENCE WAS LESS IMPORTANT THAN THESE MERE PLANTS...
IF YOU JUST CAME TO BE AN ASS, I'M GOING TO THROW YOU OUT.
DON'T YOU HAVE THE SLIGHTEST CLUE HOW OBNOXIOUS YOU ARE?
WHAT'S SO FUNNY?
WHY ISN'T IT ME?

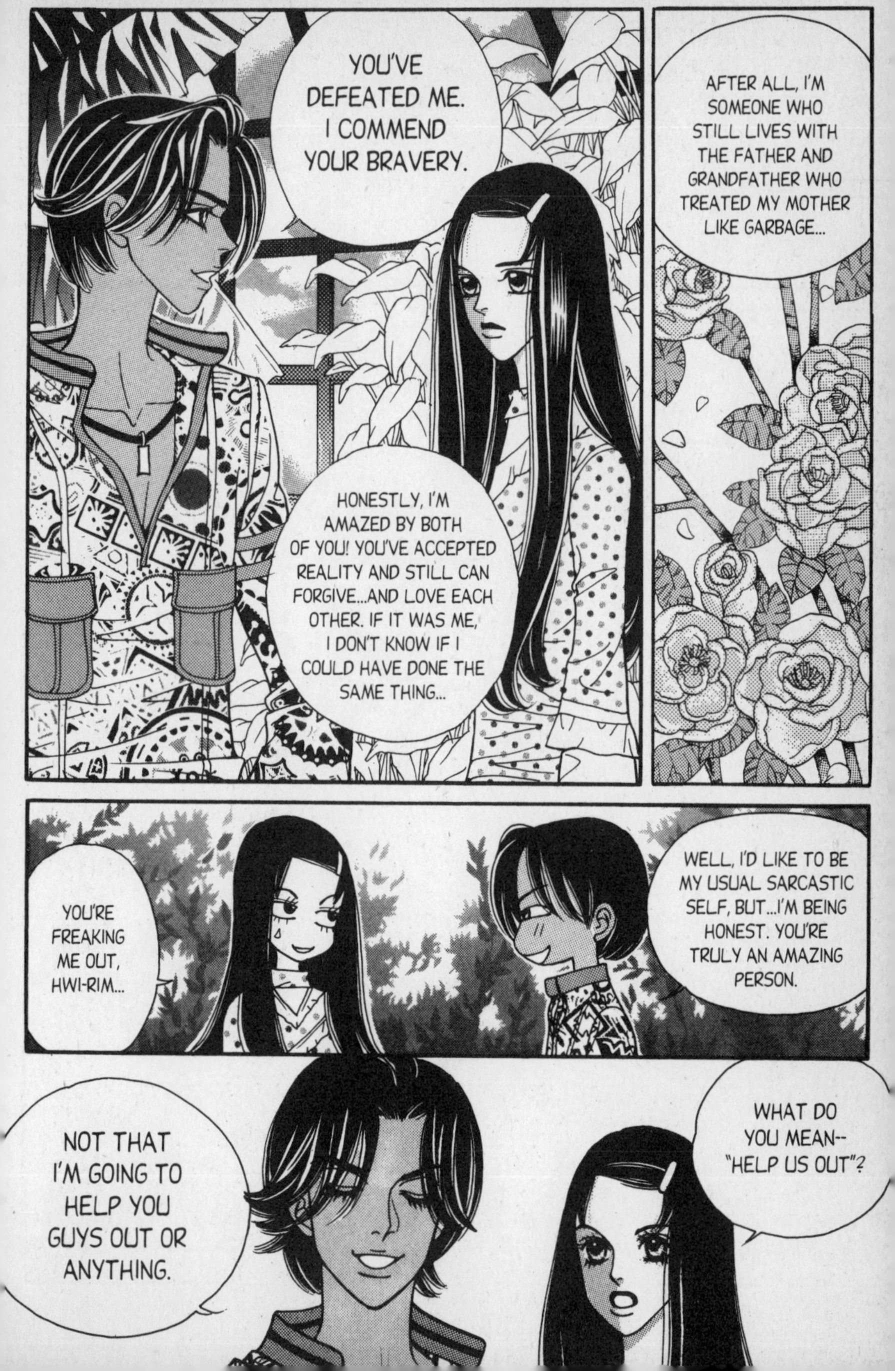
YOU'VE DEFEATED ME. I COMMEND YOUR BRAVERY.
HONESTLY, I'M AMAZED BY BOTH OF YOU! YOU'VE ACCEPTED REALITY AND STILL CAN FORGIVE...AND LOVE EACH OTHER. IF IT WAS ME, I DON'T KNOW IF I COULD HAVE DONE THE SAME THING...
AFTER ALL, I'M SOMEONE WHO STILL LIVES WITH THE FATHER AND GRANDFATHER WHO TREATED MY MOTHER LIKE GARBAGE...
YOU'RE FREAKING ME OUT, HWI-RIM...
WELL, I'D LIKE TO BE MY USUAL SARCASTIC SELF, BUT...I'M BEING HONEST. YOU'RE TRULY AN AMAZING PERSON.
NOT THAT I'M GOING TO HELP YOU GUYS OUT OR ANYTHING.
WHAT DO YOU MEAN-- "HELP US OUT"?

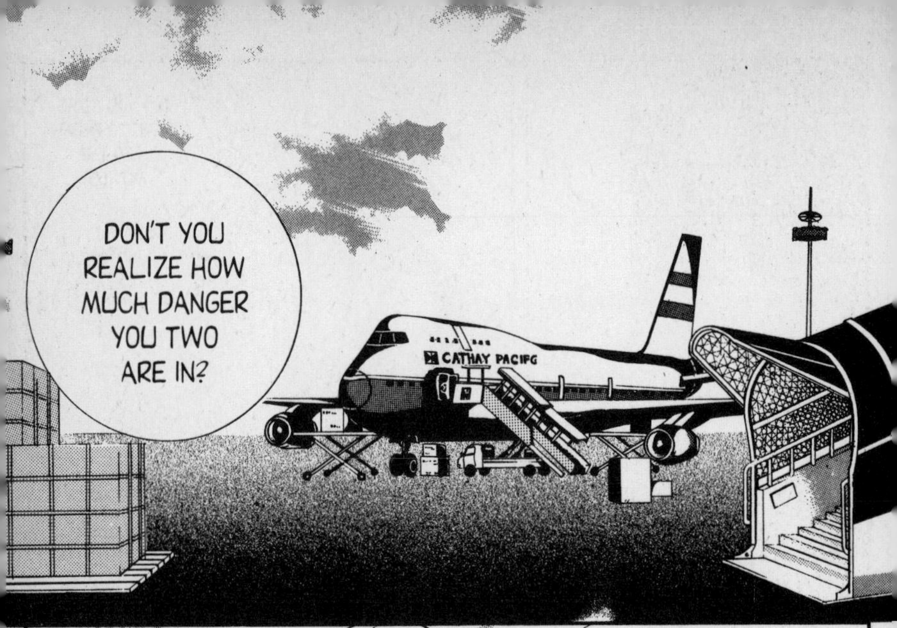
DON'T YOU REALIZE HOW MUCH DANGER YOU TWO ARE IN?
CATHAY PACIFIC

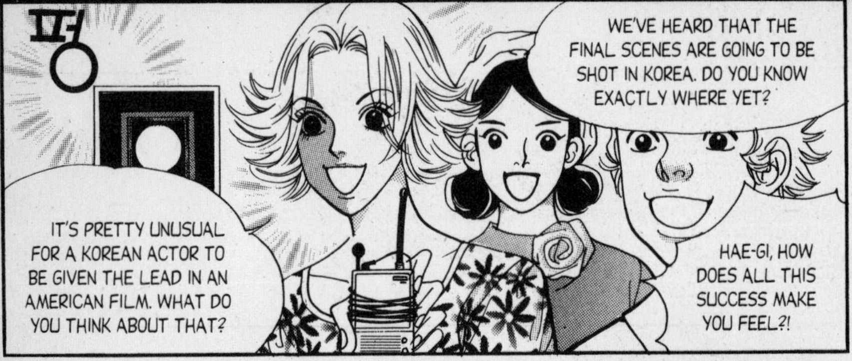
WE'VE HEARD THAT THE FINAL SCENES ARE GOING TO BE SHOT IN KOREA. DO YOU KNOW EXACTLY WHERE YET?
IT'S PRETTY UNUSUAL FOR A KOREAN ACTOR TO BE GIVEN THE LEAD IN AN AMERICAN FILM. WHAT DO YOU THINK ABOUT THAT?
HAE-GI, HOW DOES ALL THIS SUCCESS MAKE YOU FEEL?!

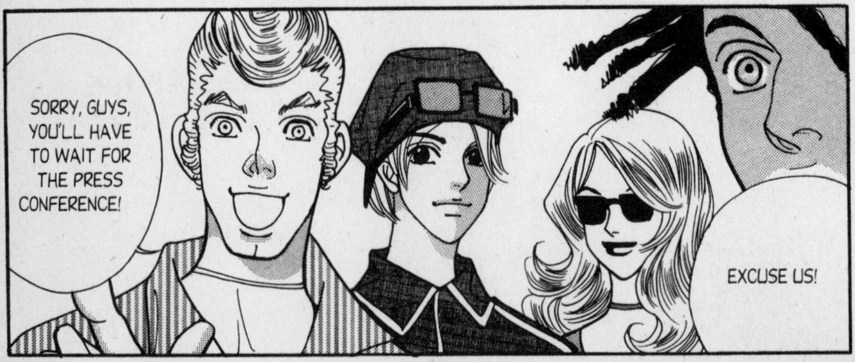
SORRY, GUYS, YOU'LL HAVE TO WAIT FOR THE PRESS CONFERENCE!
EXCUSE US!

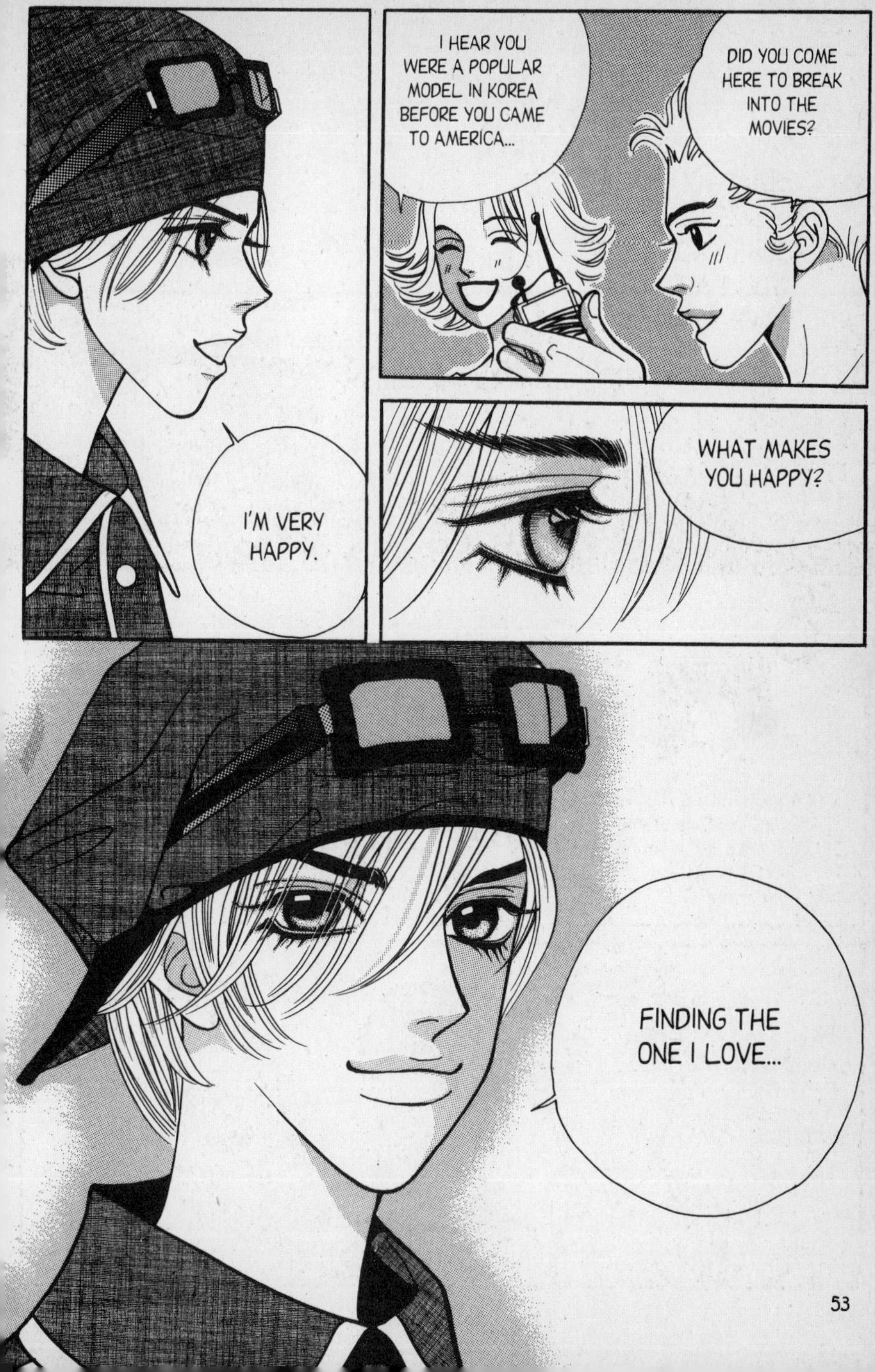
I HEAR YOU WERE A POPULAR MODEL IN KOREA BEFORE YOU CAME TO AMERICA...
DID YOU COME HERE TO BREAK INTO THE MOVIES?
I'M VERY HAPPY.
WHAT MAKES YOU HAPPY?
FINDING THE ONE I LOVE...

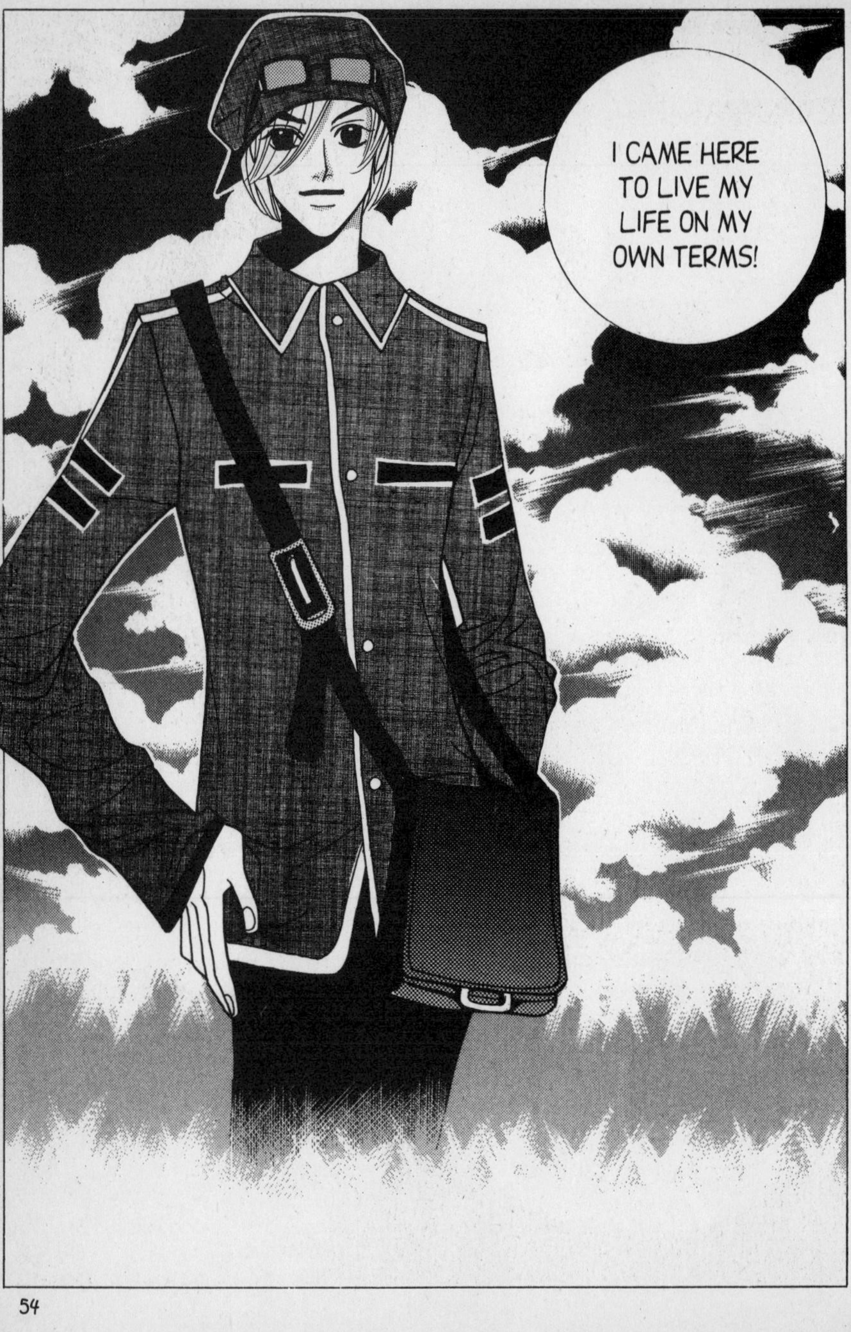
I CAME HERE TO LIVE MY LIFE ON MY OWN TERMS!

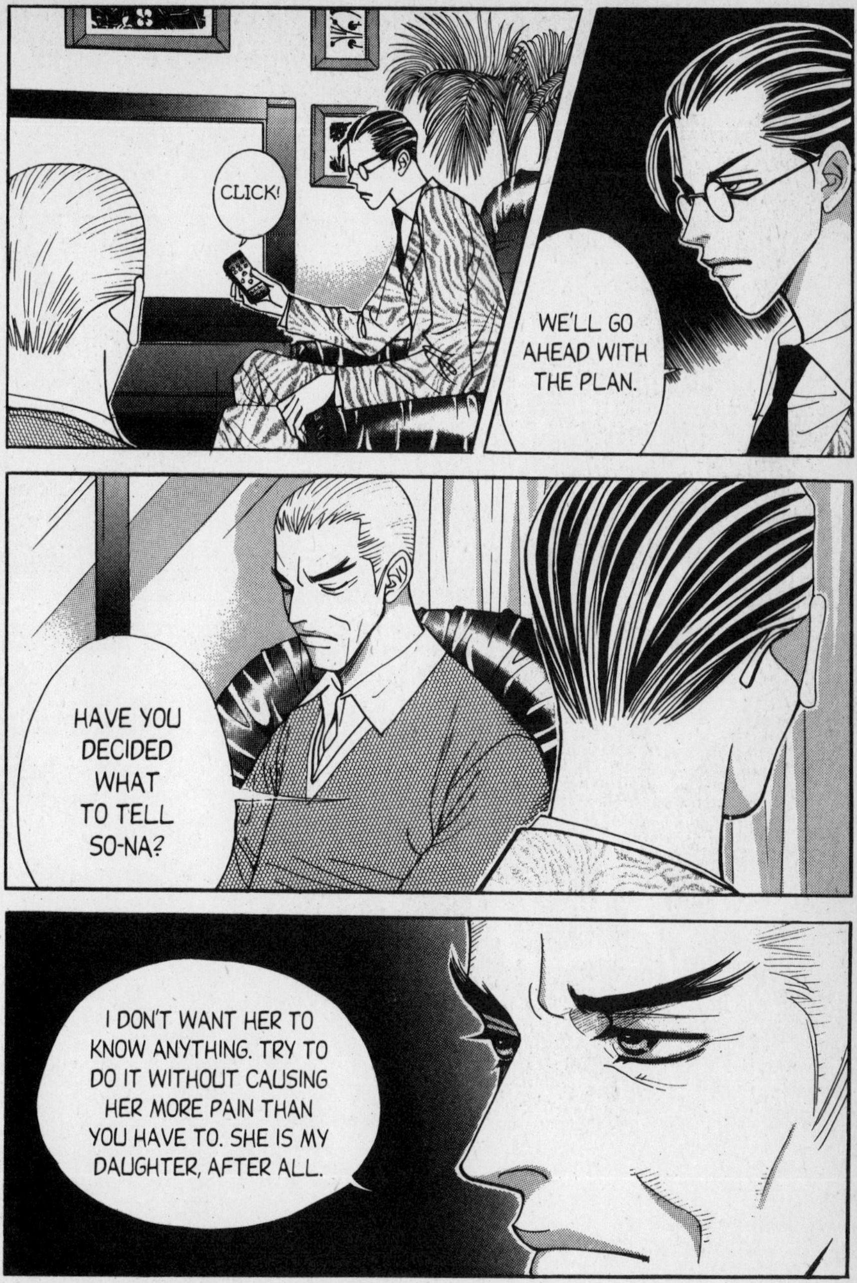
CLICK!
WE'LL GO AHEAD WITH THE PLAN.
HAVE YOU DECIDED WHAT TO TELL SO-NA?
I DON'T WANT HER TO KNOW ANYTHING. TRY TO DO IT WITHOUT CAUSING HER MORE PAIN THAN YOU HAVE TO. SHE IS MY DAUGHTER, AFTER ALL.

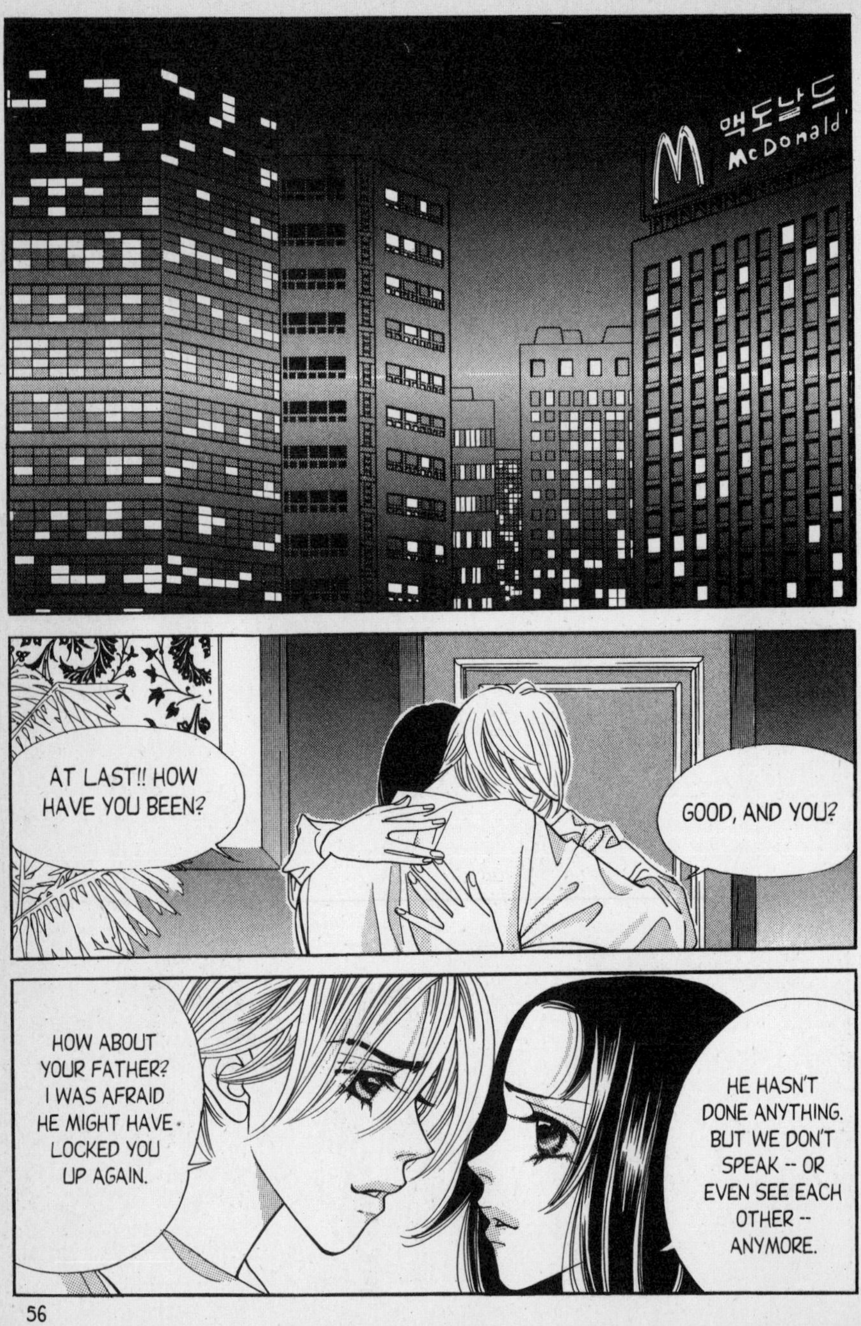
맥도날드
McDonald's
AT LAST!! HOW HAVE YOU BEEN?
GOOD, AND YOU?
HOW ABOUT YOUR FATHER? I WAS AFRAID HE MIGHT HAVE LOCKED YOU UP AGAIN.
HE HASN'T DONE ANYTHING. BUT WE DON'T SPEAK -- OR EVEN SEE EACH OTHER -- ANYMORE.

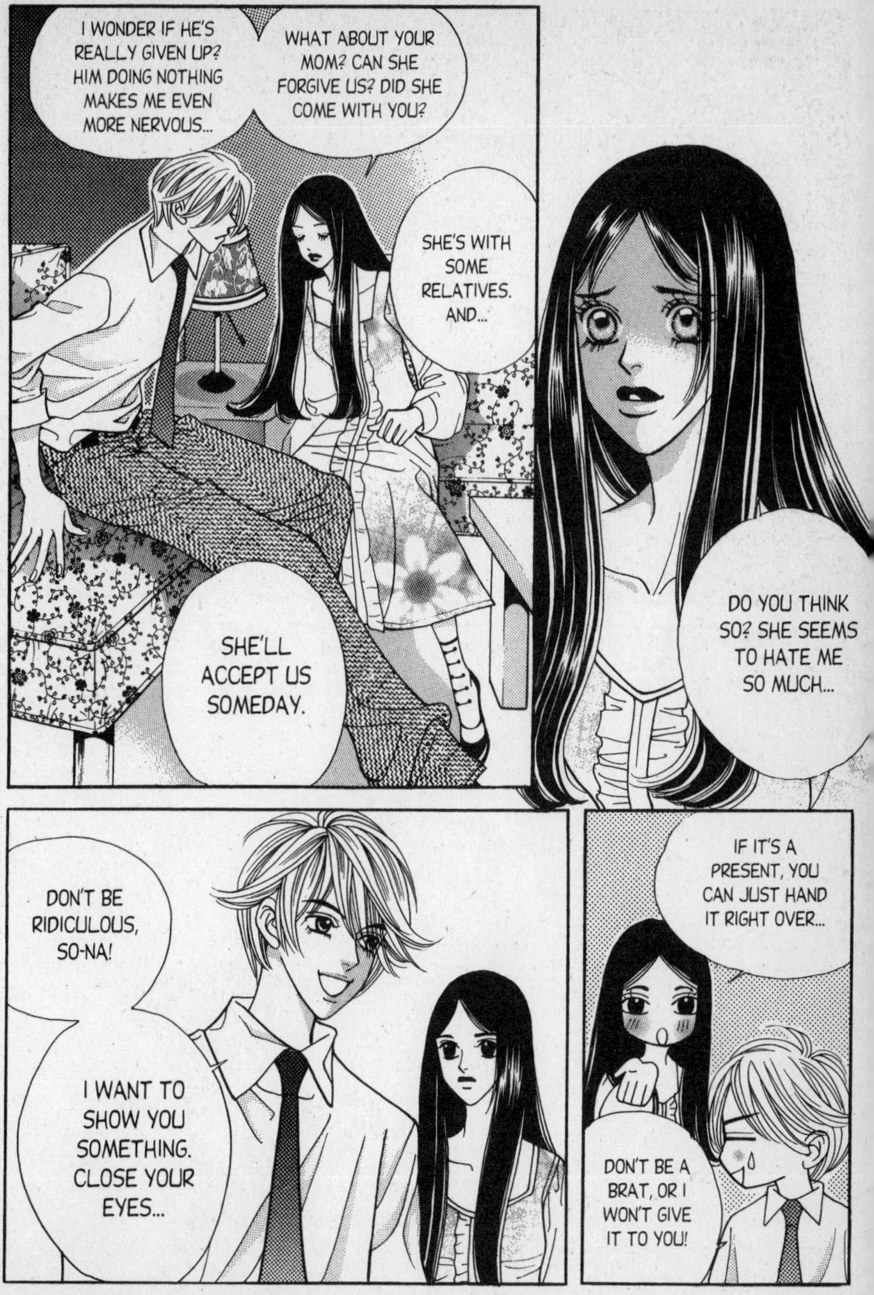
I WONDER IF HE'S REALLY GIVEN UP? HIM DOING NOTHING MAKES ME EVEN MORE NERVOUS...
WHAT ABOUT YOUR MOM? CAN SHE FORGIVE US? DID SHE COME WITH YOU?
SHE'S WITH SOME RELATIVES. AND...
SHE'LL ACCEPT US SOMEDAY.
DO YOU THINK SO? SHE SEEMS TO HATE ME SO MUCH...
DON'T BE RIDICULOUS, SO-NA!
I WANT TO SHOW YOU SOMETHING. CLOSE YOUR EYES...
IF IT'S A PRESENT, YOU CAN JUST HAND IT RIGHT OVER...
DON'T BE A BRAT, OR I WON'T GIVE IT TO YOU!

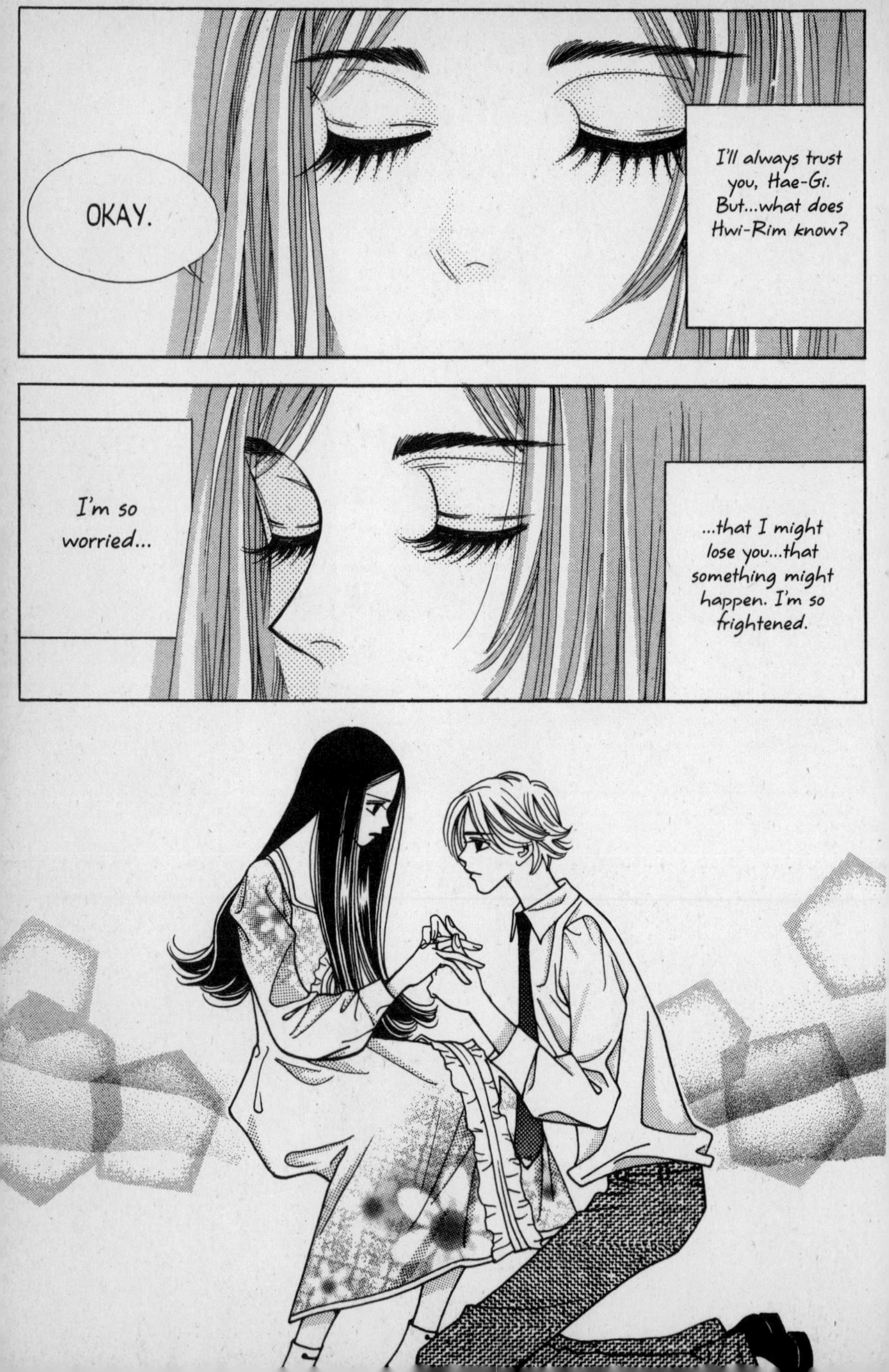
OKAY.
I'll always trust you, Hae-Gi. But...what does Hwi-Rim know?
I'm so worried...
...that I might lose you...that something might happen. I'm so frightened.

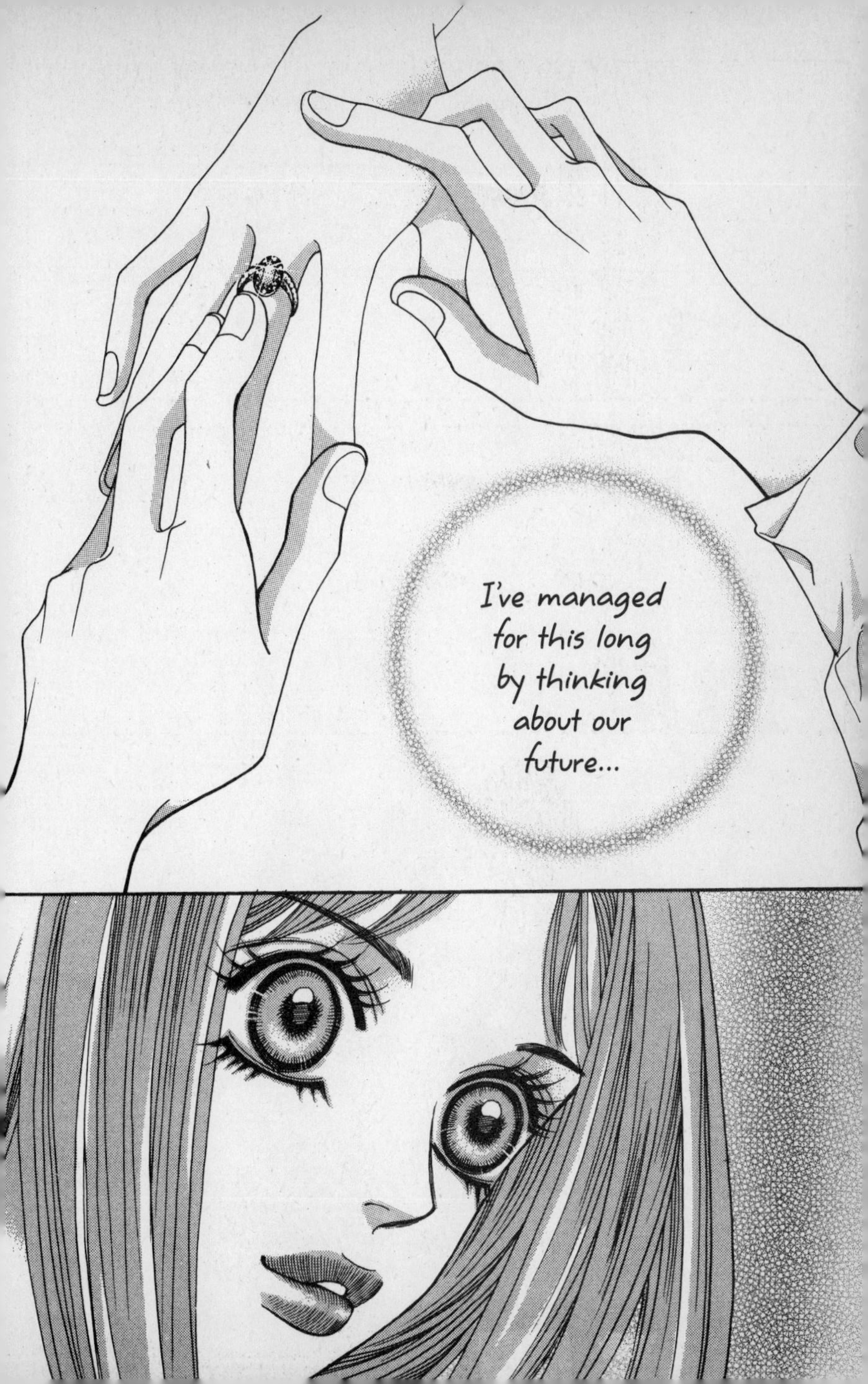
I've managed for this long by thinking about our future...

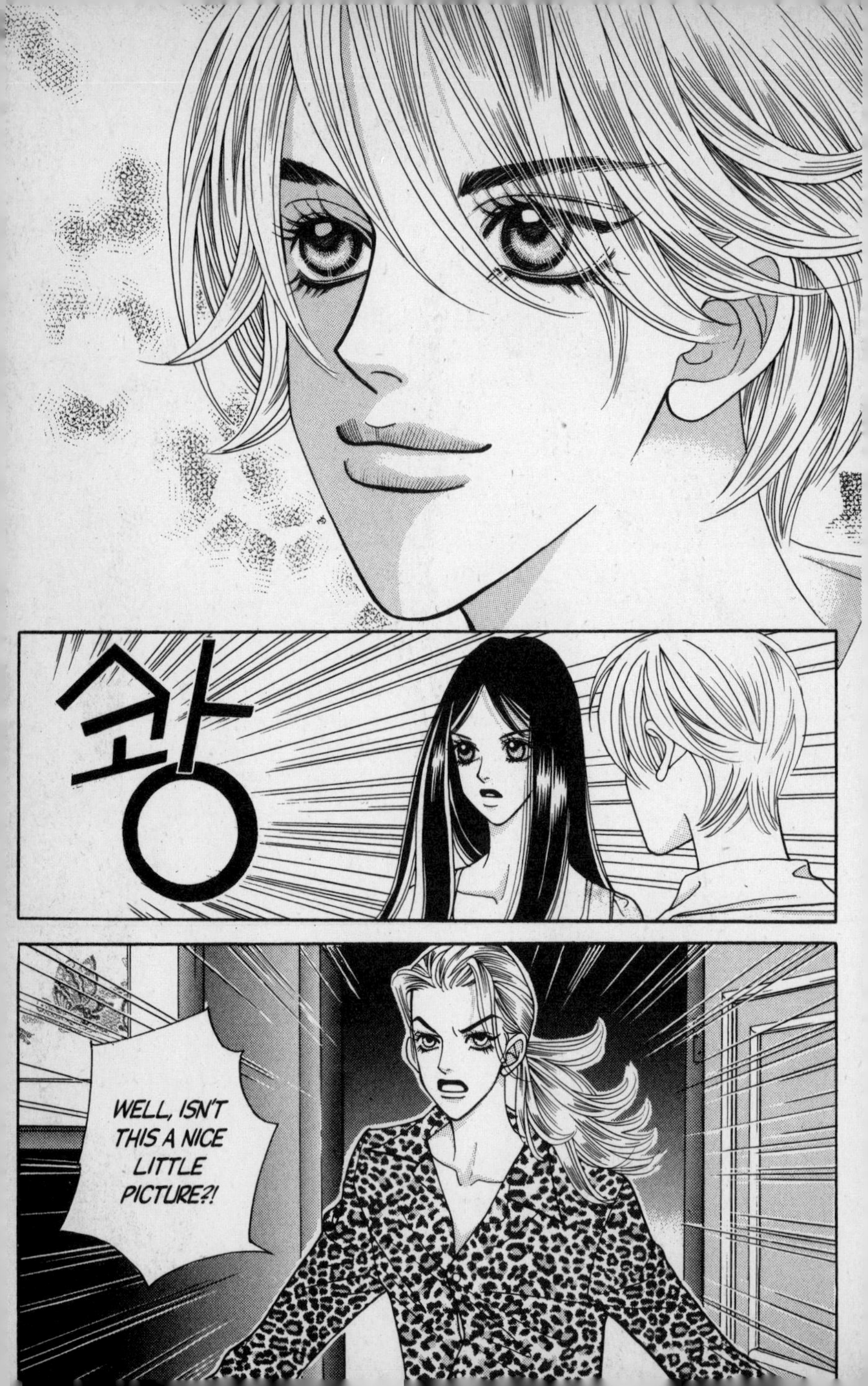
쾅
WELL, ISN'T THIS A NICE LITTLE PICTURE?!

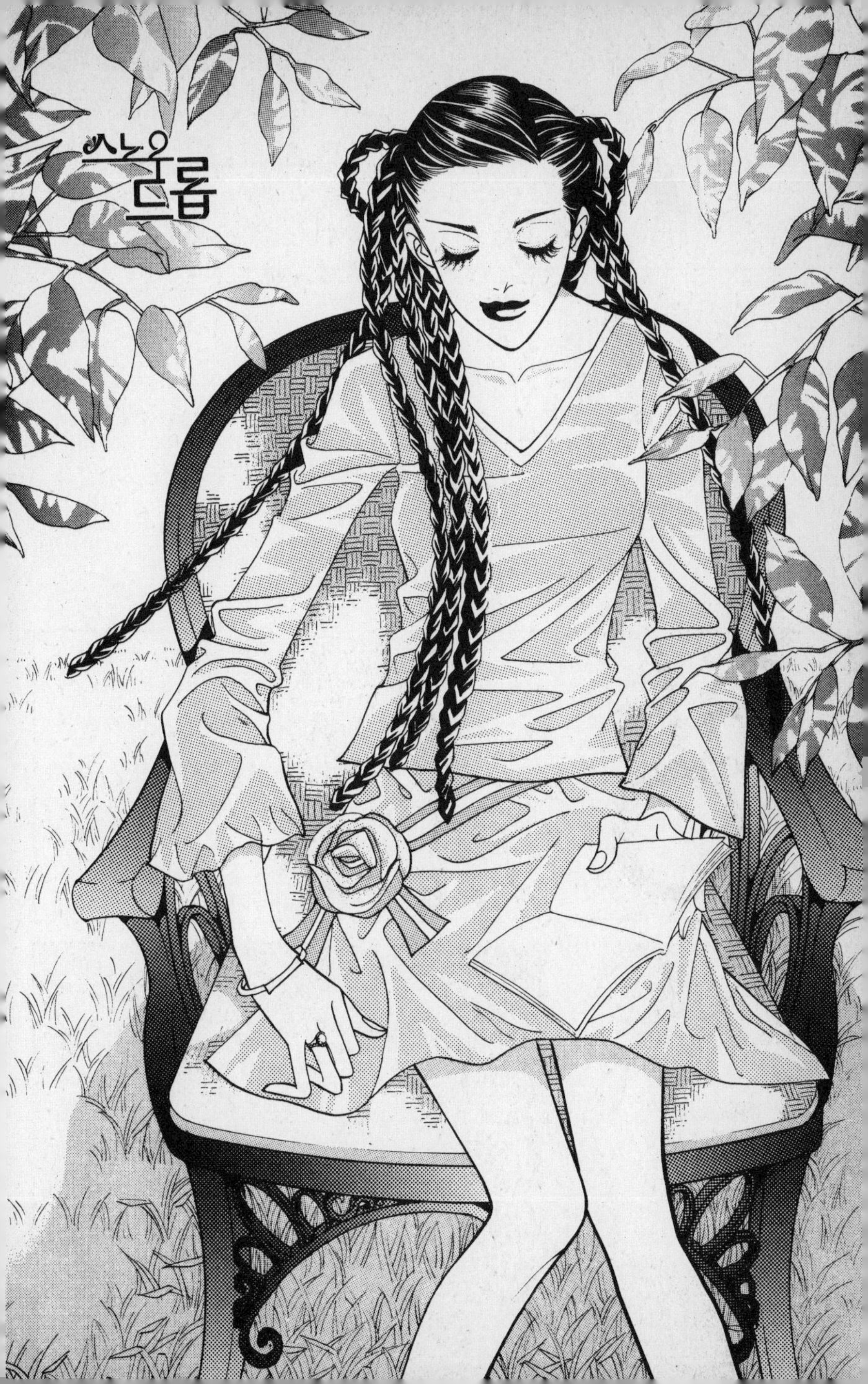
스노우드롭

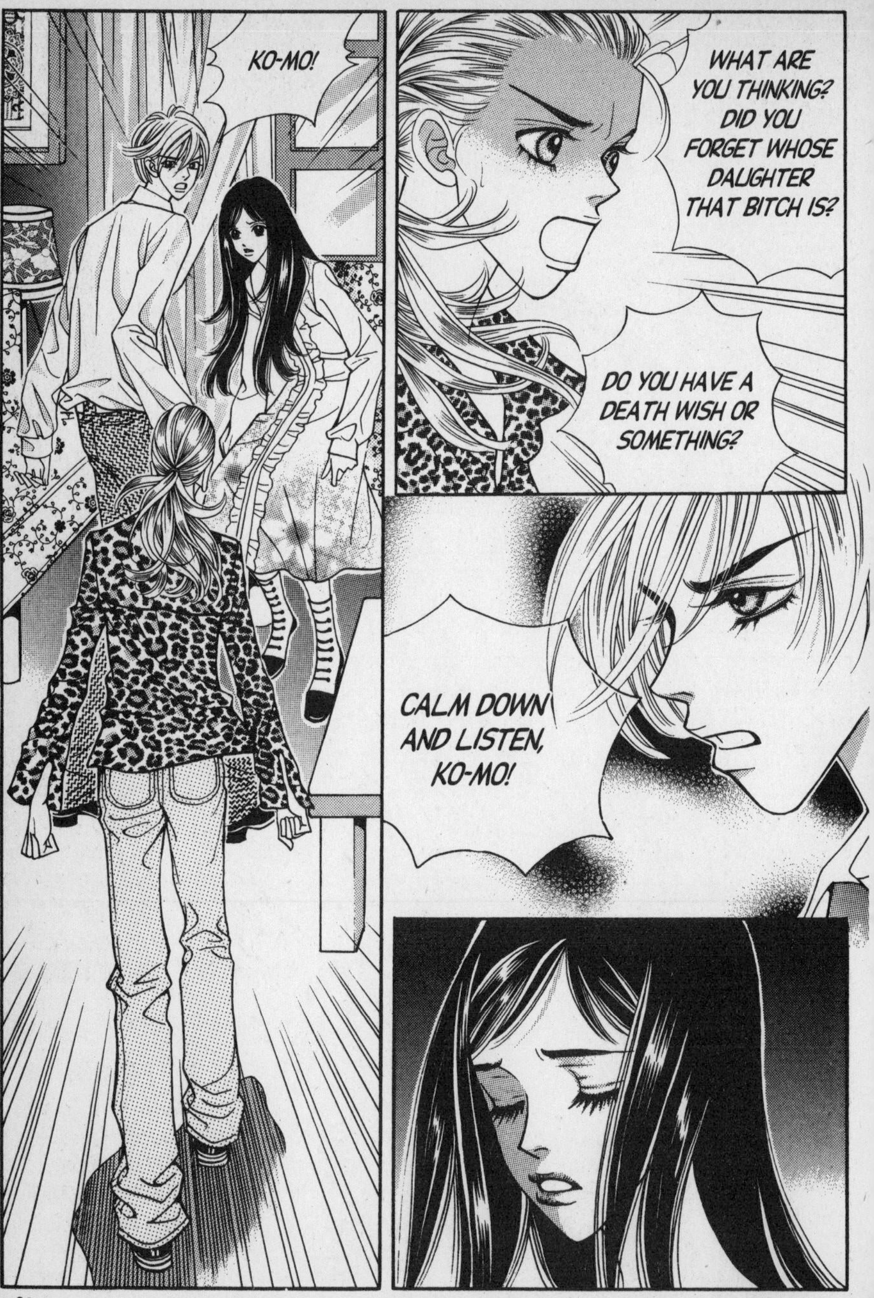
KO-MO!
WHAT ARE YOU THINKING? DID YOU FORGET WHOSE DAUGHTER THAT BITCH IS?
DO YOU HAVE A DEATH WISH OR SOMETHING?
CALM DOWN AND LISTEN, KO-MO!

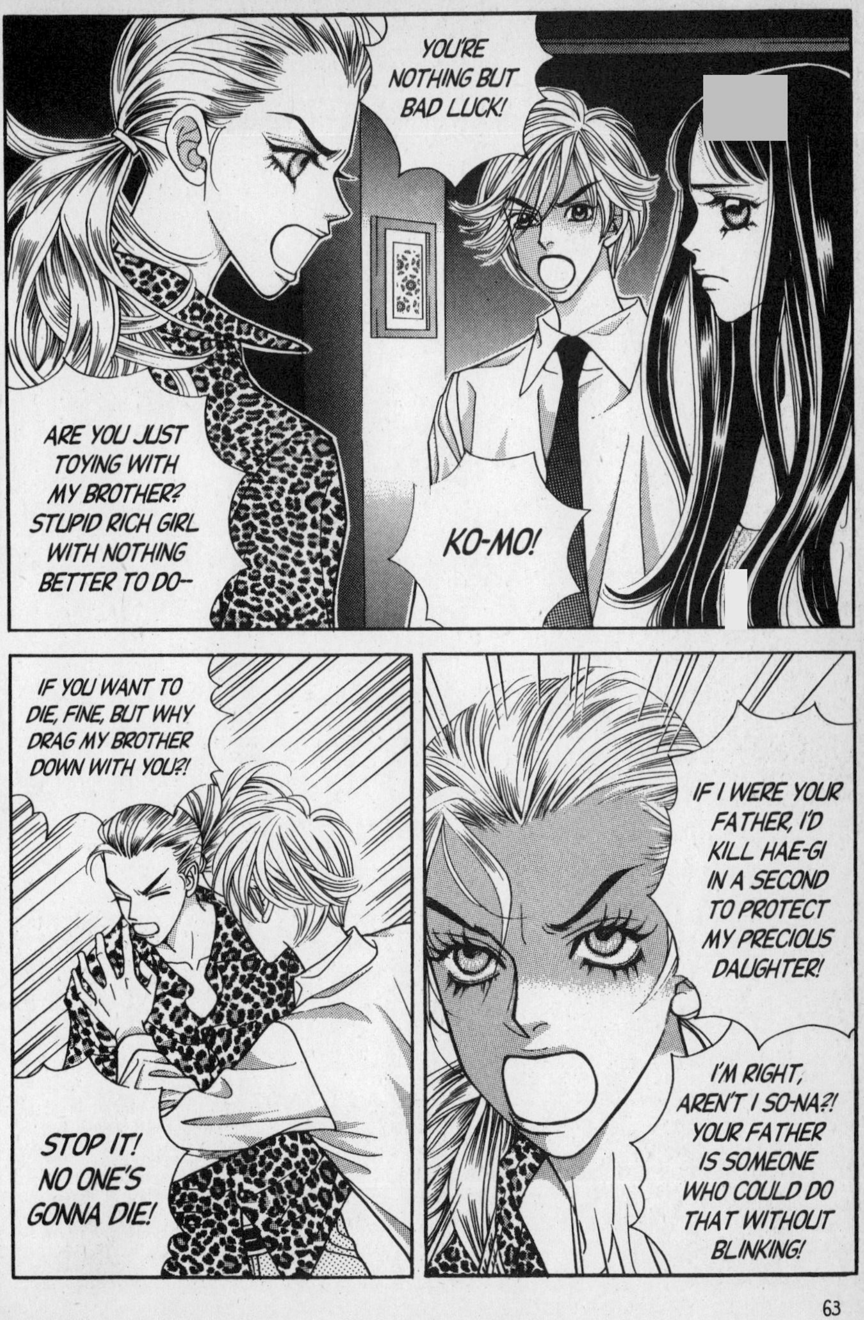
ARE YOU JUST TOYING WITH MY BROTHER? STUPID RICH GIRL WITH NOTHING BETTER TO DO--
YOU'RE NOTHING BUT BAD LUCK!
KO-MO!
IF YOU WANT TO DIE, FINE, BUT WHY DRAG MY BROTHER DOWN WITH YOU?!
STOP IT! NO ONE'S GONNA DIE!
IF I WERE YOUR FATHER, I'D KILL HAE-GI IN A SECOND TO PROTECT MY PRECIOUS DAUGHTER!
I'M RIGHT, AREN'T I SO-NA?! YOUR FATHER IS SOMEONE WHO COULD DO THAT WITHOUT BLINKING!

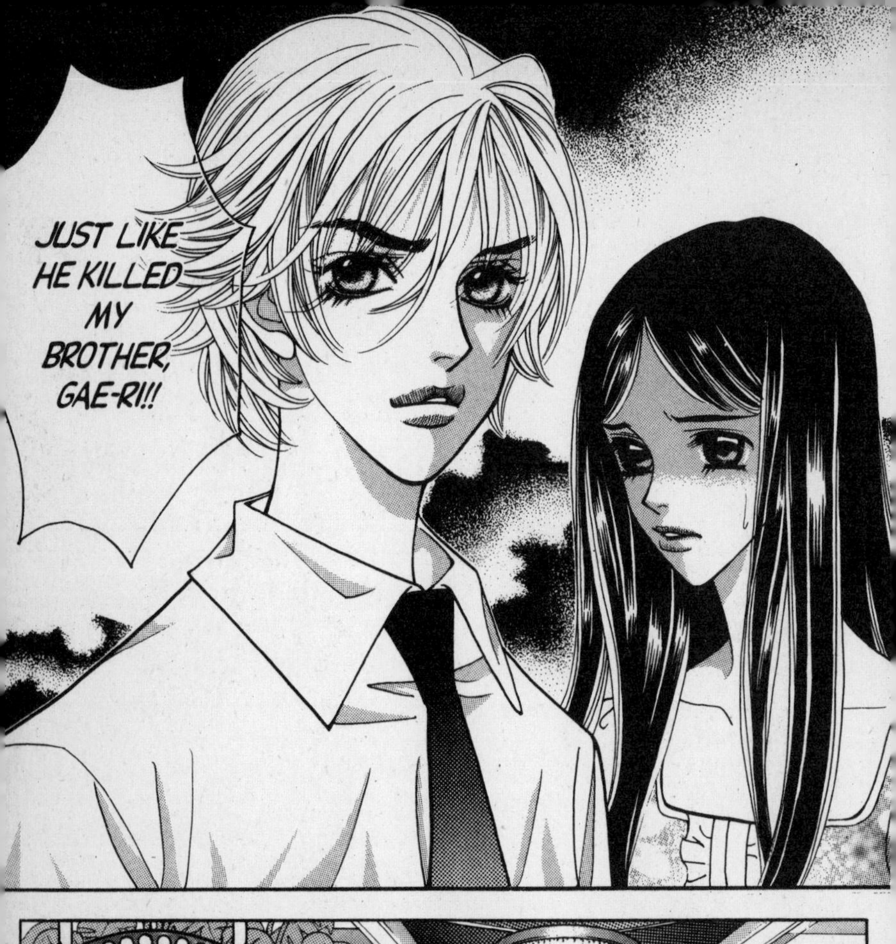
JUST LIKE HE KILLED MY BROTHER, GAE-RI!!

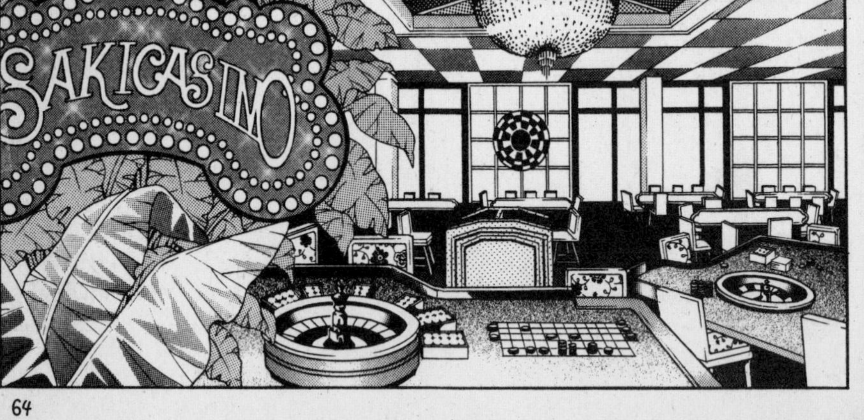
SAKICASINO

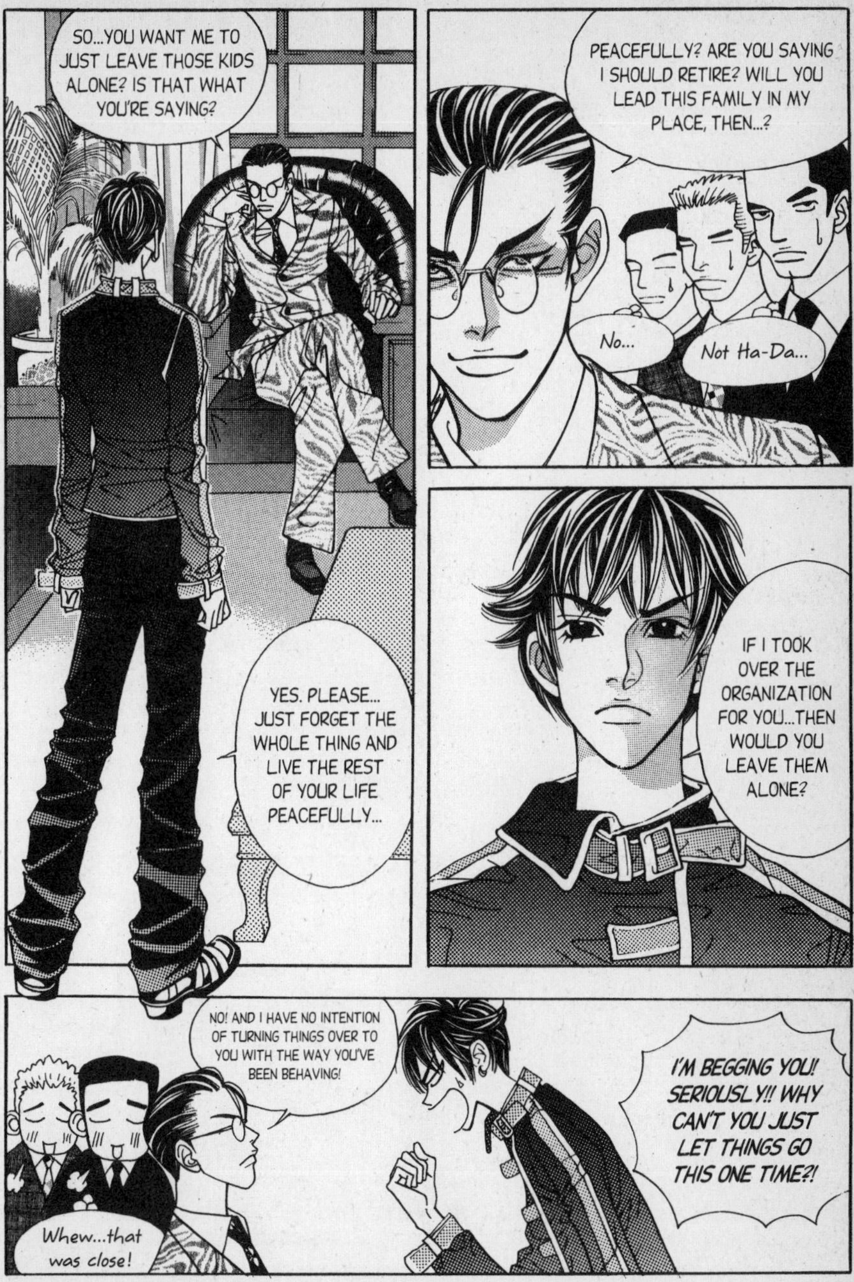

SO...YOU WANT ME TO JUST LEAVE THOSE KIDS ALONE? IS THAT WHAT YOU'RE SAYING?
YES. PLEASE... JUST FORGET THE WHOLE THING AND LIVE THE REST OF YOUR LIFE PEACEFULLY...
PEACEFULLY? ARE YOU SAYING I SHOULD RETIRE? WILL YOU LEAD THIS FAMILY IN MY PLACE, THEN...?
No...
Not Ha-Da...
IF I TOOK OVER THE ORGANIZATION FOR YOU...THEN WOULD YOU LEAVE THEM ALONE?
NO! AND I HAVE NO INTENTION OF TURNING THINGS OVER TO YOU WITH THE WAY YOU'VE BEEN BEHAVING!
Whew...that was close!
I'M BEGGING YOU! SERIOUSLY!! WHY CAN'T YOU JUST LET THINGS GO THIS ONE TIME?!

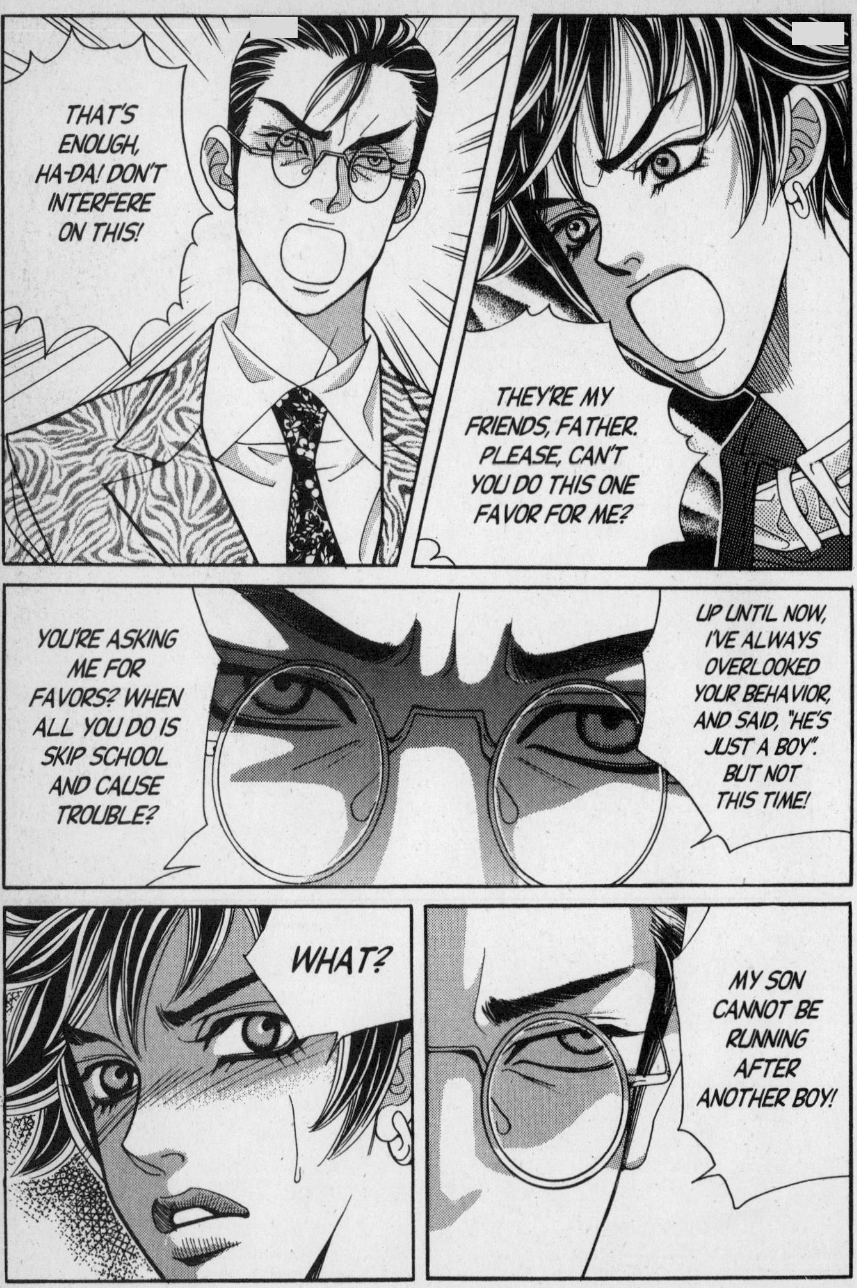
THAT'S ENOUGH, HA-DA! DON'T INTERFERE ON THIS!
THEY'RE MY FRIENDS, FATHER. PLEASE, CAN'T YOU DO THIS ONE FAVOR FOR ME?
YOU'RE ASKING ME FOR FAVORS? WHEN ALL YOU DO IS SKIP SCHOOL AND CAUSE TROUBLE?
UP UNTIL NOW, I'VE ALWAYS OVERLOOKED YOUR BEHAVIOR, AND SAID, "HE'S JUST A BOY". BUT NOT THIS TIME!
WHAT?
MY SON CANNOT BE RUNNING AFTER ANOTHER BOY!

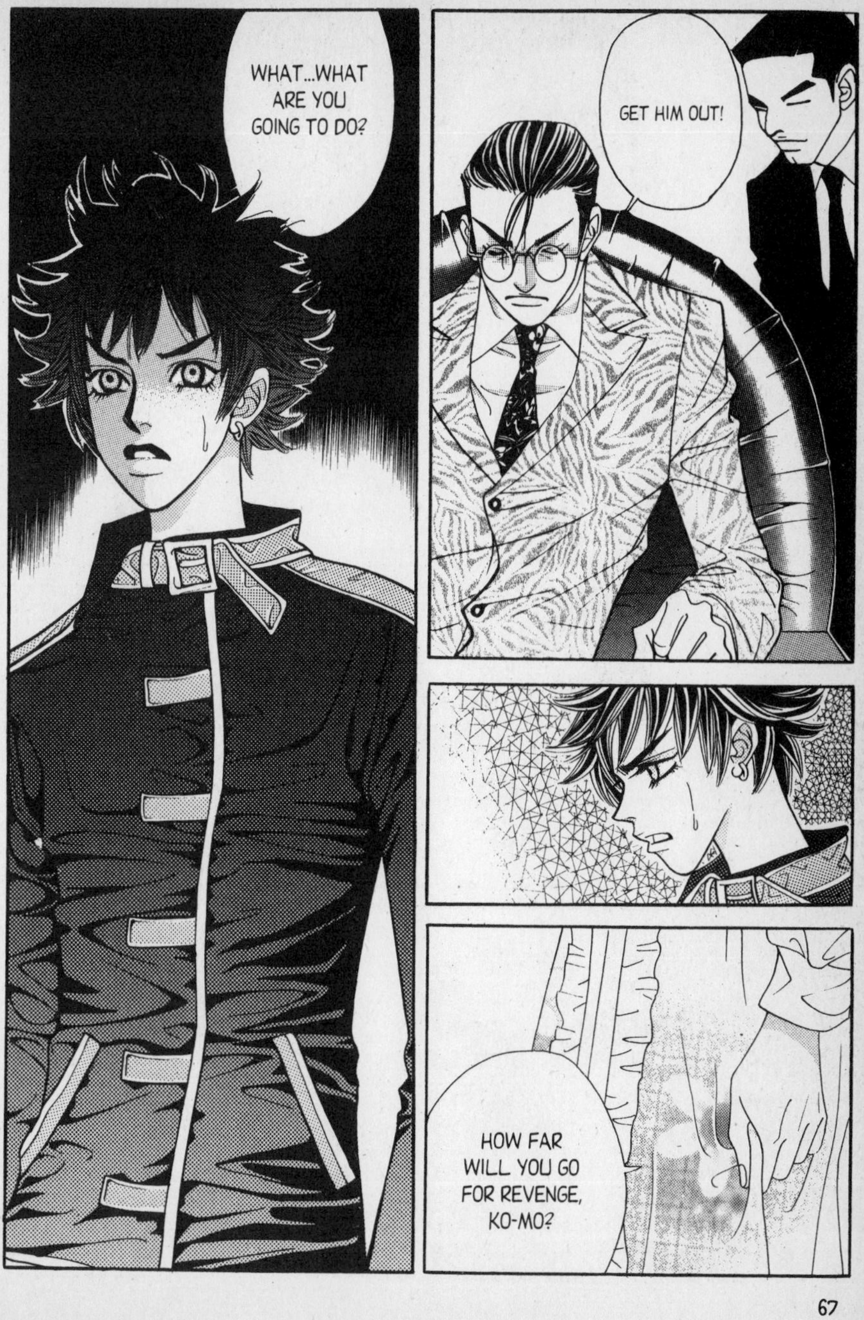
WHAT...WHAT ARE YOU GOING TO DO?
GET HIM OUT!
HOW FAR WILL YOU GO FOR REVENGE, KO-MO?

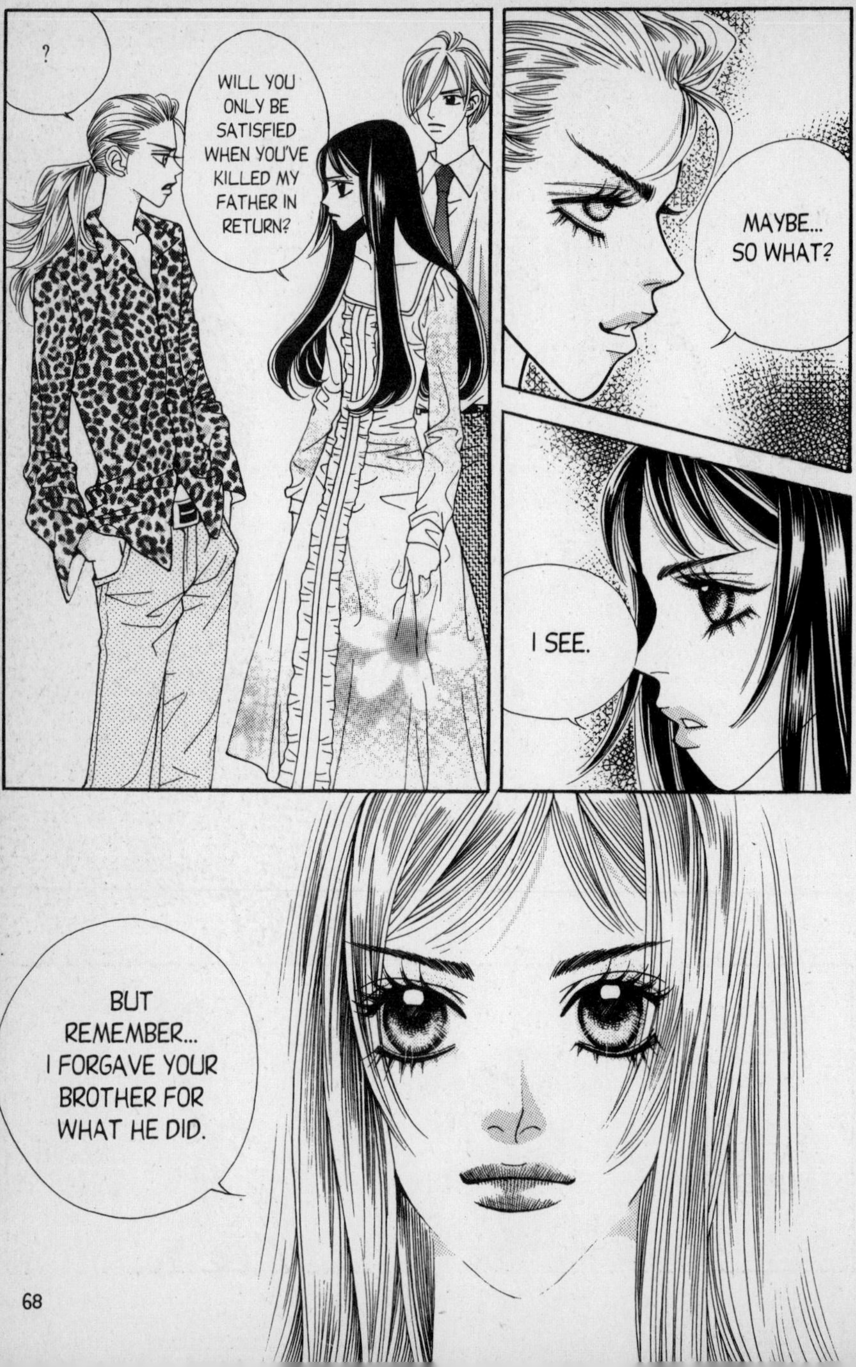
?
WILL YOU ONLY BE SATISFIED WHEN YOU'VE KILLED MY FATHER IN RETURN?
MAYBE... SO WHAT?
I SEE.
BUT REMEMBER... I FORGAVE YOUR BROTHER FOR WHAT HE DID.

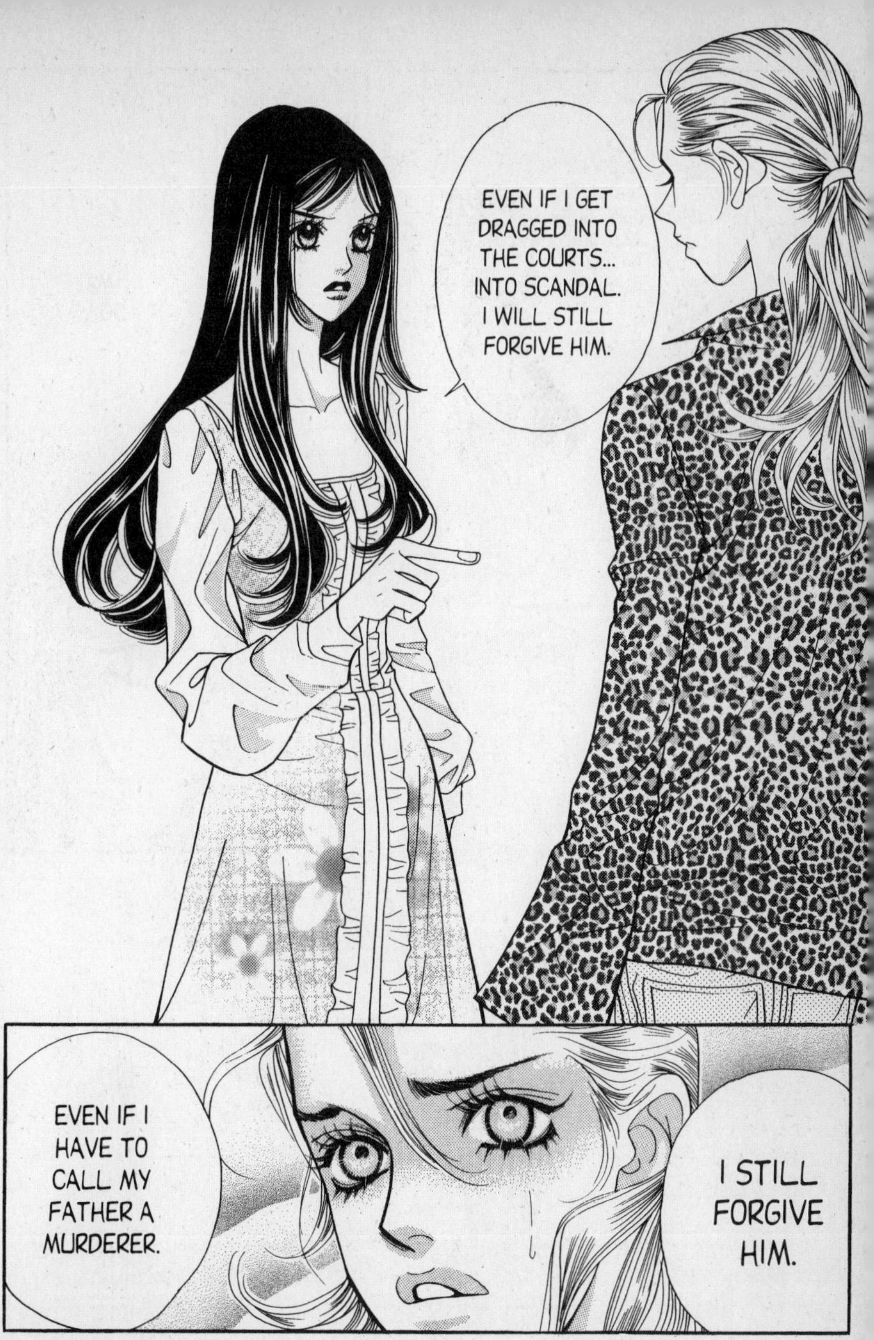
EVEN IF I GET DRAGGED INTO THE COURTS... INTO SCANDAL. I WILL STILL FORGIVE HIM.
EVEN IF I HAVE TO CALL MY FATHER A MURDERER.
I STILL FORGIVE HIM.

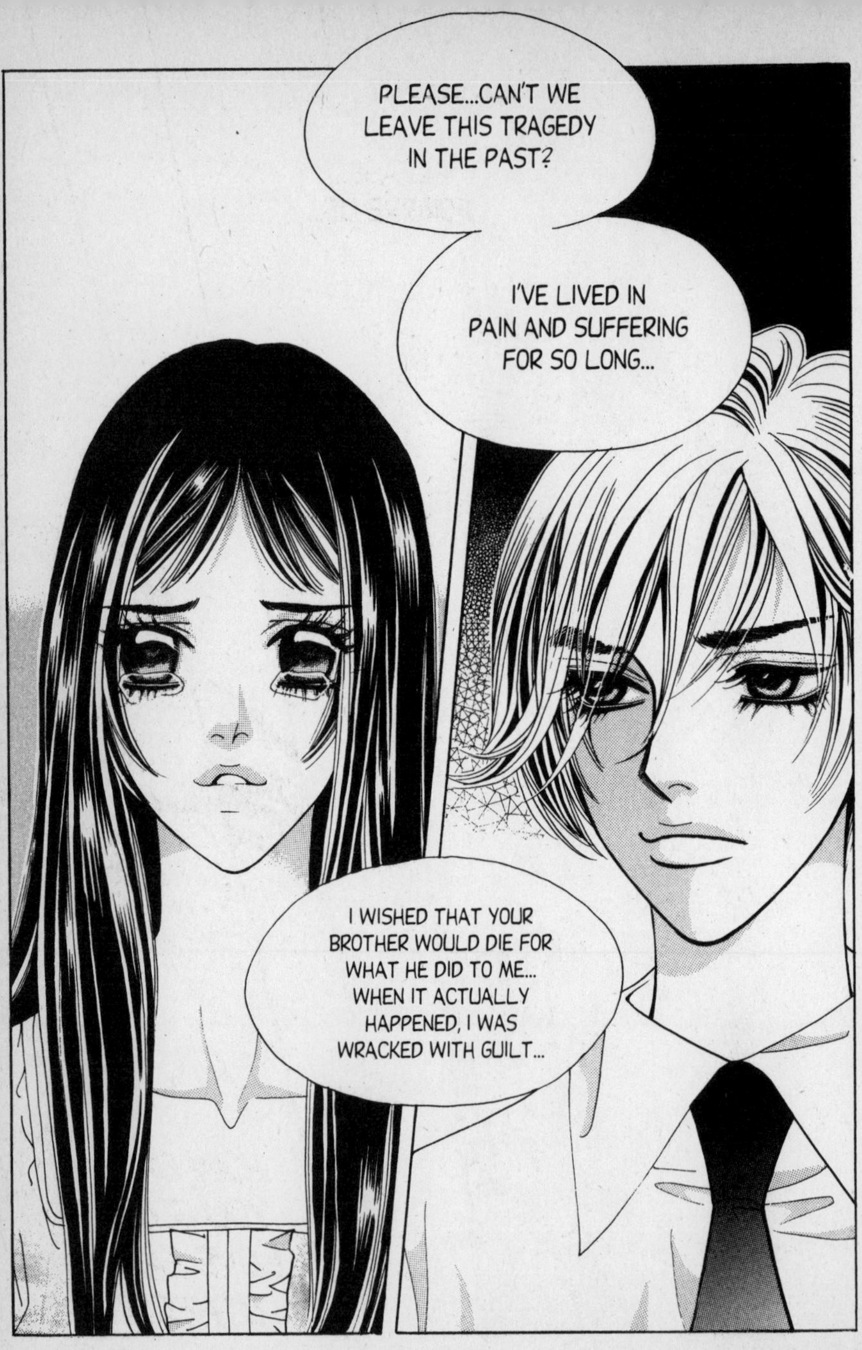
PLEASE...CAN'T WE LEAVE THIS TRAGEDY IN THE PAST?
I'VE LIVED IN PAIN AND SUFFERING FOR SO LONG...
I WISHED THAT YOUR BROTHER WOULD DIE FOR WHAT HE DID TO ME... WHEN IT ACTUALLY HAPPENED, I WAS WRACKED WITH GUILT...

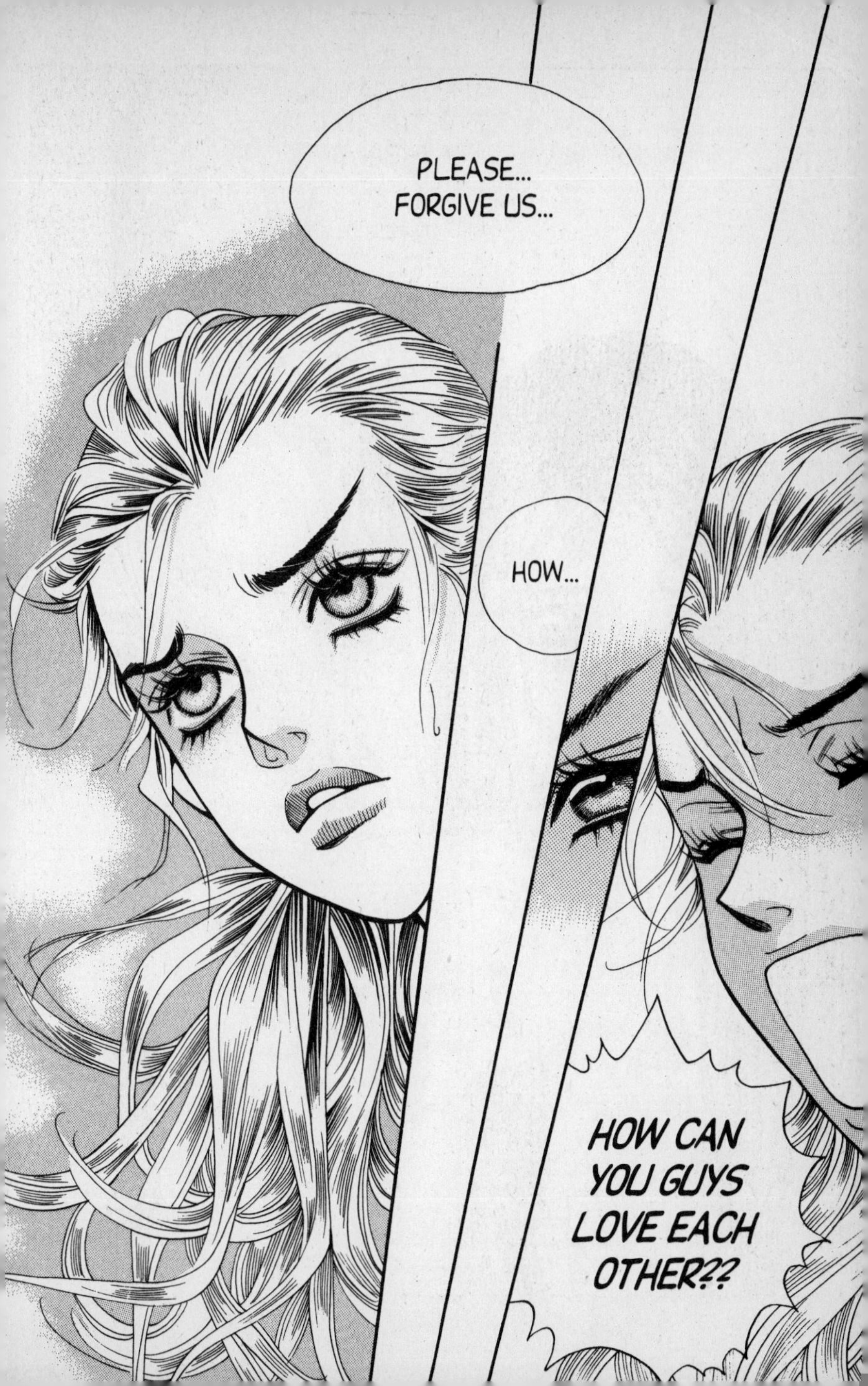
PLEASE... FORGIVE US...
HOW...
HOW CAN YOU GUYS LOVE EACH OTHER??

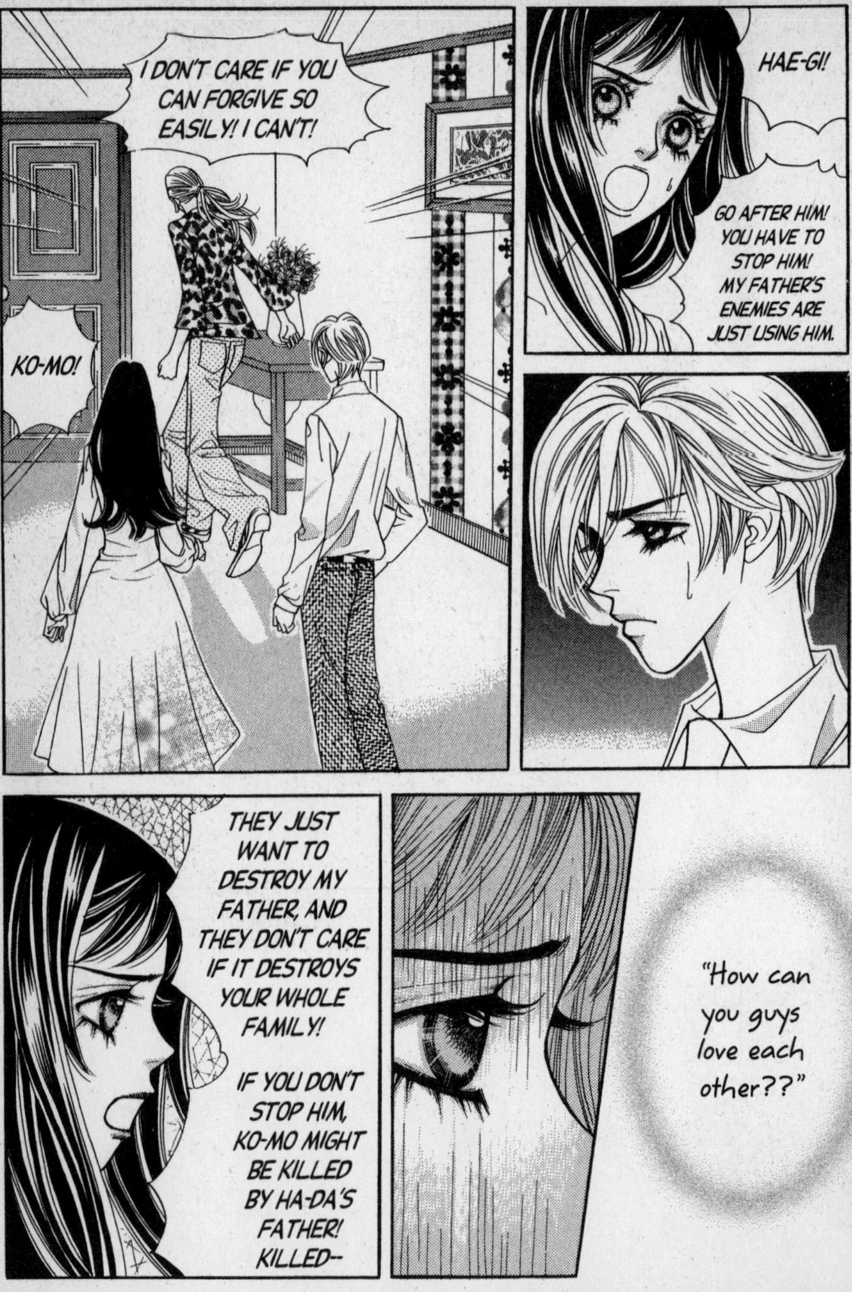
I DON'T CARE IF YOU CAN FORGIVE SO EASILY! I CAN'T!
KO-MO!
HAE-GI!
GO AFTER HIM! YOU HAVE TO STOP HIM! MY FATHER'S ENEMIES ARE JUST USING HIM.
THEY JUST WANT TO DESTROY MY FATHER, AND THEY DON'T CARE IF IT DESTROYS YOUR WHOLE FAMILY!
IF YOU DON'T STOP HIM, KO-MO MIGHT BE KILLED BY HA-DA'S FATHER! KILLED--
"How can you guys love each other??"

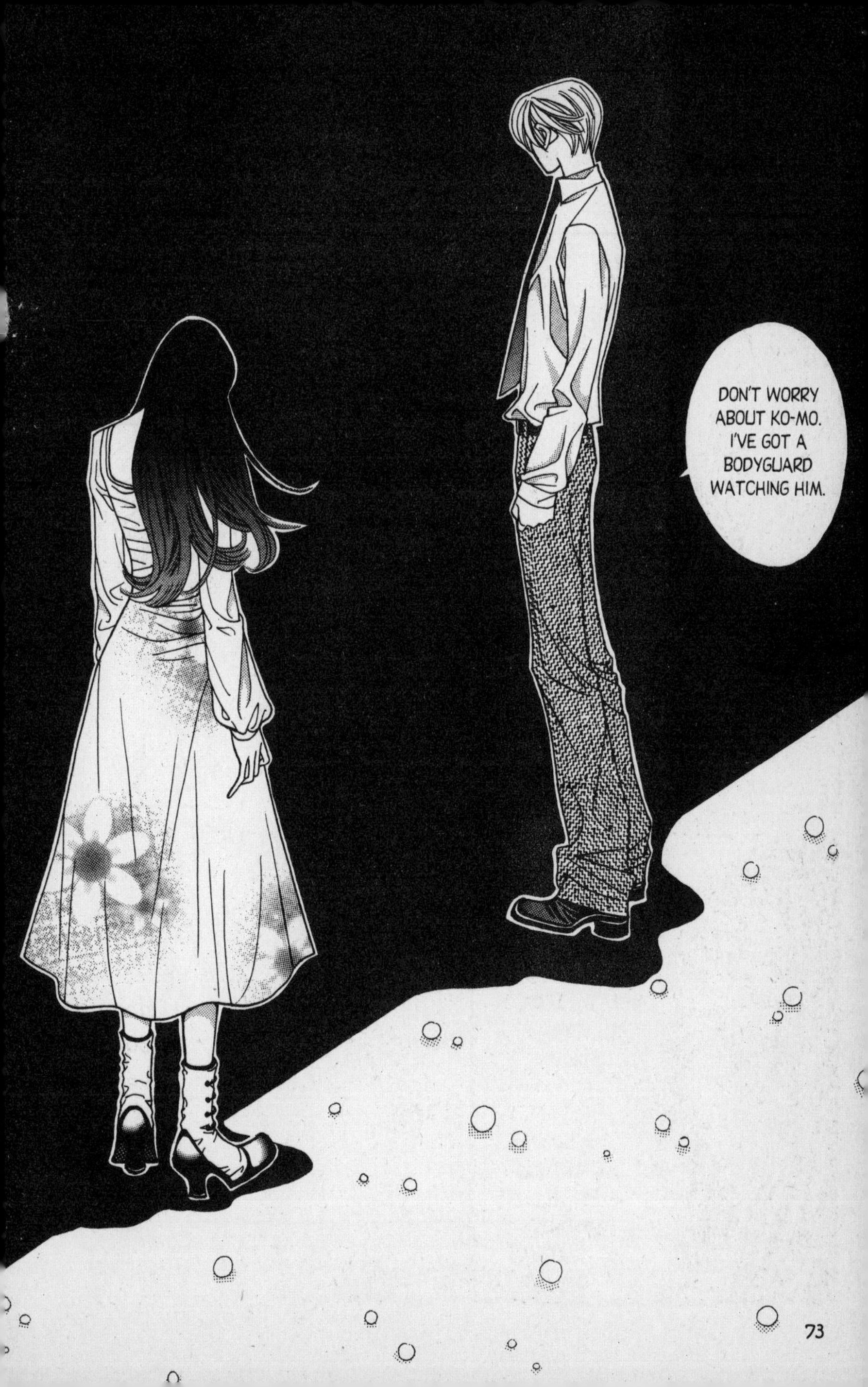
DON'T WORRY ABOUT KO-MO. I'VE GOT A BODYGUARD WATCHING HIM.

Part 36 : Eve Feels Cold for the Very First Time

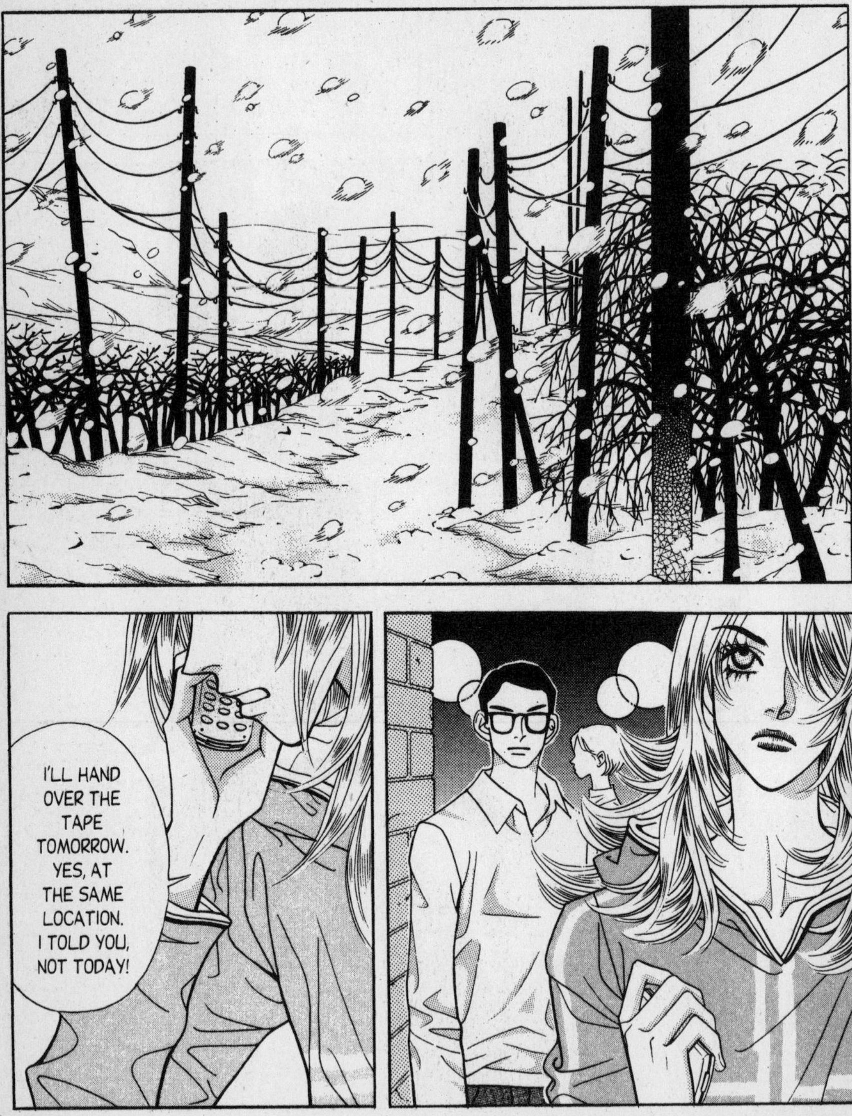
I'LL HAND OVER THE TAPE TOMORROW. YES, AT THE SAME LOCATION. I TOLD YOU, NOT TODAY!

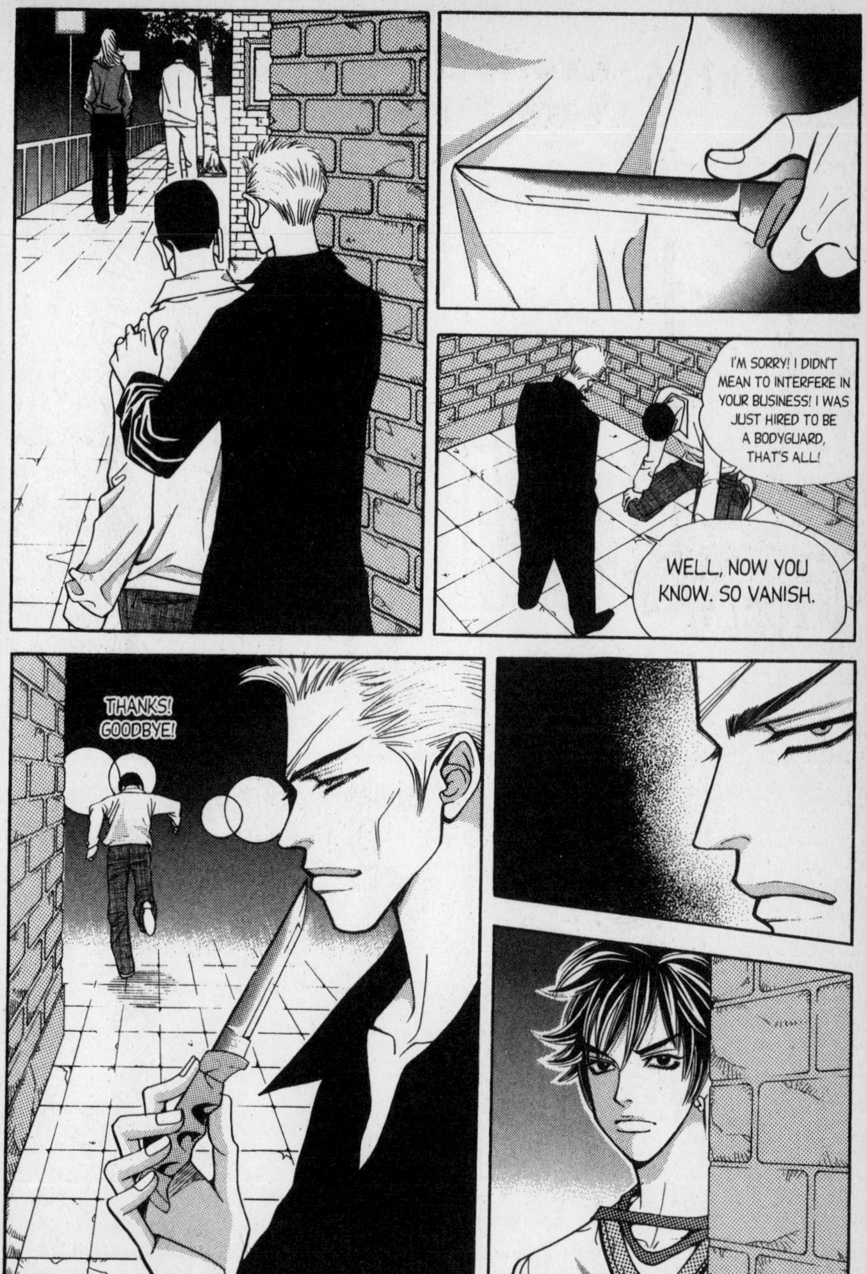
I'M SORRY! I DIDN'T MEAN TO INTERFERE IN YOUR BUSINESS! I WAS JUST HIRED TO BE A BODYGUARD, THAT'S ALL!
WELL, NOW YOU KNOW. SO VANISH.
THANKS! GOODBYE!

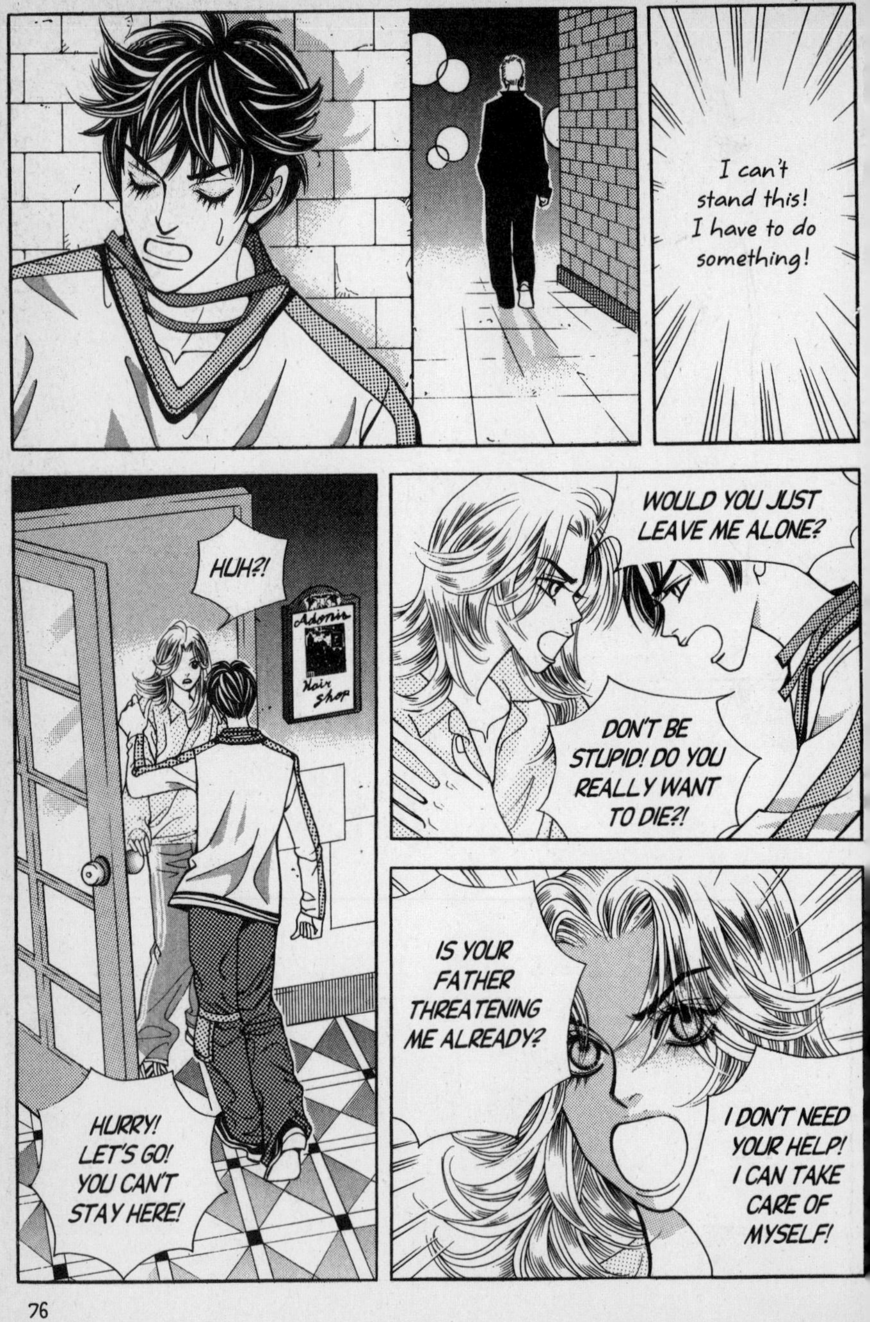
I can't stand this! I have to do something!
HUH?!
Adonis Hair Shop
HURRY! LET'S GO! YOU CAN'T STAY HERE!
WOULD YOU JUST LEAVE ME ALONE?
DON'T BE STUPID! DO YOU REALLY WANT TO DIE?!
IS YOUR FATHER THREATENING ME ALREADY?
I DON'T NEED YOUR HELP! I CAN TAKE CARE OF MYSELF!

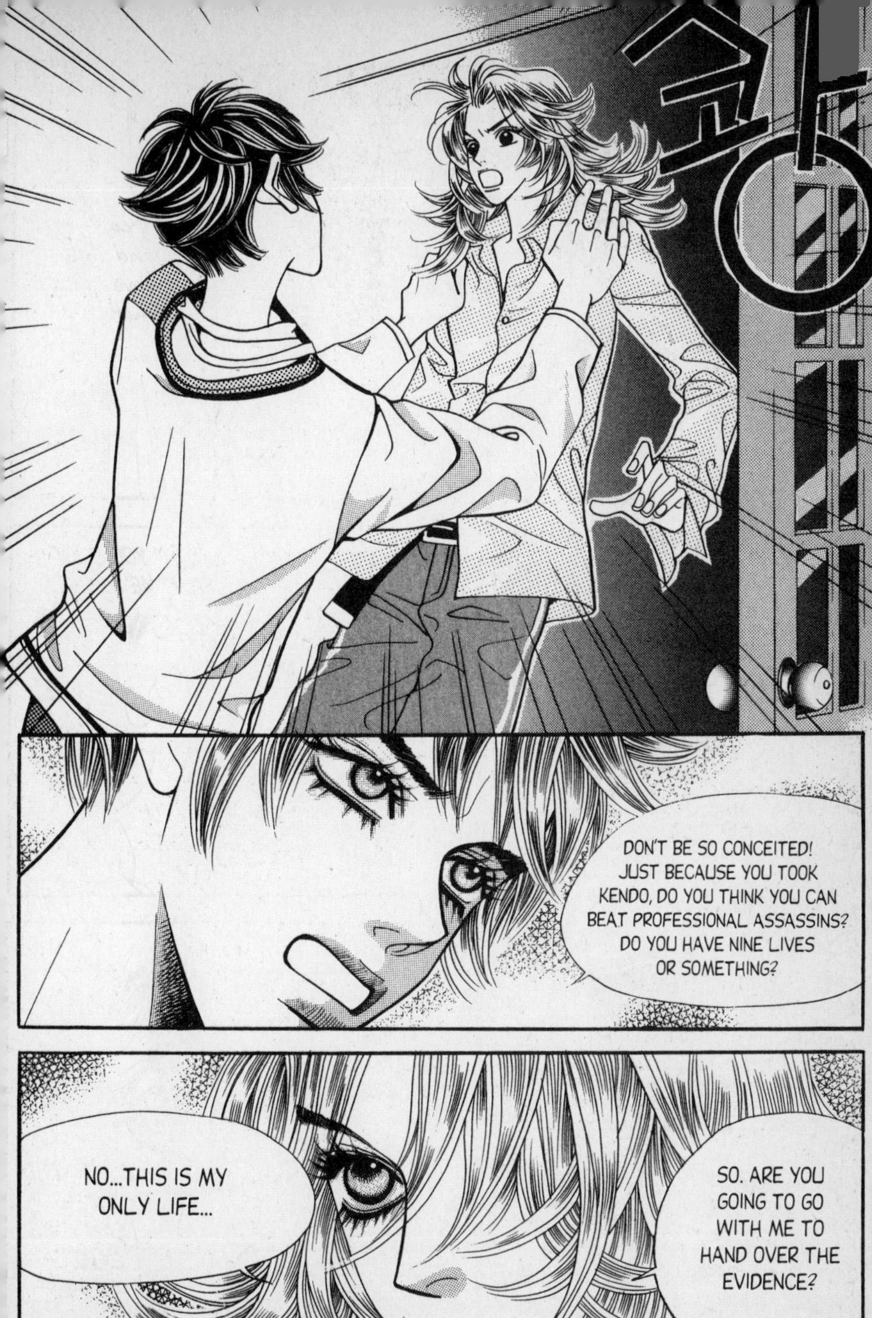
쾅
DON'T BE SO CONCEITED! JUST BECAUSE YOU TOOK KENDO, DO YOU THINK YOU CAN BEAT PROFESSIONAL ASSASSINS? DO YOU HAVE NINE LIVES OR SOMETHING?
NO...THIS IS MY ONLY LIFE...
SO. ARE YOU GOING TO GO WITH ME TO HAND OVER THE EVIDENCE?

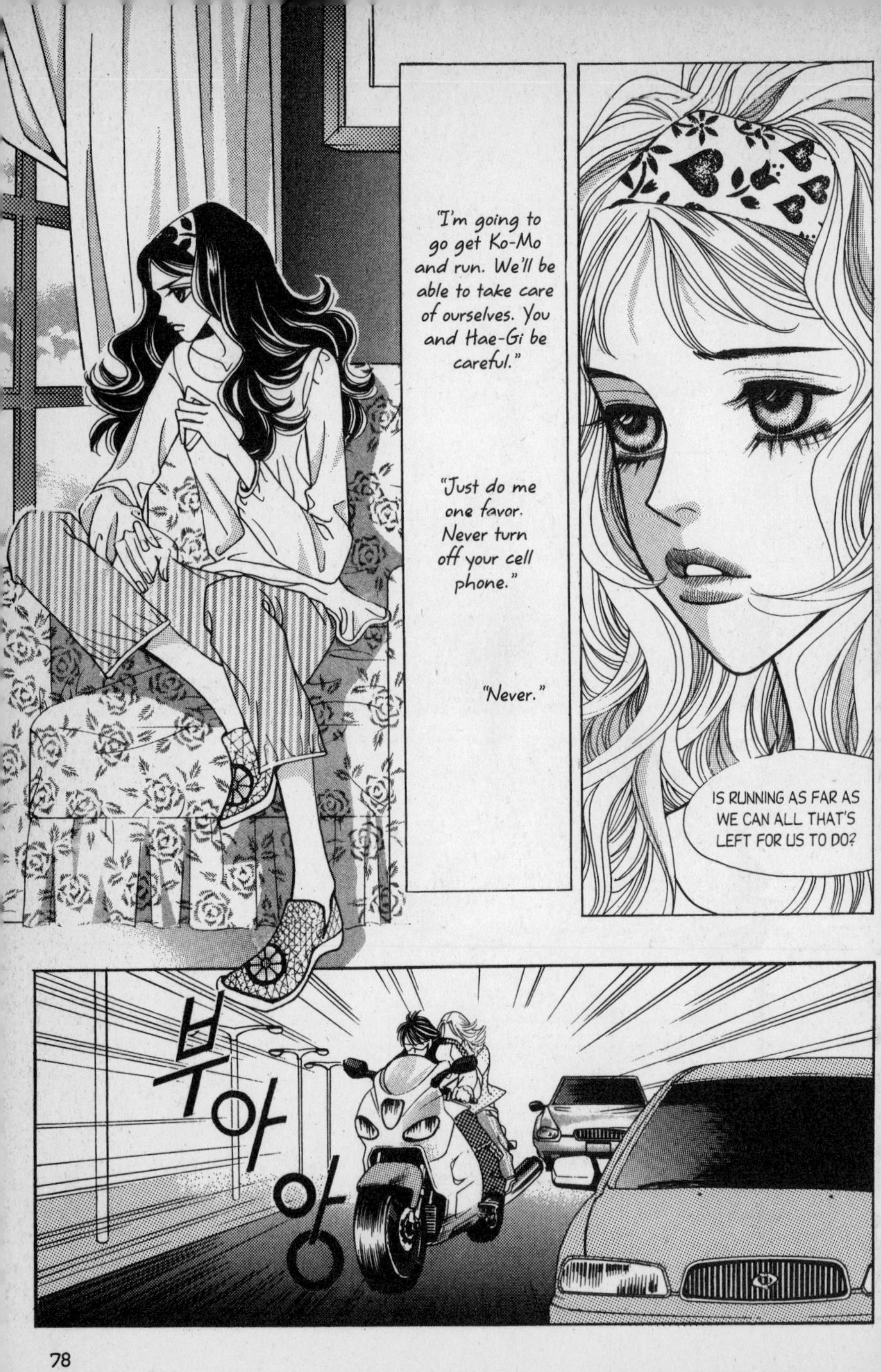
"I'm going to go get Ko-Mo and run. We'll be able to take care of ourselves. You and Hae-Gi be careful."
"Just do me one favor. Never turn off your cell phone."
"Never."
IS RUNNING AS FAR AS WE CAN ALL THAT'S LEFT FOR US TO DO?

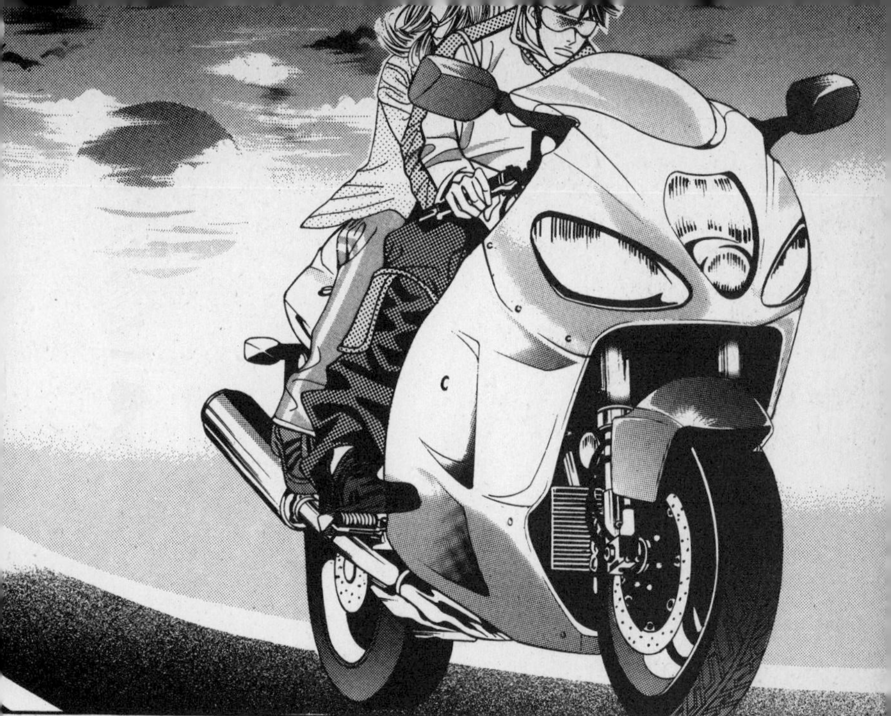

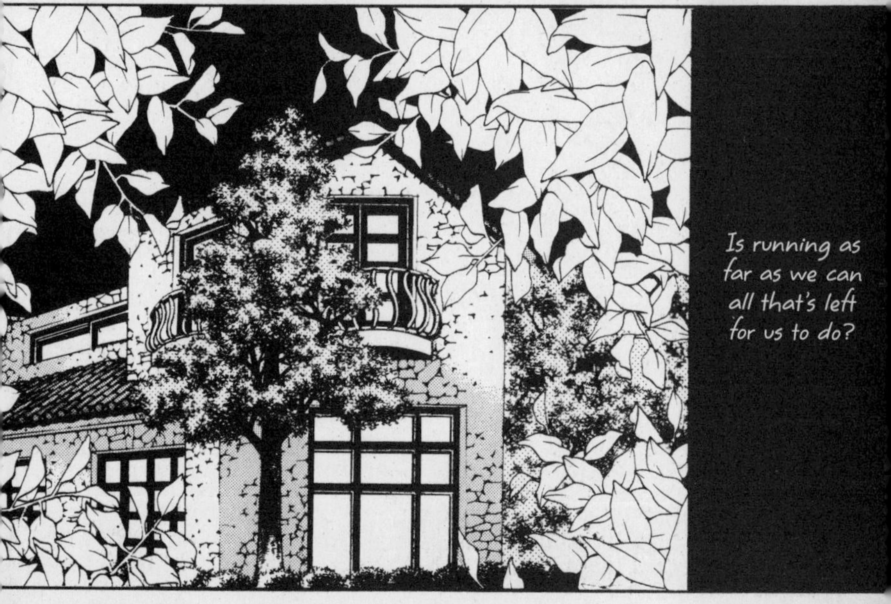
Is running as far as we can all that's left for us to do?

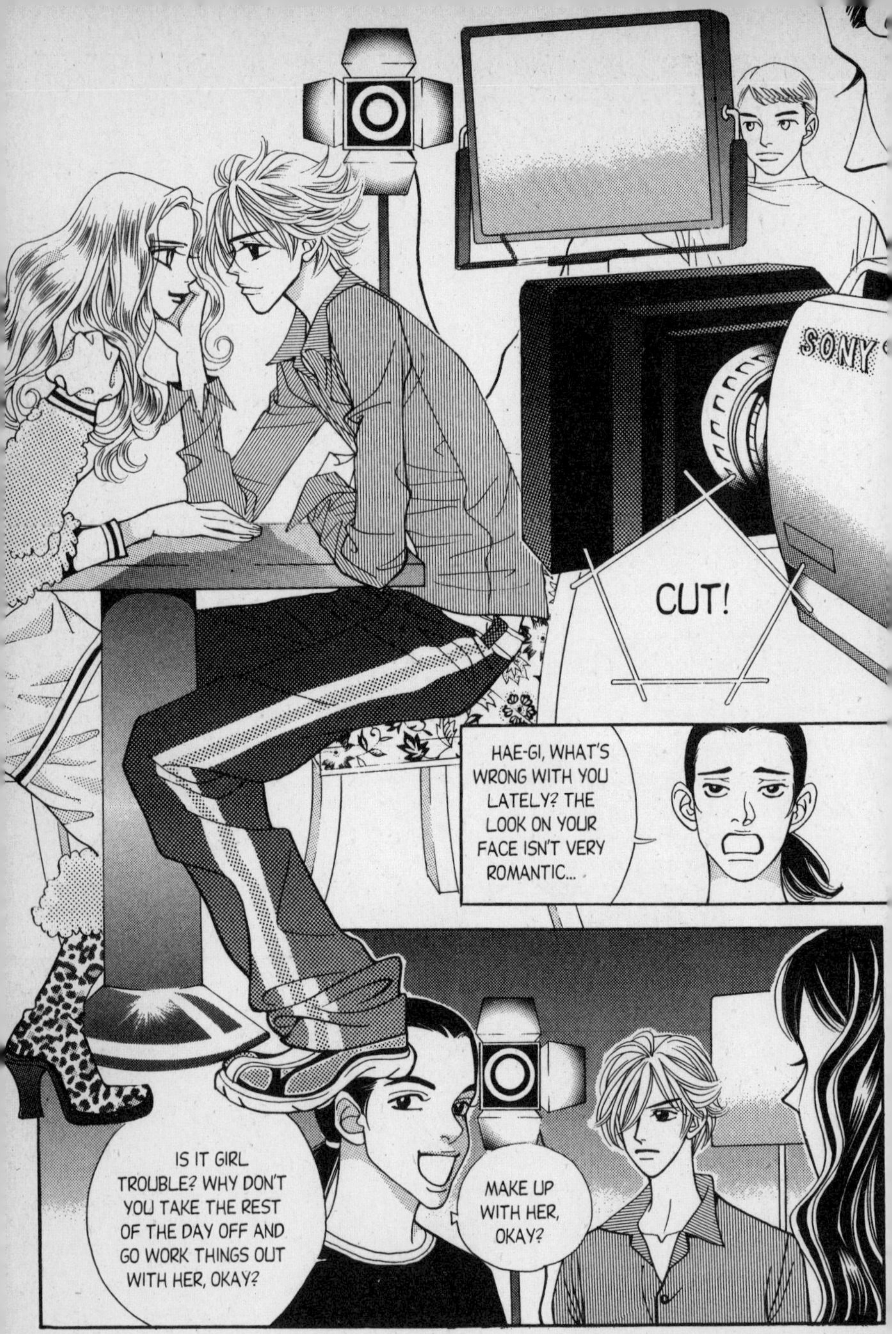
CUT!
HAE-GI, WHAT'S WRONG WITH YOU LATELY? THE LOOK ON YOUR FACE ISN'T VERY ROMANTIC...
IS IT GIRL TROUBLE? WHY DON'T YOU TAKE THE REST OF THE DAY OFF AND GO WORK THINGS OUT WITH HER, OKAY?
MAKE UP WITH HER, OKAY?

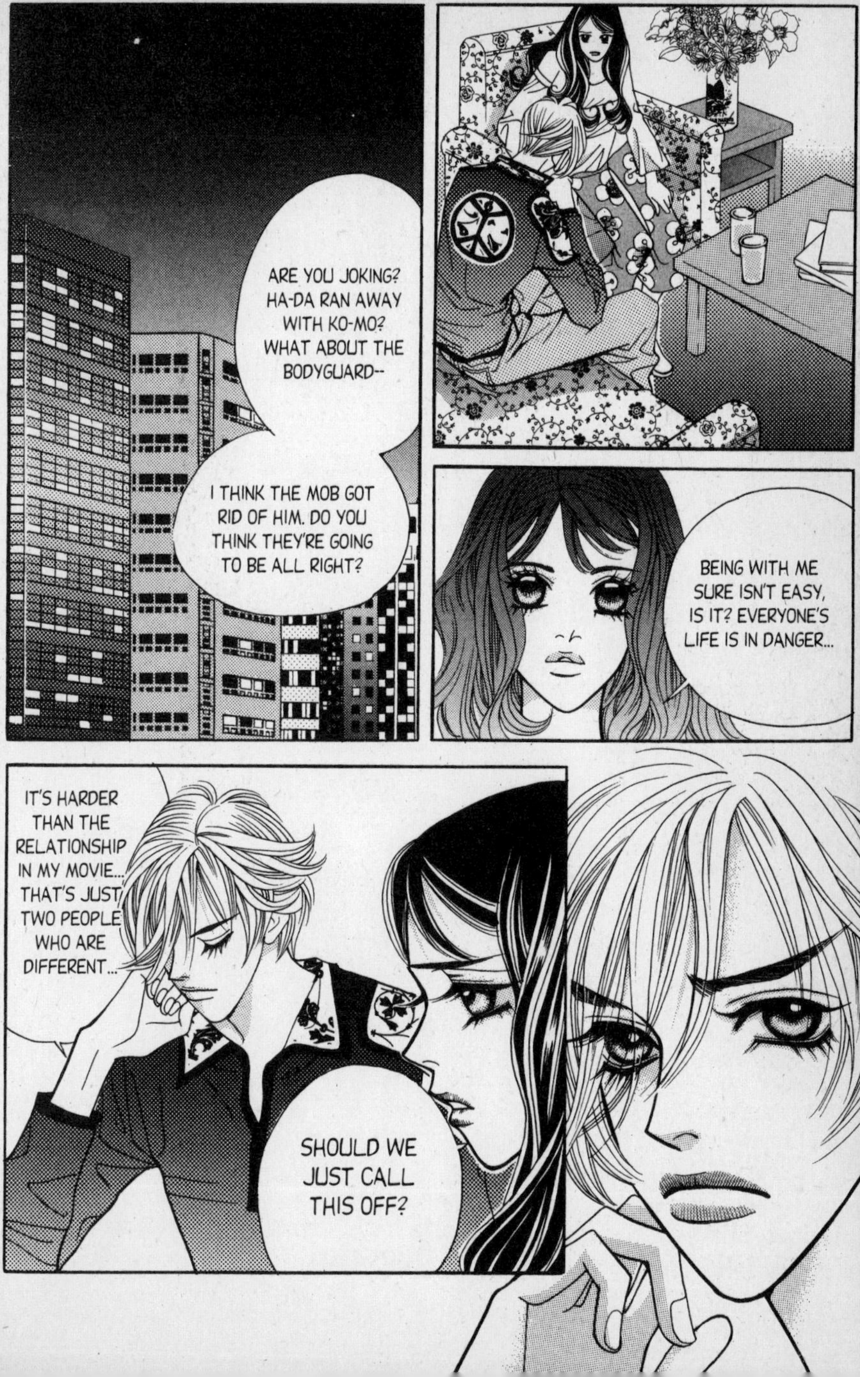
ARE YOU JOKING? HA-DA RAN AWAY WITH KO-MO? WHAT ABOUT THE BODYGUARD--
I THINK THE MOB GOT RID OF HIM. DO YOU THINK THEY'RE GOING TO BE ALL RIGHT?
BEING WITH ME SURE ISN'T EASY, IS IT? EVERYONE'S LIFE IS IN DANGER...
IT'S HARDER THAN THE RELATIONSHIP IN MY MOVIE... THAT'S JUST TWO PEOPLE WHO ARE DIFFERENT...
SHOULD WE JUST CALL THIS OFF?

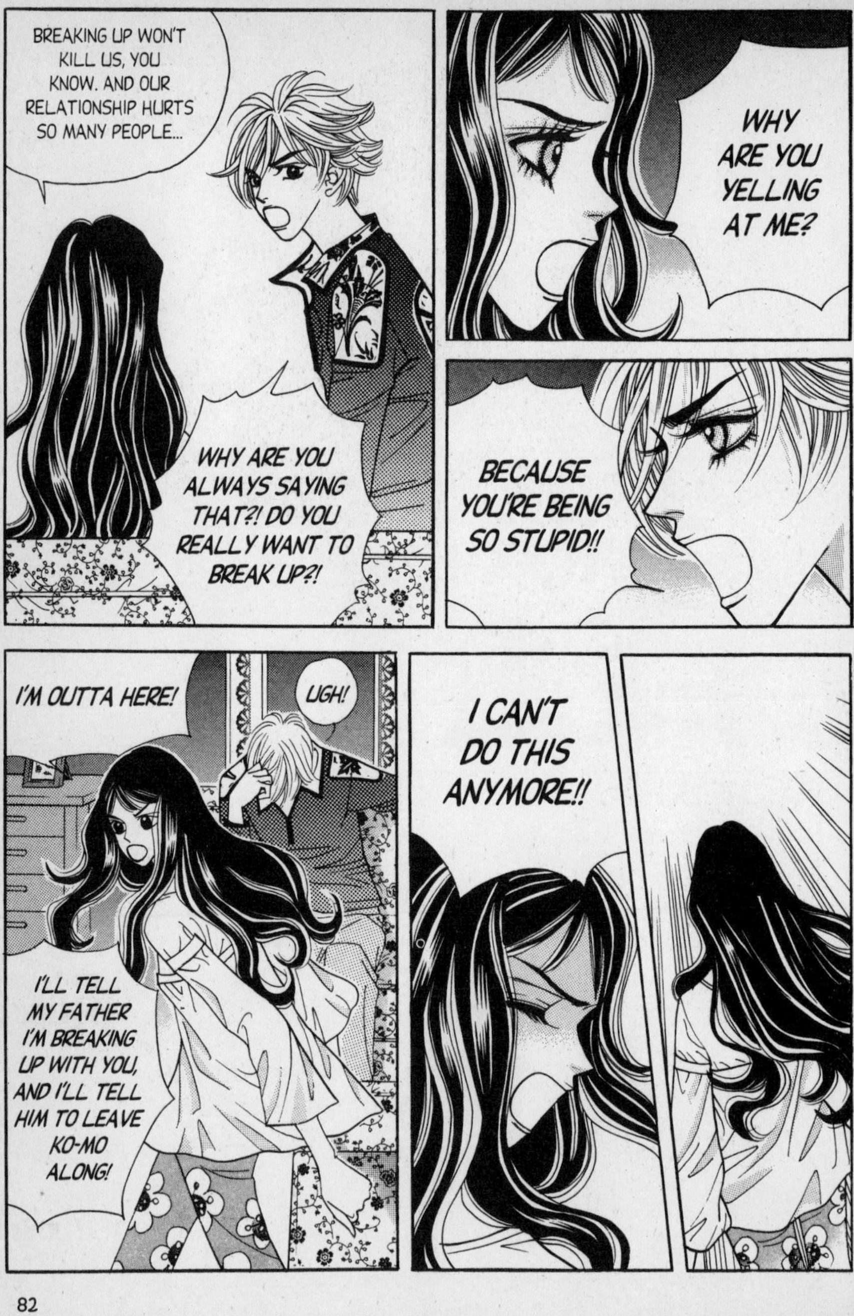
BREAKING UP WON'T KILL US, YOU KNOW. AND OUR RELATIONSHIP HURTS SO MANY PEOPLE...
WHY ARE YOU ALWAYS SAYING THAT?! DO YOU REALLY WANT TO BREAK UP?!
WHY ARE YOU YELLING AT ME?
BECAUSE YOU'RE BEING SO STUPID!!
I'M OUTTA HERE!
UGH!
I'LL TELL MY FATHER I'M BREAKING UP WITH YOU, AND I'LL TELL HIM TO LEAVE KO-MO ALONG!
I CAN'T DO THIS ANYMORE!!

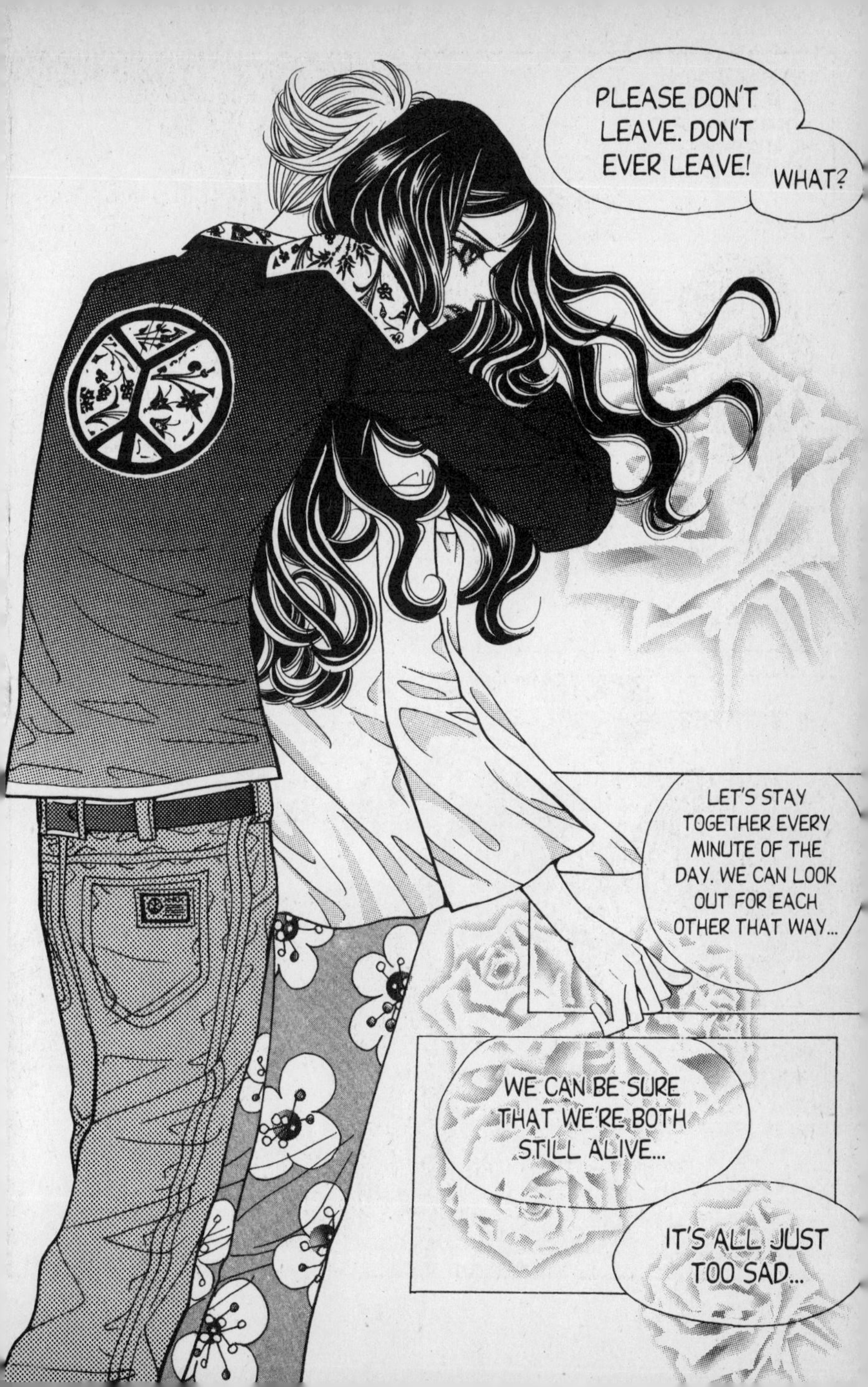
PLEASE DON'T LEAVE. DON'T EVER LEAVE!
WHAT?
LET'S STAY TOGETHER EVERY MINUTE OF THE DAY. WE CAN LOOK OUT FOR EACH OTHER THAT WAY...
WE CAN BE SURE THAT WE'RE BOTH STILL ALIVE...
IT'S ALL JUST TOO SAD...

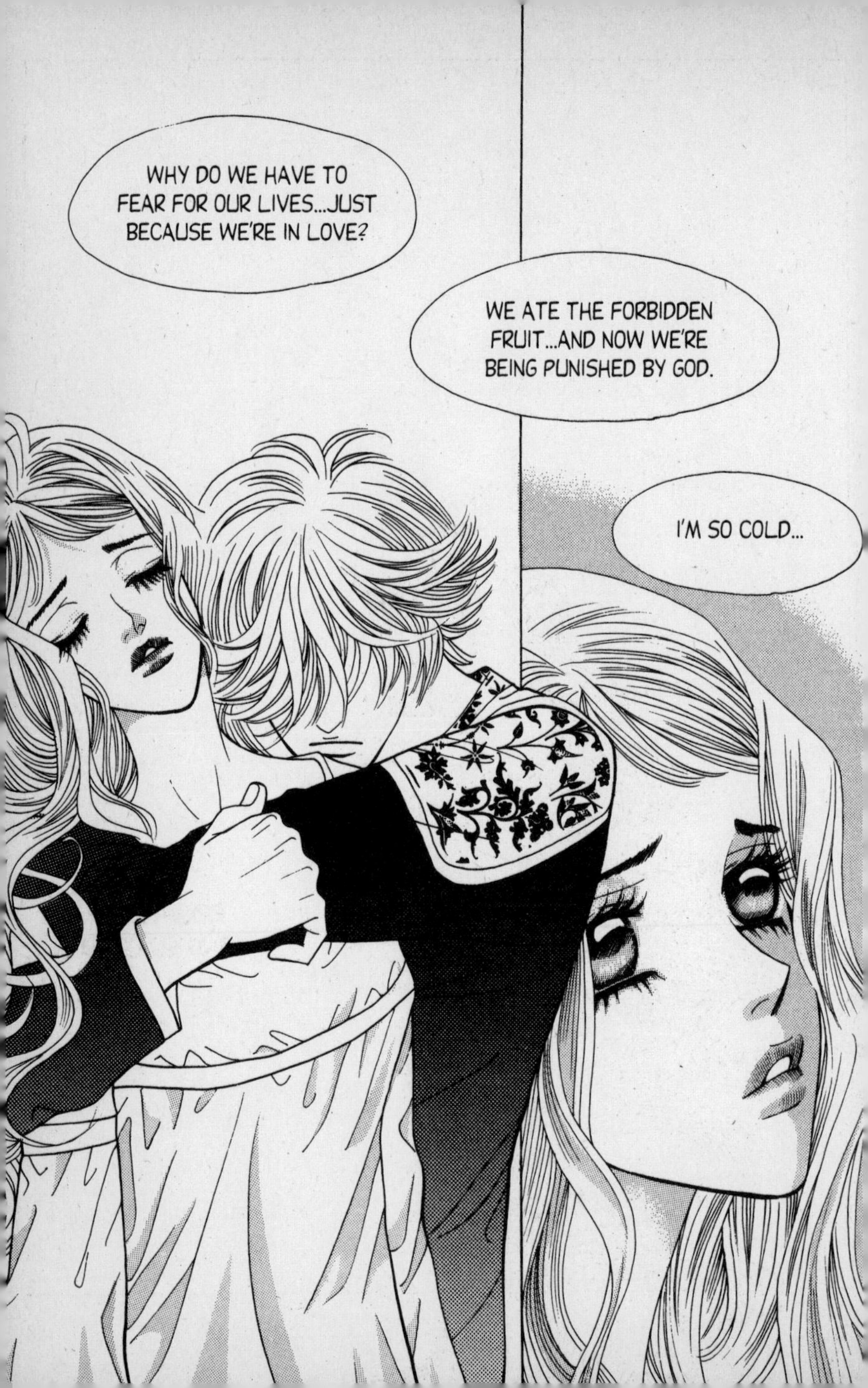
WHY DO WE HAVE TO FEAR FOR OUR LIVES...JUST BECAUSE WE'RE IN LOVE?
WE ATE THE FORBIDDEN FRUIT...AND NOW WE'RE BEING PUNISHED BY GOD.
I'M SO COLD...

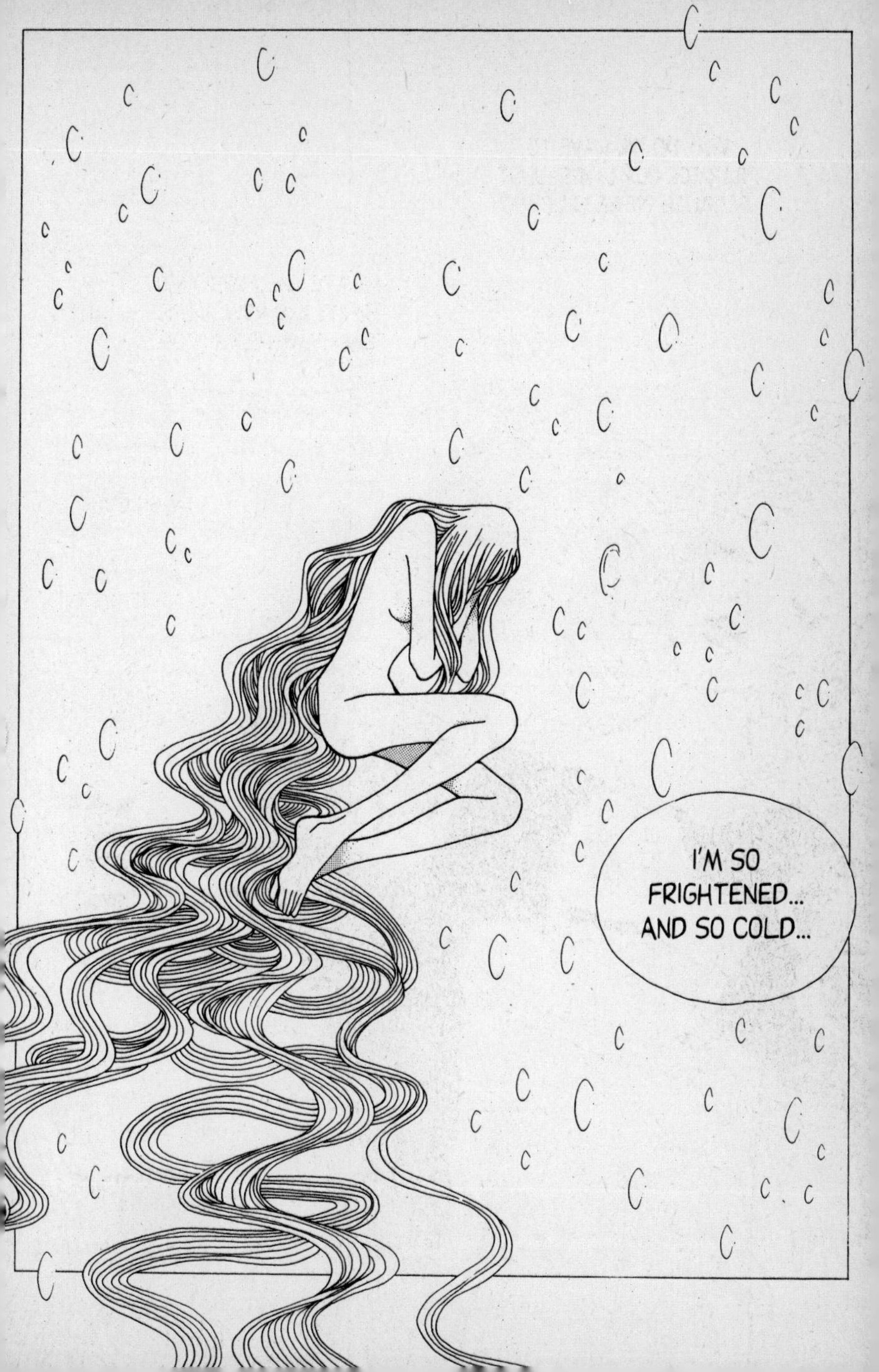
I'M SO FRIGHTENED... AND SO COLD...

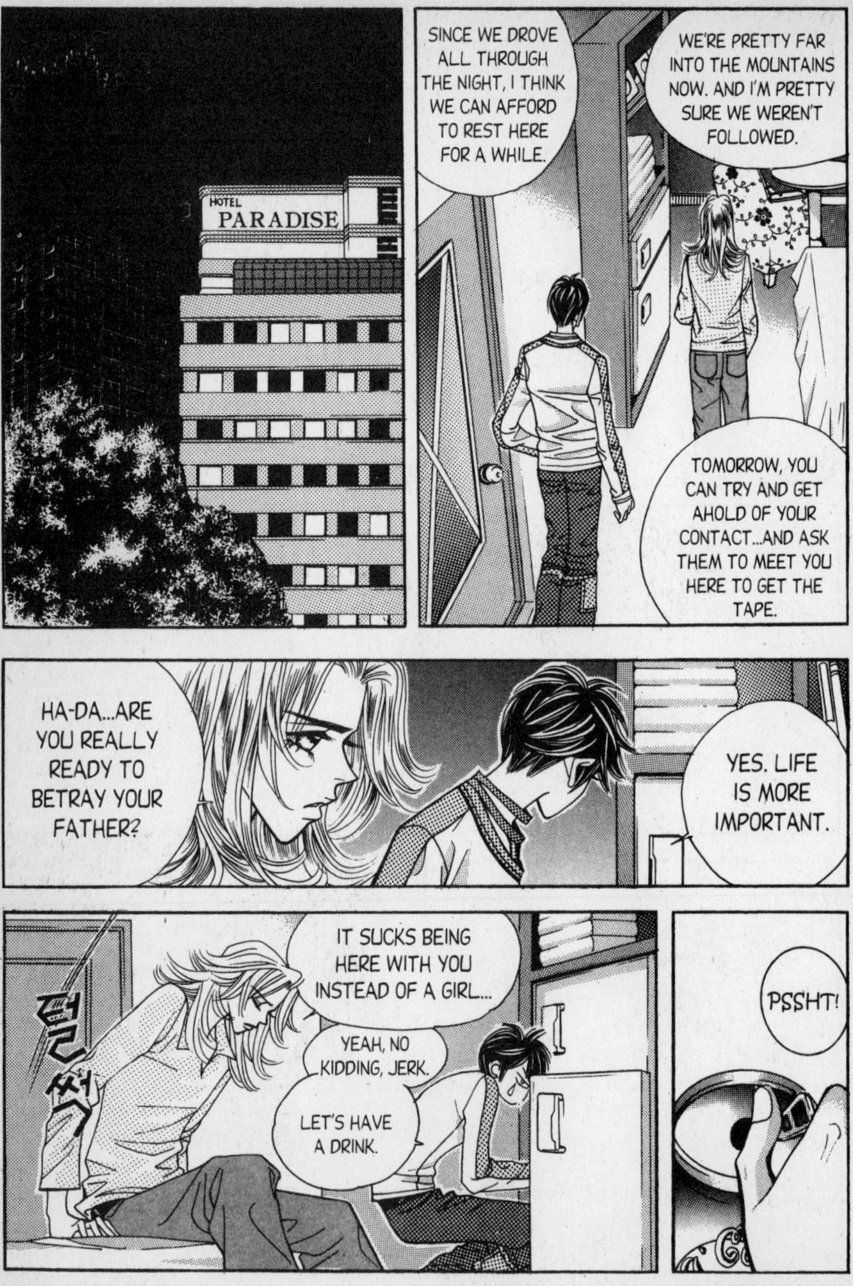
HOTEL
PARADISE
SINCE WE DROVE ALL THROUGH THE NIGHT, I THINK WE CAN AFFORD TO REST HERE FOR A WHILE.
WE'RE PRETTY FAR INTO THE MOUNTAINS NOW. AND I'M PRETTY SURE WE WEREN'T FOLLOWED.
TOMORROW, YOU CAN TRY AND GET AHOLD OF YOUR CONTACT...AND ASK THEM TO MEET YOU HERE TO GET THE TAPE.
HA-DA...ARE YOU REALLY READY TO BETRAY YOUR FATHER?
YES. LIFE IS MORE IMPORTANT.
IT SUCKS BEING HERE WITH YOU INSTEAD OF A GIRL...
YEAH, NO KIDDING, JERK.
LET'S HAVE A DRINK.
PSSHT!

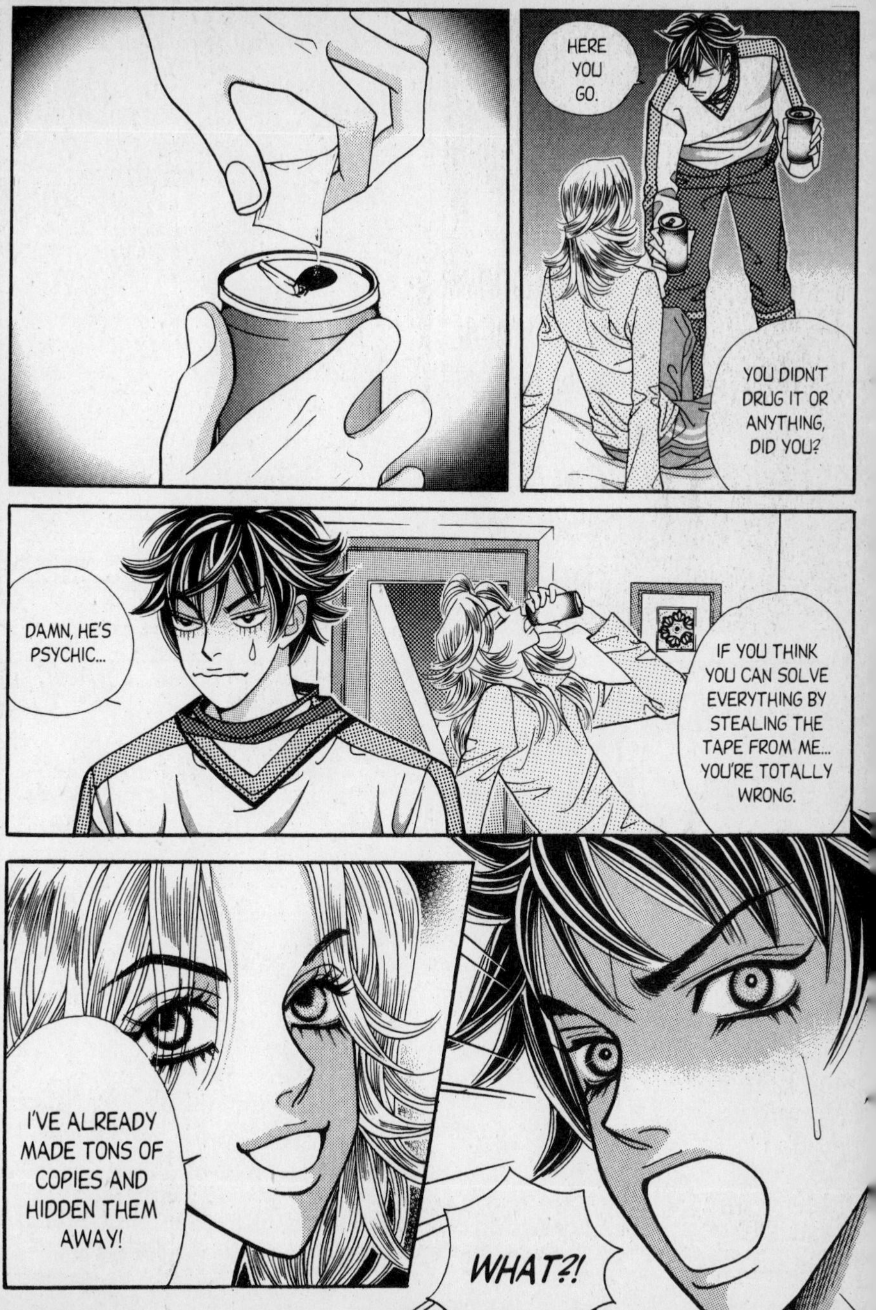
HERE YOU GO.
YOU DIDN'T DRUG IT OR ANYTHING, DID YOU?
DAMN, HE'S PSYCHIC...
IF YOU THINK YOU CAN SOLVE EVERYTHING BY STEALING THE TAPE FROM ME... YOU'RE TOTALLY WRONG.
I'VE ALREADY MADE TONS OF COPIES AND HIDDEN THEM AWAY!
WHAT?!

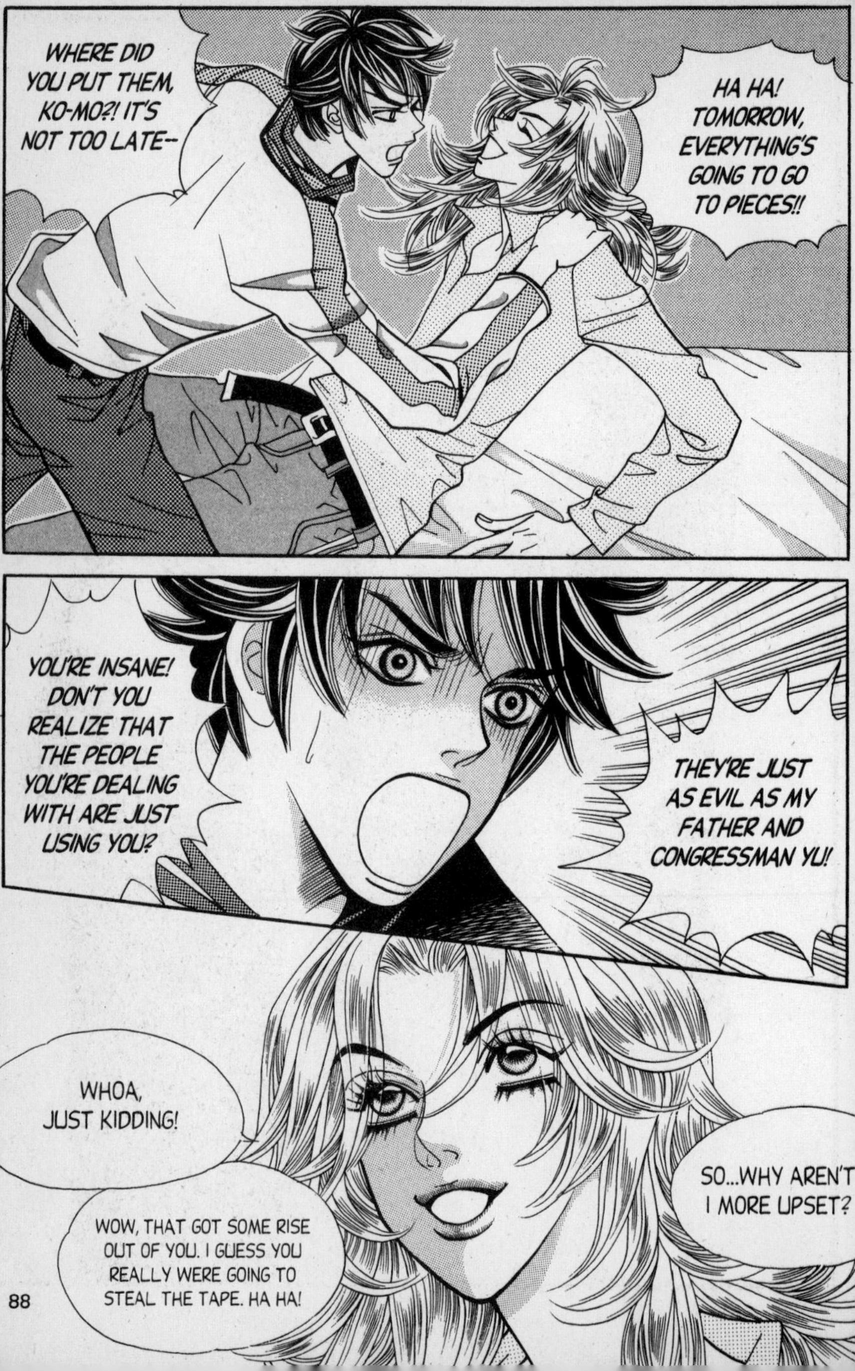
WHERE DID YOU PUT THEM, KO-MO?! IT'S NOT TOO LATE--
HA HA! TOMORROW, EVERYTHING'S GOING TO GO TO PIECES!!
YOU'RE INSANE! DON'T YOU REALIZE THAT THE PEOPLE YOU'RE DEALING WITH ARE JUST USING YOU?
THEY'RE JUST AS EVIL AS MY FATHER AND CONGRESSMAN YU!
WHOA, JUST KIDDING!
WOW, THAT GOT SOME RISE OUT OF YOU. I GUESS YOU REALLY WERE GOING TO STEAL THE TAPE. HA HA!
SO...WHY AREN'T I MORE UPSET?

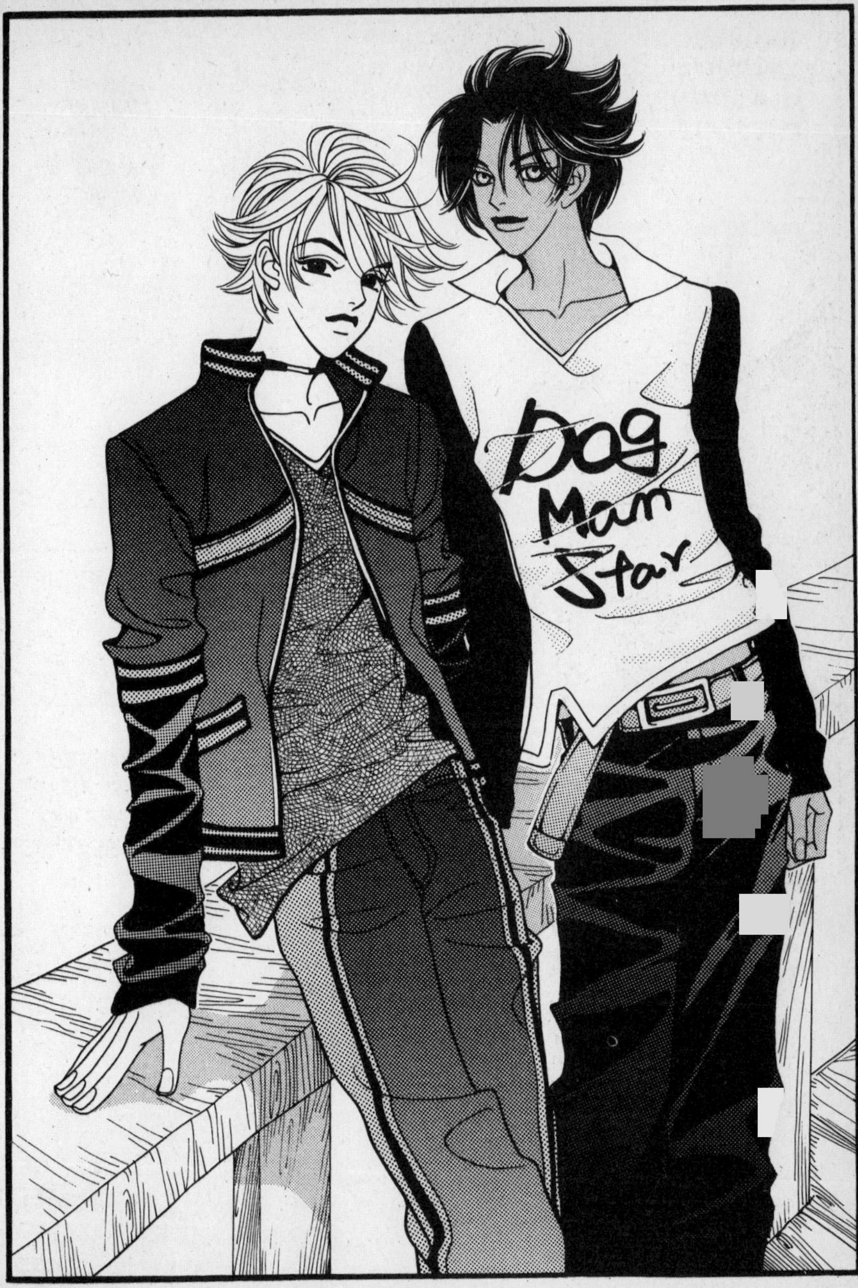
Dog
Man
Star

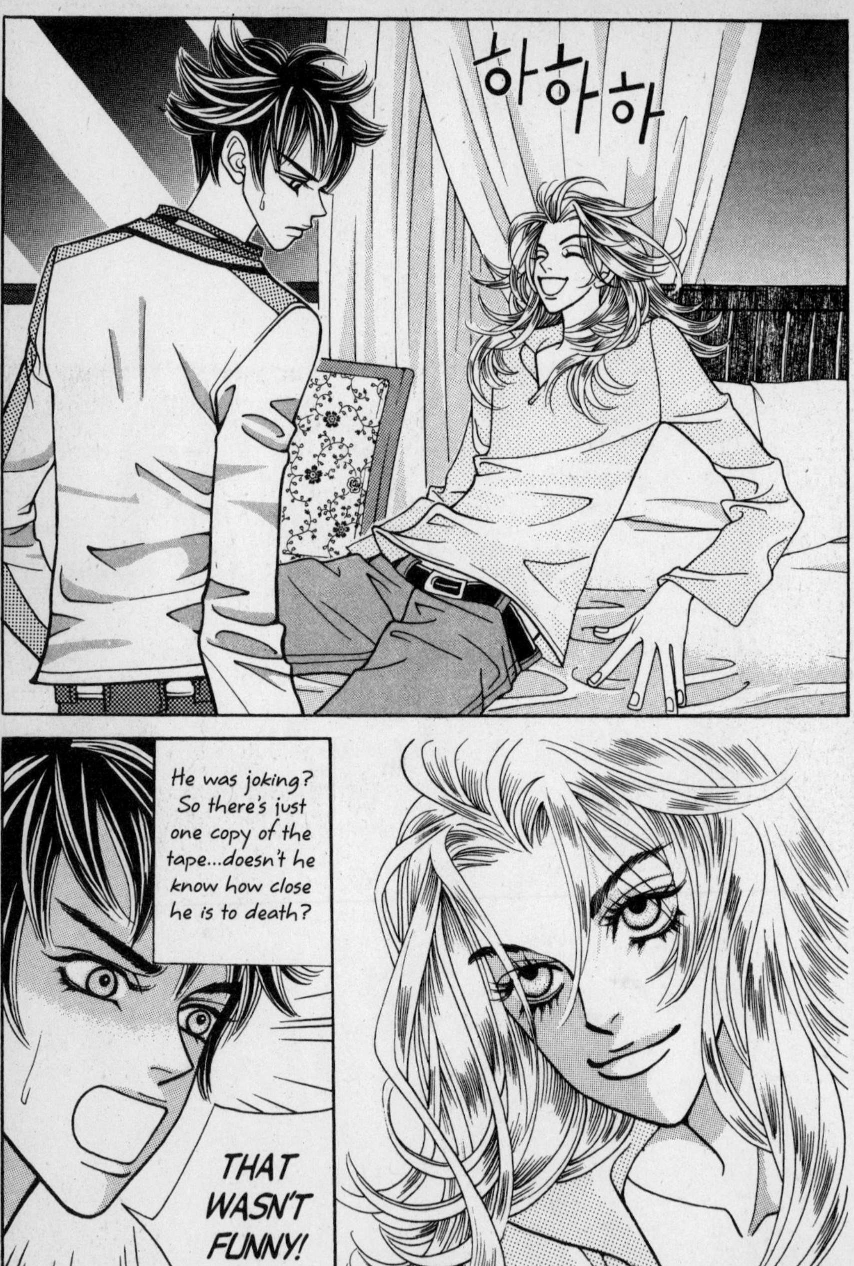

하하하
He was joking? So there's just one copy of the tape...doesn't he know how close he is to death?
THAT WASN'T FUNNY!

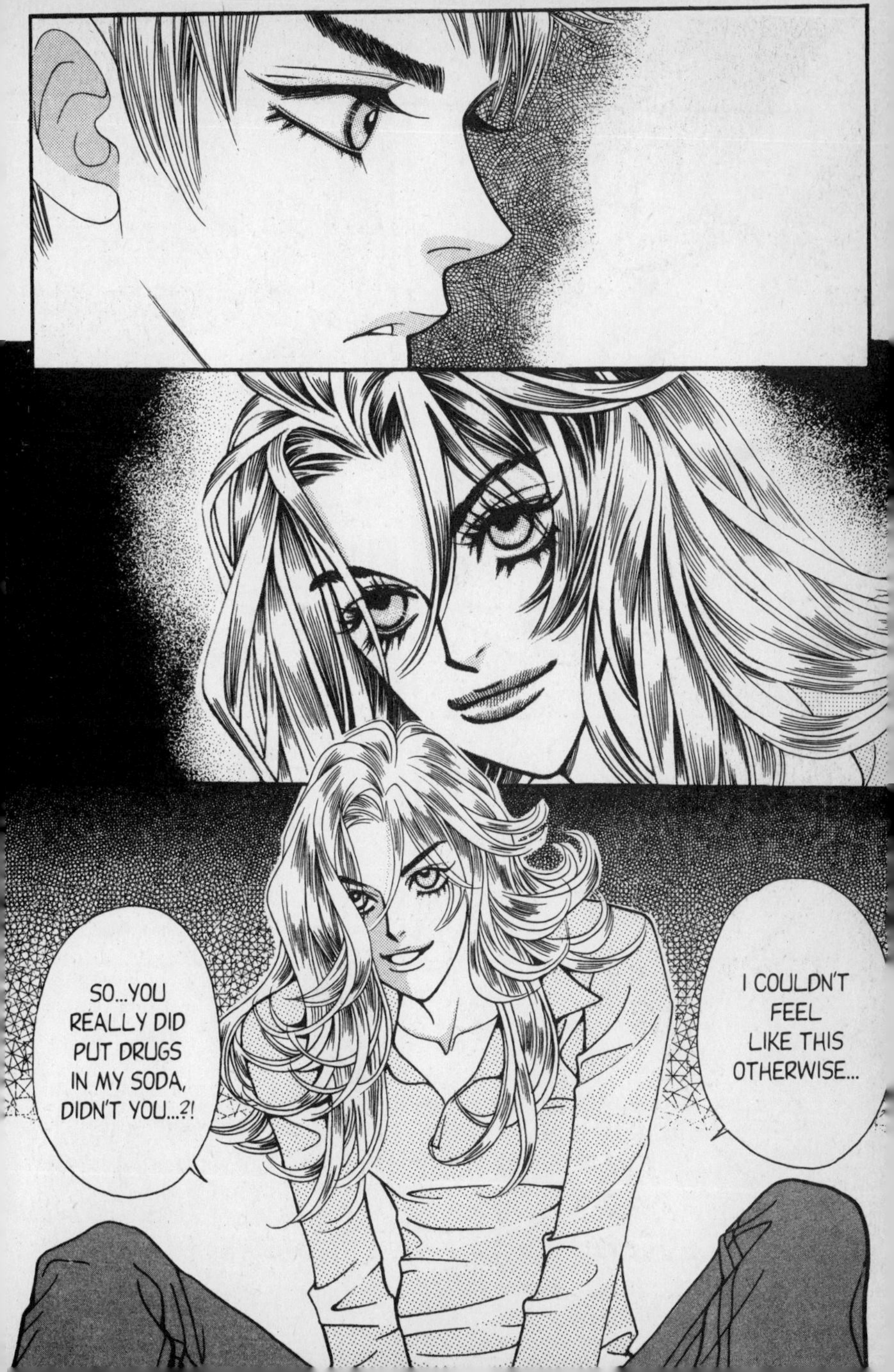
SO...YOU REALLY DID PUT DRUGS IN MY SODA, DIDN'T YOU...?!
I COULDN'T FEEL LIKE THIS OTHERWISE...

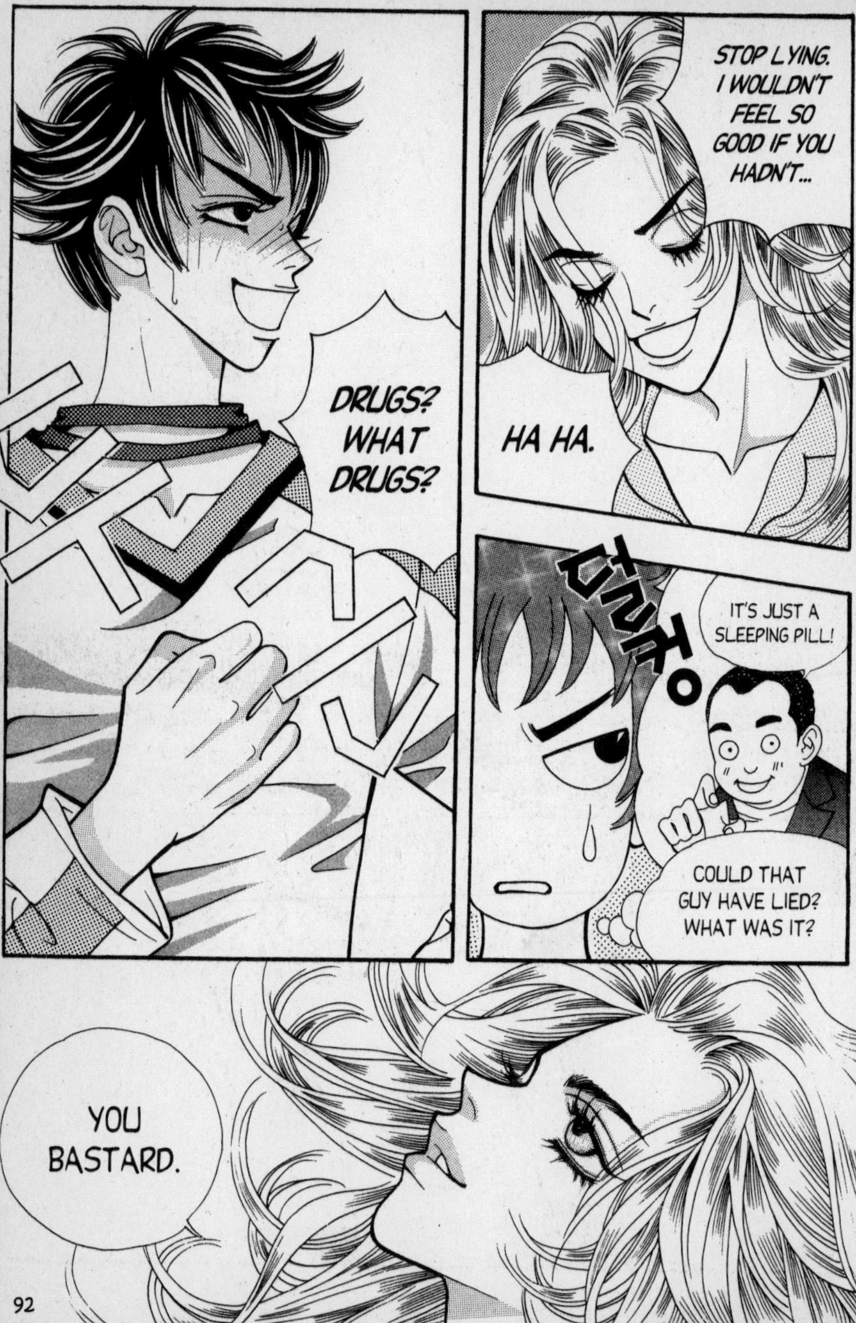
DRUGS? WHAT DRUGS?
STOP LYING. I WOULDN'T FEEL SO GOOD IF YOU HADN'T...
HA HA.
IT'S JUST A SLEEPING PILL!
COULD THAT GUY HAVE LIED? WHAT WAS IT?
YOU BASTARD.

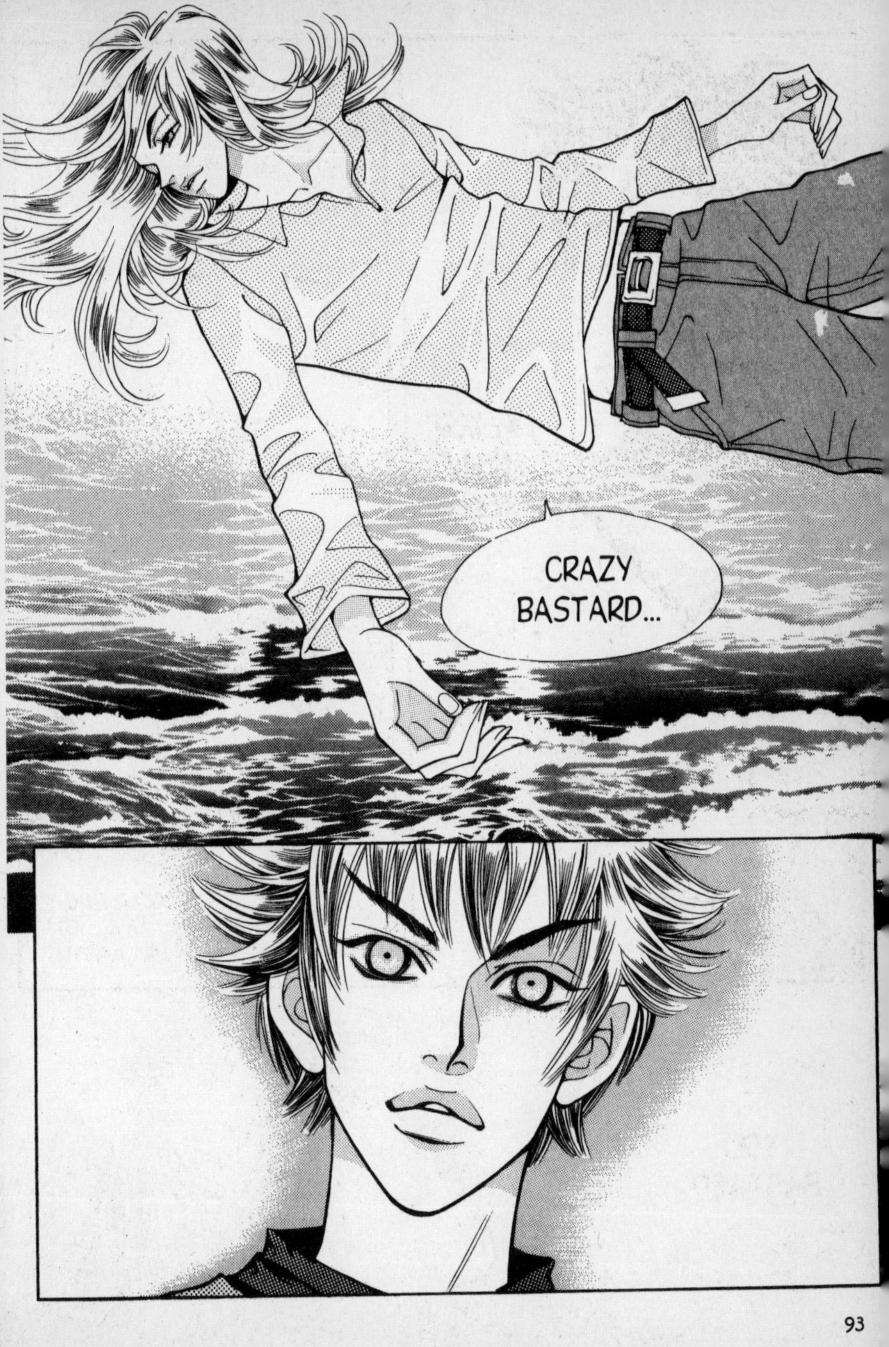
CRAZY BASTARD...

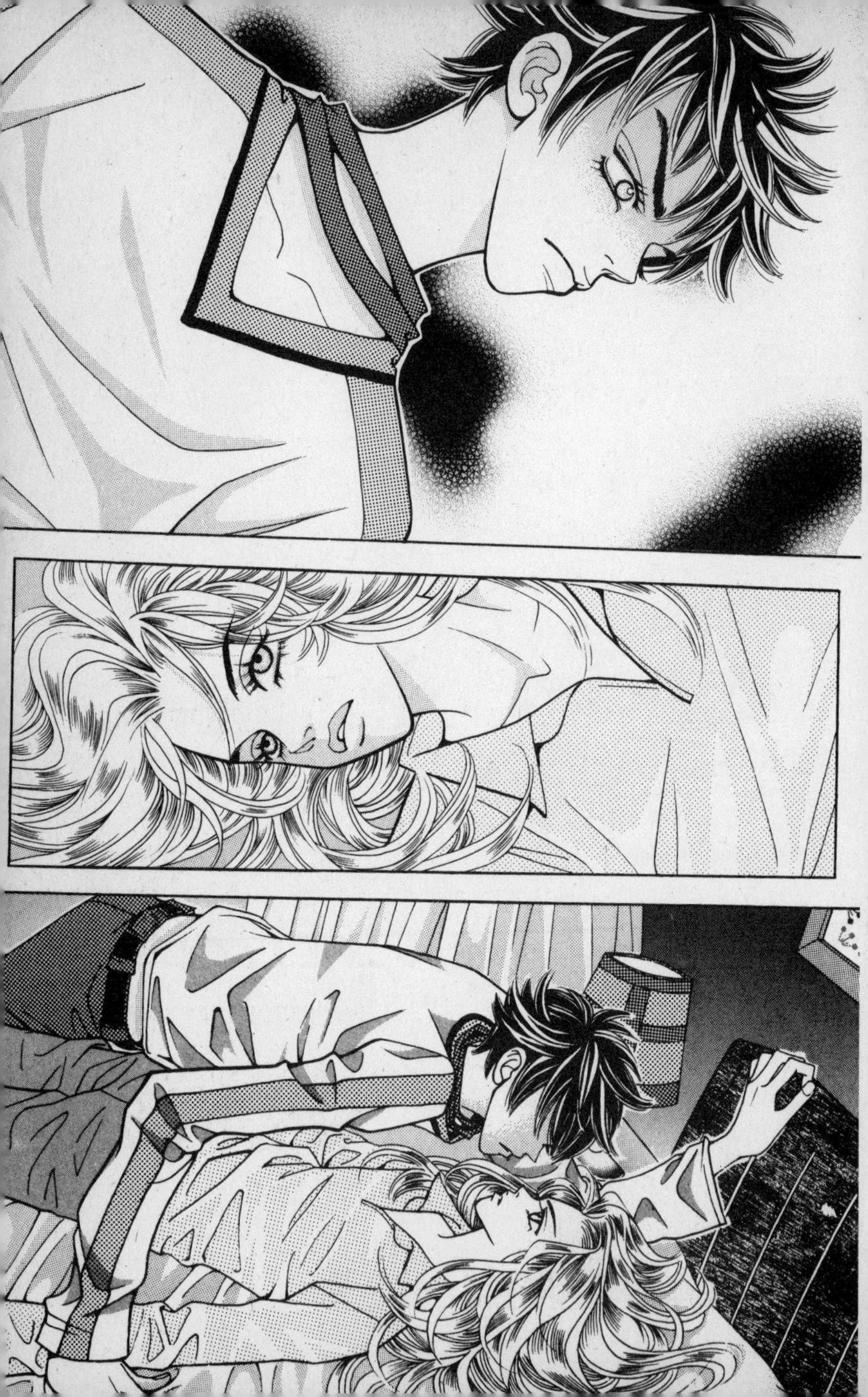

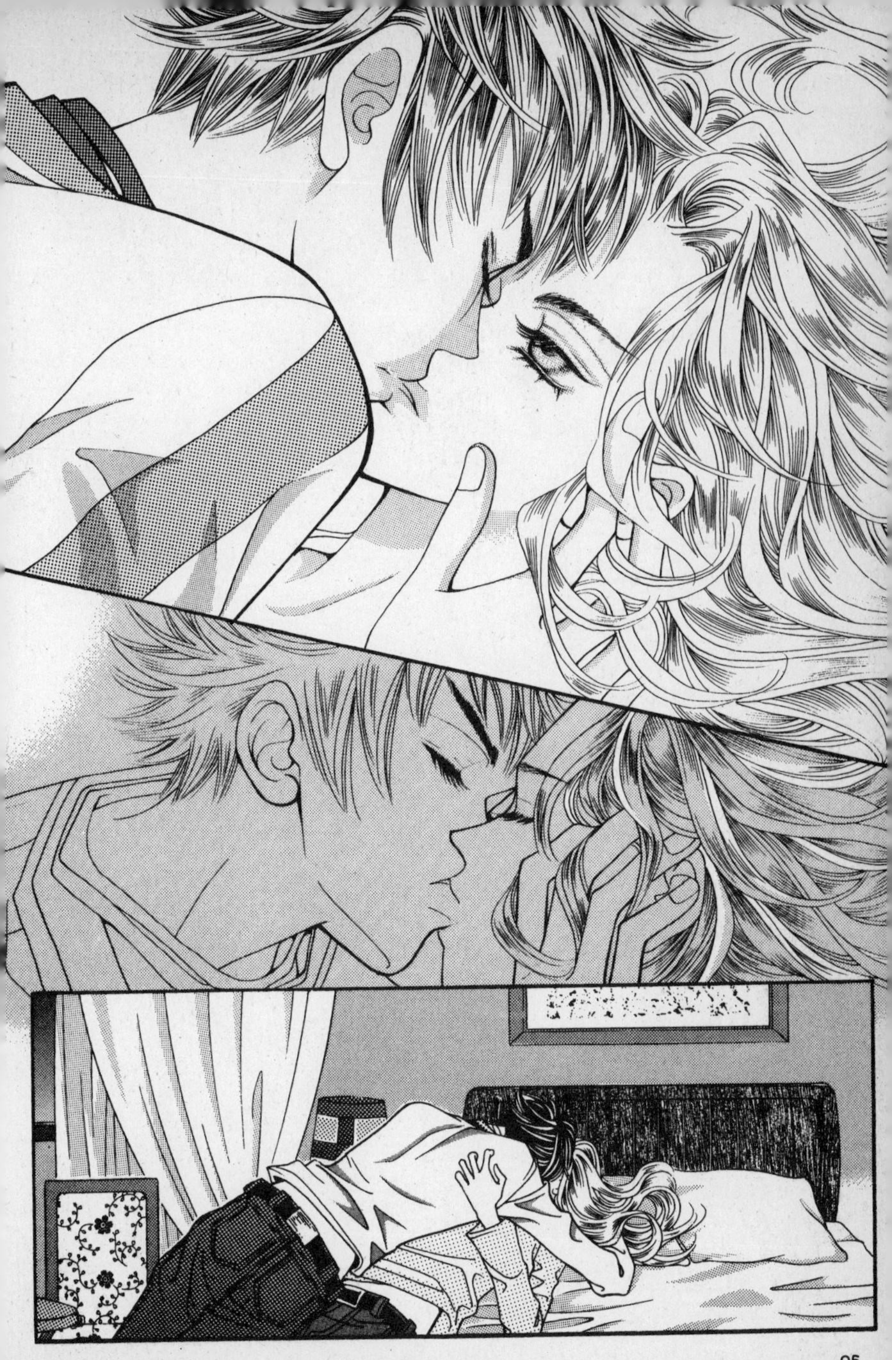

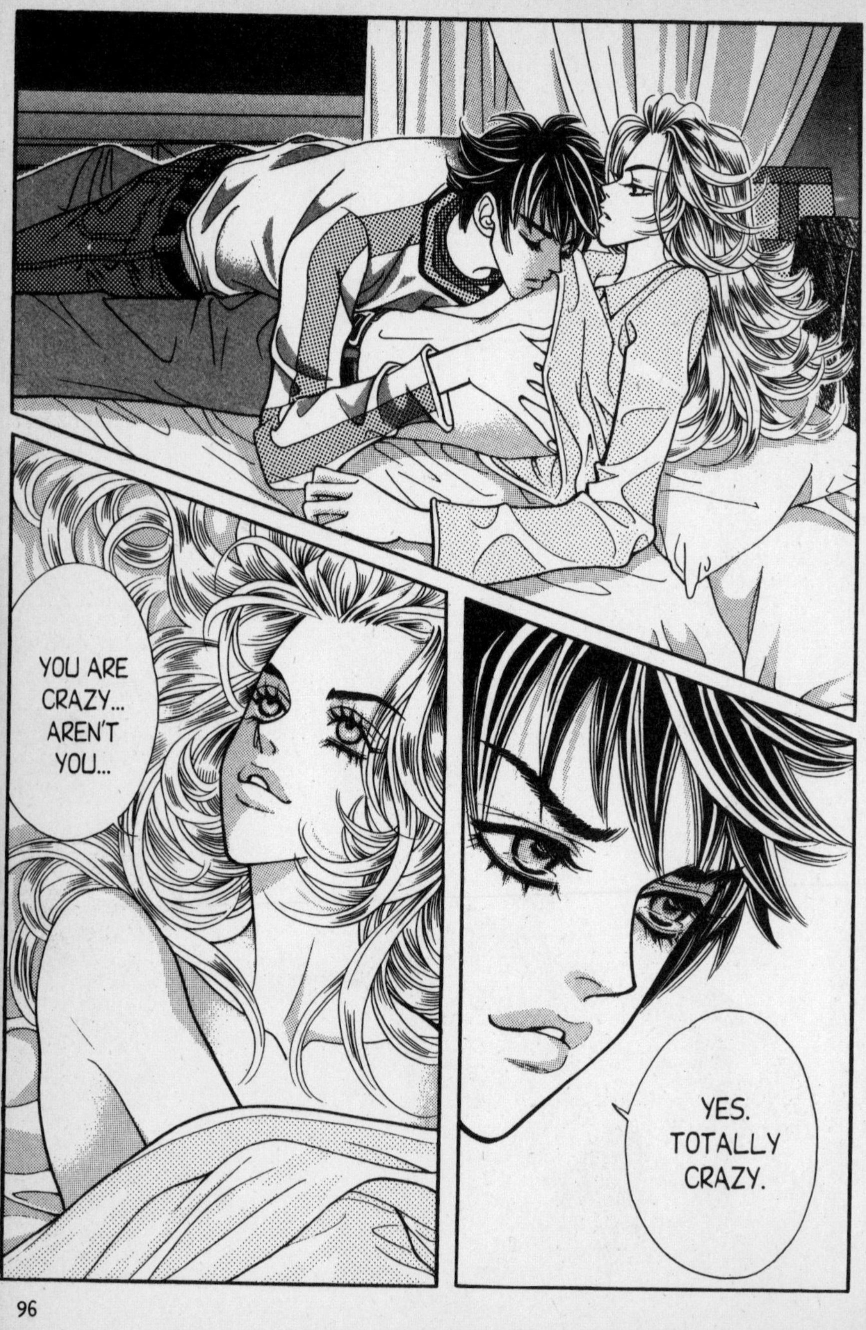
YOU ARE CRAZY... AREN'T YOU...
YES. TOTALLY CRAZY.

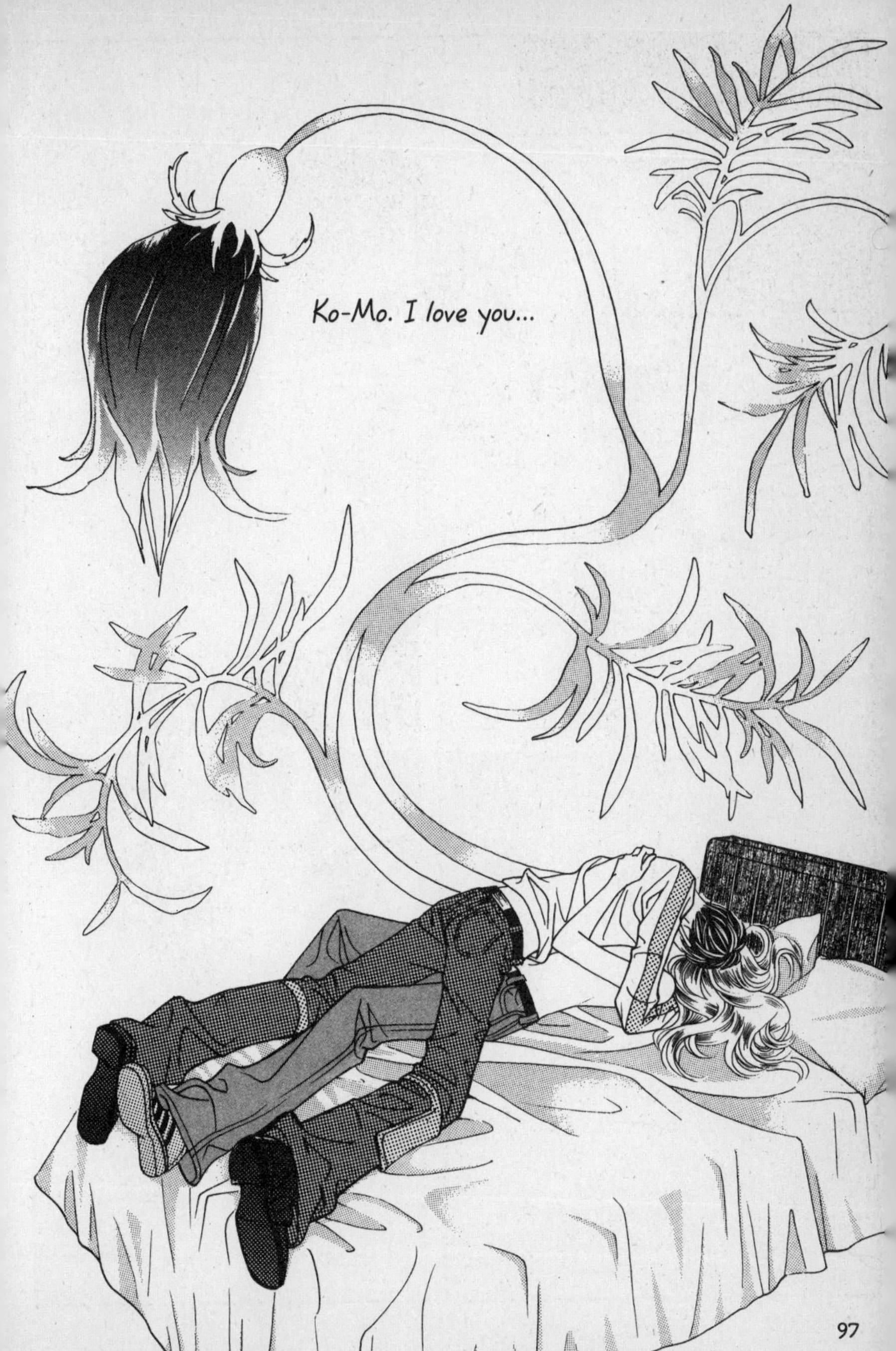
Ko-Mo. I love you...

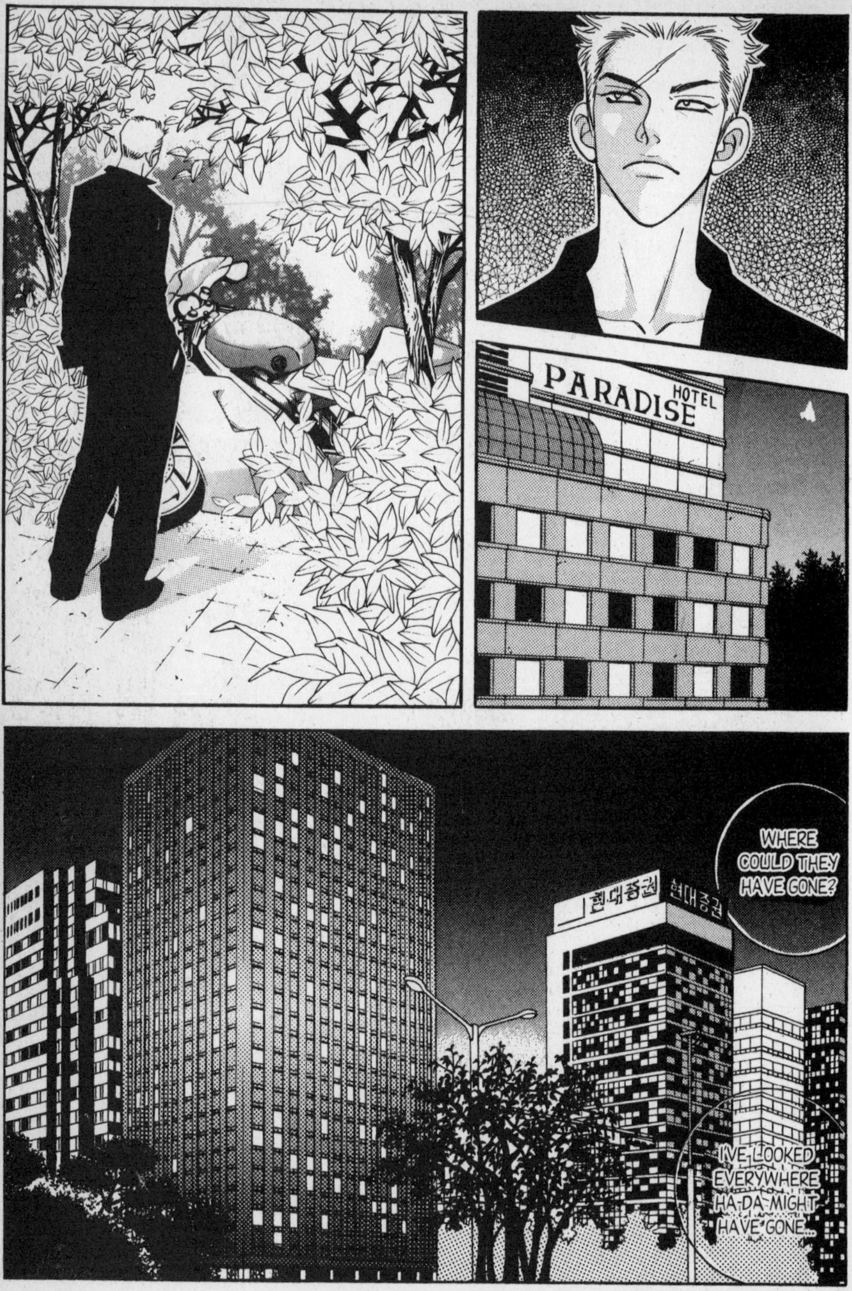
PARADISE HOTEL
현대증권
현대증권
WHERE COULD THEY HAVE GONE?
I'VE LOOKED EVERYWHERE HA-DA MIGHT HAVE GONE...

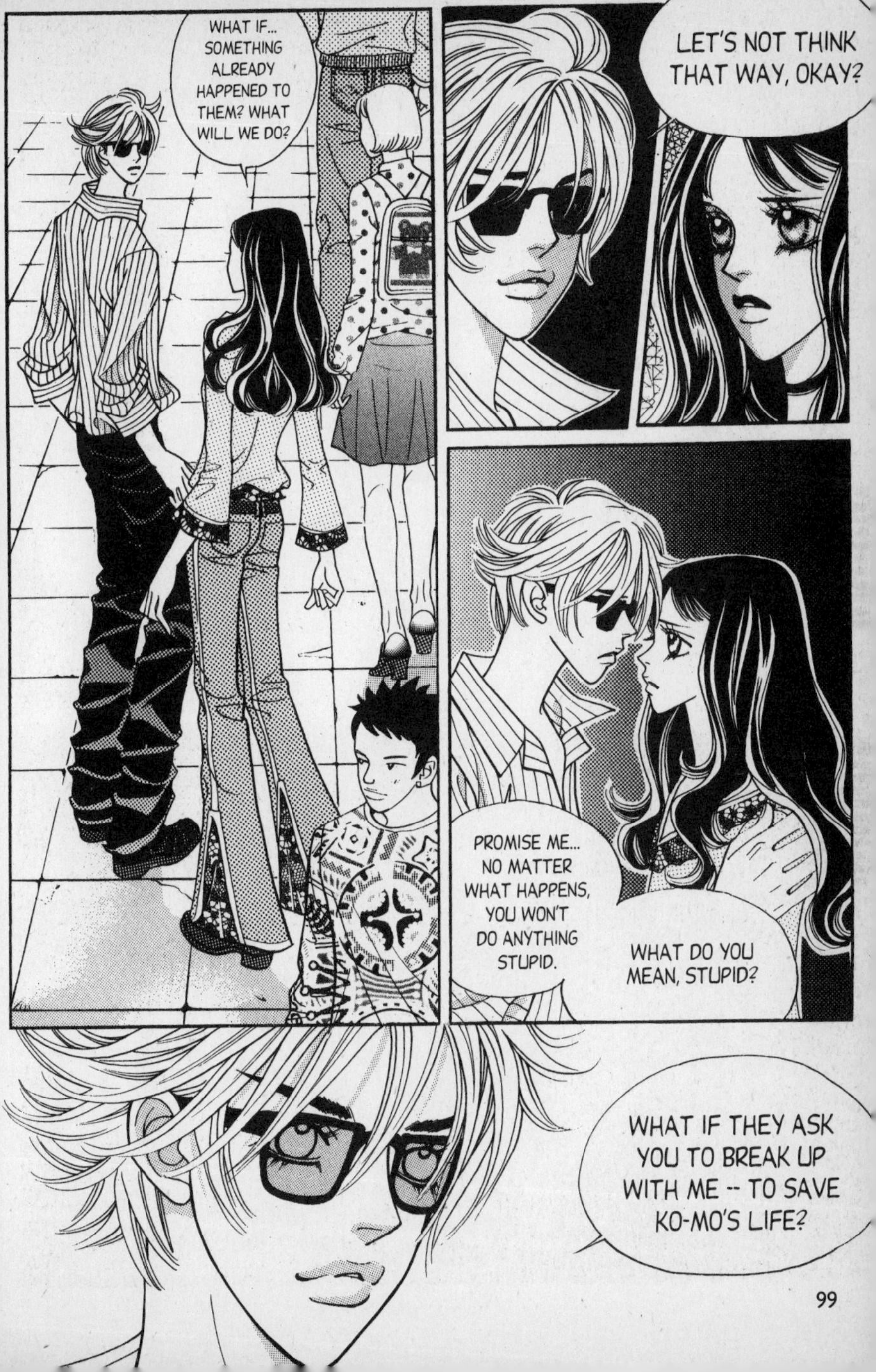
WHAT IF... SOMETHING ALREADY HAPPENED TO THEM? WHAT WILL WE DO?
LET'S NOT THINK THAT WAY, OKAY?
PROMISE ME... NO MATTER WHAT HAPPENS, YOU WON'T DO ANYTHING STUPID.
WHAT DO YOU MEAN, STUPID?
WHAT IF THEY ASK YOU TO BREAK UP WITH ME -- TO SAVE KO-MO'S LIFE?

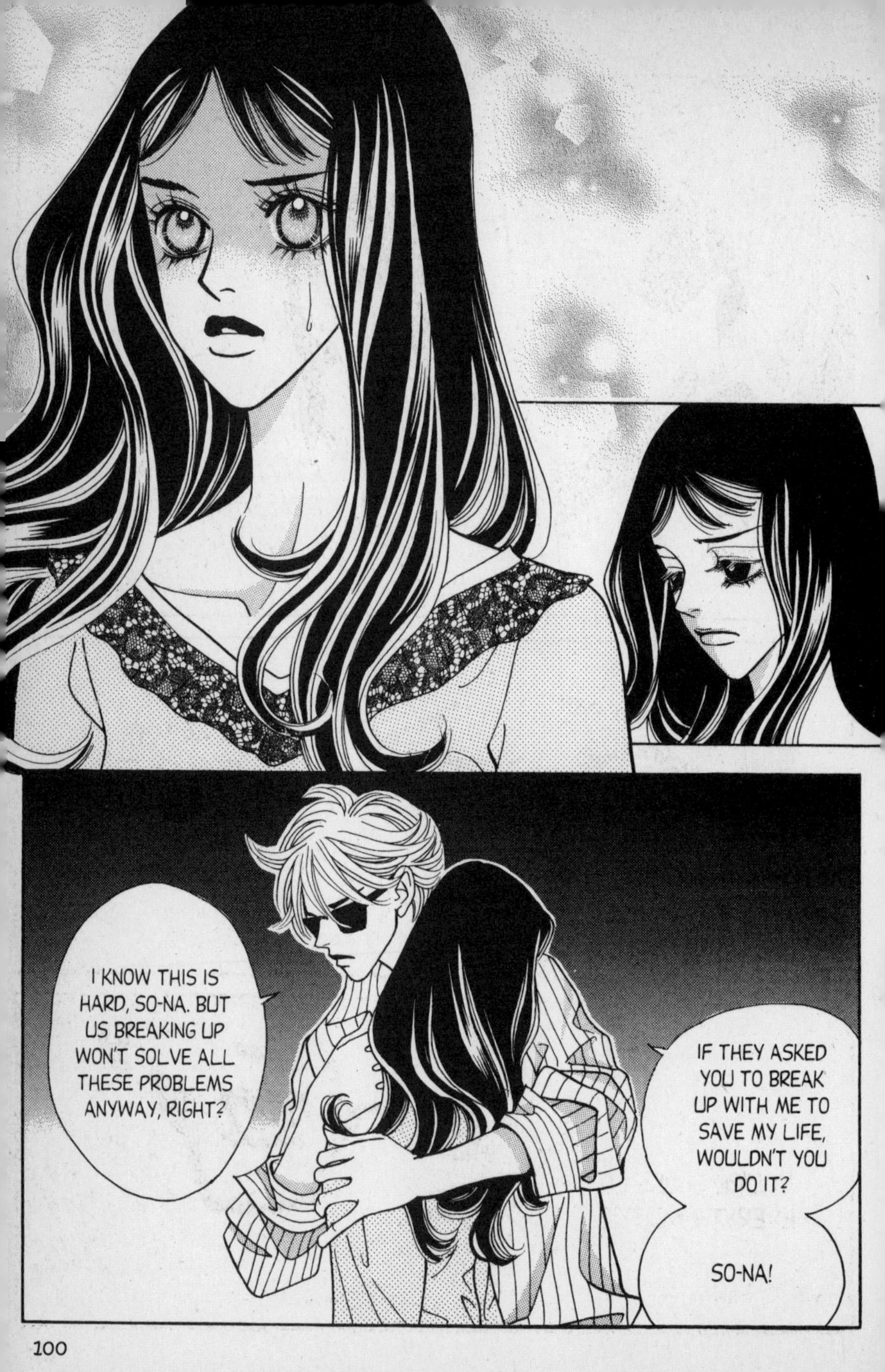
I KNOW THIS IS HARD, SO-NA. BUT US BREAKING UP WON'T SOLVE ALL THESE PROBLEMS ANYWAY, RIGHT?
IF THEY ASKED YOU TO BREAK UP WITH ME TO SAVE MY LIFE, WOULDN'T YOU DO IT?
SO-NA!

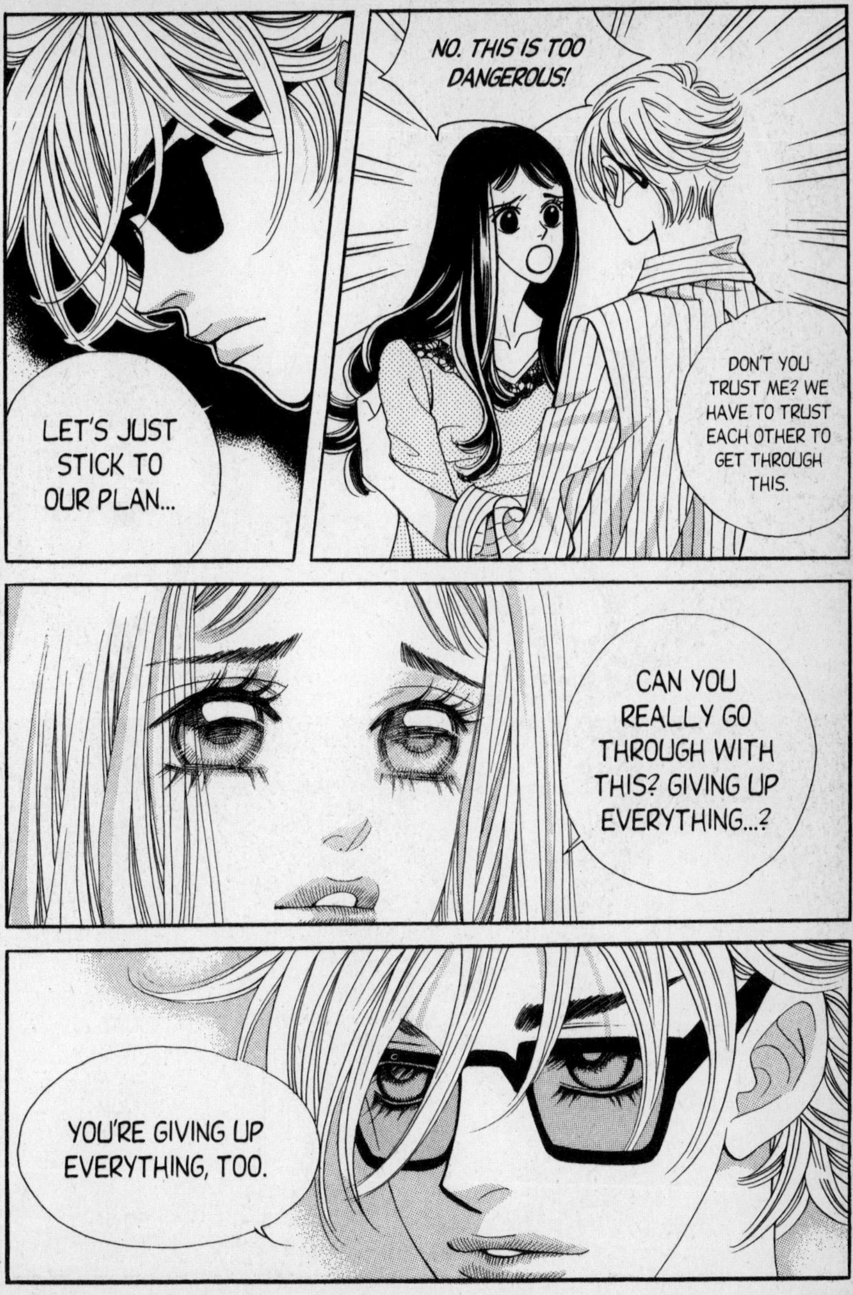
LET'S JUST STICK TO OUR PLAN...
NO. THIS IS TOO DANGEROUS!
DON'T YOU TRUST ME? WE HAVE TO TRUST EACH OTHER TO GET THROUGH THIS.
CAN YOU REALLY GO THROUGH WITH THIS? GIVING UP EVERYTHING...?
YOU'RE GIVING UP EVERYTHING, TOO.

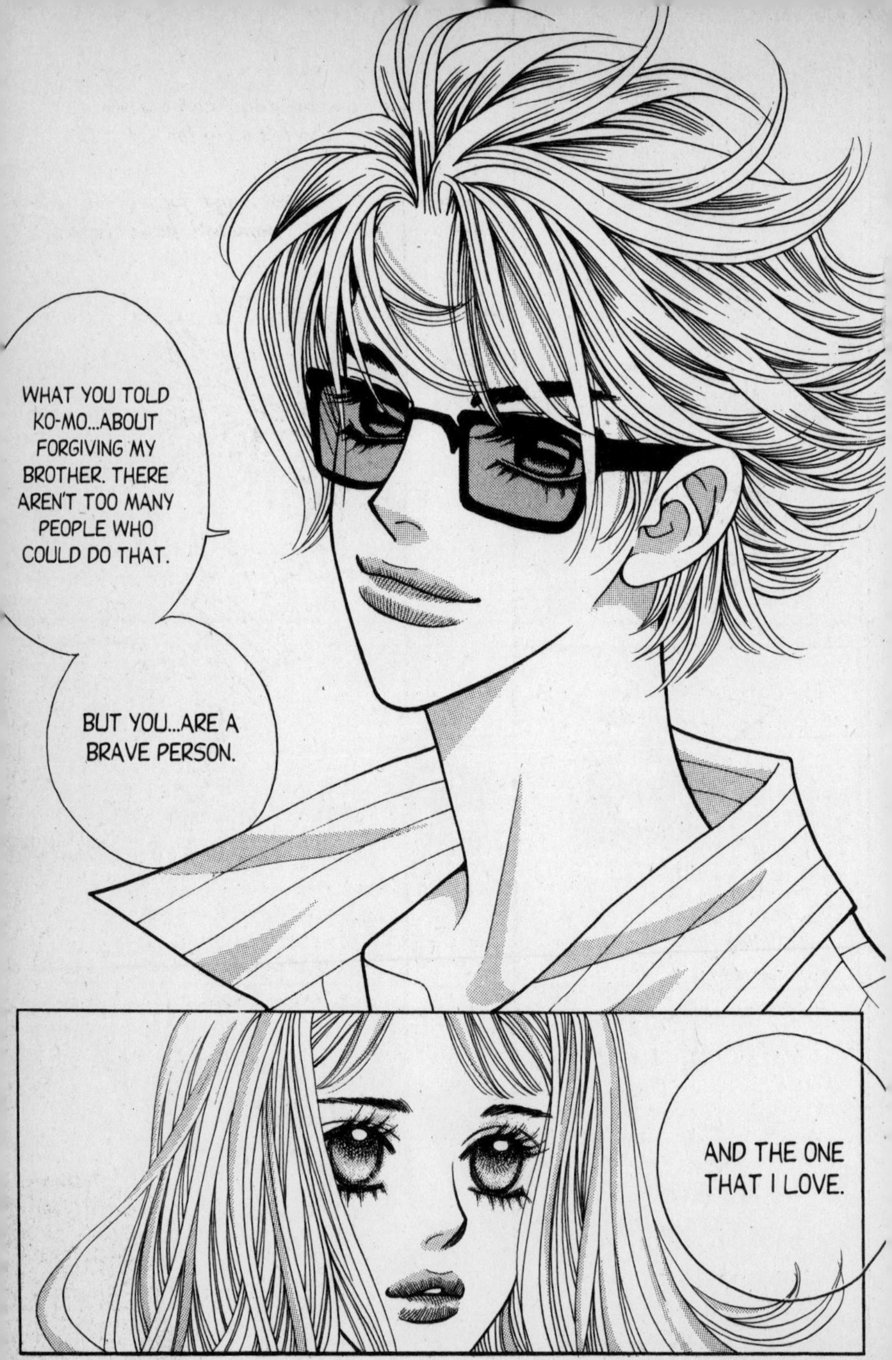
WHAT YOU TOLD KO-MO...ABOUT FORGIVING MY BROTHER. THERE AREN'T TOO MANY PEOPLE WHO COULD DO THAT.
BUT YOU...ARE A BRAVE PERSON.
AND THE ONE THAT I LOVE.

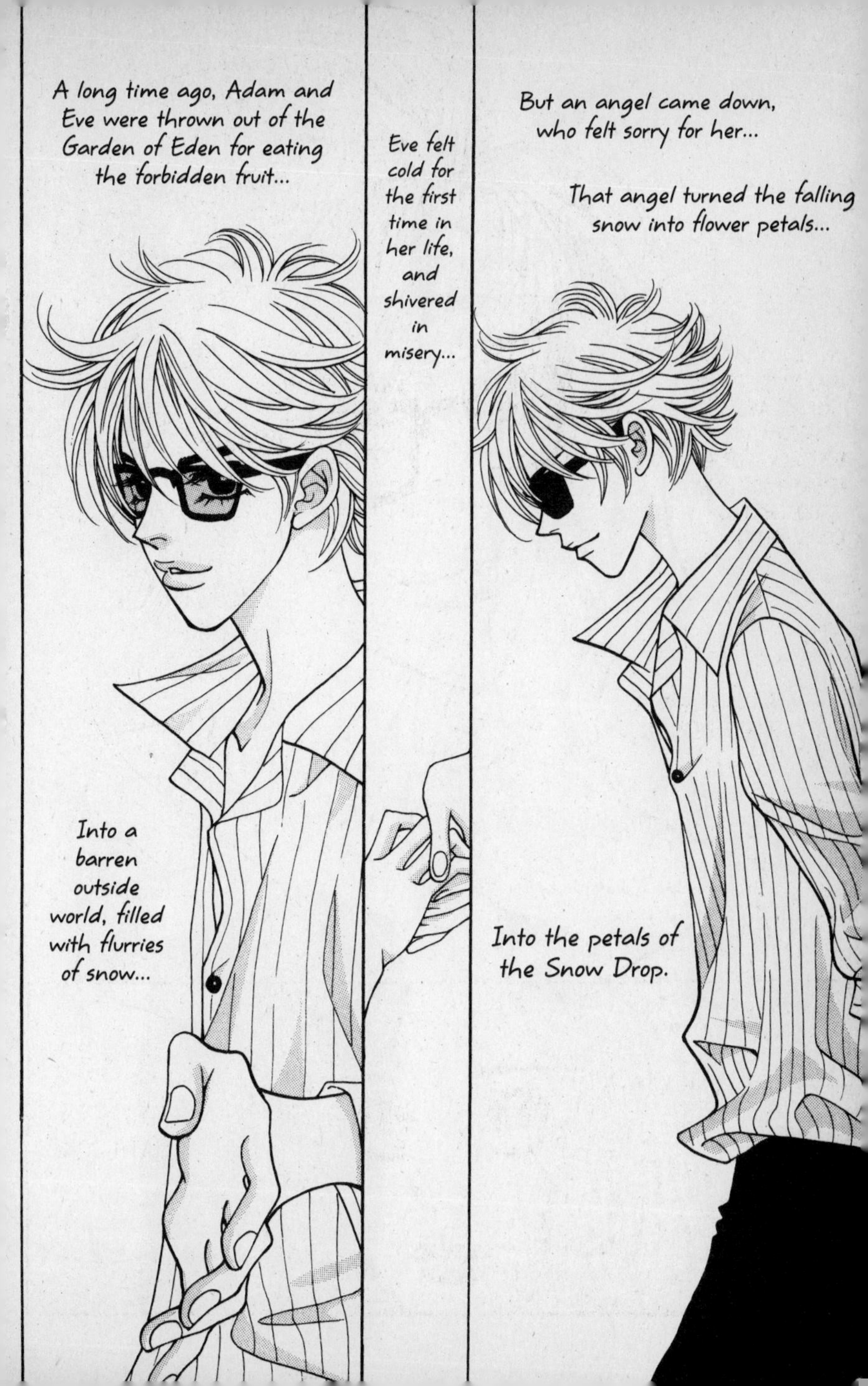
A long time ago, Adam and Eve were thrown out of the Garden of Eden for eating the forbidden fruit...
Into a barren outside world, filled with flurries of snow...
Eve felt cold for the first time in her life, and shivered in misery...
But an angel came down, who felt sorry for her...
That angel turned the falling snow into flower petals...
Into the petals of the Snow Drop.

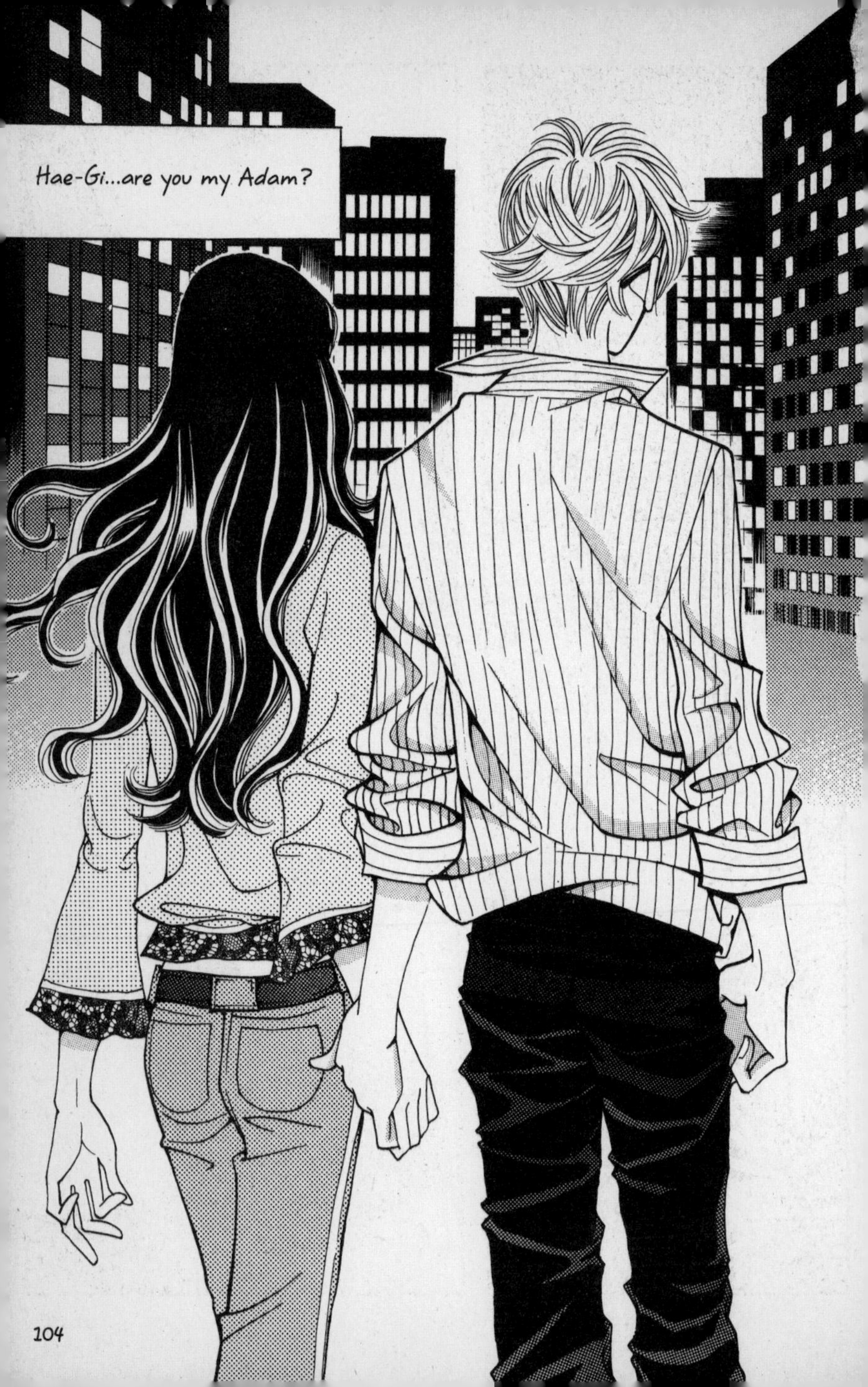
Hae-Gi...are you my Adam?

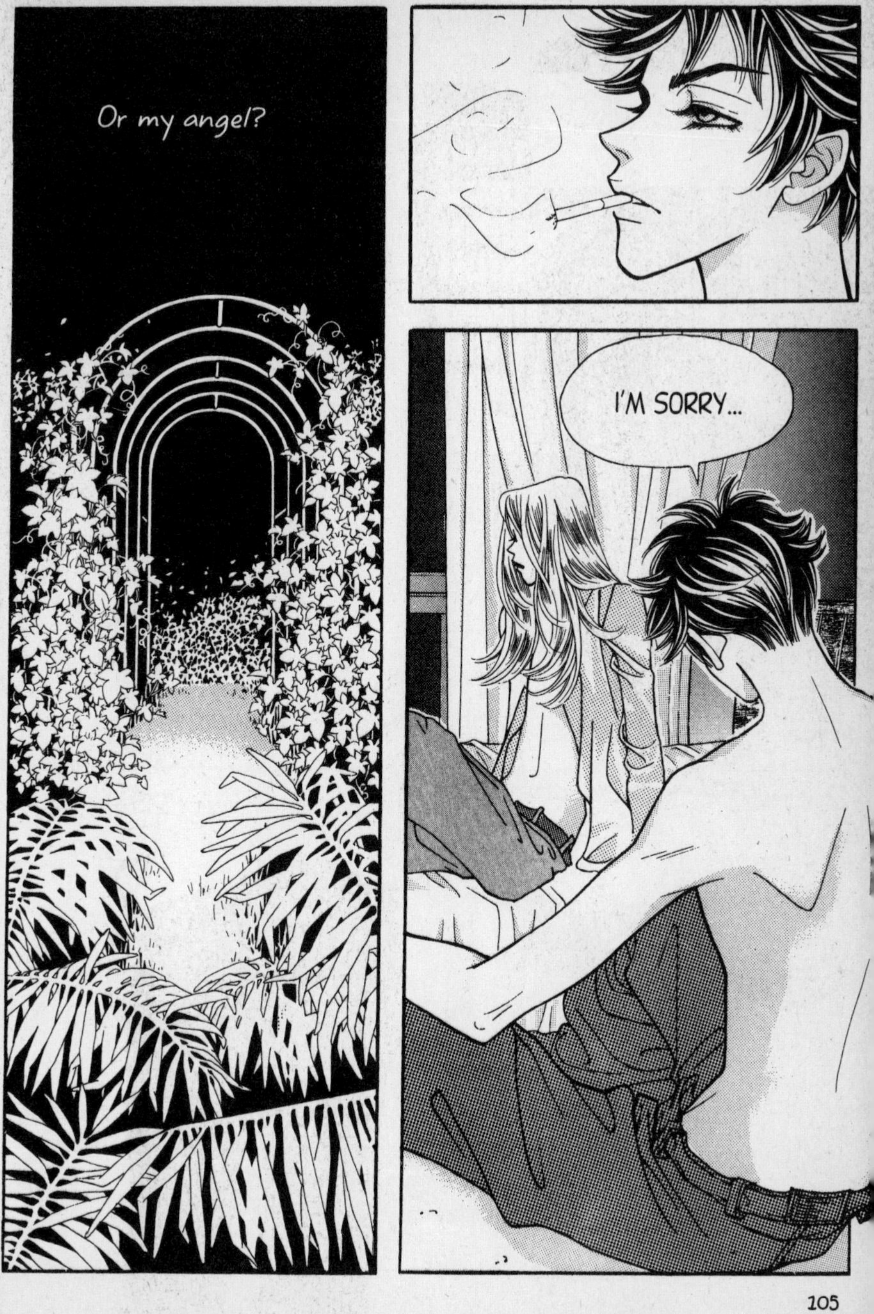
Or my angel?
I'M SORRY...

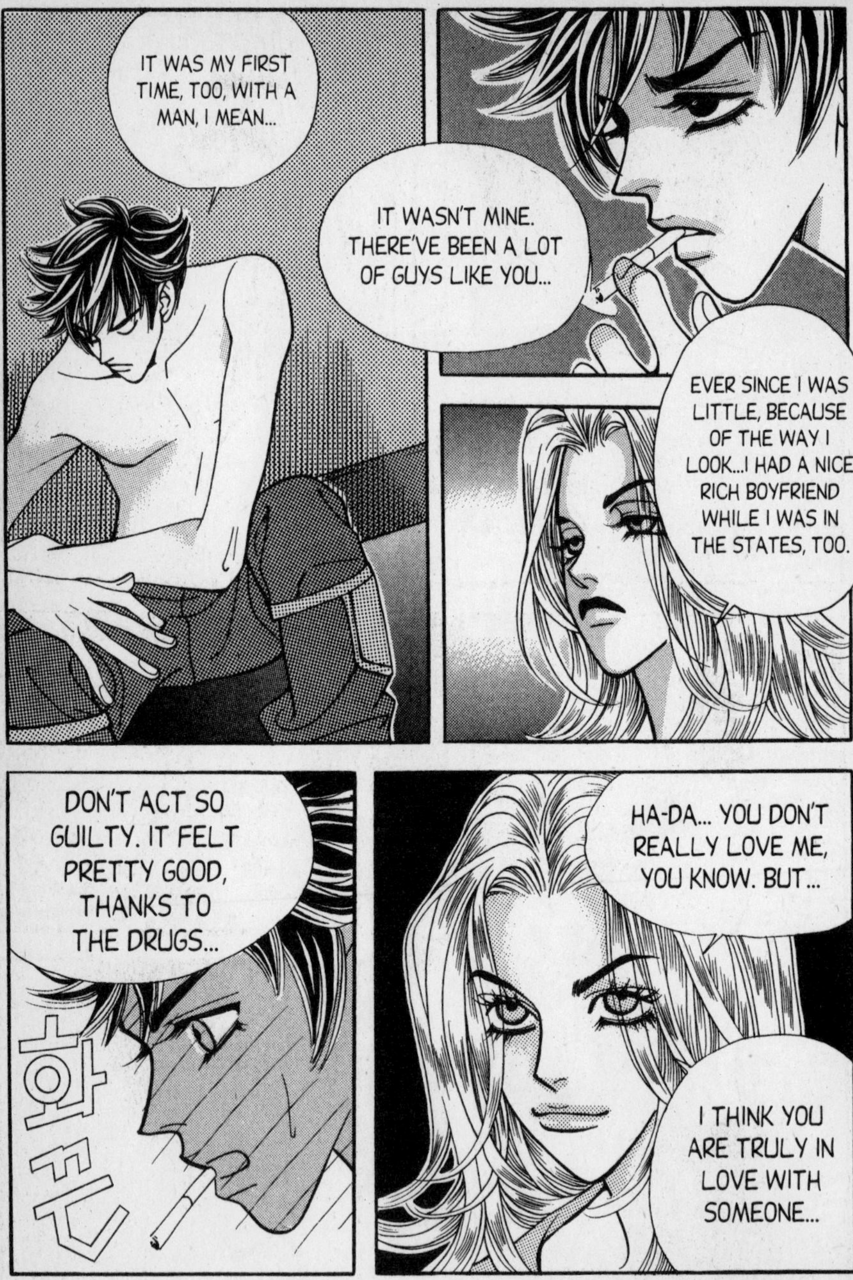
IT WAS MY FIRST TIME, TOO, WITH A MAN, I MEAN...
IT WASN'T MINE. THERE'VE BEEN A LOT OF GUYS LIKE YOU...
EVER SINCE I WAS LITTLE, BECAUSE OF THE WAY I LOOK...I HAD A NICE RICH BOYFRIEND WHILE I WAS IN THE STATES, TOO.
DON'T ACT SO GUILTY. IT FELT PRETTY GOOD, THANKS TO THE DRUGS...
HA-DA... YOU DON'T REALLY LOVE ME, YOU KNOW. BUT...
I THINK YOU ARE TRULY IN LOVE WITH SOMEONE...

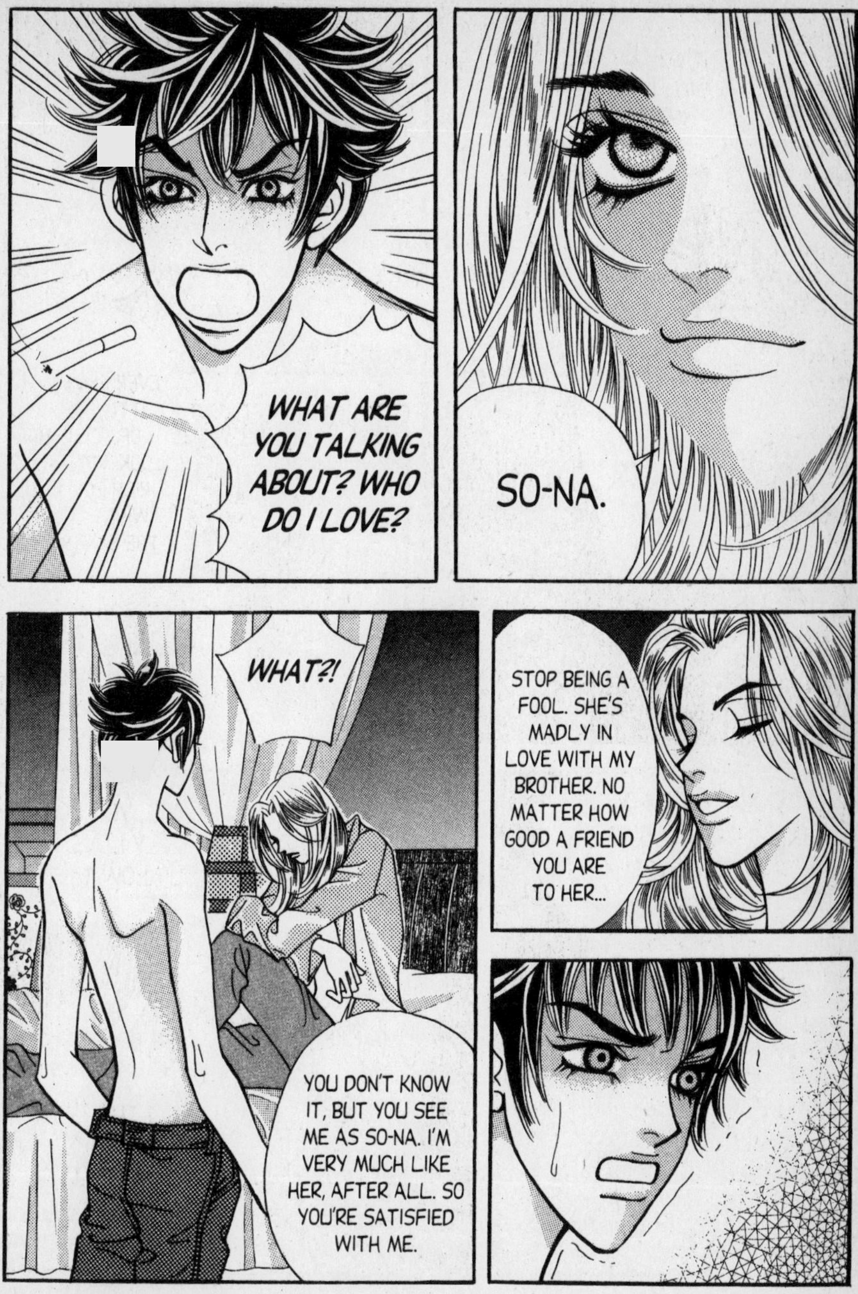
WHAT ARE YOU TALKING ABOUT? WHO DO I LOVE?
SO-NA.
WHAT?!
YOU DON'T KNOW IT, BUT YOU SEE ME AS SO-NA. I'M VERY MUCH LIKE HER, AFTER ALL. SO YOU'RE SATISFIED WITH ME.
STOP BEING A FOOL. SHE'S MADLY IN LOVE WITH MY BROTHER. NO MATTER HOW GOOD A FRIEND YOU ARE TO HER...

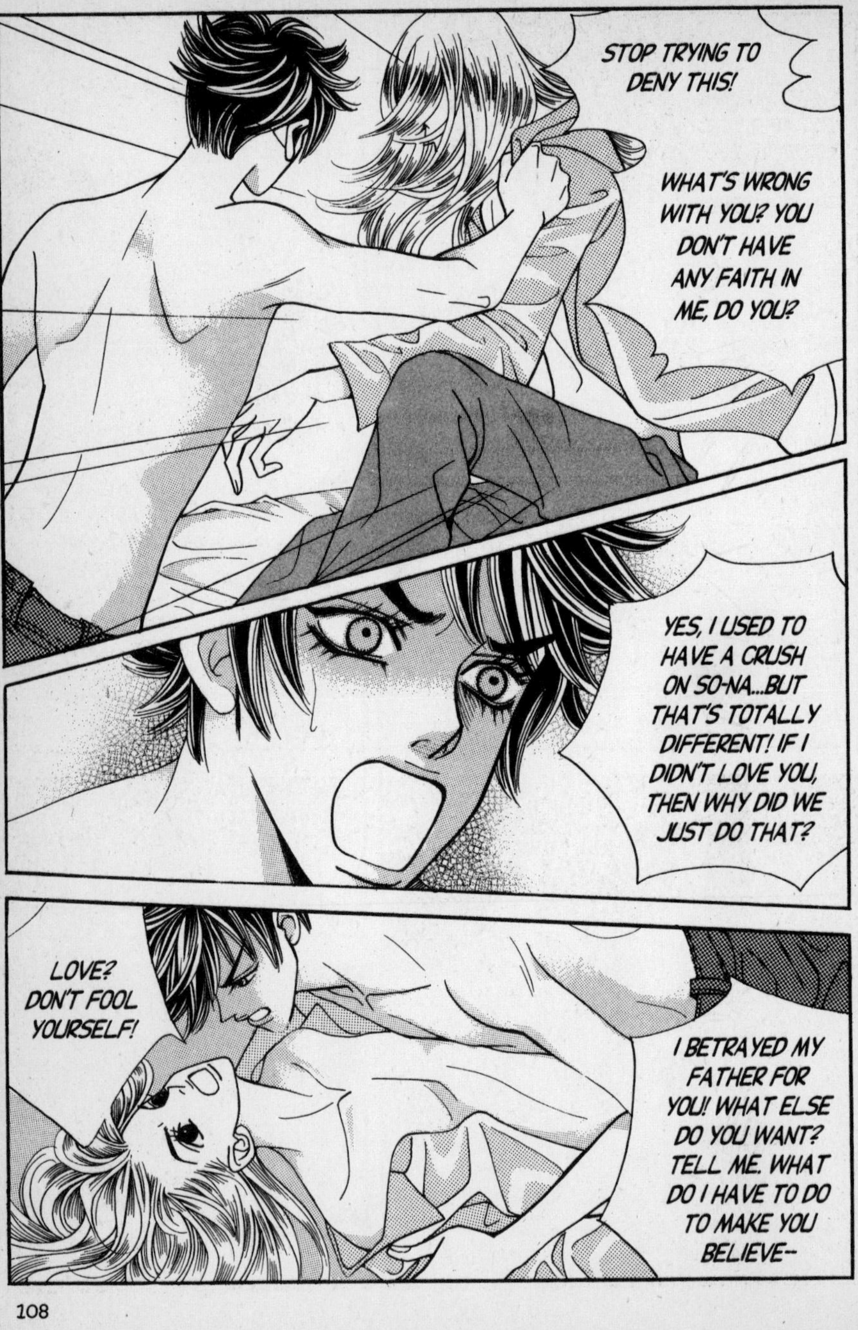
STOP TRYING TO DENY THIS!
WHAT'S WRONG WITH YOU? YOU DON'T HAVE ANY FAITH IN ME, DO YOU?
YES, I USED TO HAVE A CRUSH ON SO-NA...BUT THAT'S TOTALLY DIFFERENT! IF I DIDN'T LOVE YOU, THEN WHY DID WE JUST DO THAT?
LOVE? DON'T FOOL YOURSELF!
I BETRAYED MY FATHER FOR YOU! WHAT ELSE DO YOU WANT? TELL ME. WHAT DO I HAVE TO DO TO MAKE YOU BELIEVE--

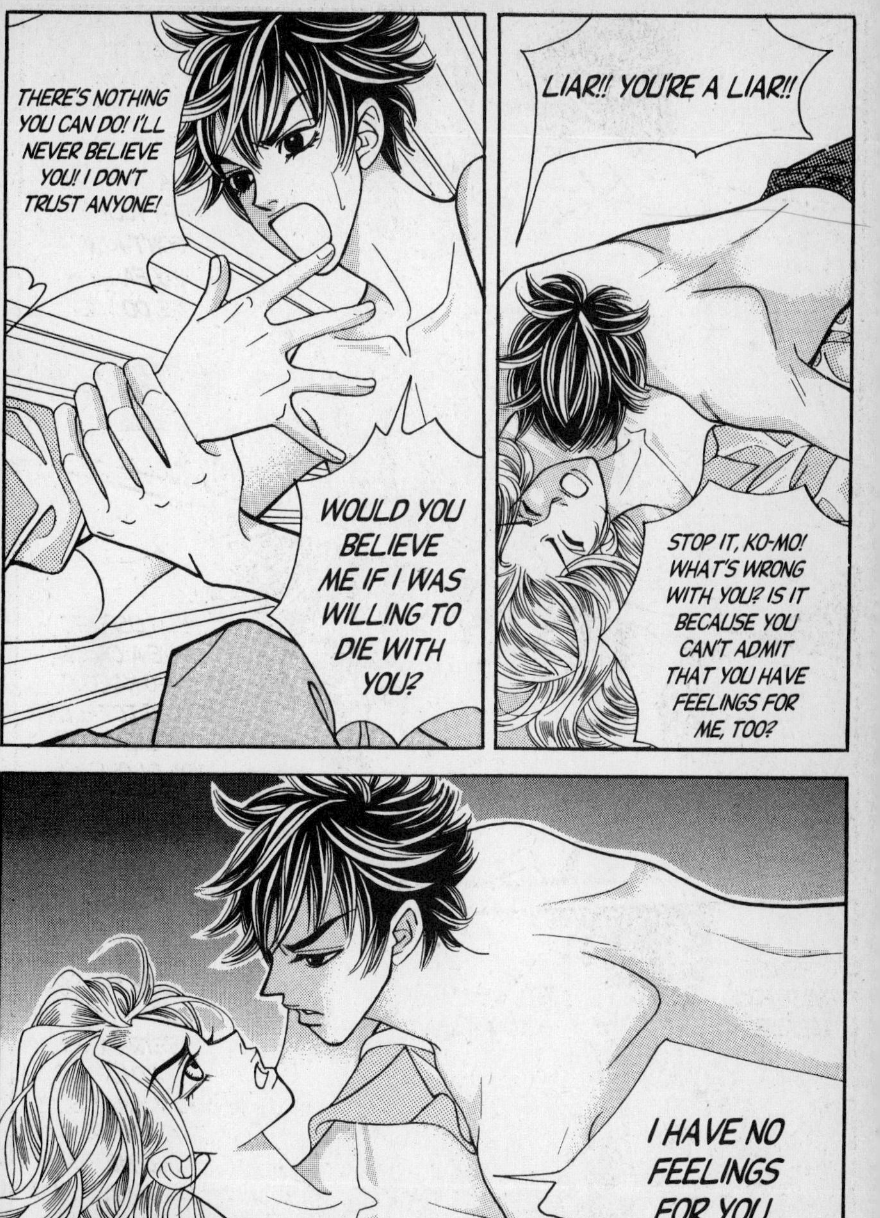
THERE'S NOTHING YOU CAN DO! I'LL NEVER BELIEVE YOU! I DON'T TRUST ANYONE!
WOULD YOU BELIEVE ME IF I WAS WILLING TO DIE WITH YOU?
LIAR!! YOU'RE A LIAR!!
STOP IT, KO-MO! WHAT'S WRONG WITH YOU? IS IT BECAUSE YOU CAN'T ADMIT THAT YOU HAVE FEELINGS FOR ME, TOO?
I HAVE NO FEELINGS FOR YOU.

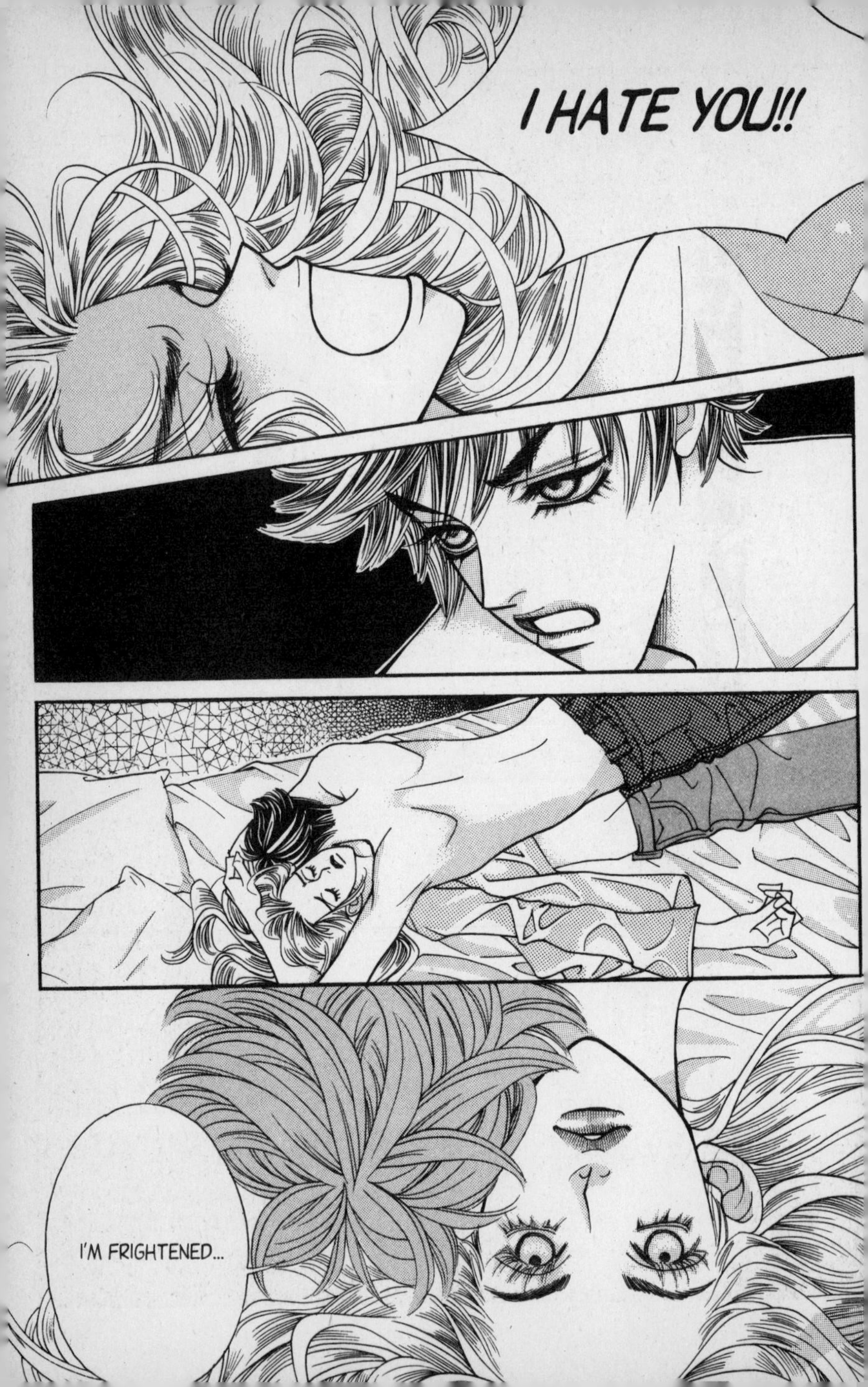
I HATE YOU!!
I'M FRIGHTENED...

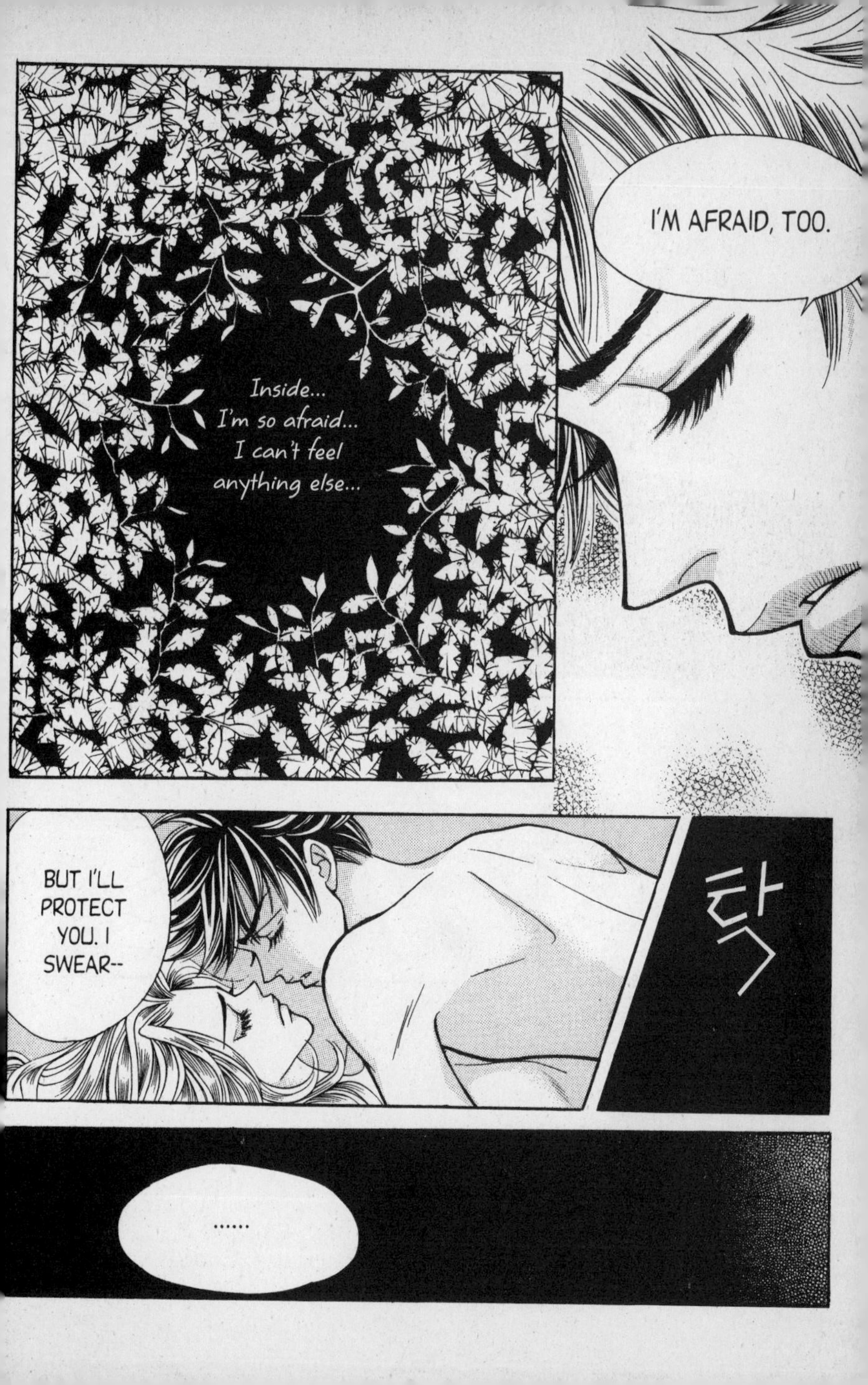
Inside... I'm so afraid... I can't feel anything else...
I'M AFRAID, TOO.
BUT I'LL PROTECT YOU. I SWEAR--
탁
......

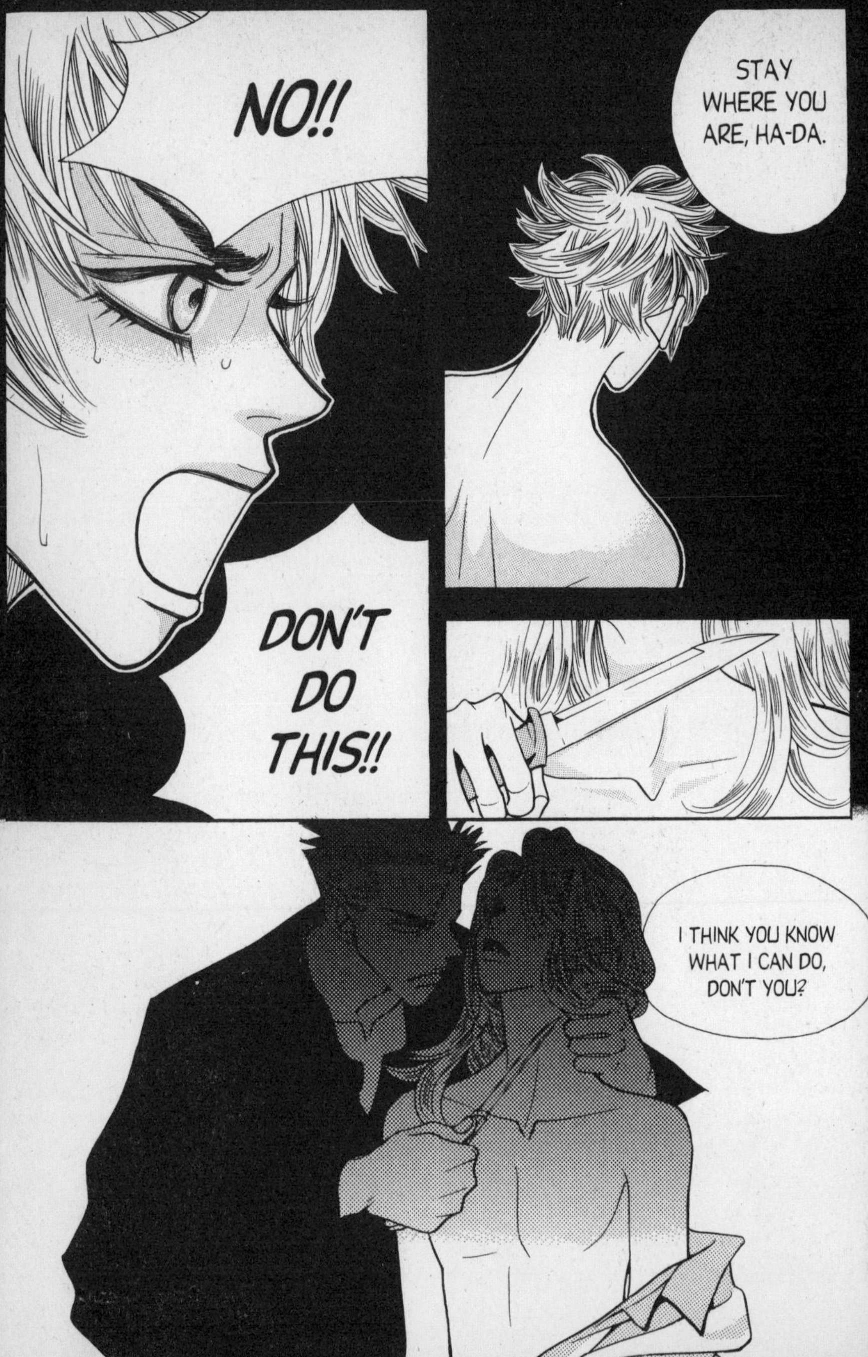
NO!!
STAY WHERE YOU ARE, HA-DA.
DON'T DO THIS!!
I THINK YOU KNOW WHAT I CAN DO, DON'T YOU?

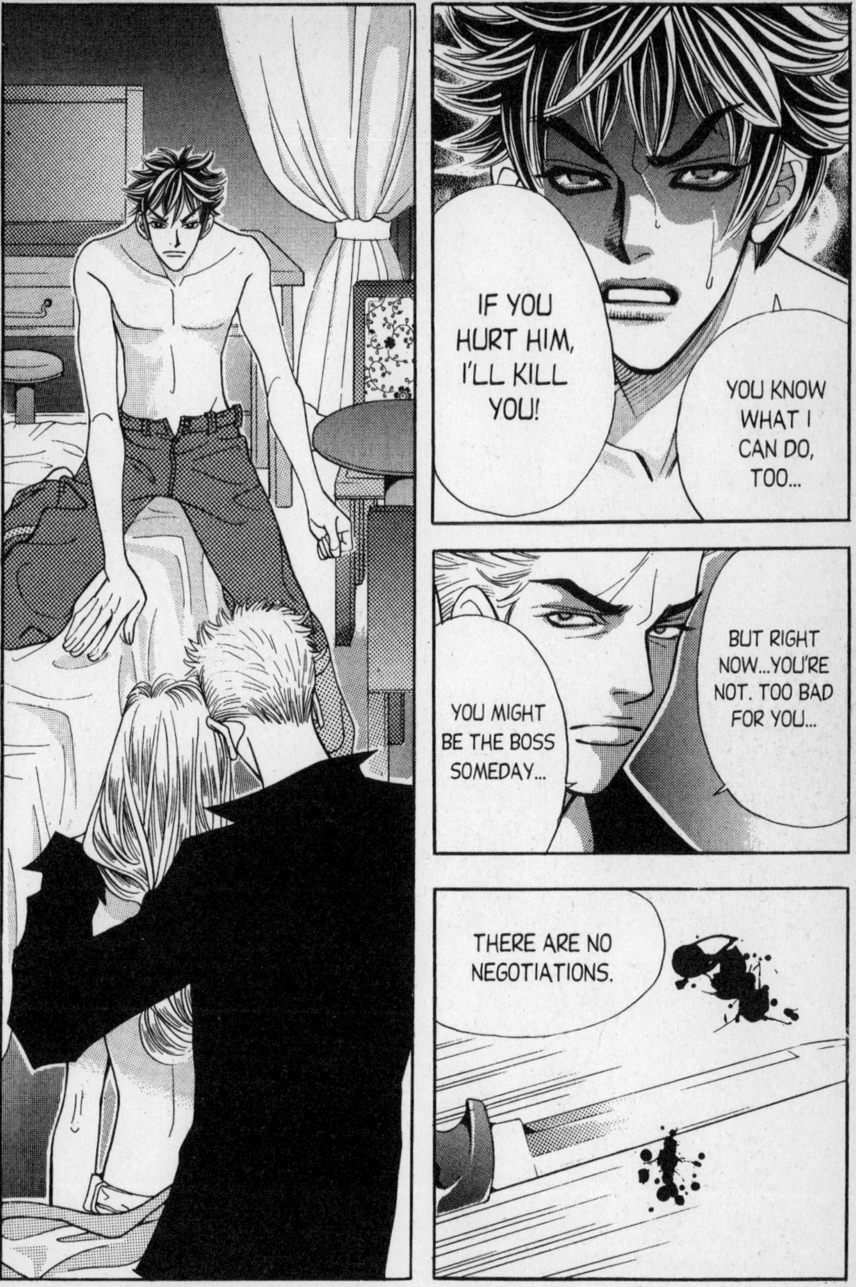
IF YOU HURT HIM, I'LL KILL YOU!
YOU KNOW WHAT I CAN DO, TOO...
YOU MIGHT BE THE BOSS SOMEDAY...
BUT RIGHT NOW...YOU'RE NOT. TOO BAD FOR YOU...
THERE ARE NO NEGOTIATIONS.

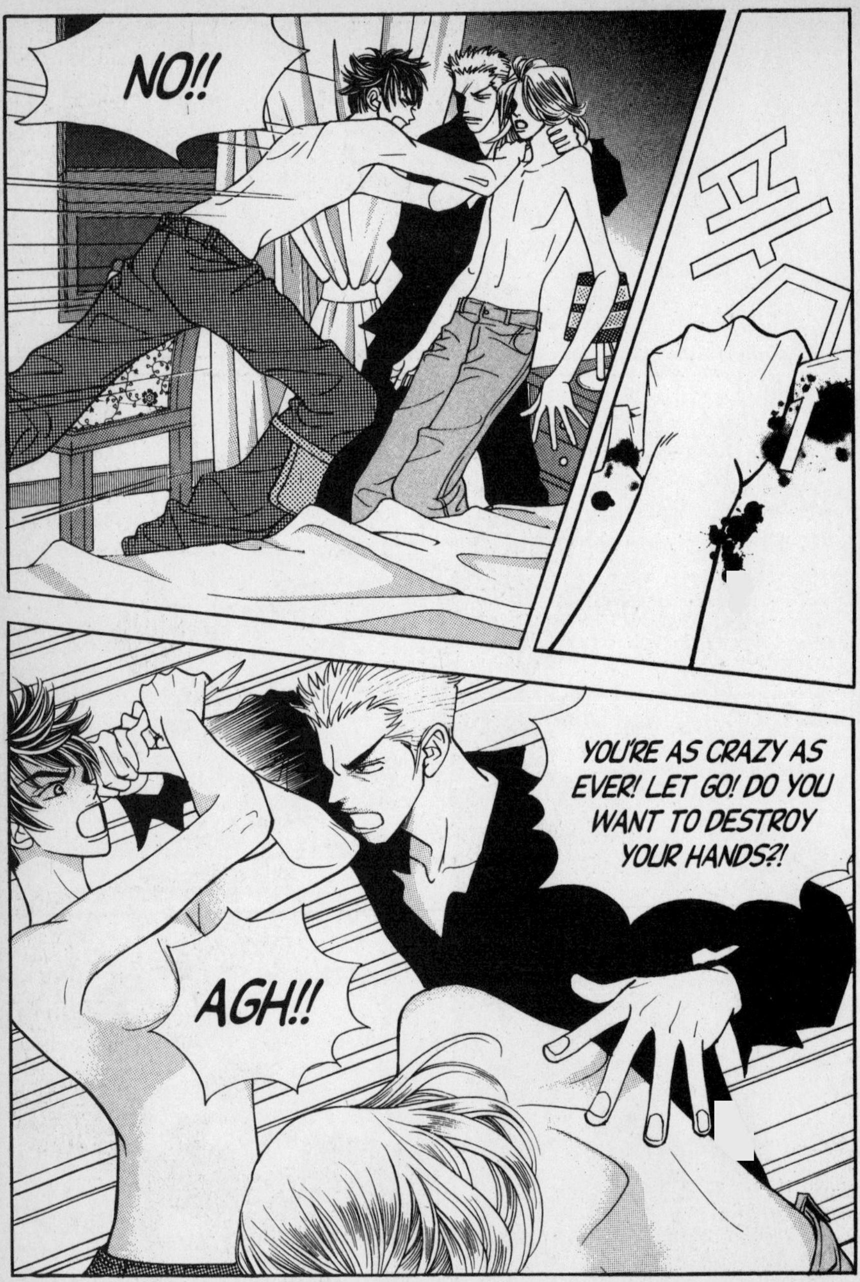
NO!!
YOU'RE AS CRAZY AS EVER! LET GO! DO YOU WANT TO DESTROY YOUR HANDS?!
AGH!!

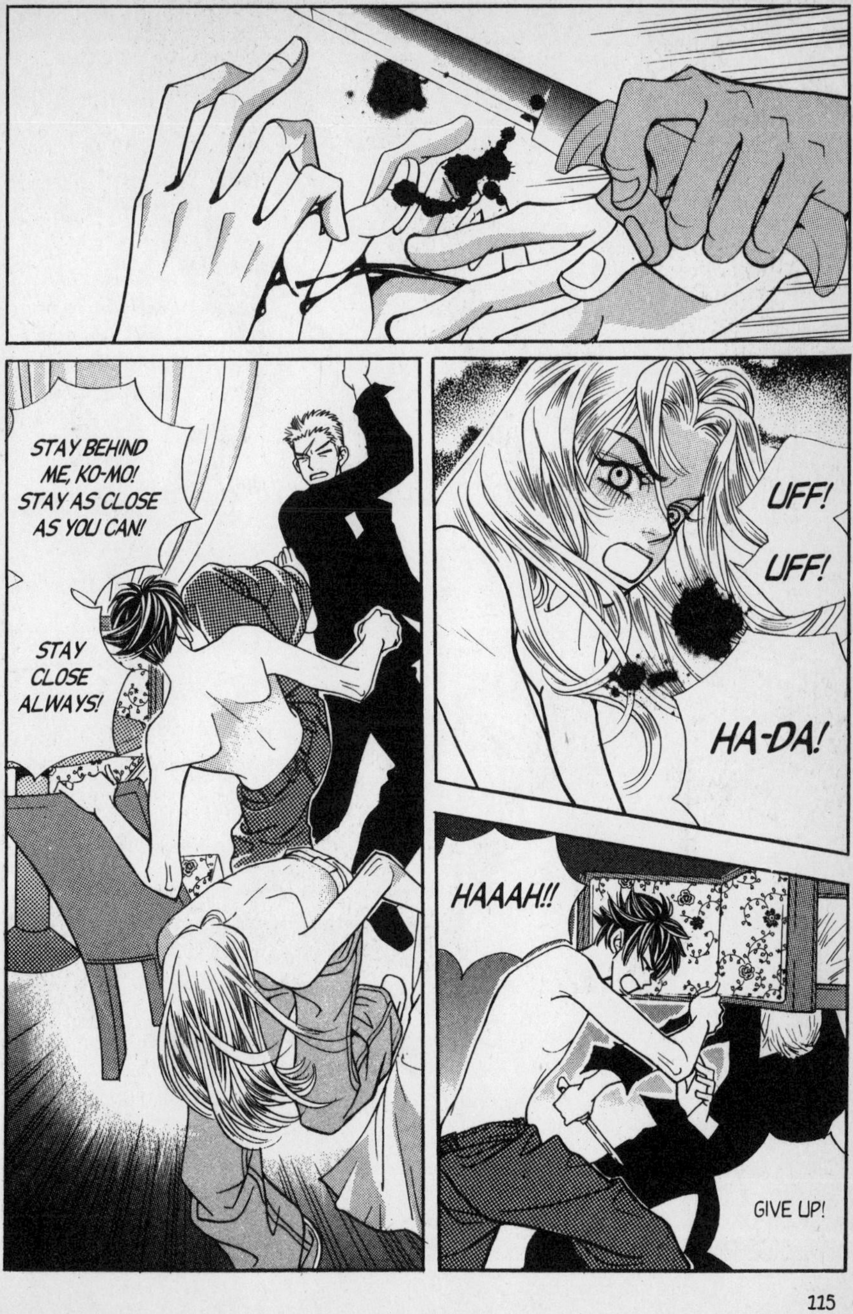
STAY BEHIND ME, KO-MO! STAY AS CLOSE AS YOU CAN!
STAY CLOSE ALWAYS!
UFF!
UFF!
HA-DA!
HAAAH!!
GIVE UP!

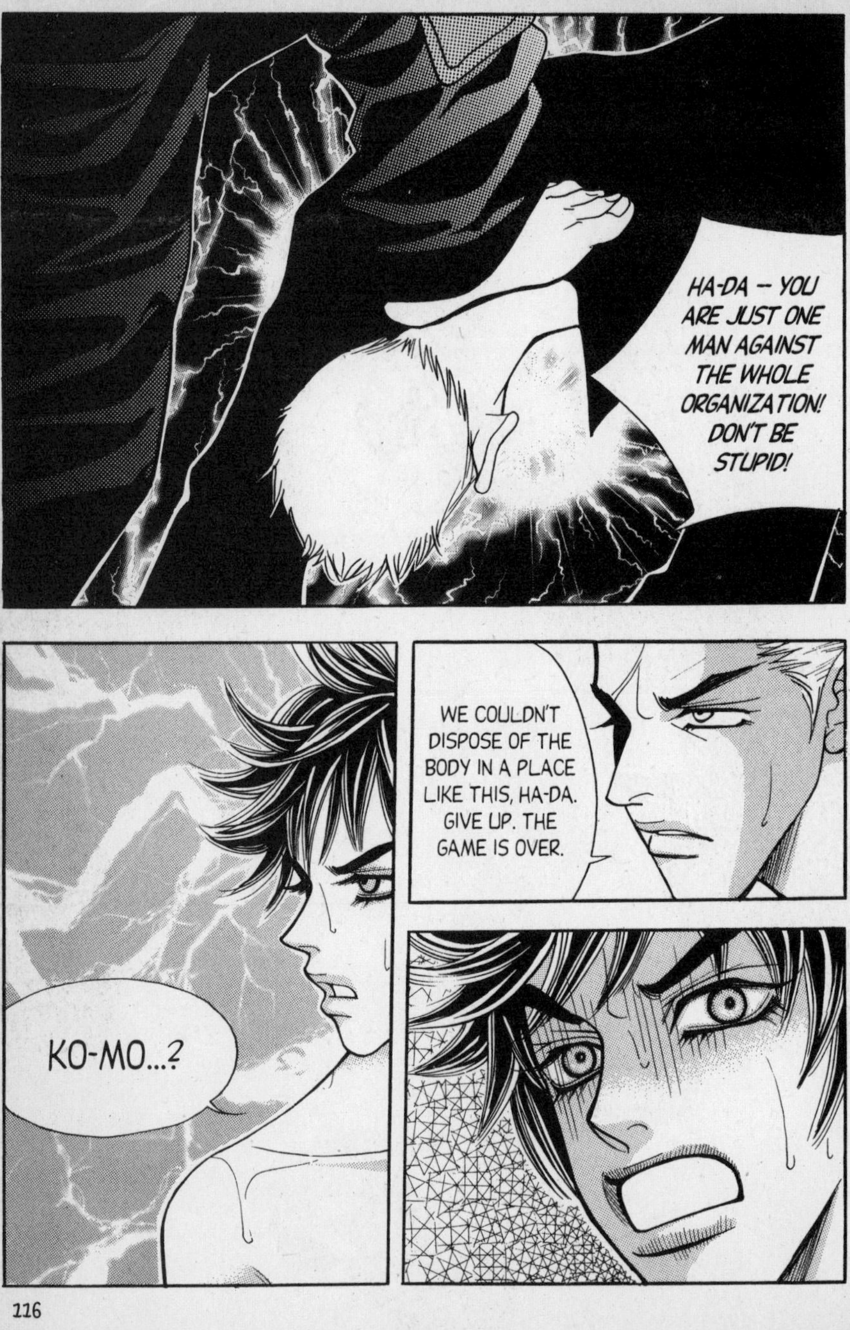
HA-DA -- YOU ARE JUST ONE MAN AGAINST THE WHOLE ORGANIZATION! DON'T BE STUPID!
KO-MO...?
WE COULDN'T DISPOSE OF THE BODY IN A PLACE LIKE THIS, HA-DA. GIVE UP. THE GAME IS OVER.

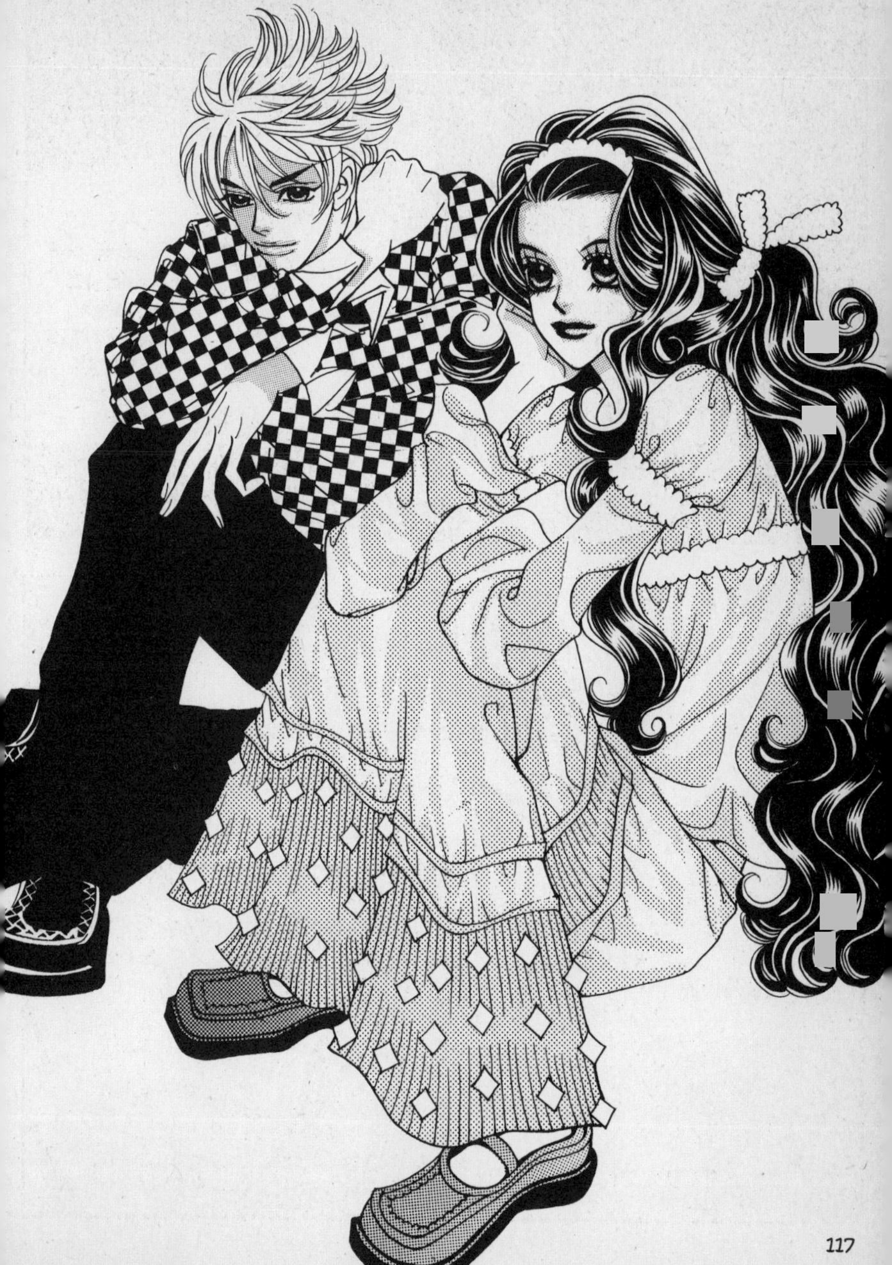

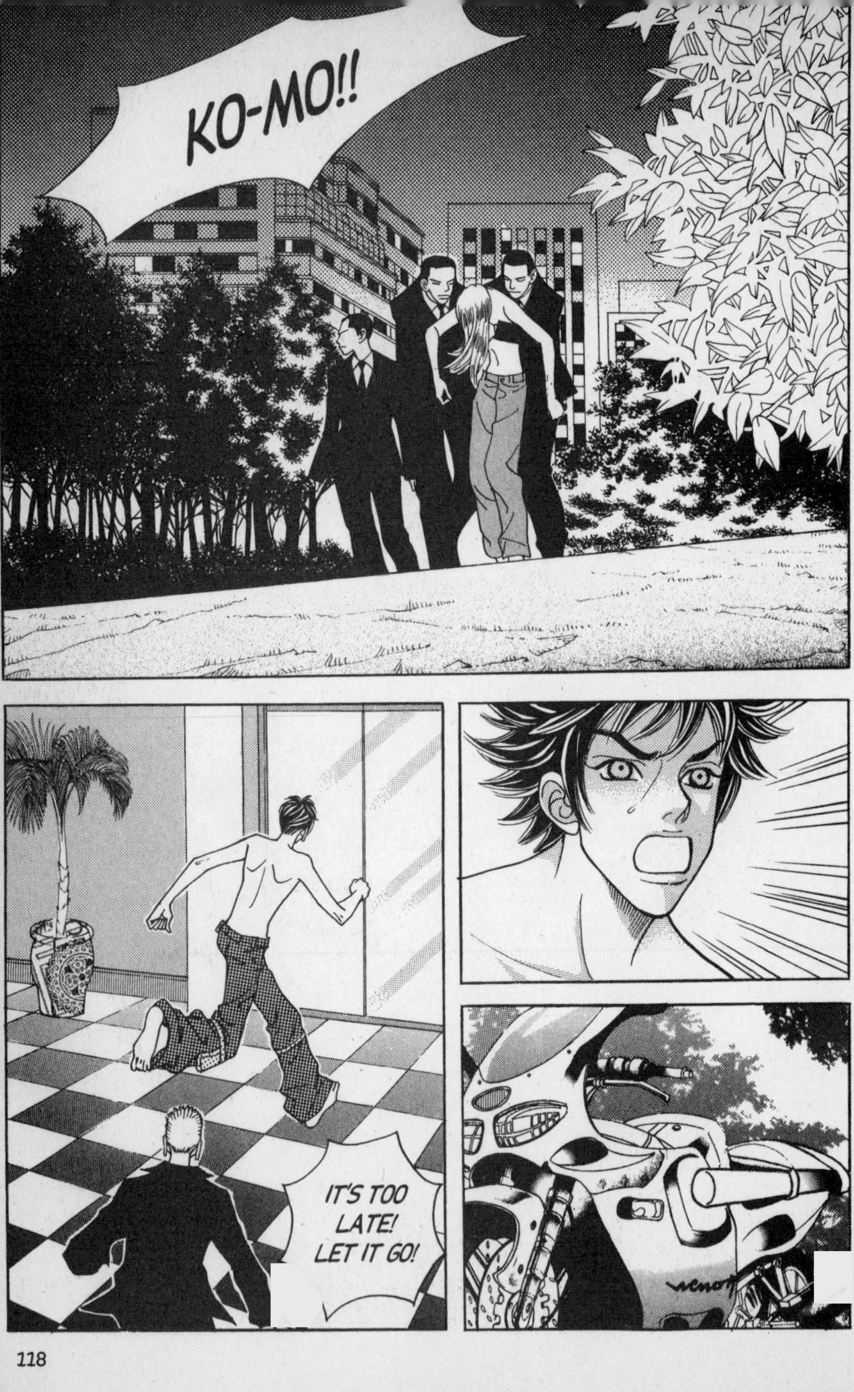
KO-MO!!
IT'S TOO LATE! LET IT GO!

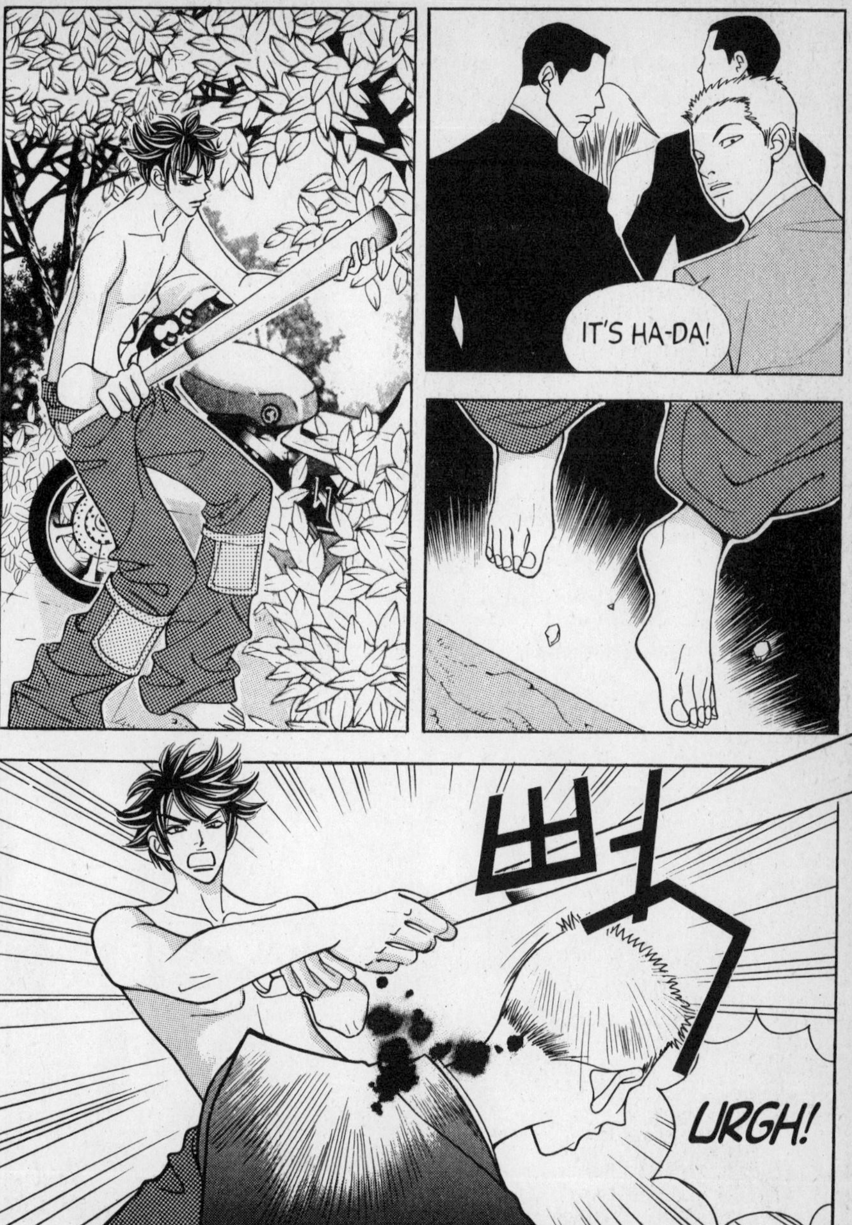
IT'S HA-DA!
URGH!

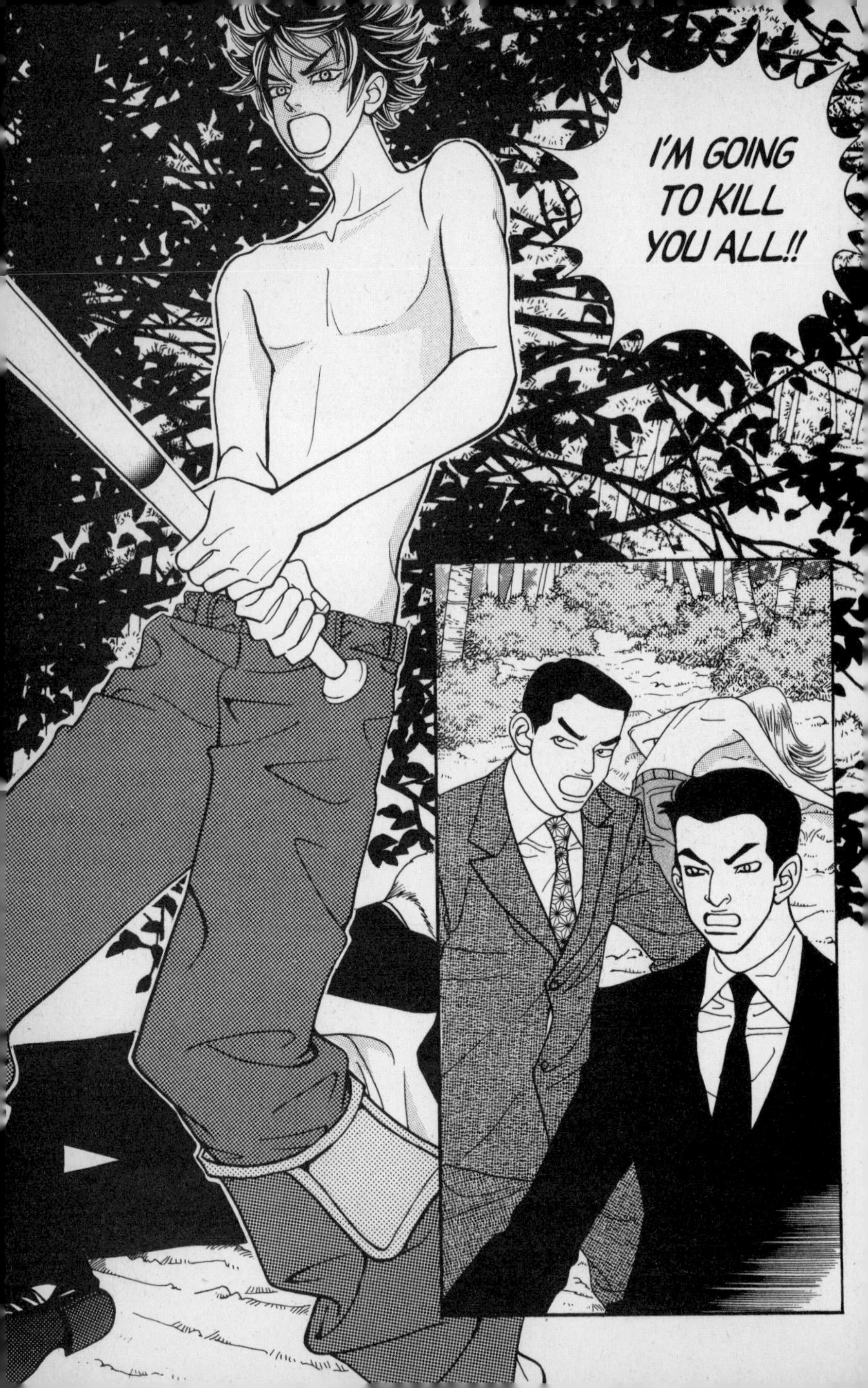
I'M GOING TO KILL YOU ALL!!

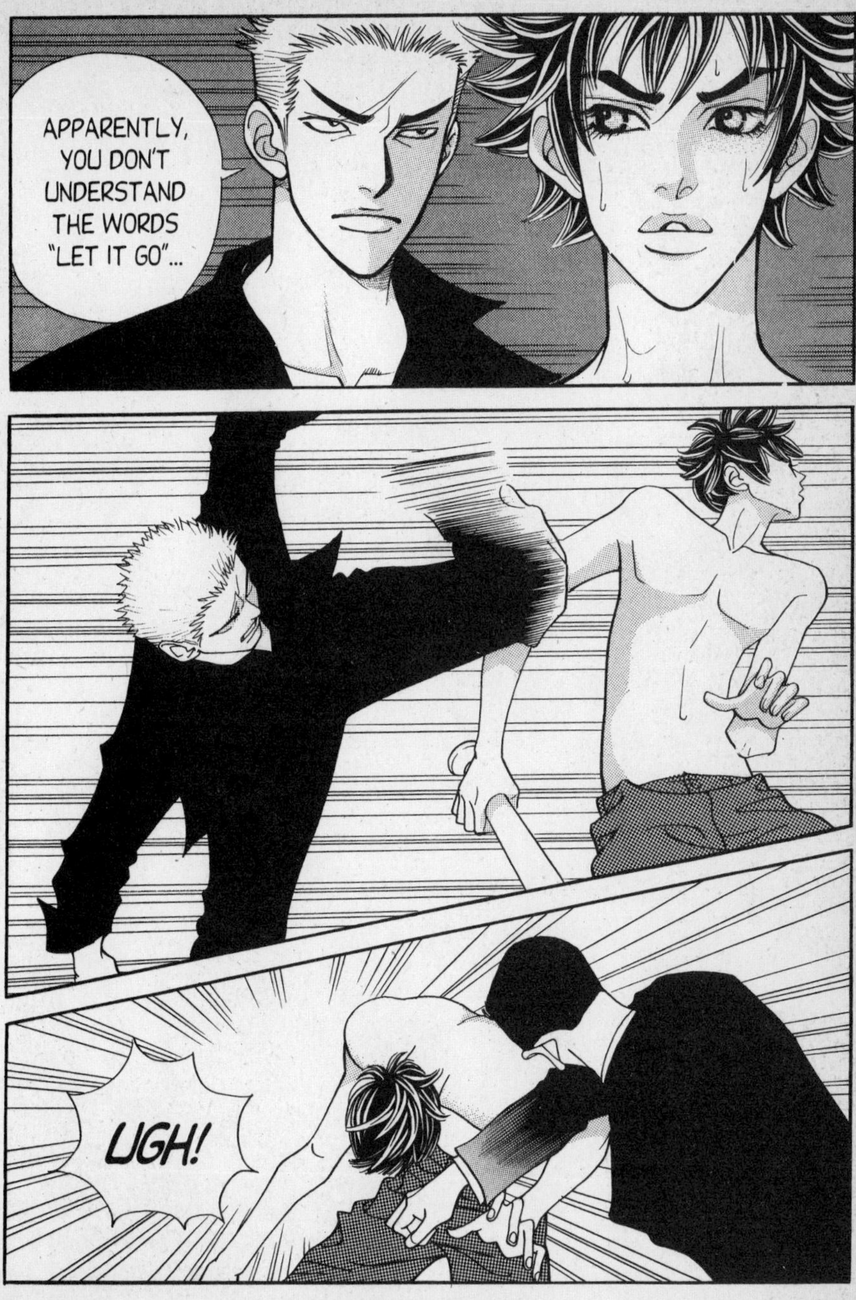
APPARENTLY, YOU DON'T UNDERSTAND THE WORDS "LET IT GO"...
UGH!

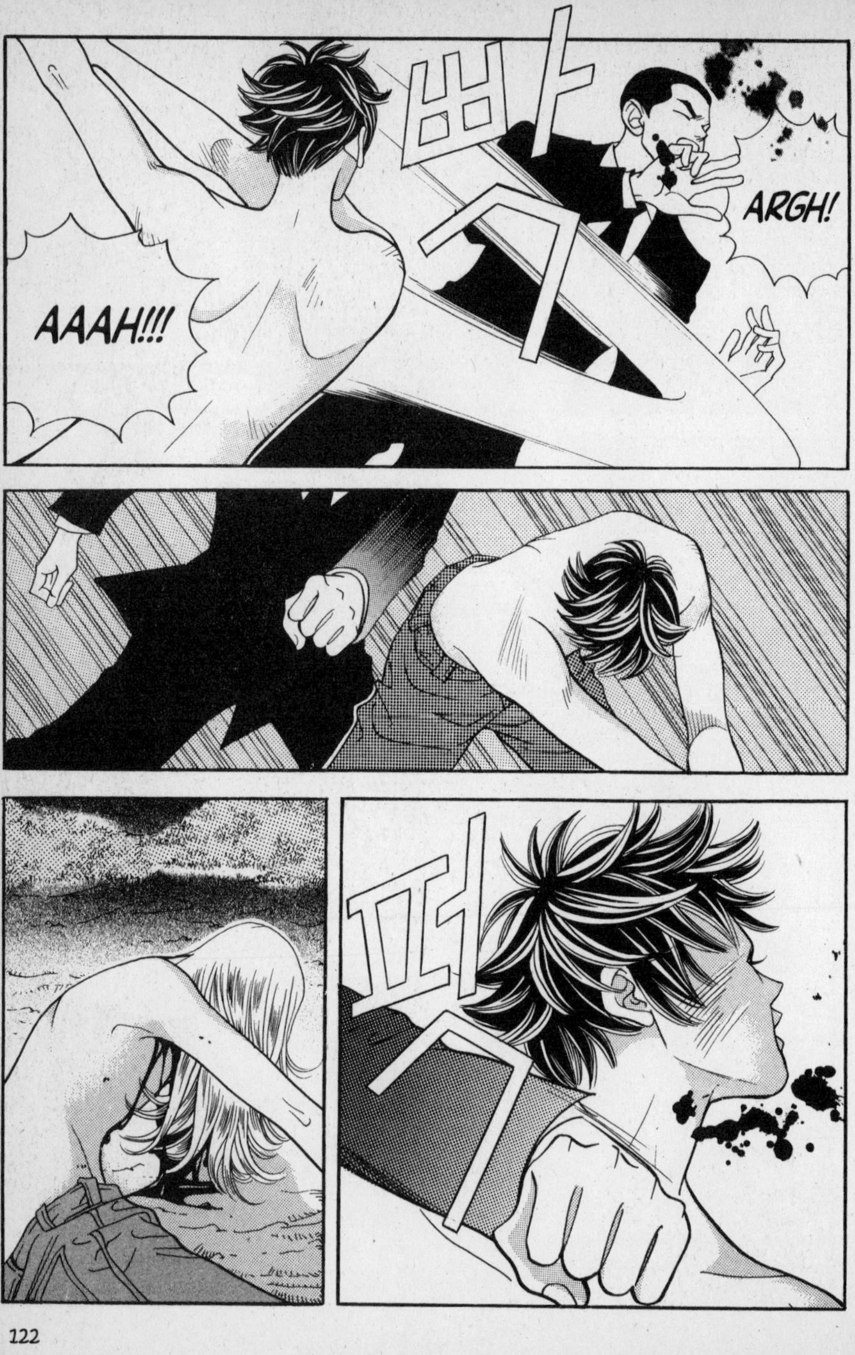
빡
ARGH!
AAAH!!!
퍽

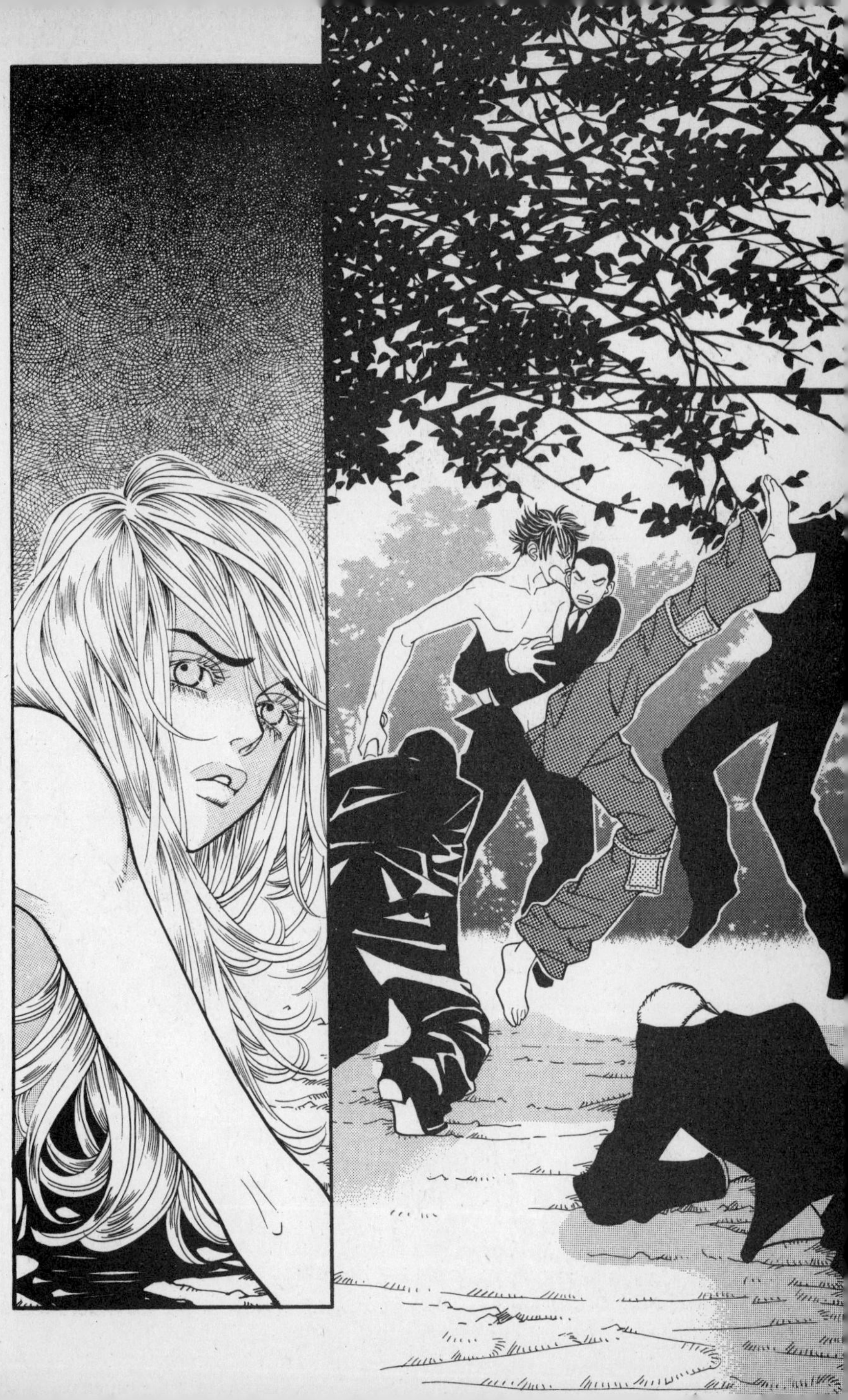

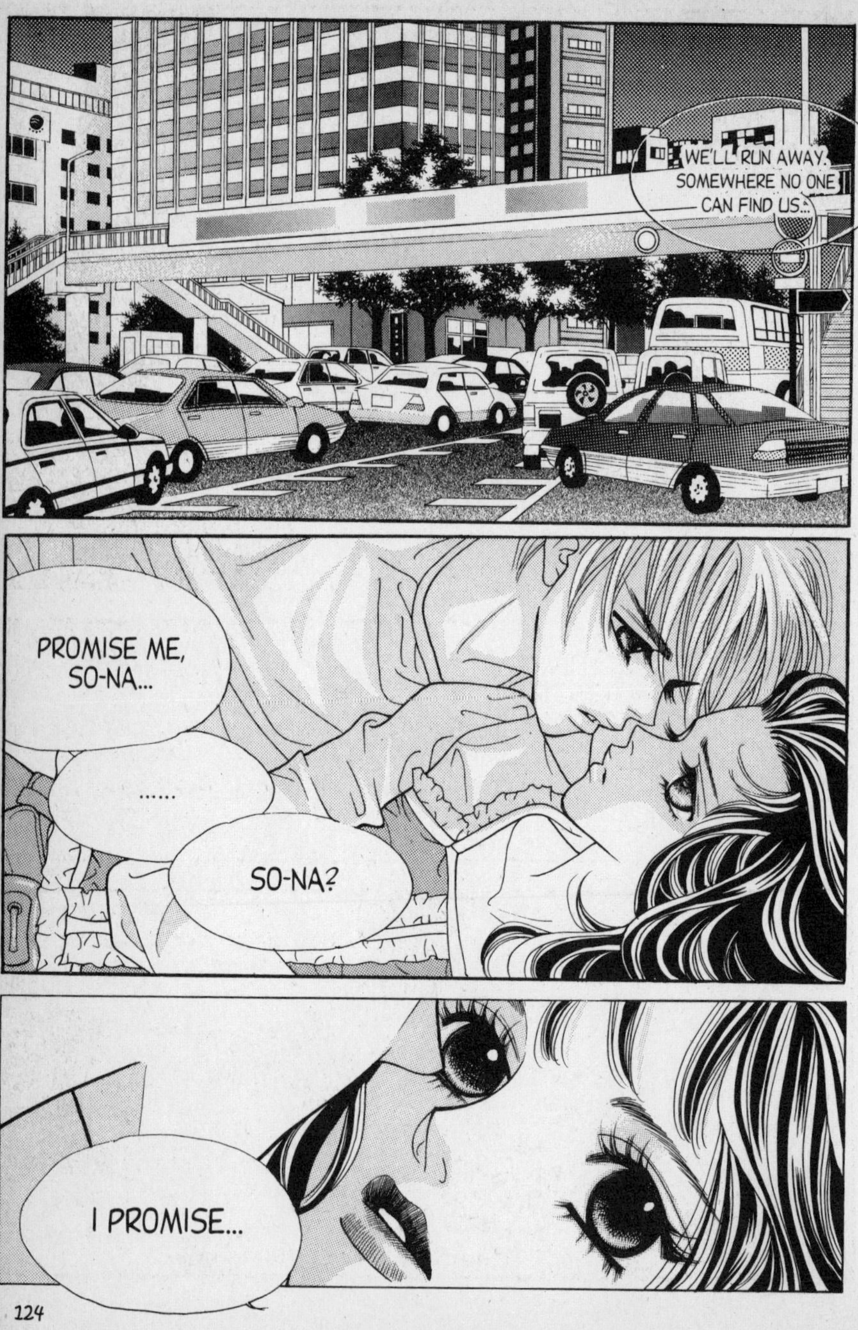
WE'LL RUN AWAY. SOMEWHERE NO ONE CAN FIND US...
PROMISE ME, SO-NA...
......
SO-NA?
I PROMISE...

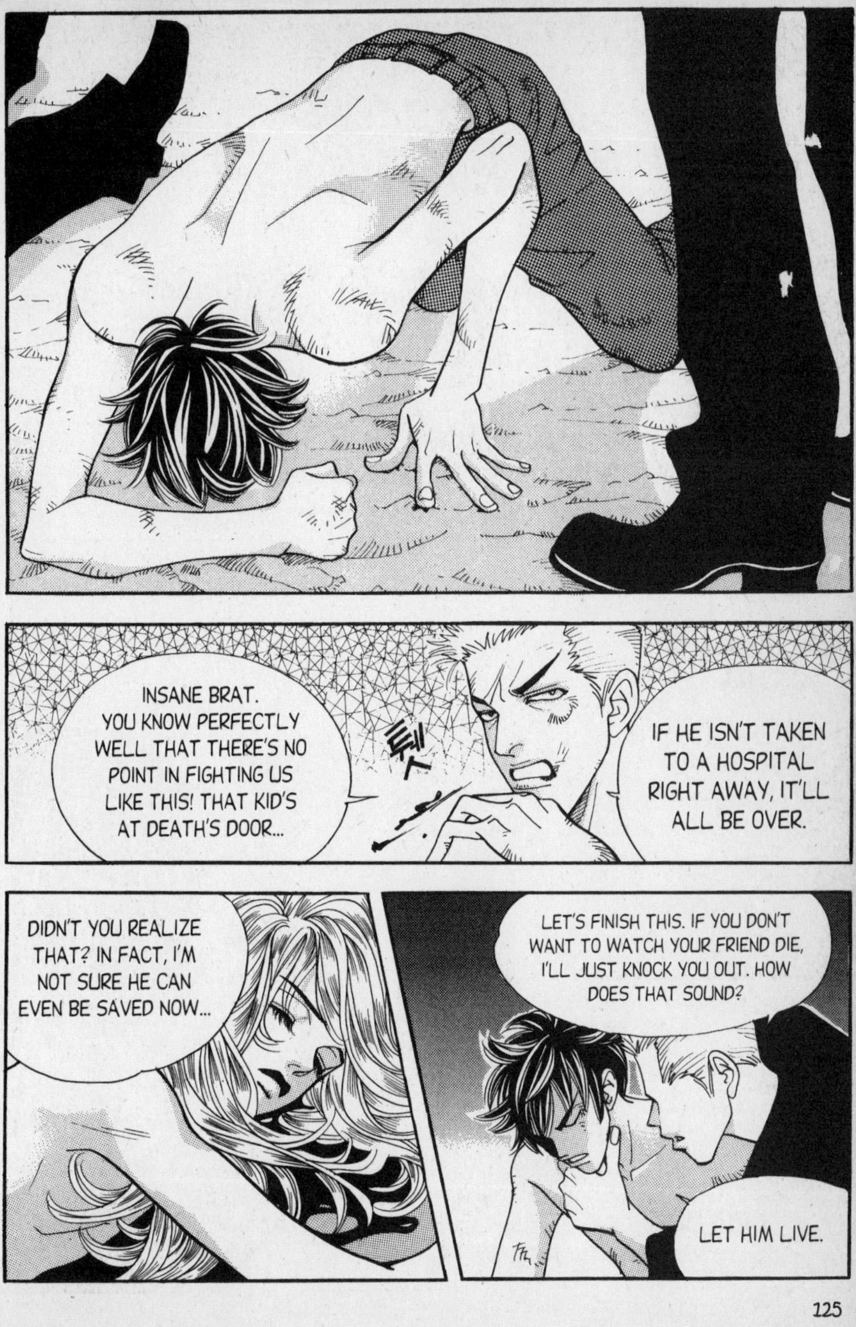
INSANE BRAT. YOU KNOW PERFECTLY WELL THAT THERE'S NO POINT IN FIGHTING US LIKE THIS! THAT KID'S AT DEATH'S DOOR...
IF HE ISN'T TAKEN TO A HOSPITAL RIGHT AWAY, IT'LL ALL BE OVER.
DIDN'T YOU REALIZE THAT? IN FACT, I'M NOT SURE HE CAN EVEN BE SAVED NOW...
LET'S FINISH THIS. IF YOU DON'T WANT TO WATCH YOUR FRIEND DIE, I'LL JUST KNOCK YOU OUT. HOW DOES THAT SOUND?
LET HIM LIVE.

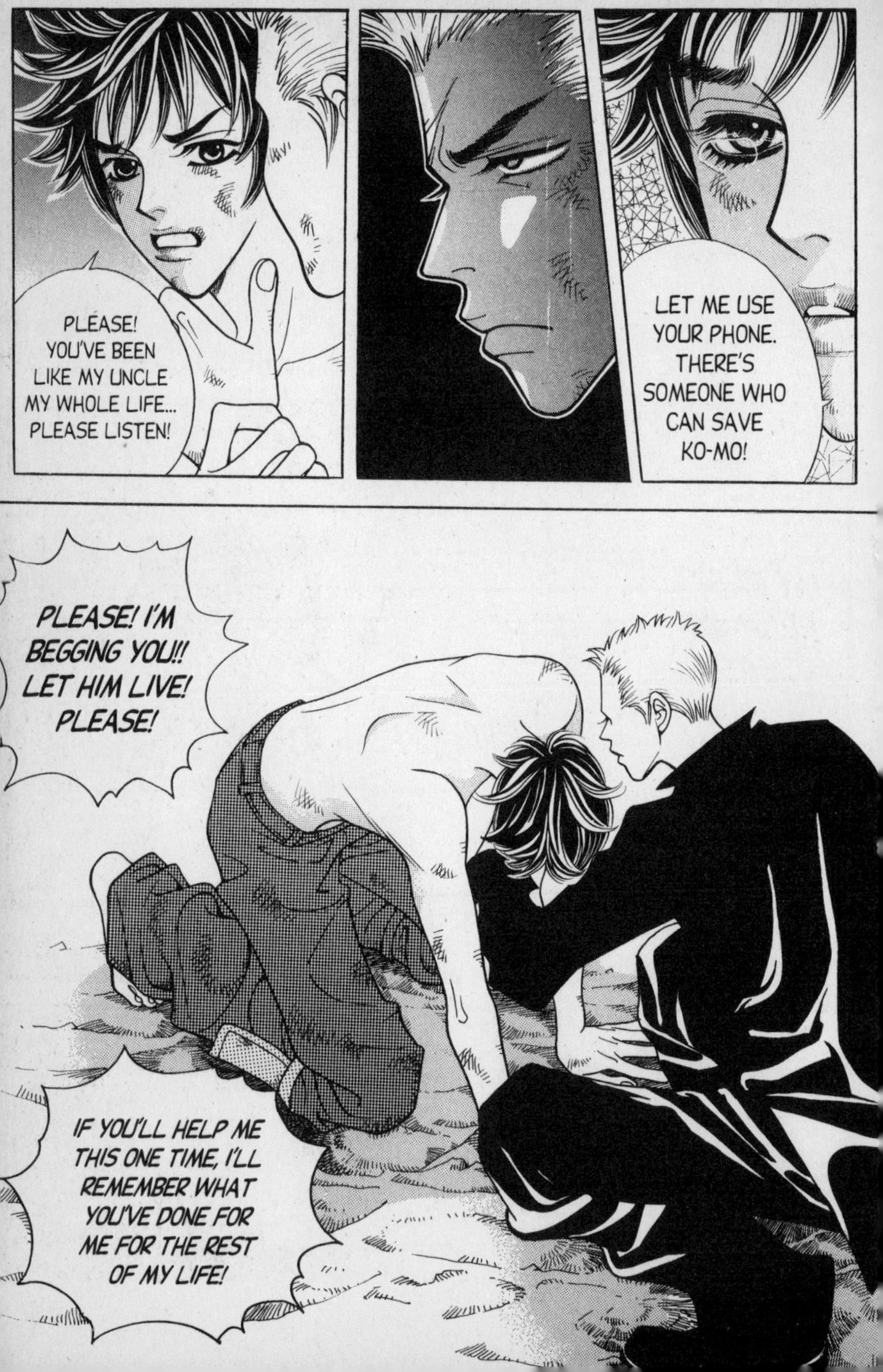
PLEASE! YOU'VE BEEN LIKE MY UNCLE MY WHOLE LIFE... PLEASE LISTEN!
LET ME USE YOUR PHONE. THERE'S SOMEONE WHO CAN SAVE KO-MO!
PLEASE! I'M BEGGING YOU!! LET HIM LIVE! PLEASE!
IF YOU'LL HELP ME THIS ONE TIME, I'LL REMEMBER WHAT YOU'VE DONE FOR ME FOR THE REST OF MY LIFE!

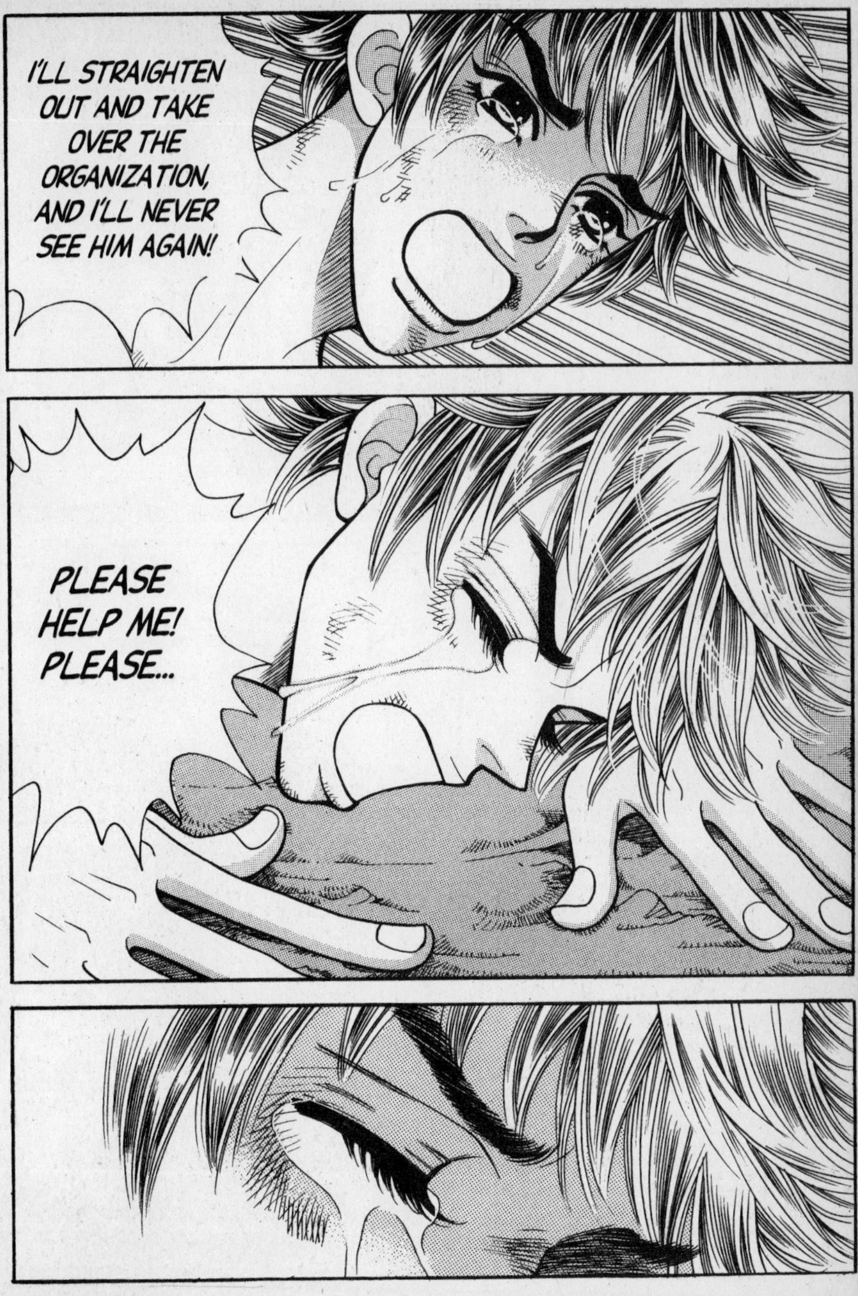
I'LL STRAIGHTEN OUT AND TAKE OVER THE ORGANIZATION, AND I'LL NEVER SEE HIM AGAIN!
PLEASE HELP ME! PLEASE...

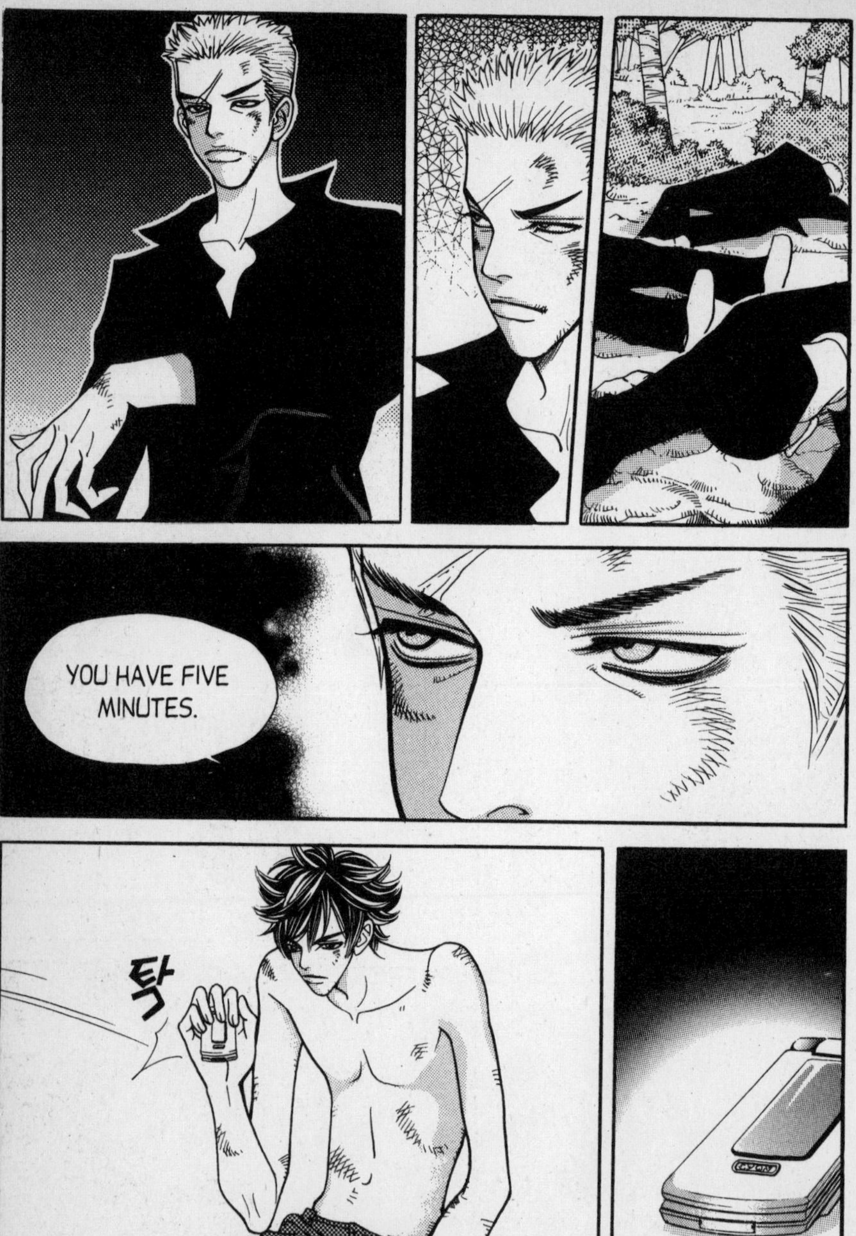
YOU HAVE FIVE MINUTES.
탁

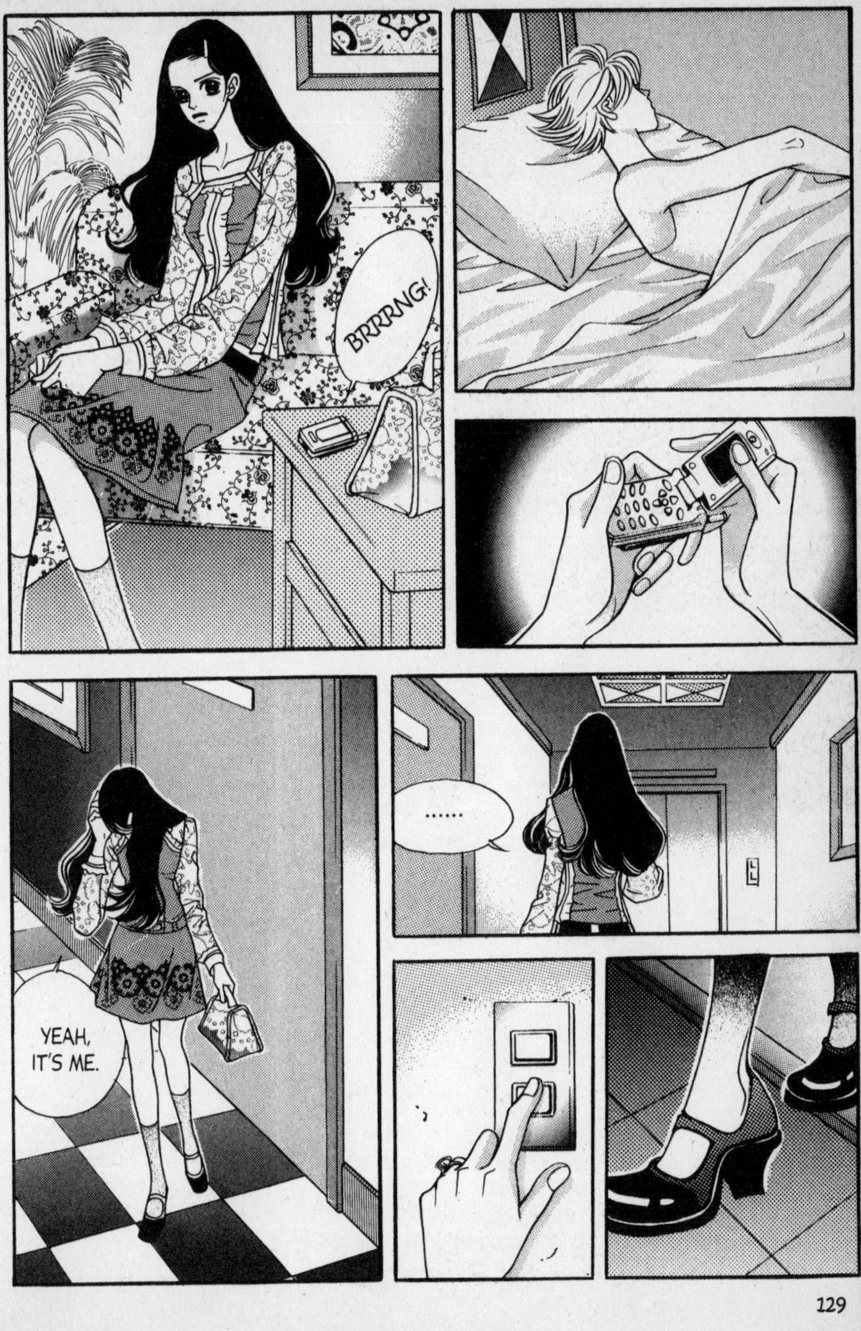
BRRRNG!
......
YEAH, IT'S ME.

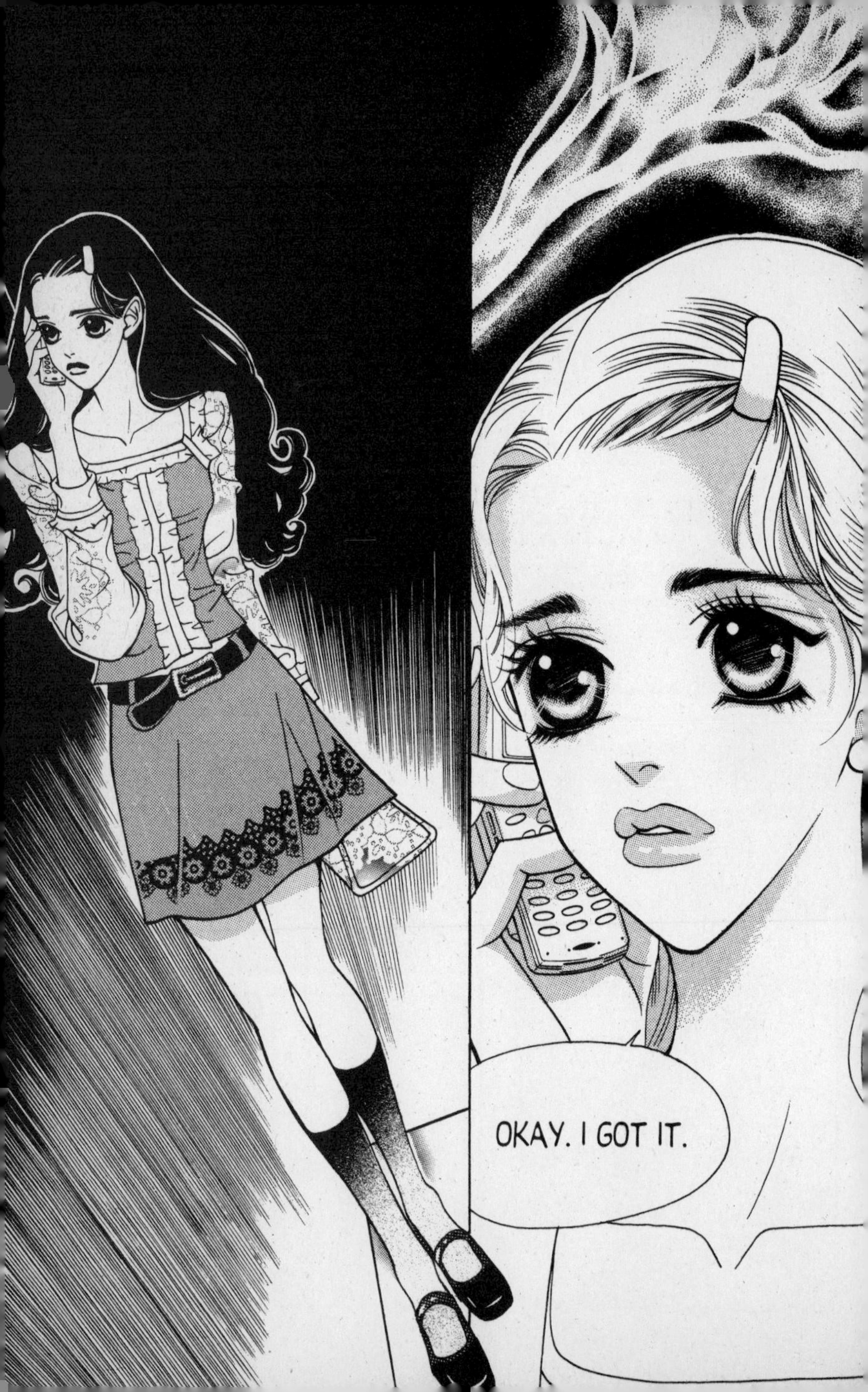
OKAY. I GOT IT.

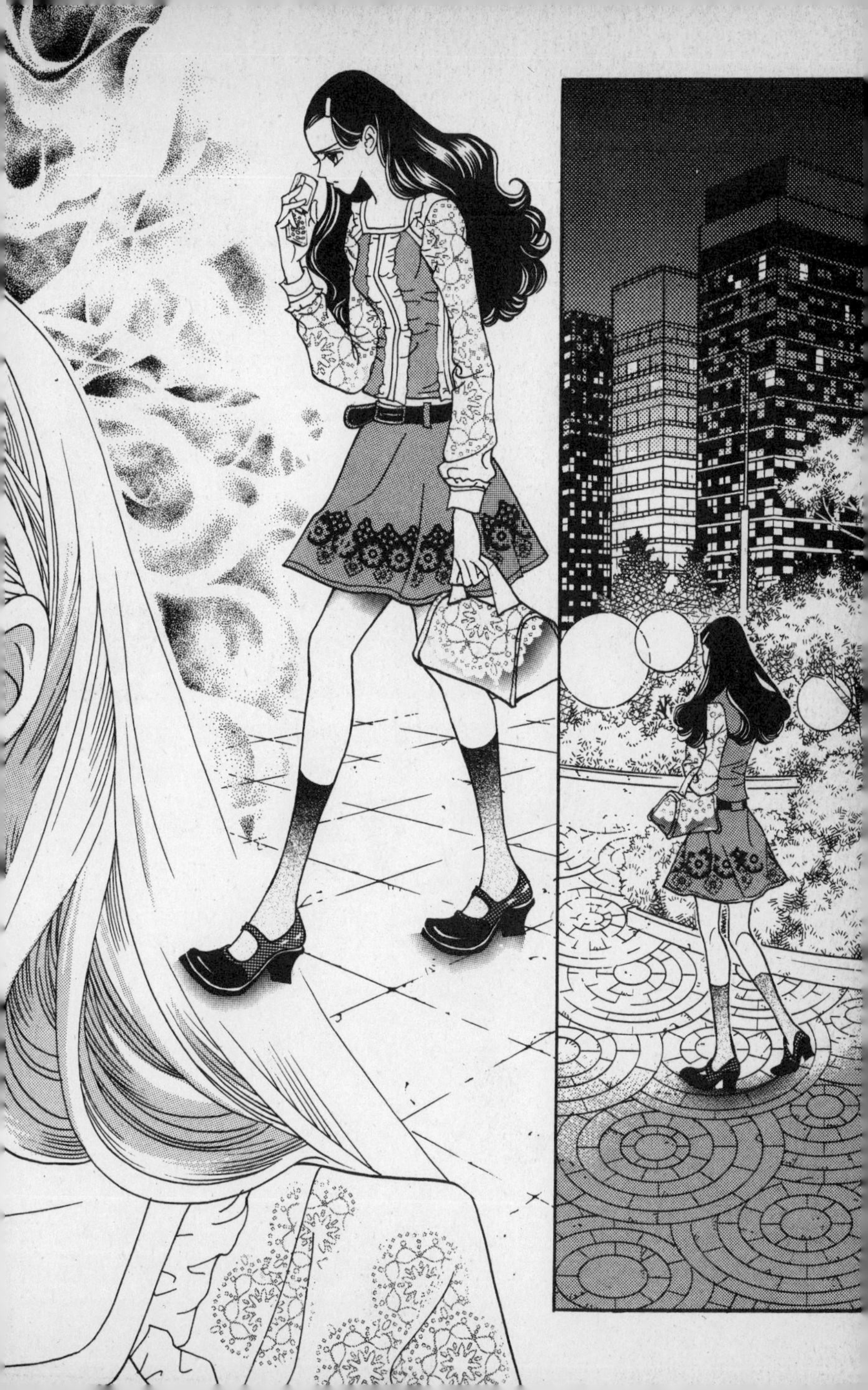

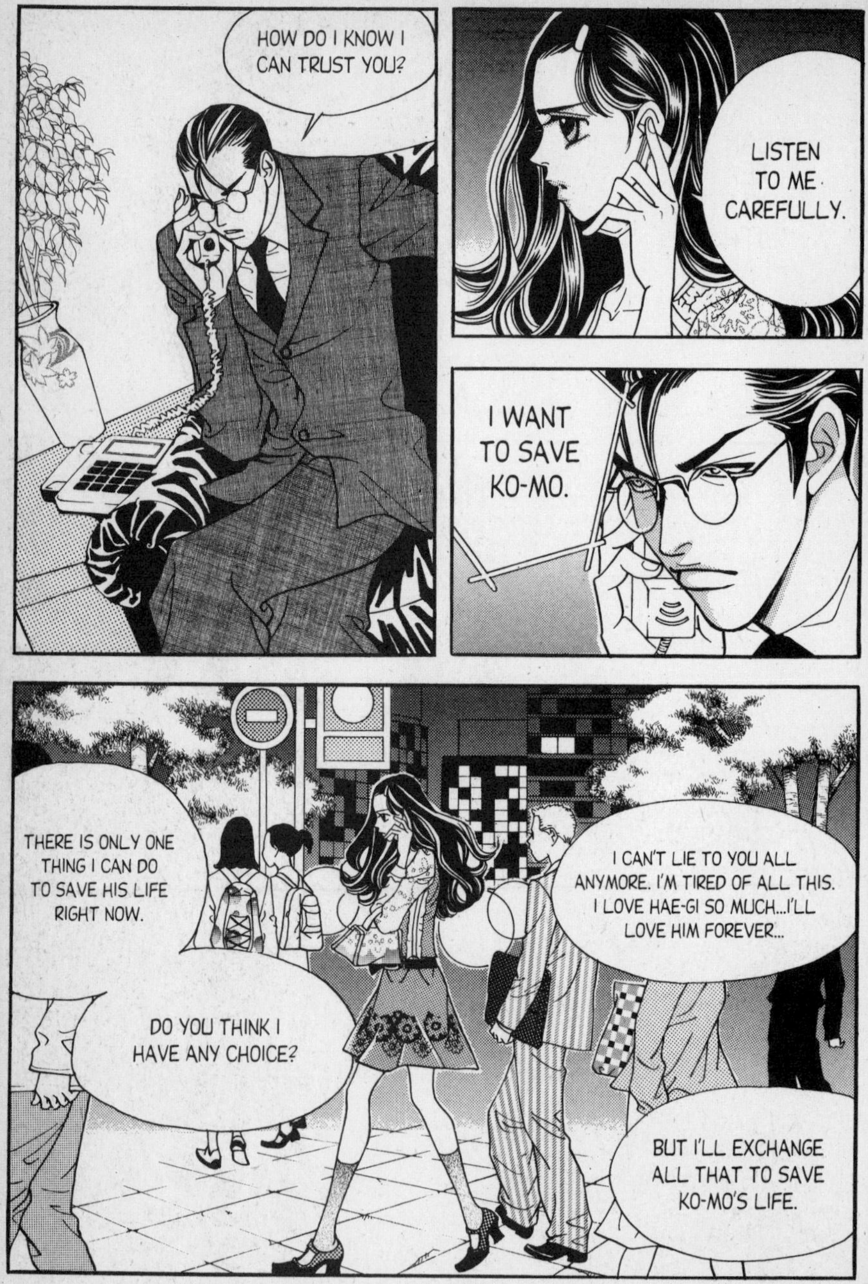
HOW DO I KNOW I CAN TRUST YOU?
LISTEN TO ME CAREFULLY.
I WANT TO SAVE KO-MO.
THERE IS ONLY ONE THING I CAN DO TO SAVE HIS LIFE RIGHT NOW.
DO YOU THINK I HAVE ANY CHOICE?
I CAN'T LIE TO YOU ALL ANYMORE. I'M TIRED OF ALL THIS. I LOVE HAE-GI SO MUCH...I'LL LOVE HIM FOREVER...
BUT I'LL EXCHANGE ALL THAT TO SAVE KO-MO'S LIFE.

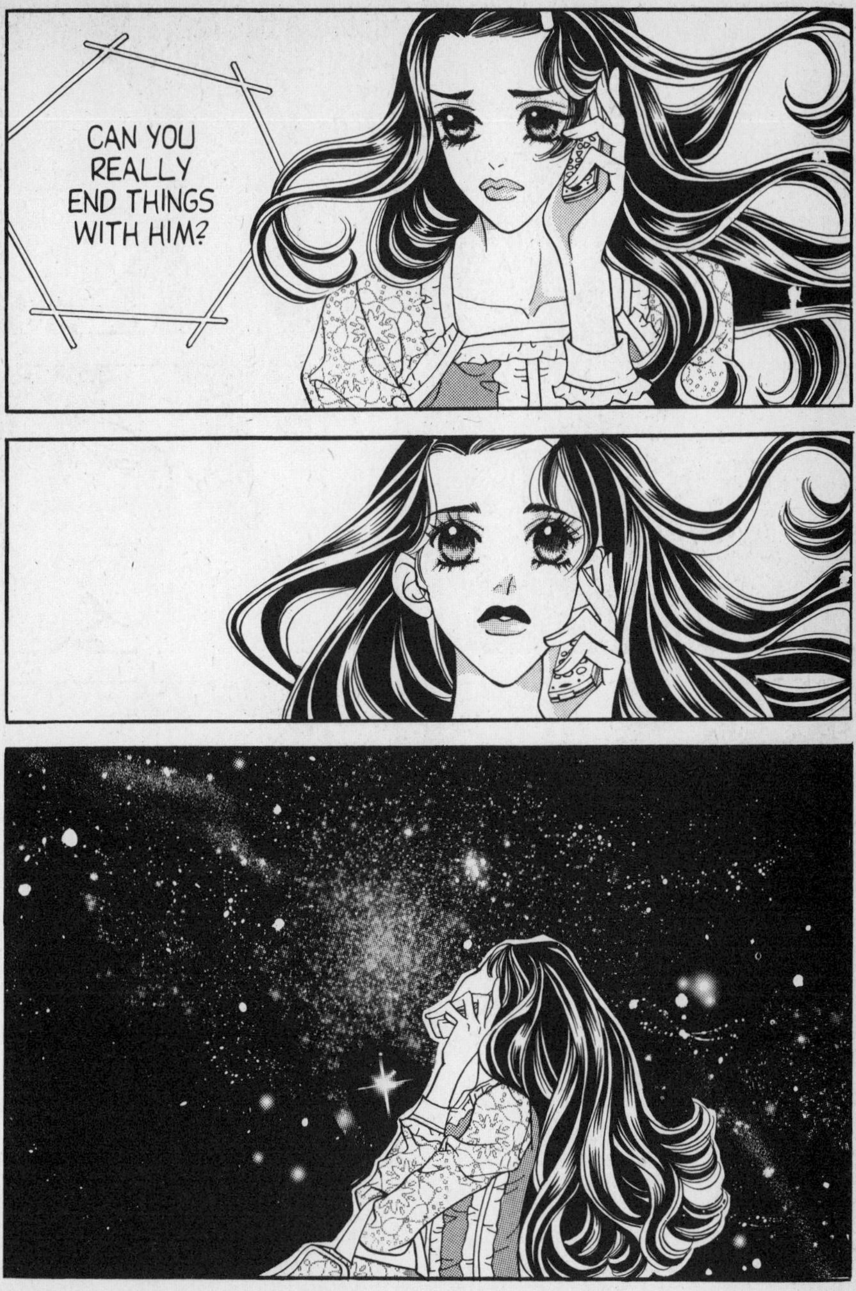
CAN YOU REALLY END THINGS WITH HIM?

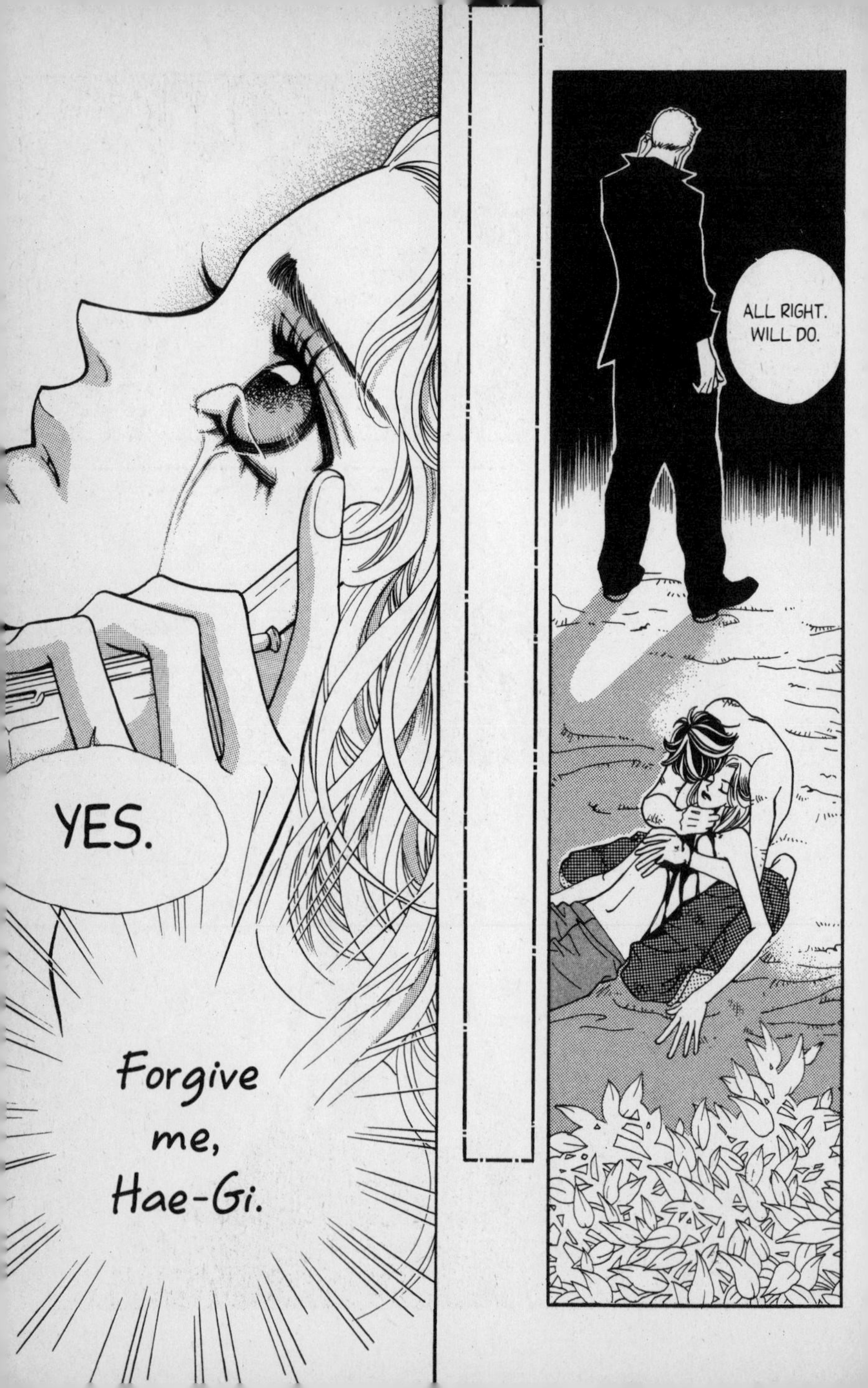
YES.
Forgive me, Hae-Gi.
ALL RIGHT. WILL DO.

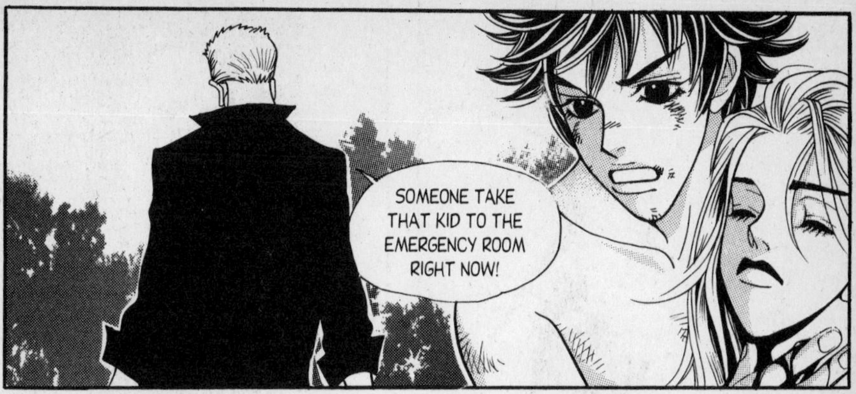
SOMEONE TAKE THAT KID TO THE EMERGENCY ROOM RIGHT NOW!
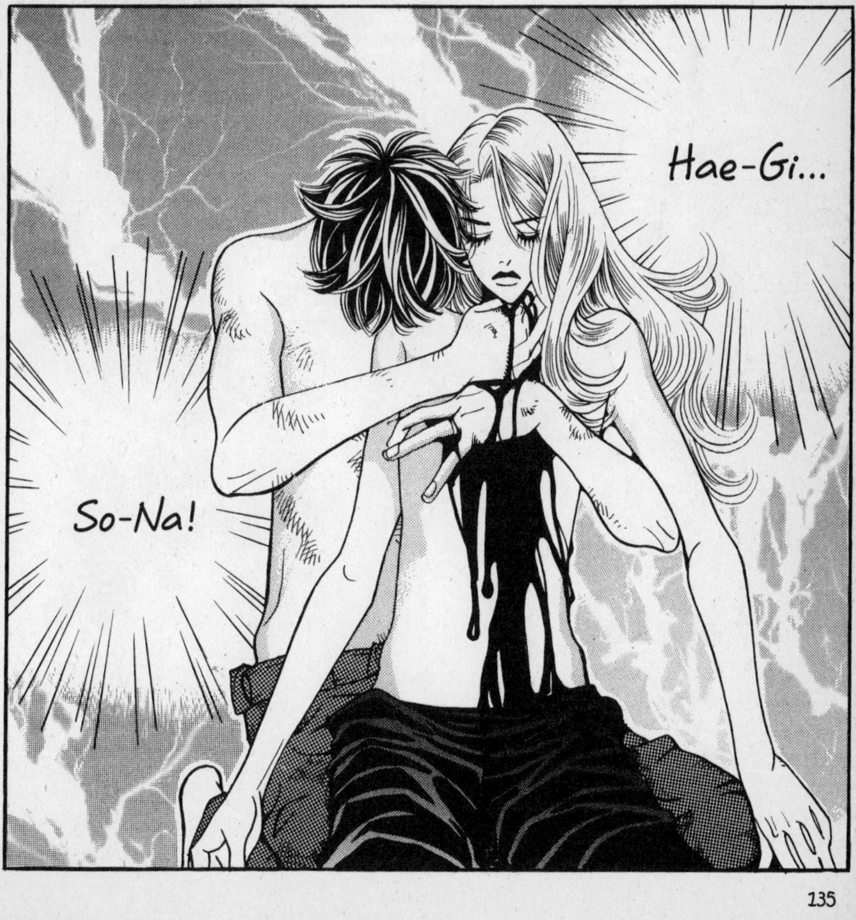
Hae-Gi...
So-Na!

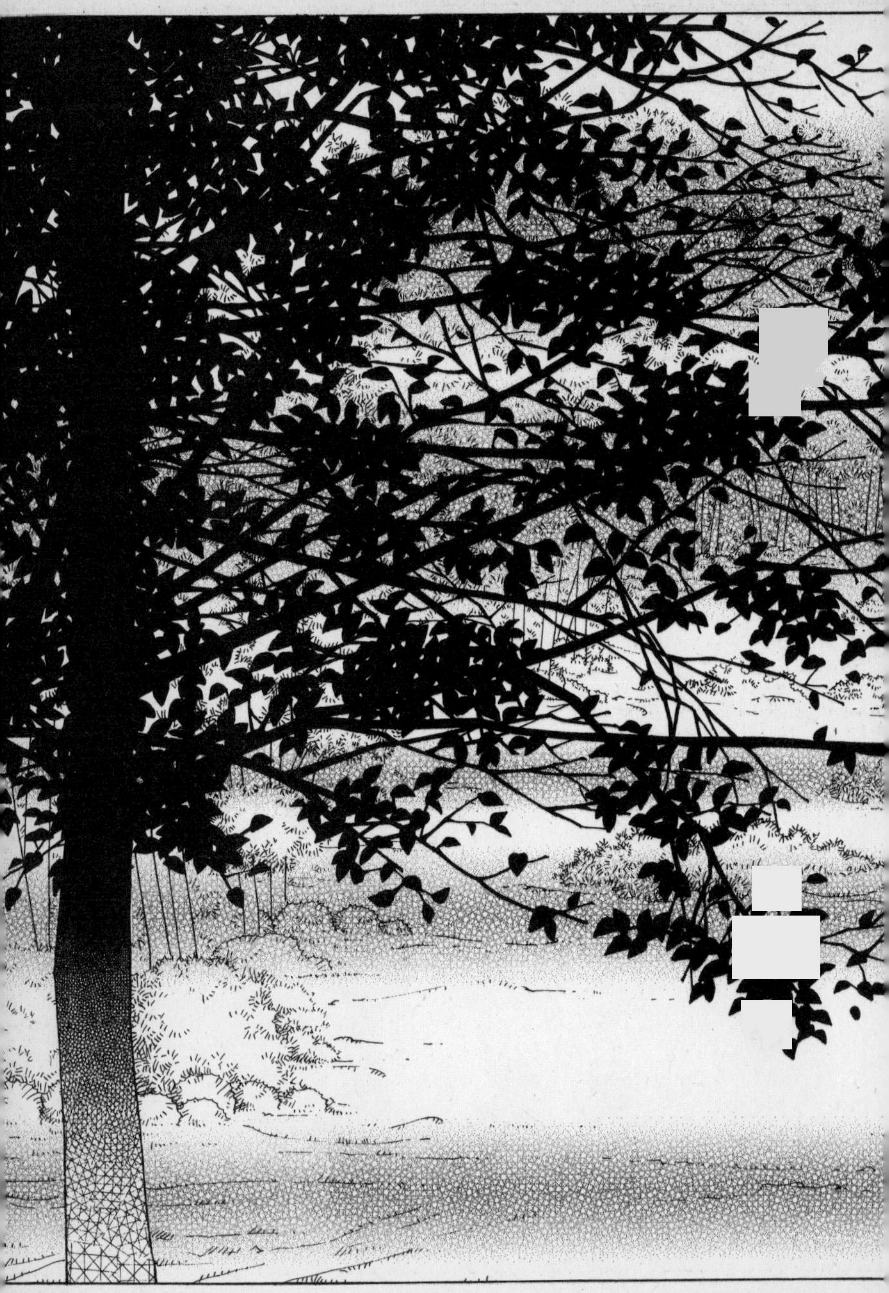

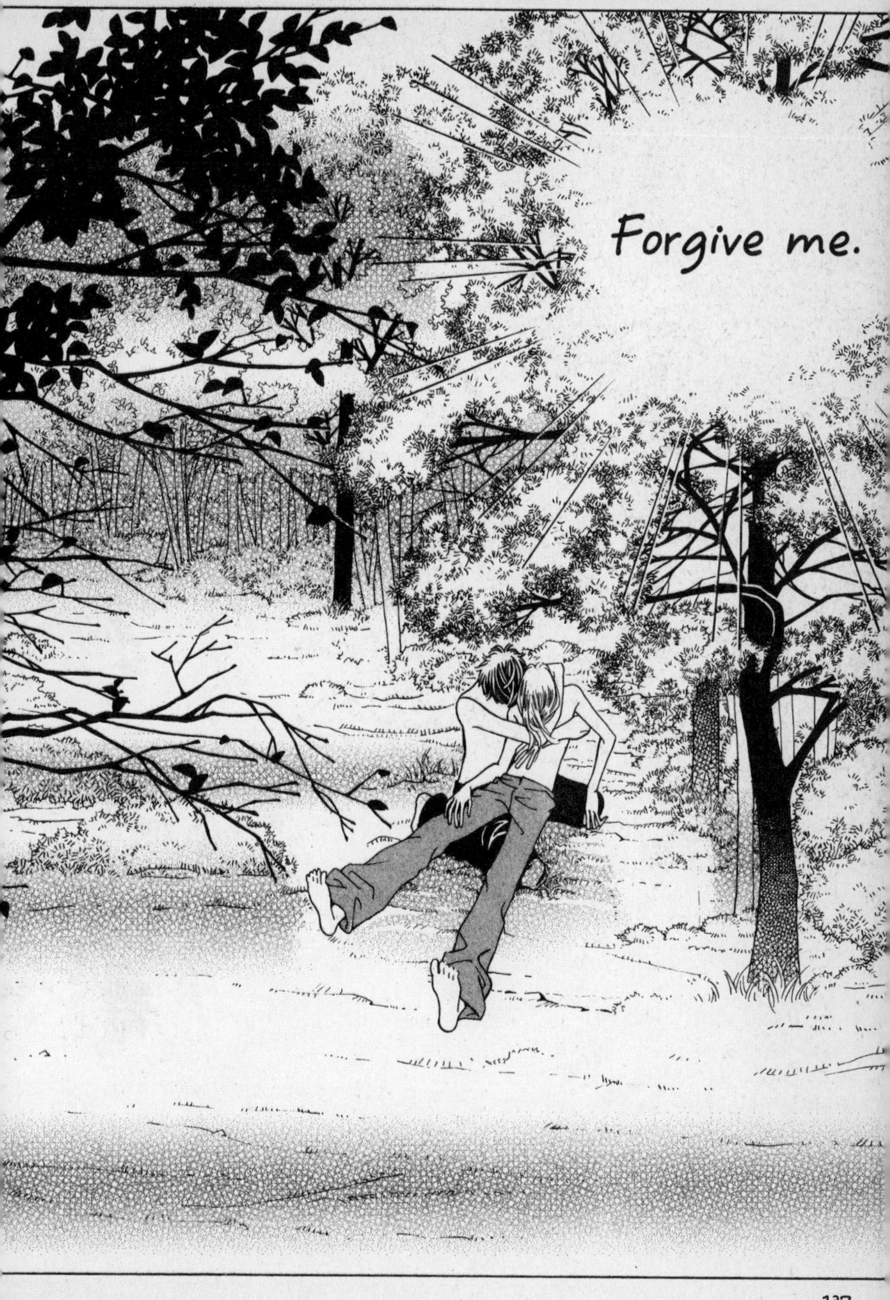
Forgive me.

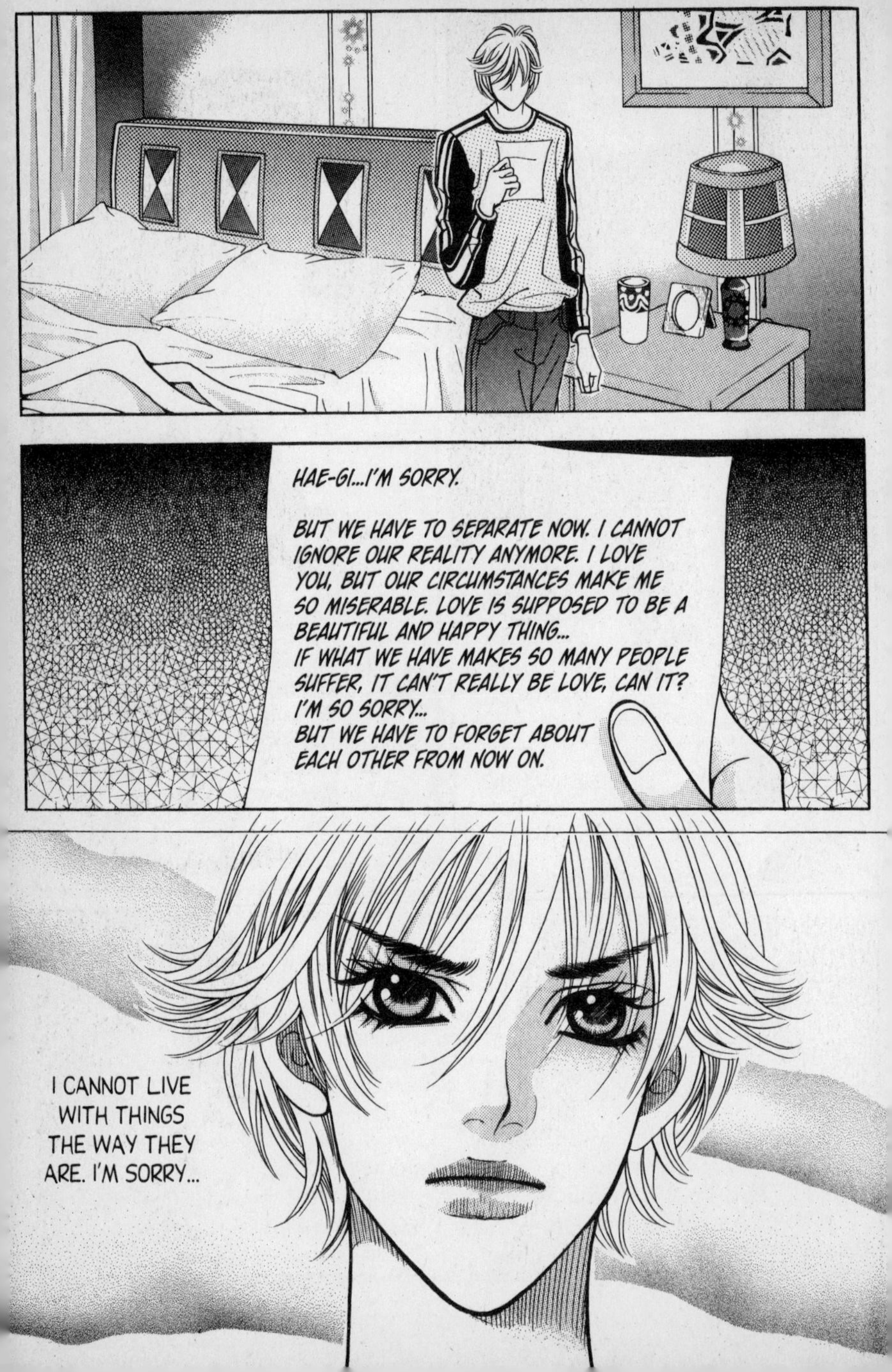
HAE-GI...I'M SORRY.
BUT WE HAVE TO SEPARATE NOW. I CANNOT IGNORE OUR REALITY ANYMORE. I LOVE YOU, BUT OUR CIRCUMSTANCES MAKE ME SO MISERABLE. LOVE IS SUPPOSED TO BE A BEAUTIFUL AND HAPPY THING... IF WHAT WE HAVE MAKES SO MANY PEOPLE SUFFER, IT CAN'T REALLY BE LOVE, CAN IT? I'M SO SORRY... BUT WE HAVE TO FORGET ABOUT EACH OTHER FROM NOW ON.
I CANNOT LIVE WITH THINGS THE WAY THEY ARE. I'M SORRY...

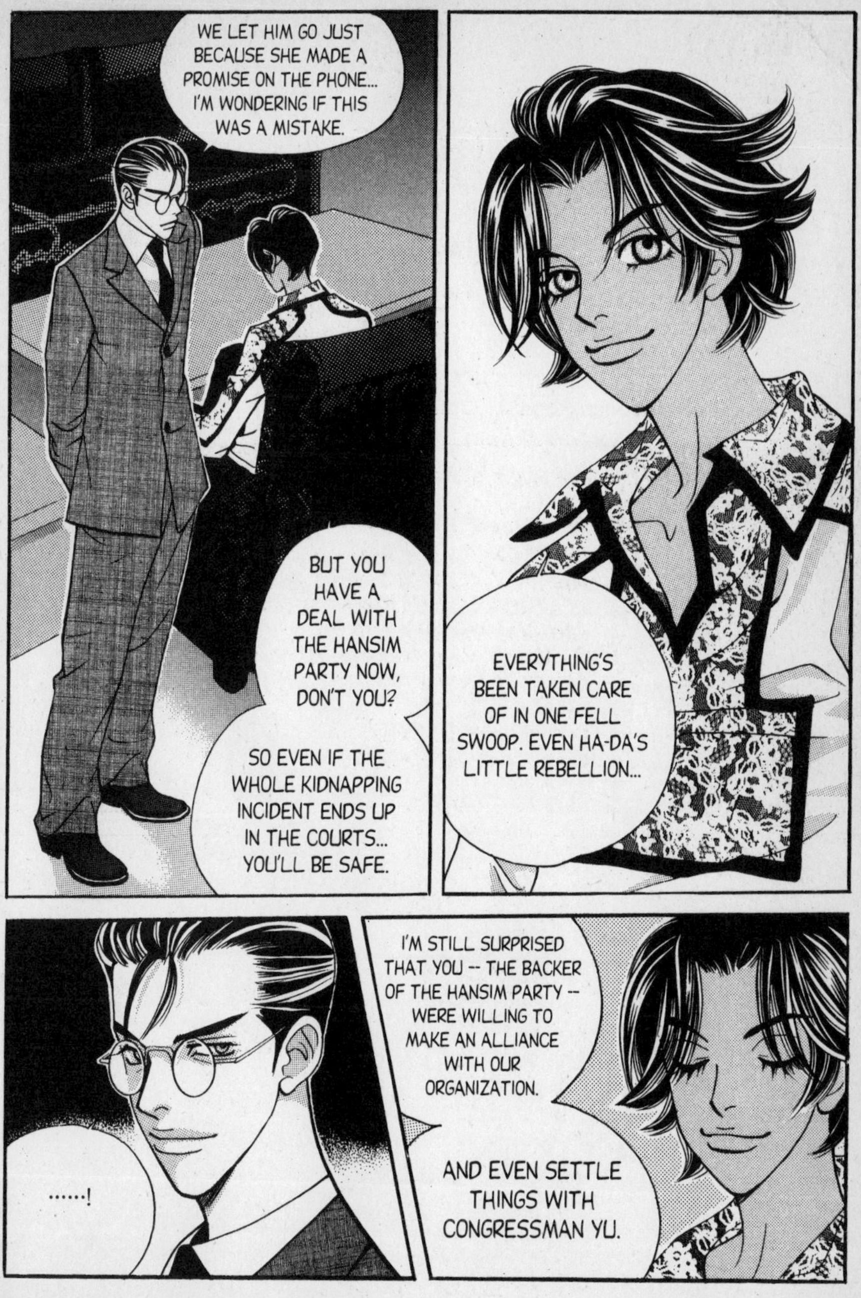
WE LET HIM GO JUST BECAUSE SHE MADE A PROMISE ON THE PHONE... I'M WONDERING IF THIS WAS A MISTAKE.
BUT YOU HAVE A DEAL WITH THE HANSIM PARTY NOW, DON'T YOU?
SO EVEN IF THE WHOLE KIDNAPPING INCIDENT ENDS UP IN THE COURTS... YOU'LL BE SAFE.
EVERYTHING'S BEEN TAKEN CARE OF IN ONE FELL SWOOP. EVEN HA-DA'S LITTLE REBELLION...
......!
I'M STILL SURPRISED THAT YOU -- THE BACKER OF THE HANSIM PARTY -- WERE WILLING TO MAKE AN ALLIANCE WITH OUR ORGANIZATION.
AND EVEN SETTLE THINGS WITH CONGRESSMAN YU.

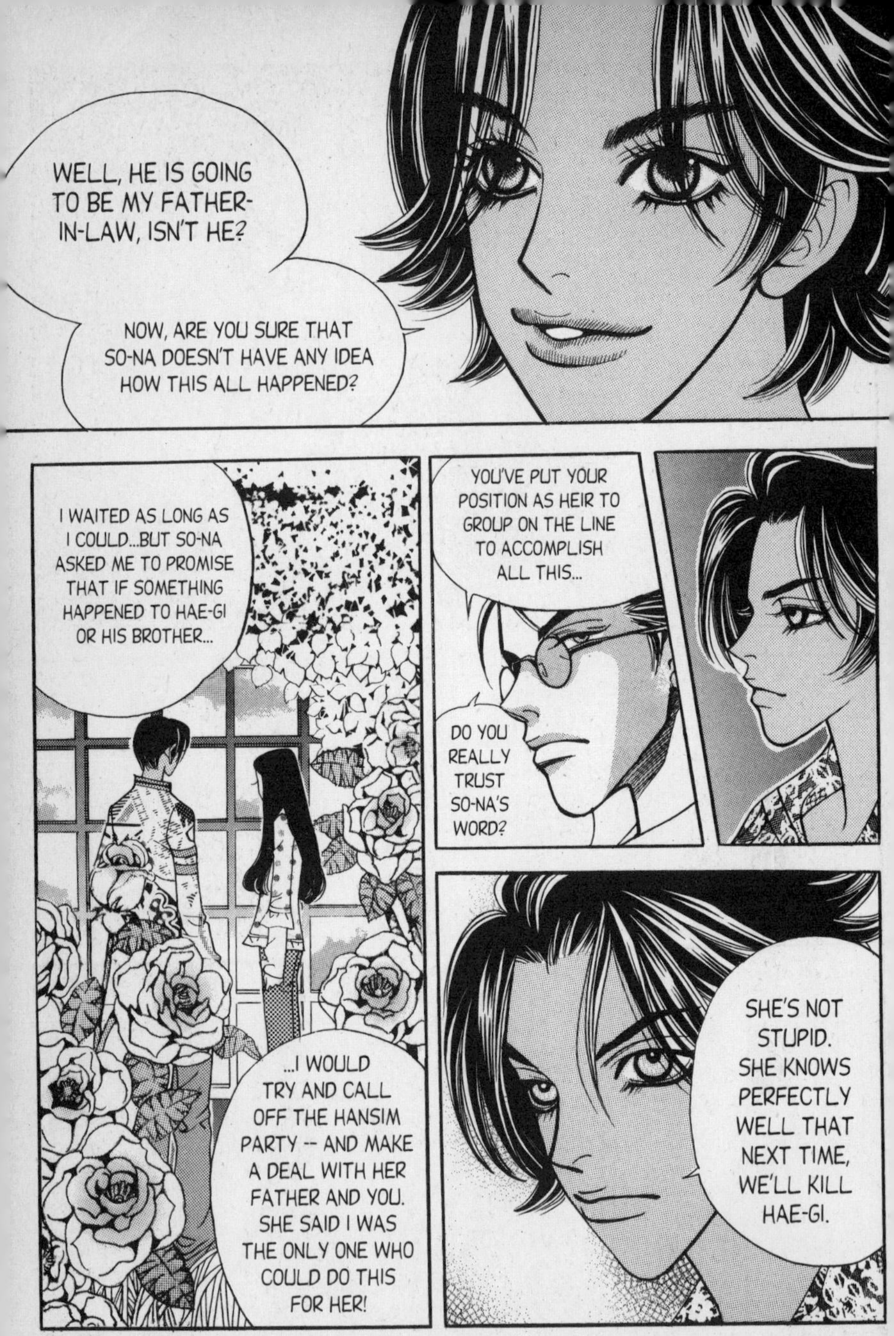
WELL, HE IS GOING TO BE MY FATHER-IN-LAW, ISN'T HE?
NOW, ARE YOU SURE THAT SO-NA DOESN'T HAVE ANY IDEA HOW THIS ALL HAPPENED?
I WAITED AS LONG AS I COULD...BUT SO-NA ASKED ME TO PROMISE THAT IF SOMETHING HAPPENED TO HAE-GI OR HIS BROTHER...
...I WOULD TRY AND CALL OFF THE HANSIM PARTY -- AND MAKE A DEAL WITH HER FATHER AND YOU. SHE SAID I WAS THE ONLY ONE WHO COULD DO THIS FOR HER!
YOU'VE PUT YOUR POSITION AS HEIR TO GROUP ON THE LINE TO ACCOMPLISH ALL THIS...
DO YOU REALLY TRUST SO-NA'S WORD?
SHE'S NOT STUPID. SHE KNOWS PERFECTLY WELL THAT NEXT TIME, WE'LL KILL HAE-GI.

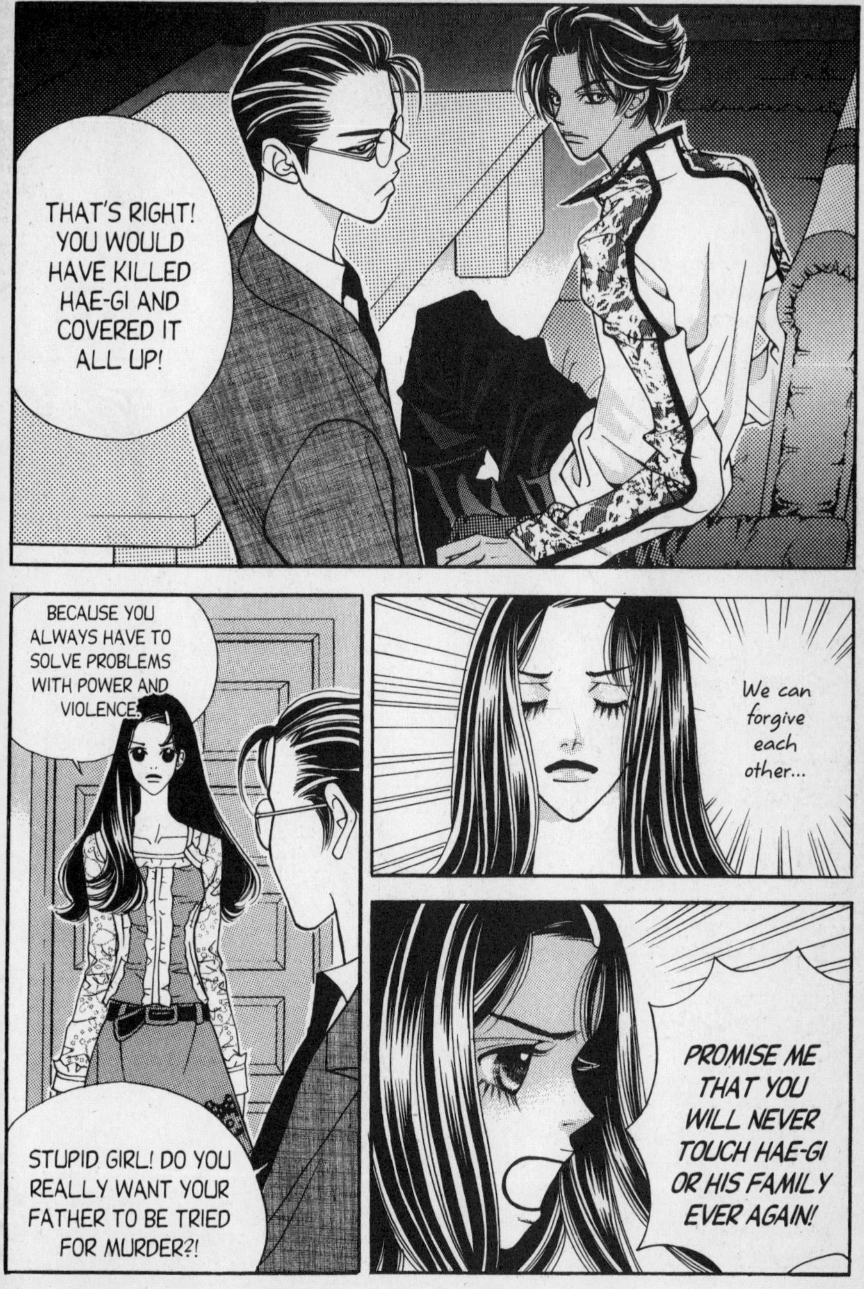
THAT'S RIGHT! YOU WOULD HAVE KILLED HAE-GI AND COVERED IT ALL UP!
BECAUSE YOU ALWAYS HAVE TO SOLVE PROBLEMS WITH POWER AND VIOLENCE.
STUPID GIRL! DO YOU REALLY WANT YOUR FATHER TO BE TRIED FOR MURDER?!
We can forgive each other...
PROMISE ME THAT YOU WILL NEVER TOUCH HAE-GI OR HIS FAMILY EVER AGAIN!

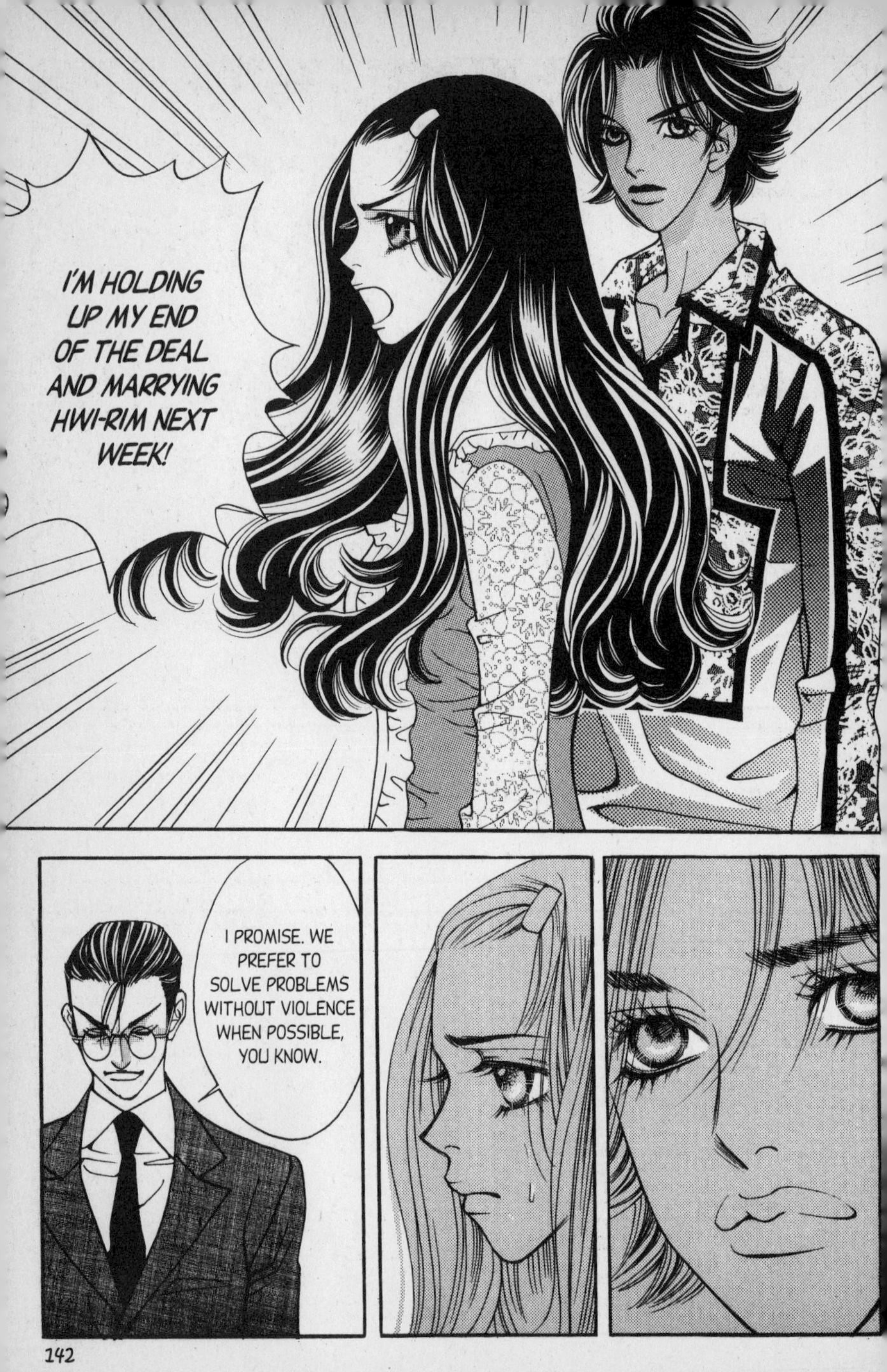
I'M HOLDING UP MY END OF THE DEAL AND MARRYING HWI-RIM NEXT WEEK!
I PROMISE. WE PREFER TO SOLVE PROBLEMS WITHOUT VIOLENCE WHEN POSSIBLE, YOU KNOW.

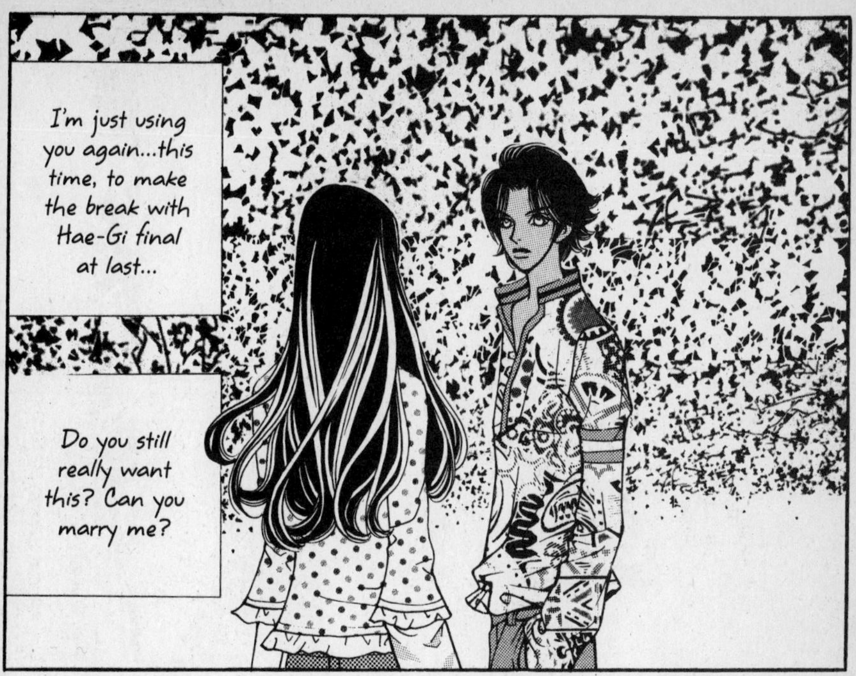
I'm just using you again...this time, to make the break with Hae-Gi final at last...
Do you still really want this? Can you marry me?

Part 37 : Angel

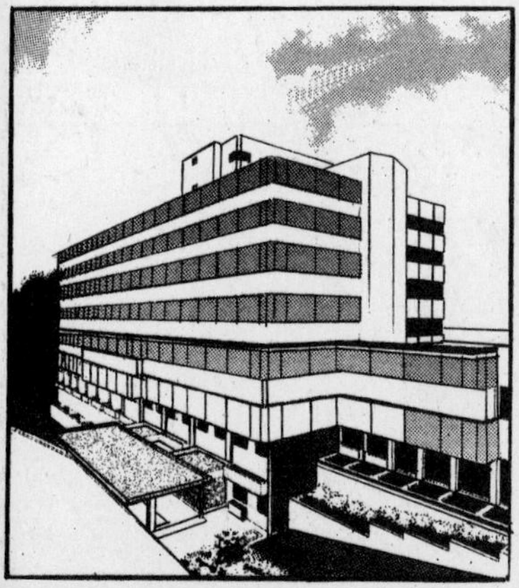

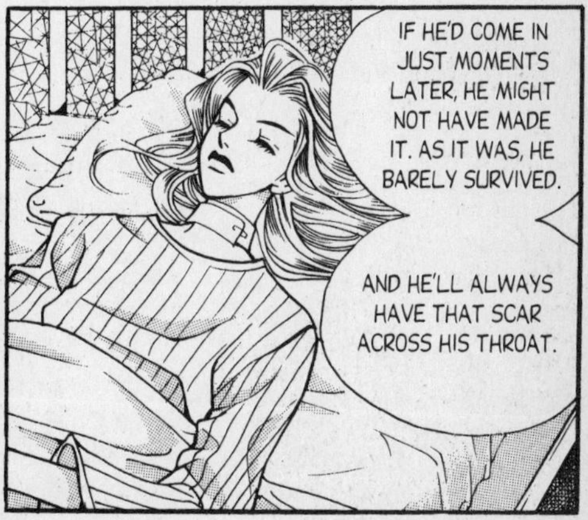
IF HE'D COME IN JUST MOMENTS LATER, HE MIGHT NOT HAVE MADE IT. AS IT WAS, HE BARELY SURVIVED.
AND HE'LL ALWAYS HAVE THAT SCAR ACROSS HIS THROAT.

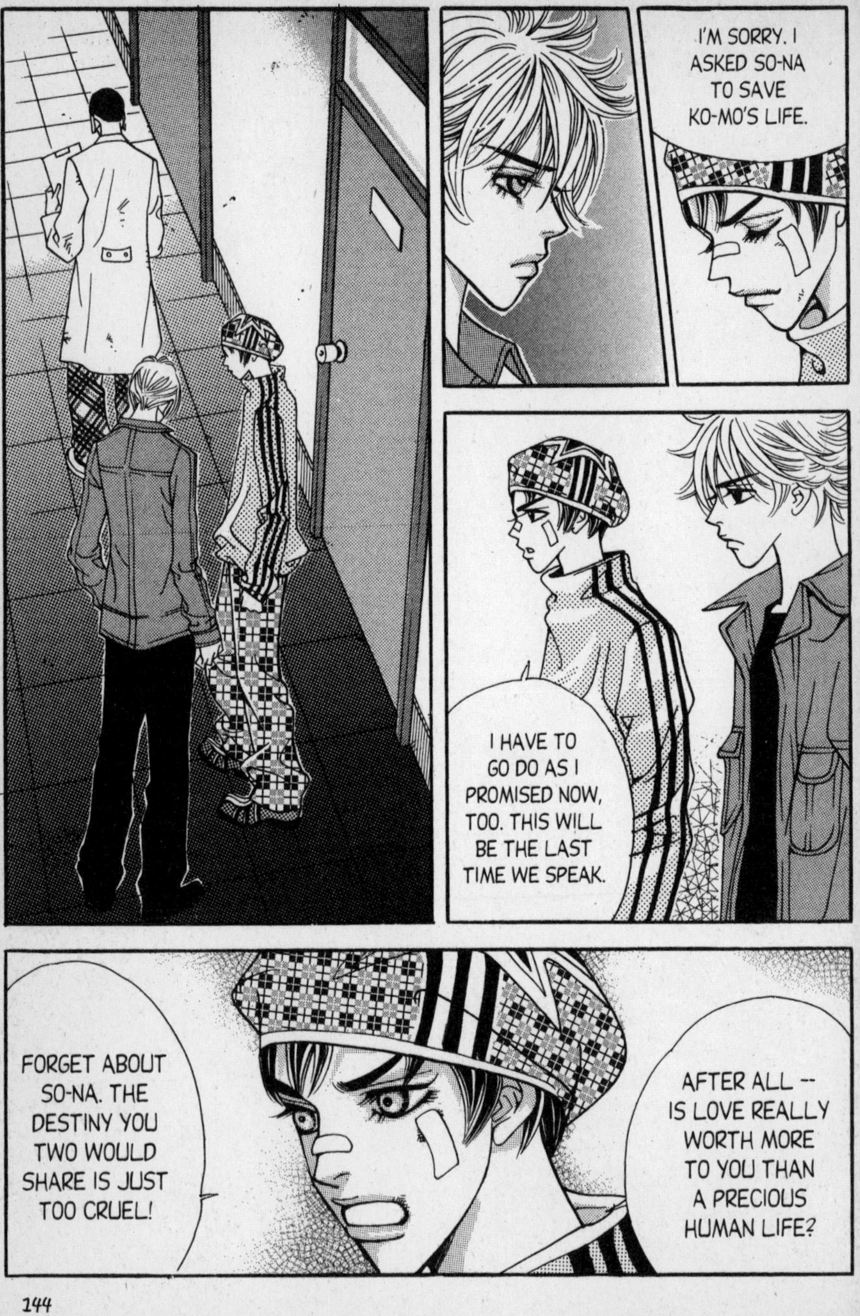
I'M SORRY. I ASKED SO-NA TO SAVE KO-MO'S LIFE.
I HAVE TO GO DO AS I PROMISED NOW, TOO. THIS WILL BE THE LAST TIME WE SPEAK.
FORGET ABOUT SO-NA. THE DESTINY YOU TWO WOULD SHARE IS JUST TOO CRUEL!
AFTER ALL -- IS LOVE REALLY WORTH MORE TO YOU THAN A PRECIOUS HUMAN LIFE?

스노우 드롭

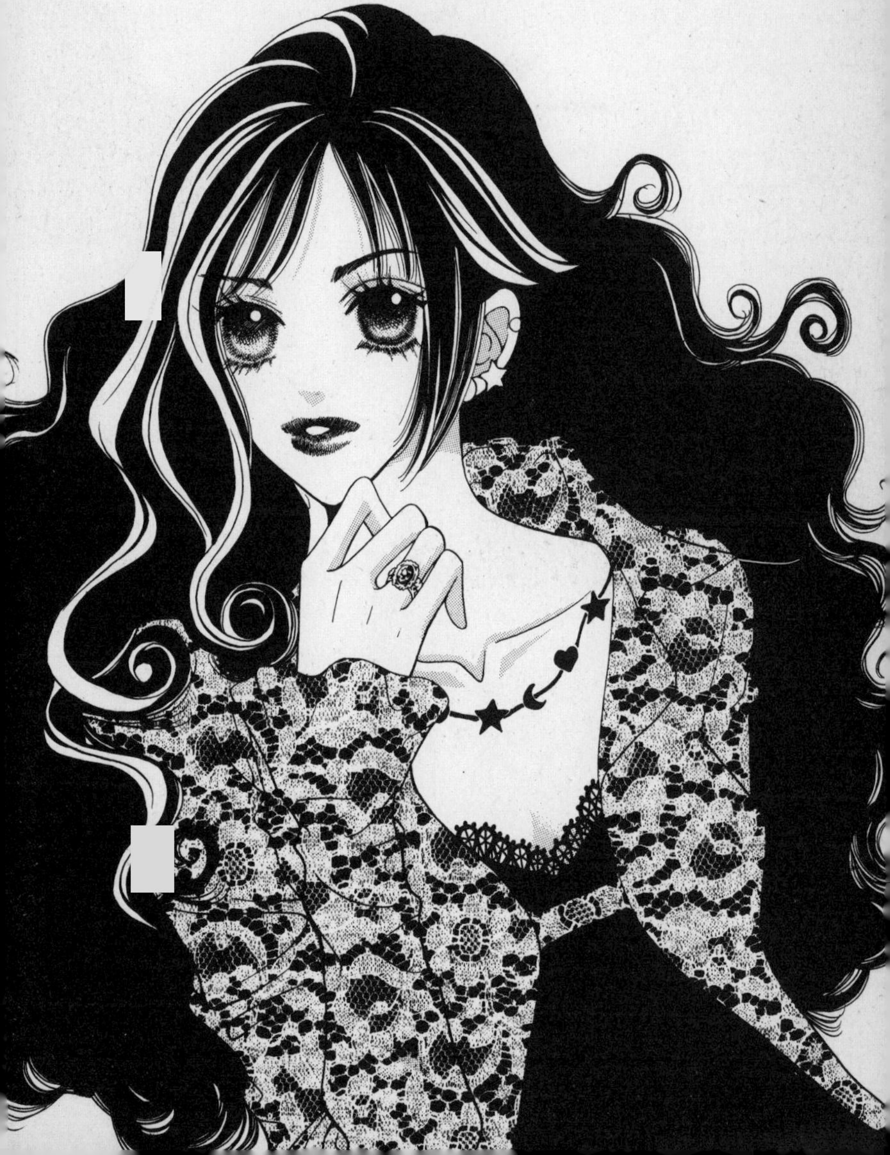

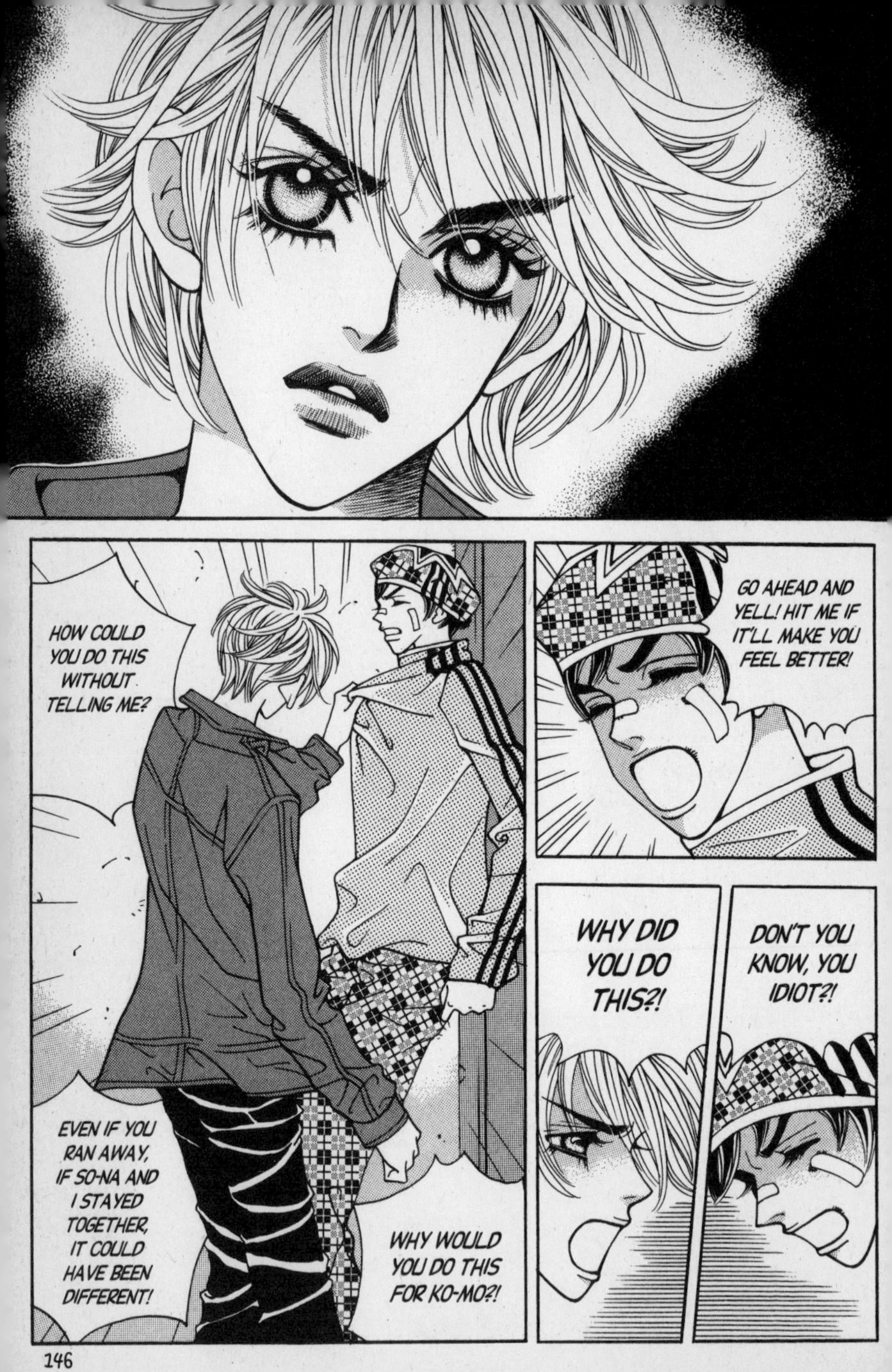

HOW COULD YOU DO THIS WITHOUT TELLING ME?
EVEN IF YOU RAN AWAY, IF SO-NA AND I STAYED TOGETHER, IT COULD HAVE BEEN DIFFERENT!
WHY WOULD YOU DO THIS FOR KO-MO?!
GO AHEAD AND YELL! HIT ME IF IT'LL MAKE YOU FEEL BETTER!
WHY DID YOU DO THIS?!
DON'T YOU KNOW, YOU IDIOT?!

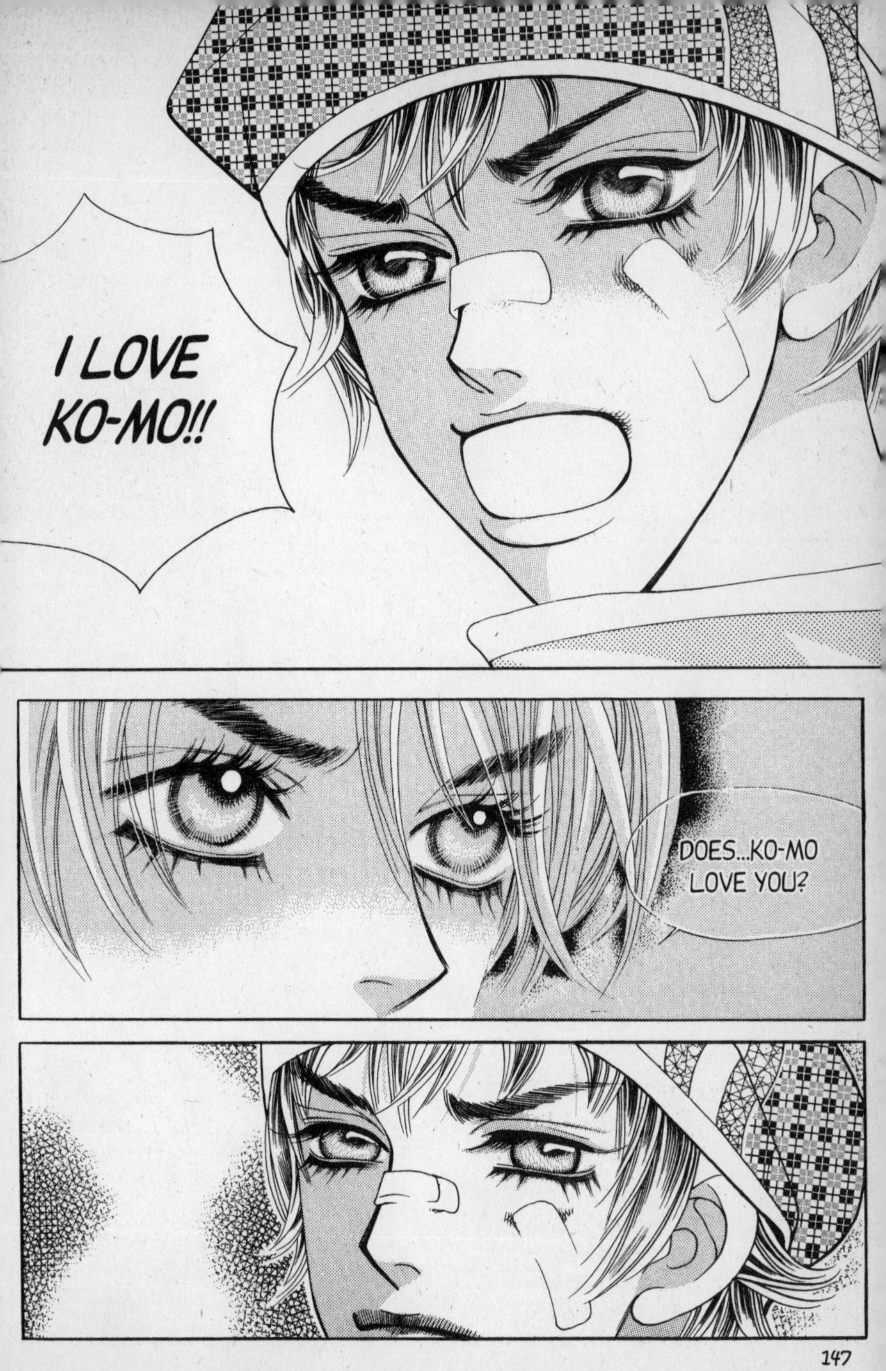
I LOVE KO-MO!!
DOES...KO-MO LOVE YOU?

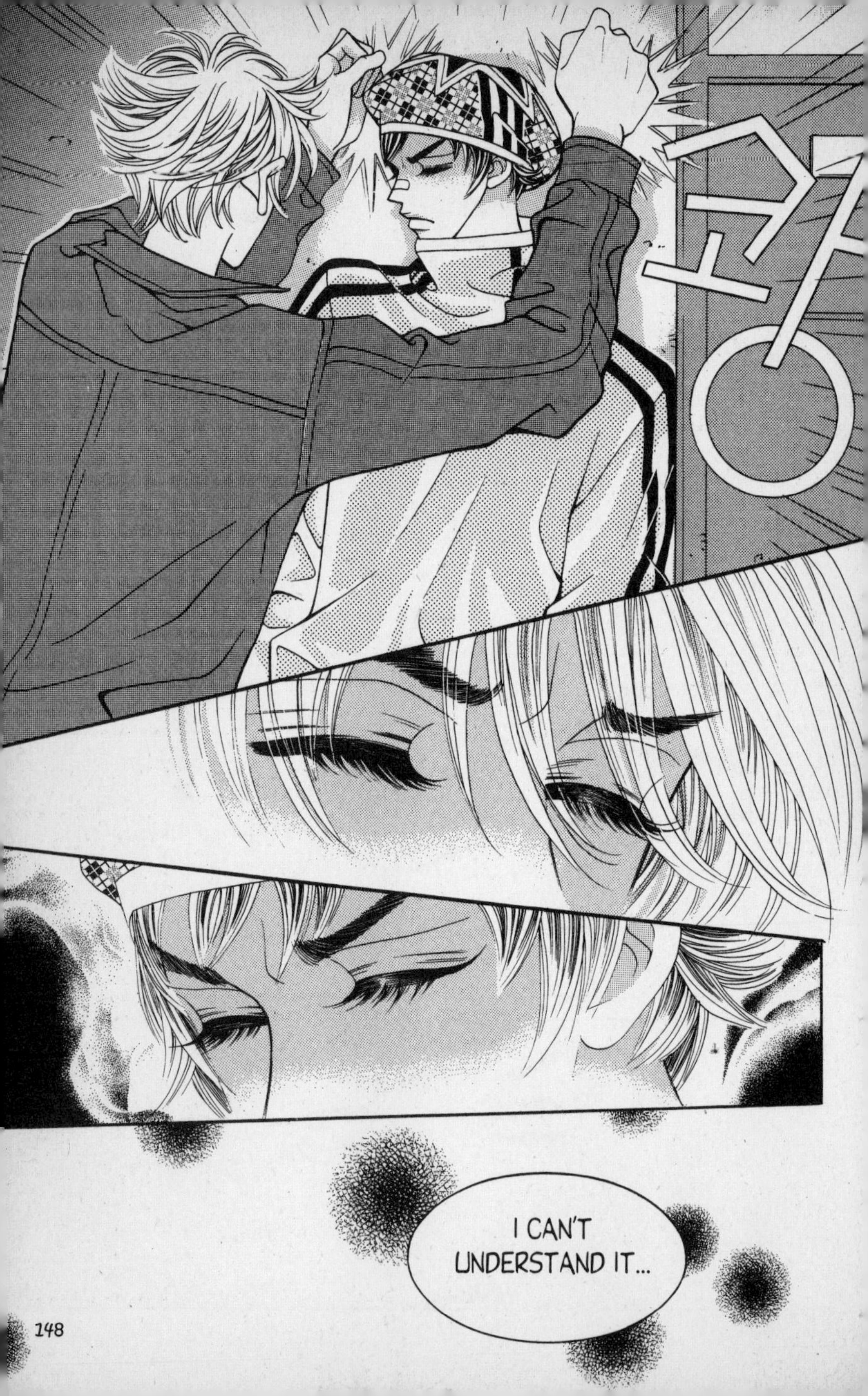
I CAN'T
UNDERSTAND IT...

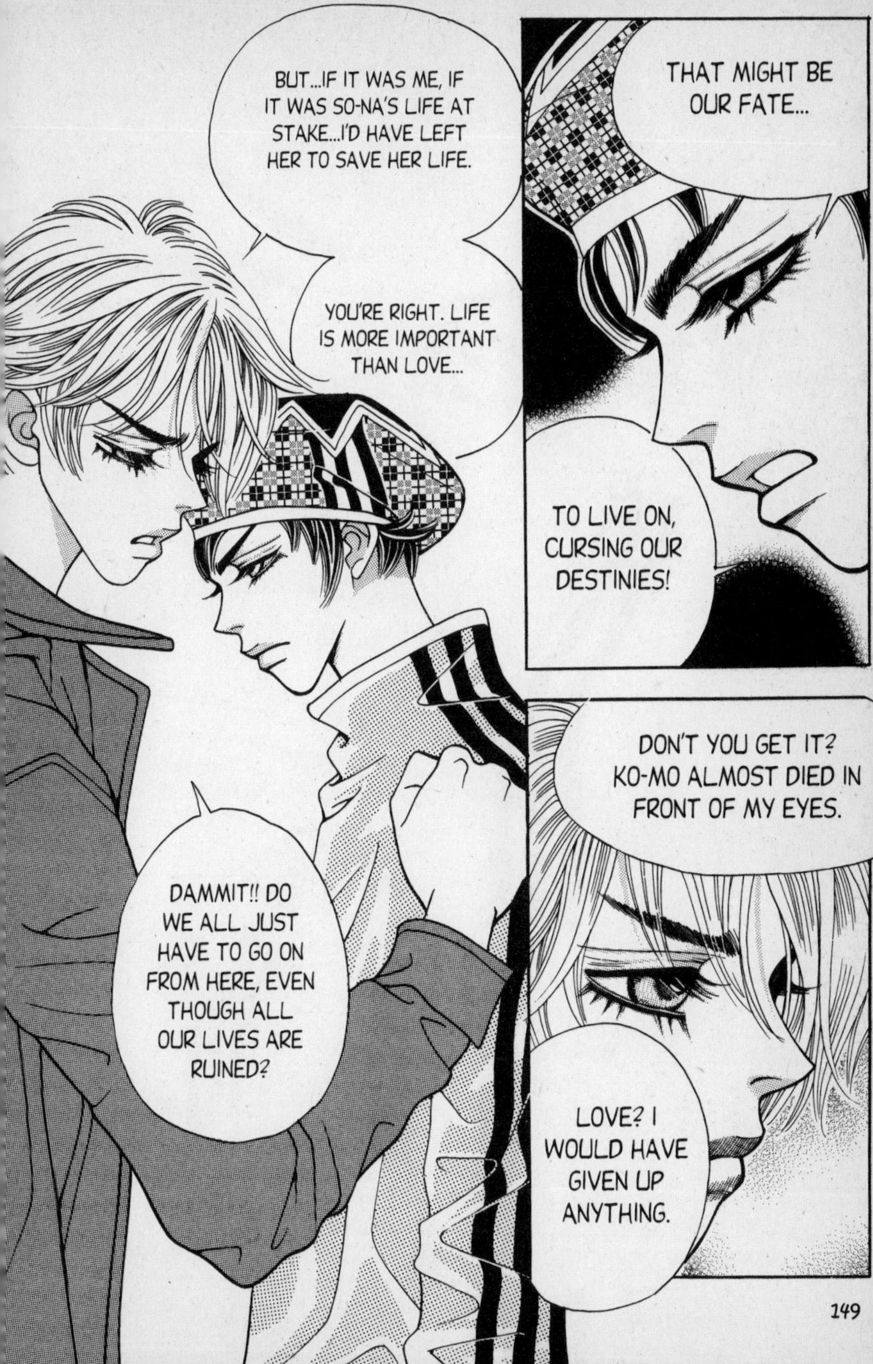

BUT...IF IT WAS ME, IF IT WAS SO-NA'S LIFE AT STAKE...I'D HAVE LEFT HER TO SAVE HER LIFE.
YOU'RE RIGHT. LIFE IS MORE IMPORTANT THAN LOVE...
DAMMIT!! DO WE ALL JUST HAVE TO GO ON FROM HERE, EVEN THOUGH ALL OUR LIVES ARE RUINED?
THAT MIGHT BE OUR FATE...
TO LIVE ON, CURSING OUR DESTINIES!
DON'T YOU GET IT? KO-MO ALMOST DIED IN FRONT OF MY EYES.
LOVE? I WOULD HAVE GIVEN UP ANYTHING.

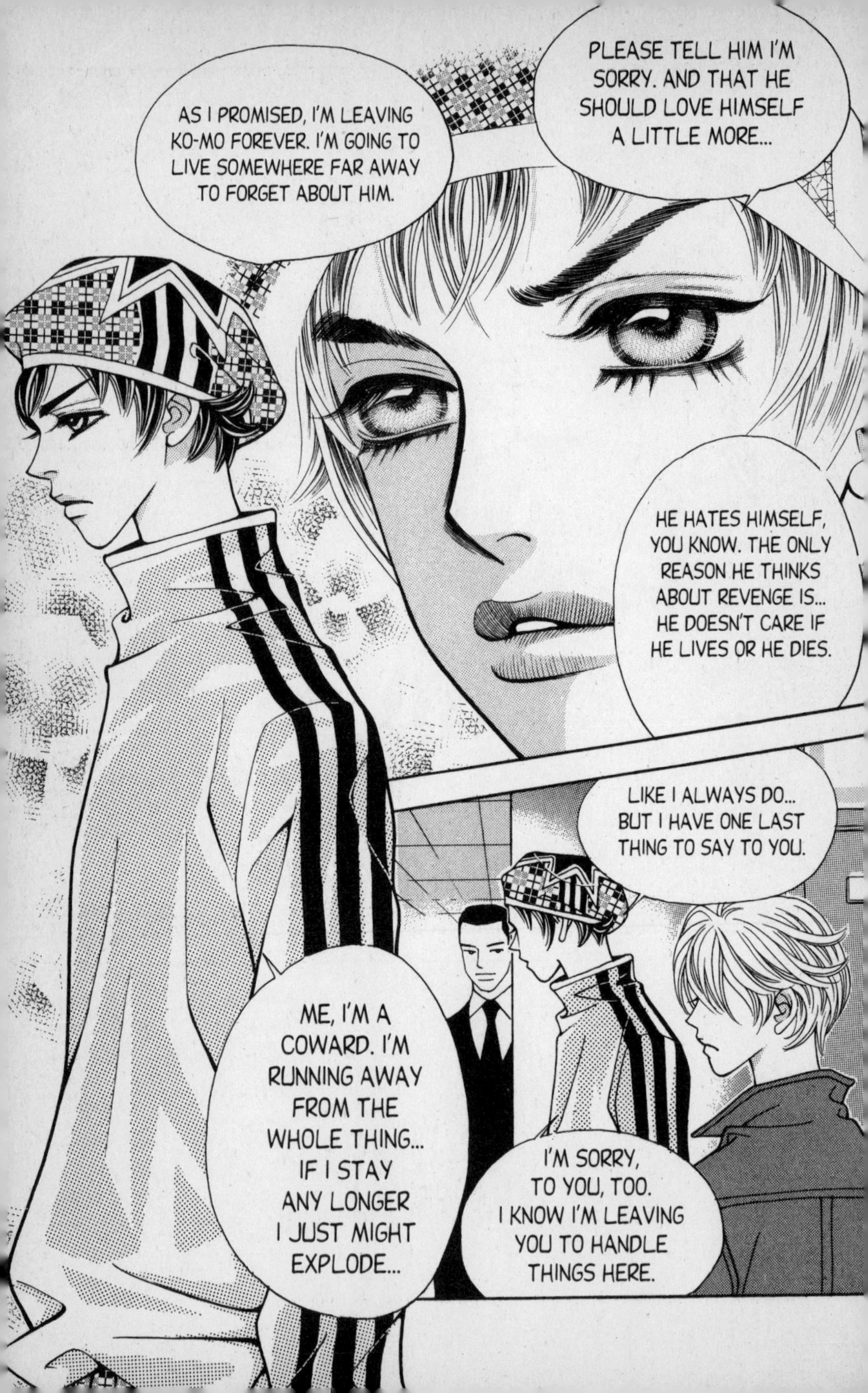
AS I PROMISED, I'M LEAVING KO-MO FOREVER. I'M GOING TO LIVE SOMEWHERE FAR AWAY TO FORGET ABOUT HIM.
PLEASE TELL HIM I'M SORRY. AND THAT HE SHOULD LOVE HIMSELF A LITTLE MORE...
HE HATES HIMSELF, YOU KNOW. THE ONLY REASON HE THINKS ABOUT REVENGE IS... HE DOESN'T CARE IF HE LIVES OR HE DIES.
LIKE I ALWAYS DO... BUT I HAVE ONE LAST THING TO SAY TO YOU.
ME, I'M A COWARD. I'M RUNNING AWAY FROM THE WHOLE THING... IF I STAY ANY LONGER I JUST MIGHT EXPLODE...
I'M SORRY, TO YOU, TOO. I KNOW I'M LEAVING YOU TO HANDLE THINGS HERE.

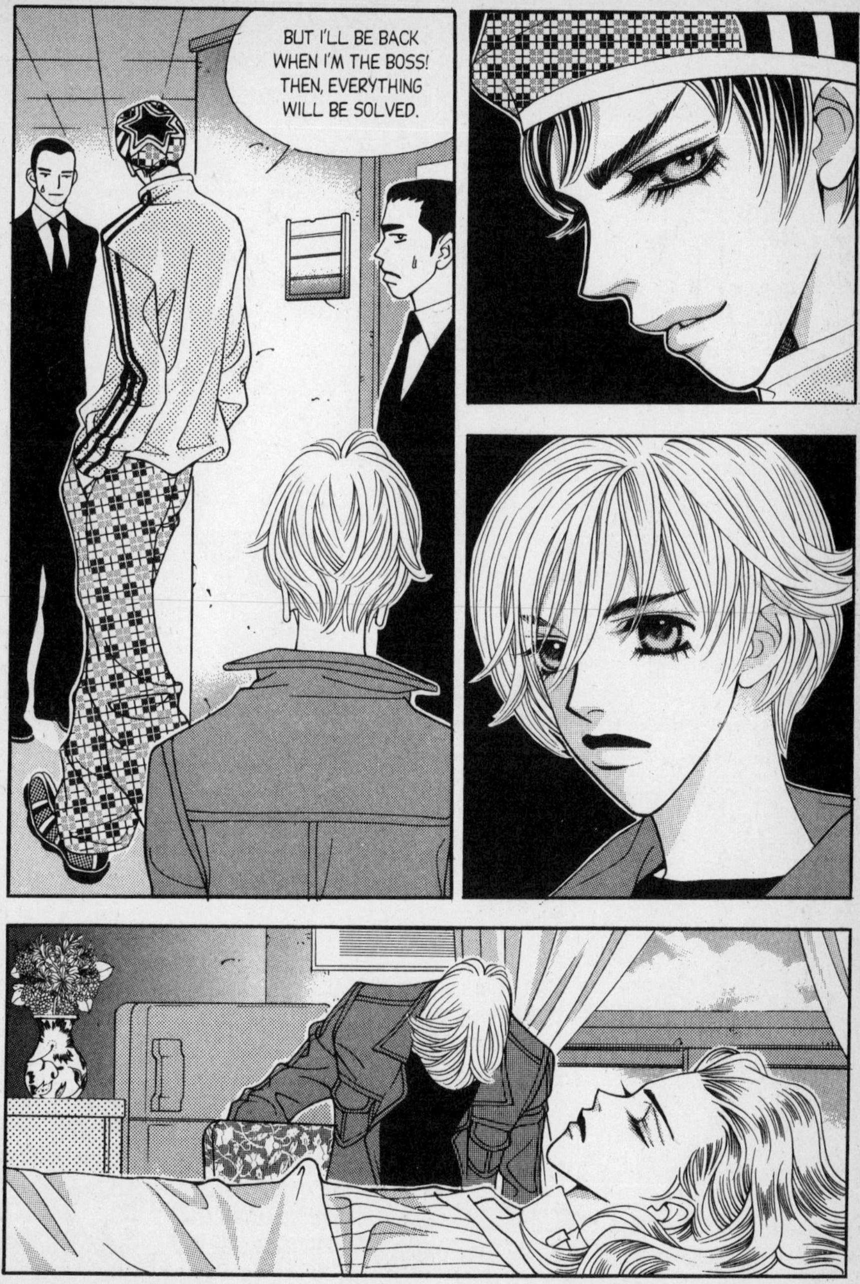
BUT I'LL BE BACK WHEN I'M THE BOSS! THEN, EVERYTHING WILL BE SOLVED.

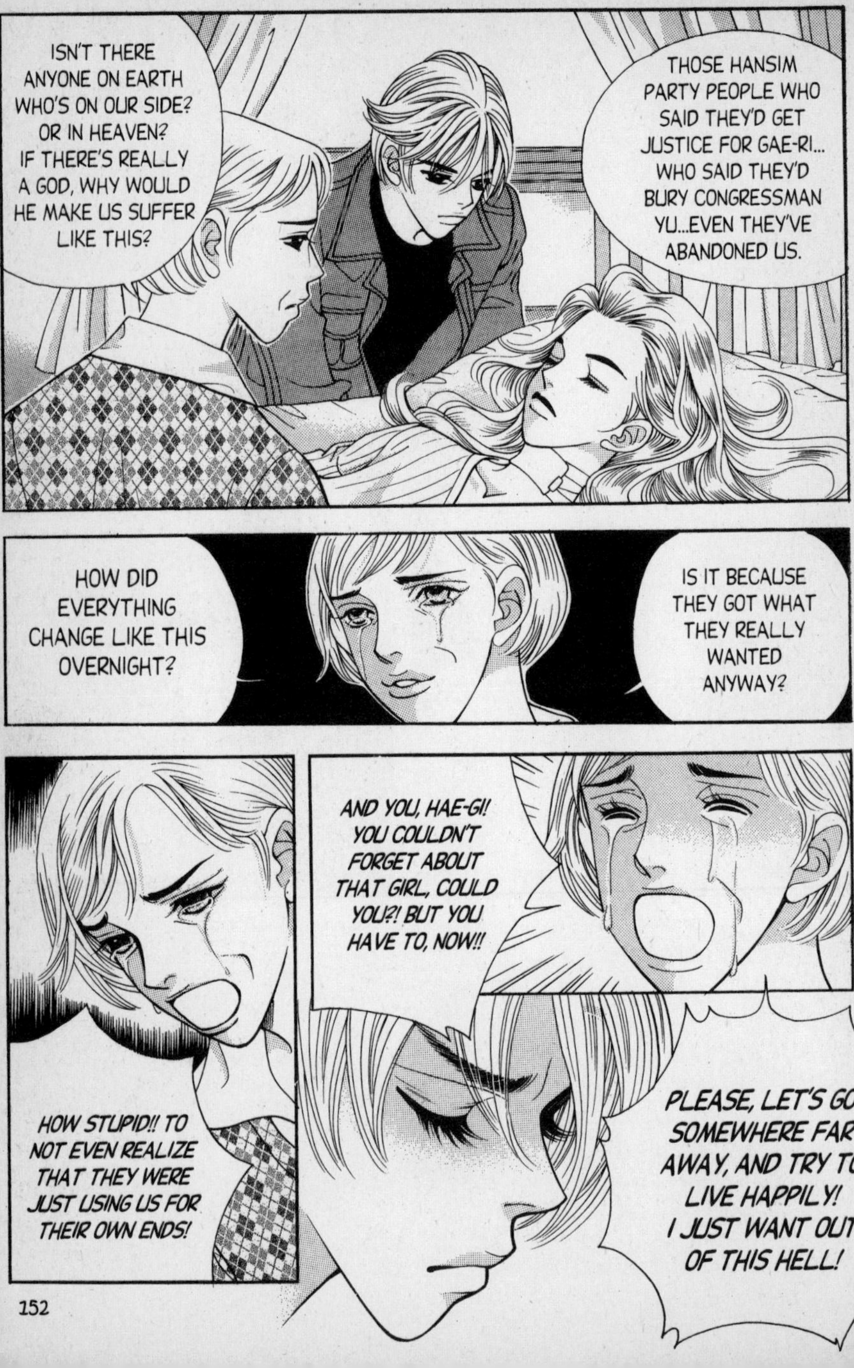
ISN'T THERE ANYONE ON EARTH WHO'S ON OUR SIDE? OR IN HEAVEN? IF THERE'S REALLY A GOD, WHY WOULD HE MAKE US SUFFER LIKE THIS?
THOSE HANSIM PARTY PEOPLE WHO SAID THEY'D GET JUSTICE FOR GAE-RI... WHO SAID THEY'D BURY CONGRESSMAN YU...EVEN THEY'VE ABANDONED US.
HOW DID EVERYTHING CHANGE LIKE THIS OVERNIGHT?
IS IT BECAUSE THEY GOT WHAT THEY REALLY WANTED ANYWAY?
HOW STUPID!! TO NOT EVEN REALIZE THAT THEY WERE JUST USING US FOR THEIR OWN ENDS!
AND YOU, HAE-GI! YOU COULDN'T FORGET ABOUT THAT GIRL, COULD YOU?! BUT YOU HAVE TO, NOW!!
PLEASE, LET'S GO SOMEWHERE FAR AWAY, AND TRY TO LIVE HAPPILY! I JUST WANT OUT OF THIS HELL!

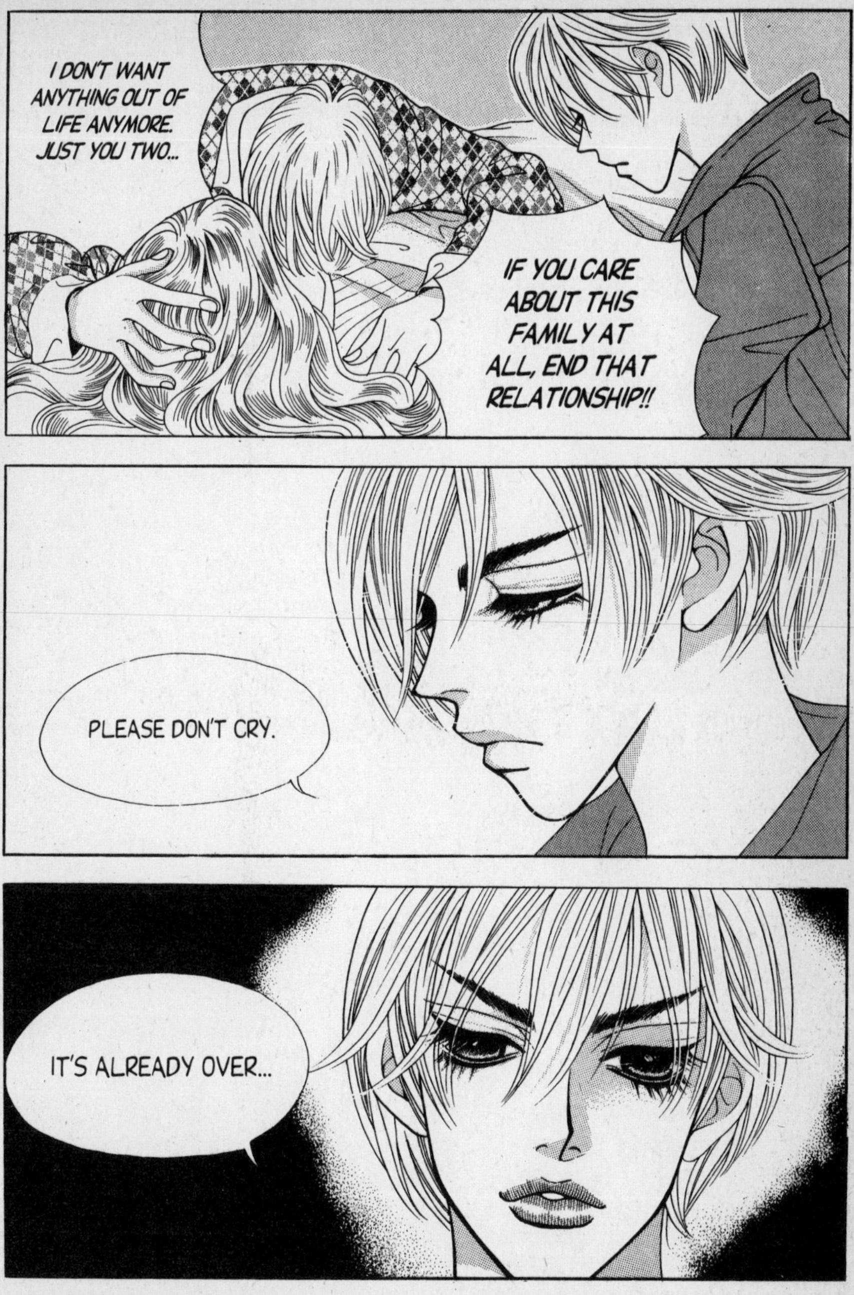
I DON'T WANT ANYTHING OUT OF LIFE ANYMORE. JUST YOU TWO...
IF YOU CARE ABOUT THIS FAMILY AT ALL, END THAT RELATIONSHIP!!
PLEASE DON'T CRY.
IT'S ALREADY OVER...

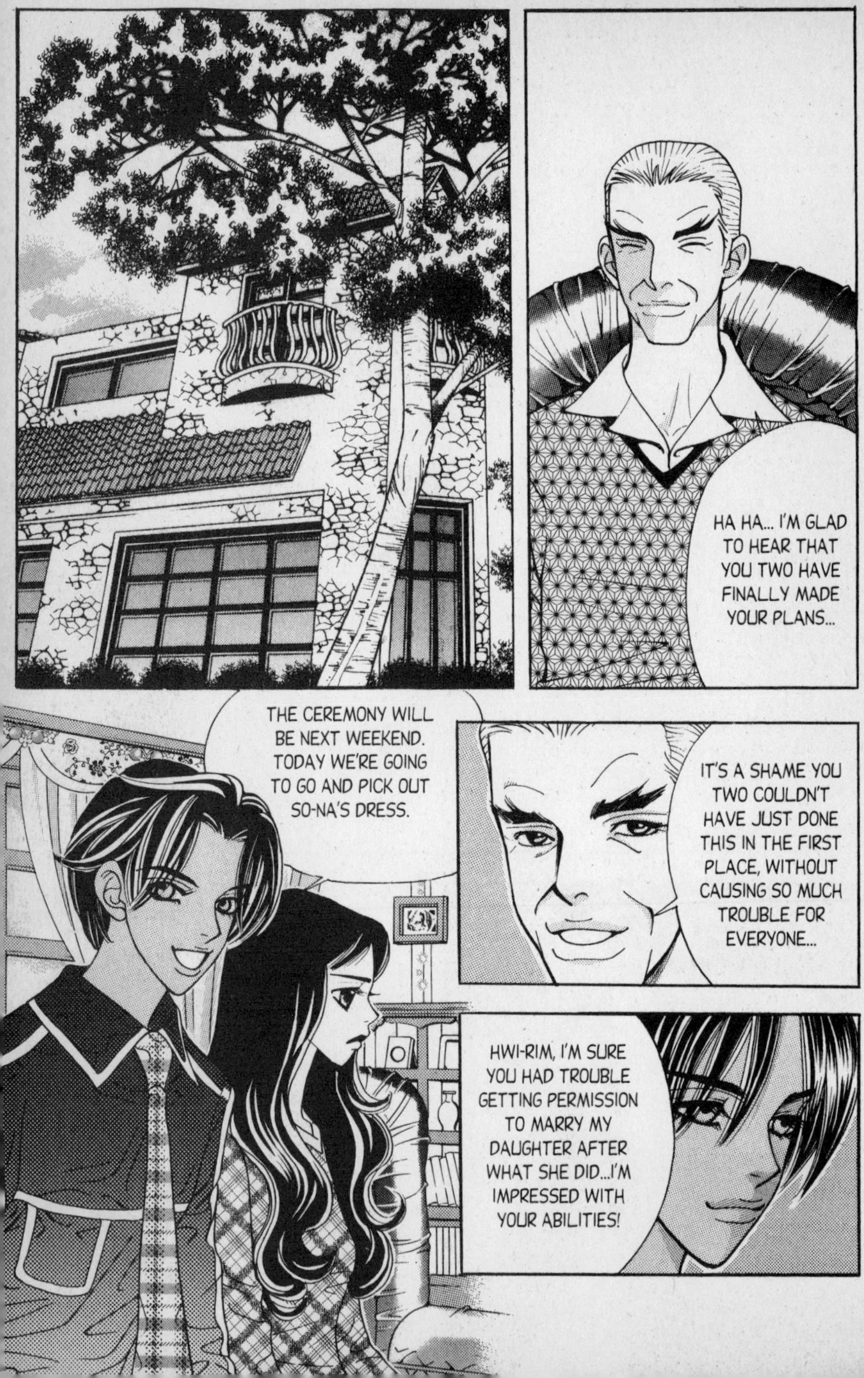
HA HA... I'M GLAD TO HEAR THAT YOU TWO HAVE FINALLY MADE YOUR PLANS...
THE CEREMONY WILL BE NEXT WEEKEND. TODAY WE'RE GOING TO GO AND PICK OUT SO-NA'S DRESS.
IT'S A SHAME YOU TWO COULDN'T HAVE JUST DONE THIS IN THE FIRST PLACE, WITHOUT CAUSING SO MUCH TROUBLE FOR EVERYONE...
HWI-RIM, I'M SURE YOU HAD TROUBLE GETTING PERMISSION TO MARRY MY DAUGHTER AFTER WHAT SHE DID...I'M IMPRESSED WITH YOUR ABILITIES!

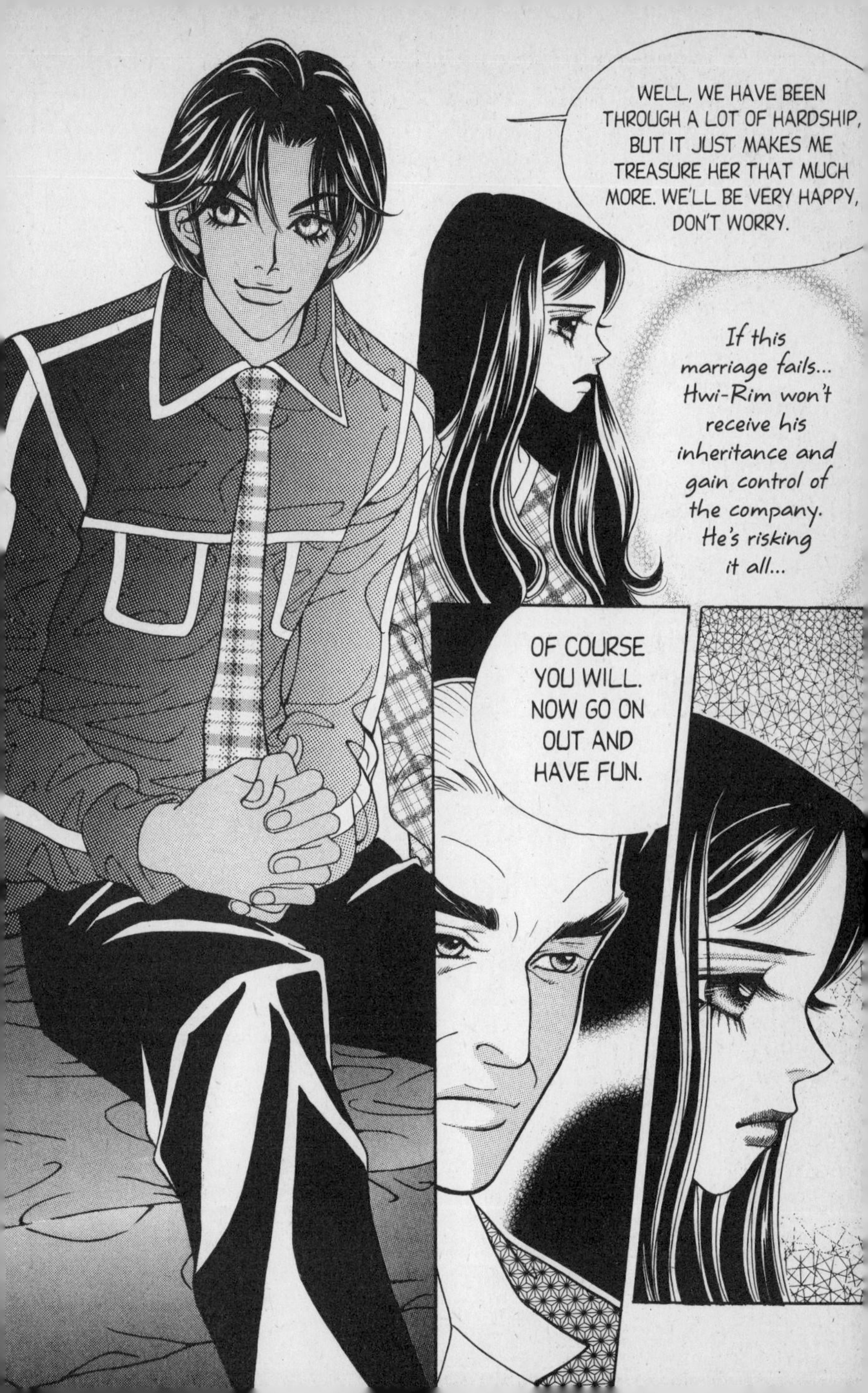
WELL, WE HAVE BEEN THROUGH A LOT OF HARDSHIP, BUT IT JUST MAKES ME TREASURE HER THAT MUCH MORE. WE'LL BE VERY HAPPY, DON'T WORRY.
If this marriage fails... Hwi-Rim won't receive his inheritance and gain control of the company. He's risking it all...
OF COURSE YOU WILL. NOW GO ON OUT AND HAVE FUN.

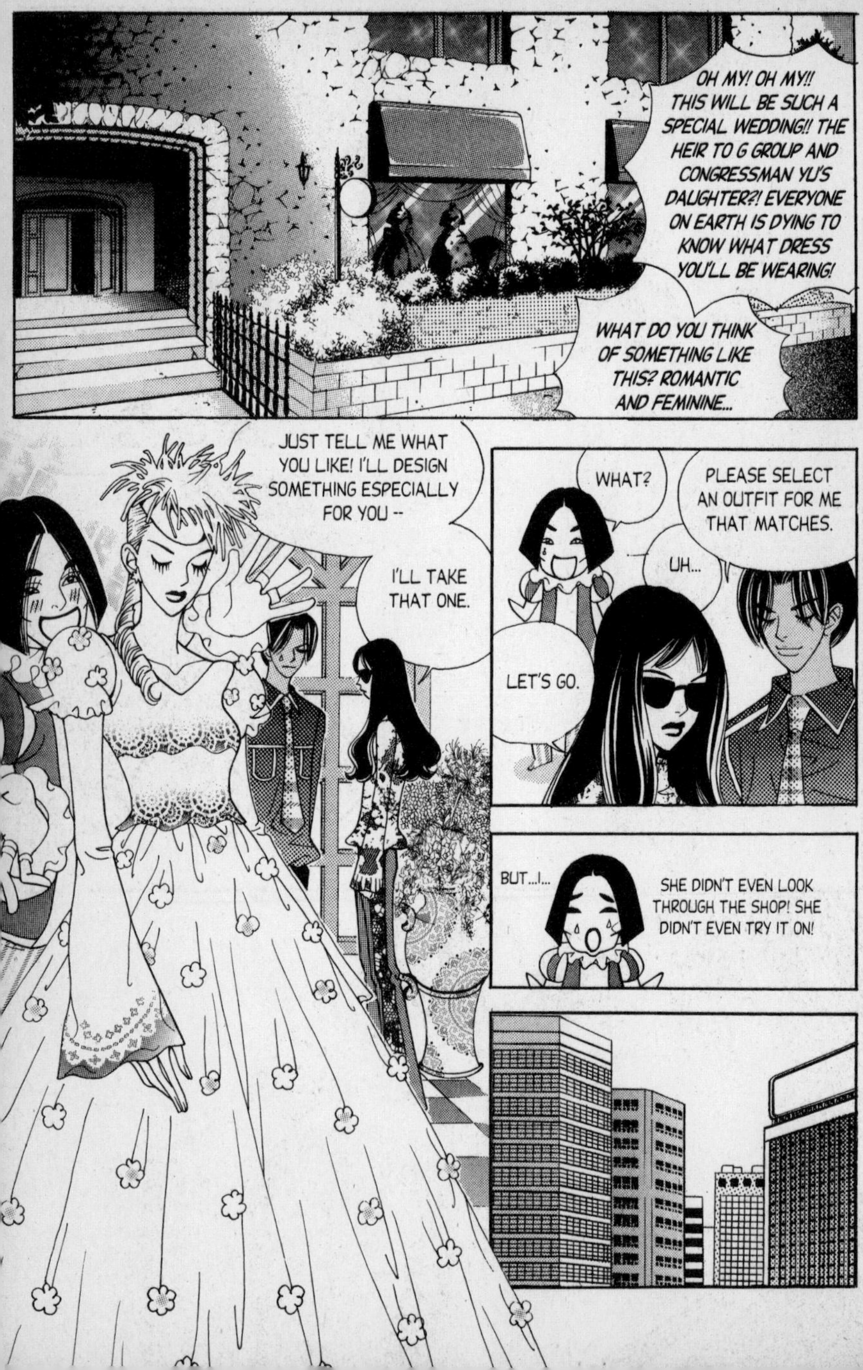
OH MY! OH MY!! THIS WILL BE SUCH A SPECIAL WEDDING!! THE HEIR TO G GROUP AND CONGRESSMAN YU'S DAUGHTER?! EVERYONE ON EARTH IS DYING TO KNOW WHAT DRESS YOU'LL BE WEARING!
WHAT DO YOU THINK OF SOMETHING LIKE THIS? ROMANTIC AND FEMININE...
JUST TELL ME WHAT YOU LIKE! I'LL DESIGN SOMETHING ESPECIALLY FOR YOU --
I'LL TAKE THAT ONE.
WHAT?
PLEASE SELECT AN OUTFIT FOR ME THAT MATCHES.
UH...
LET'S GO.
BUT...I...
SHE DIDN'T EVEN LOOK THROUGH THE SHOP! SHE DIDN'T EVEN TRY IT ON!

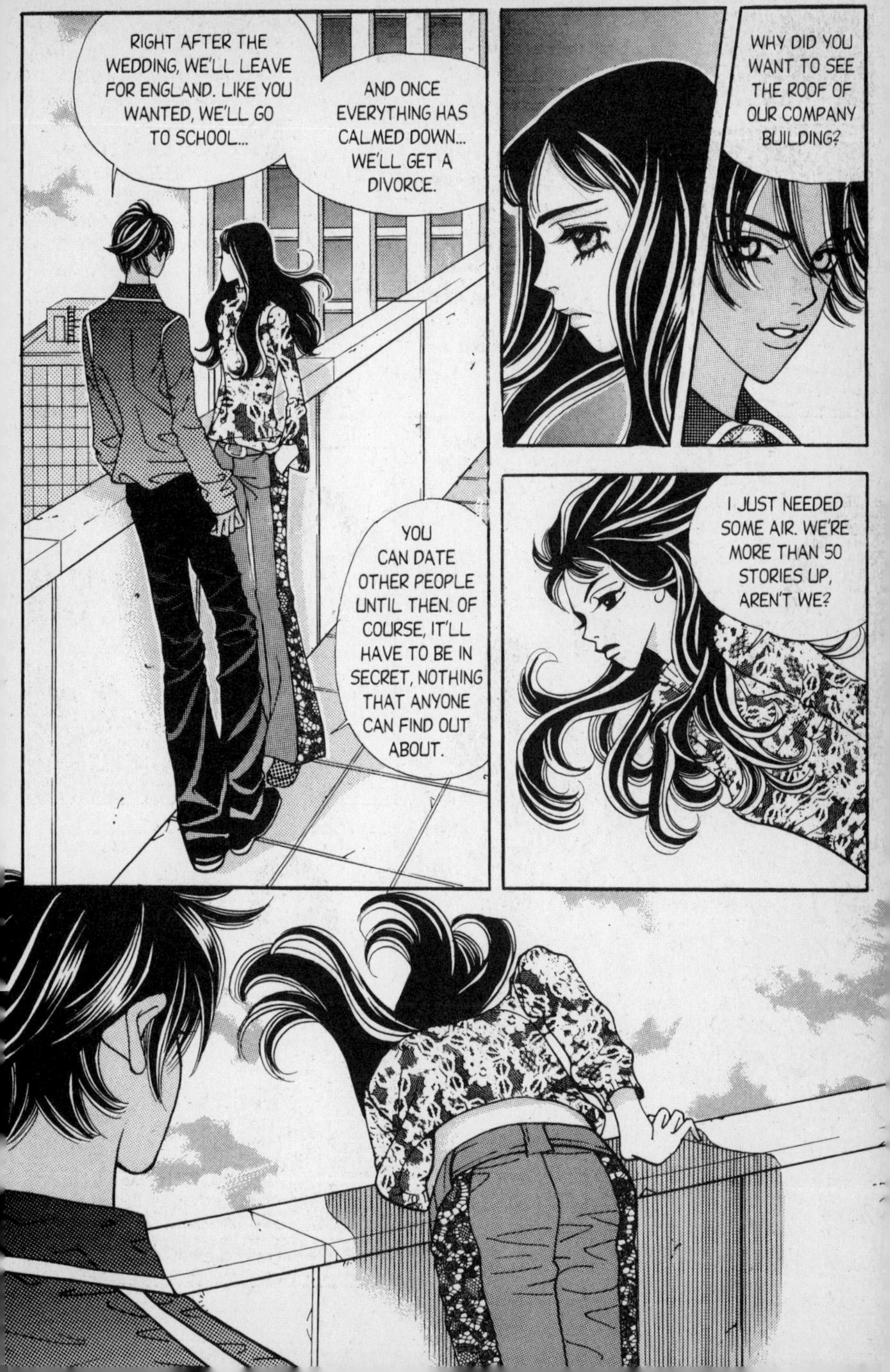
RIGHT AFTER THE WEDDING, WE'LL LEAVE FOR ENGLAND. LIKE YOU WANTED, WE'LL GO TO SCHOOL...
AND ONCE EVERYTHING HAS CALMED DOWN... WE'LL GET A DIVORCE.
YOU CAN DATE OTHER PEOPLE UNTIL THEN. OF COURSE, IT'LL HAVE TO BE IN SECRET, NOTHING THAT ANYONE CAN FIND OUT ABOUT.
WHY DID YOU WANT TO SEE THE ROOF OF OUR COMPANY BUILDING?
I JUST NEEDED SOME AIR. WE'RE MORE THAN 50 STORIES UP, AREN'T WE?

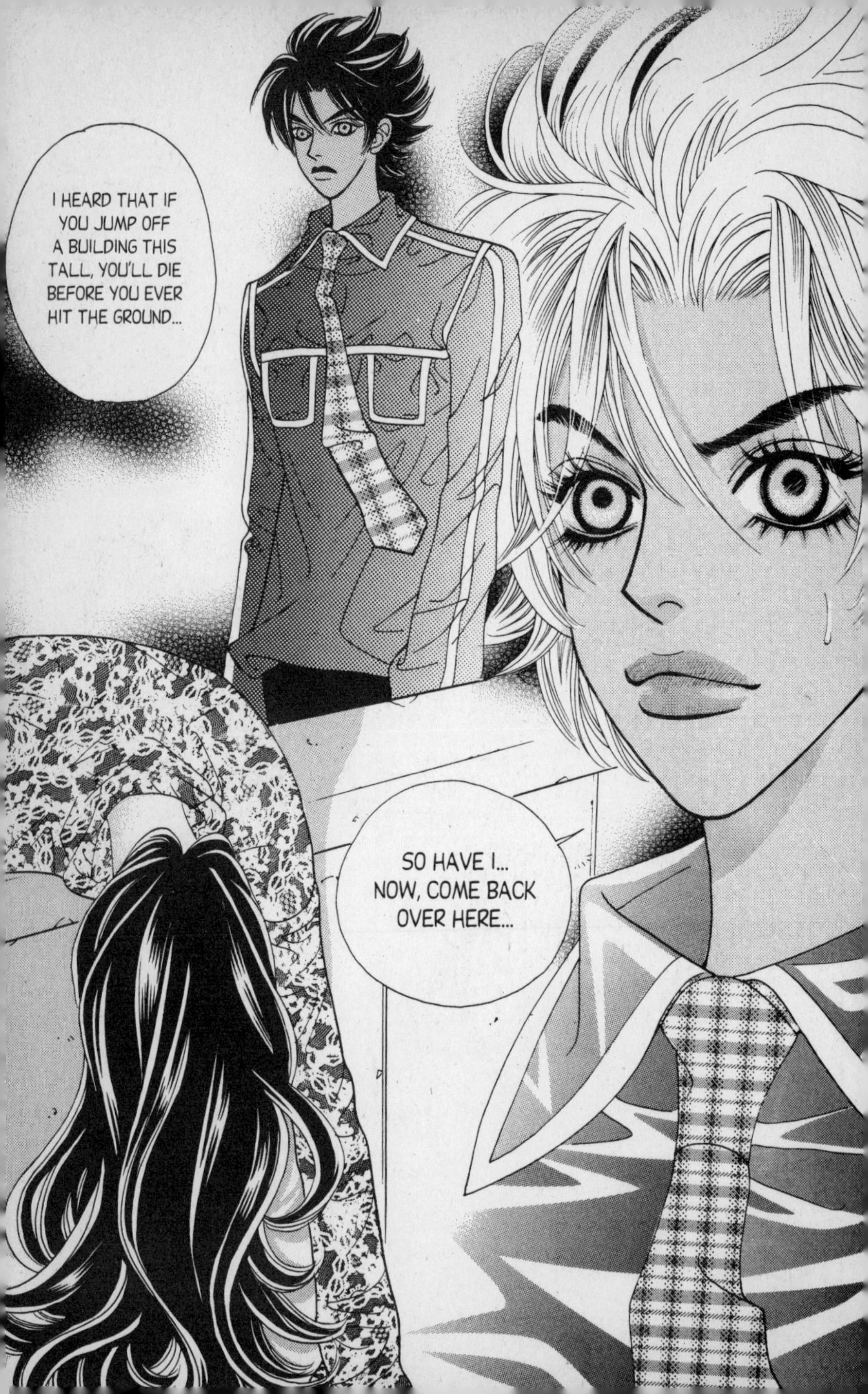
I HEARD THAT IF YOU JUMP OFF A BUILDING THIS TALL, YOU'LL DIE BEFORE YOU EVER HIT THE GROUND...
SO HAVE I... NOW, COME BACK OVER HERE...

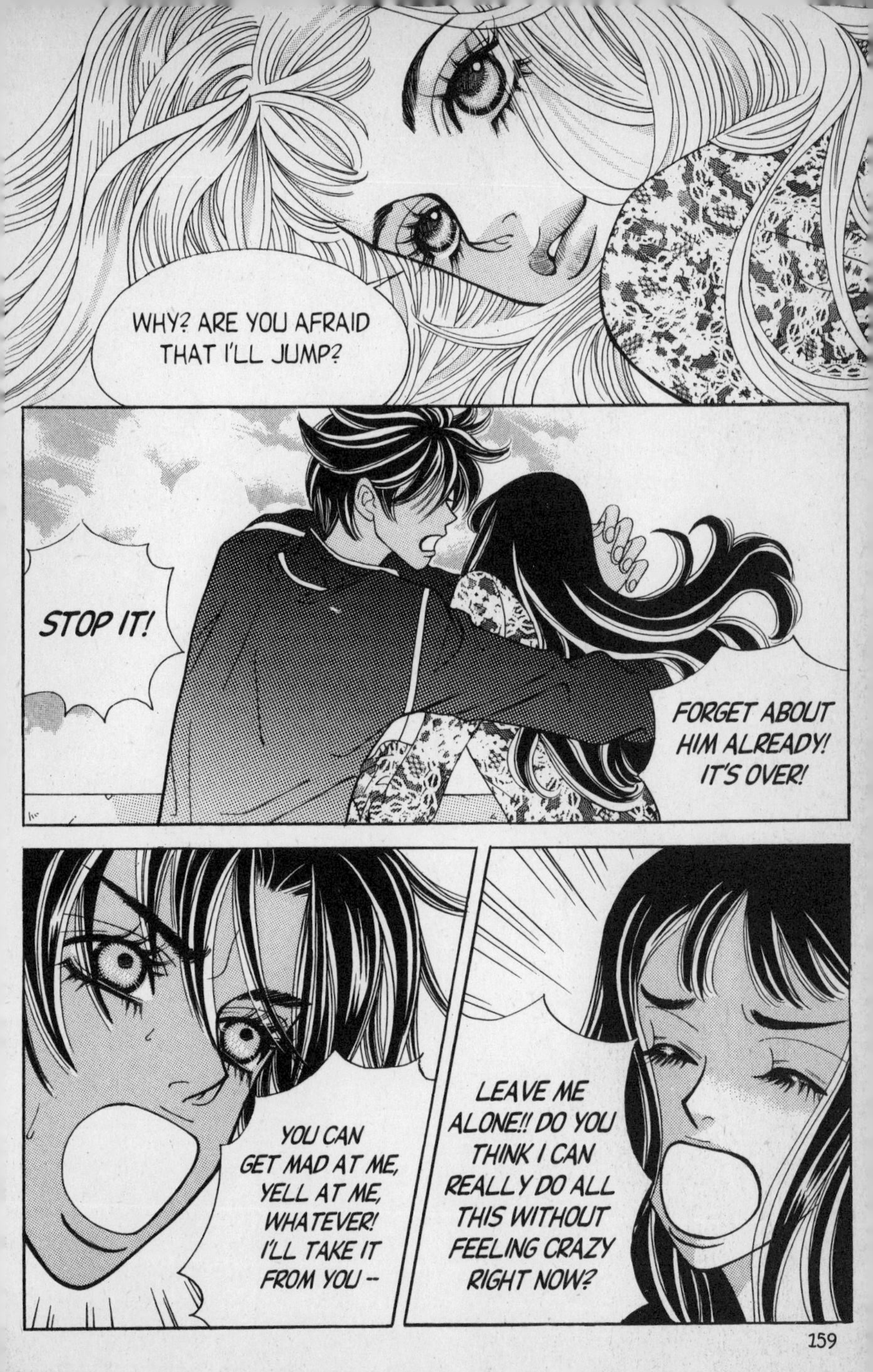
WHY? ARE YOU AFRAID THAT I'LL JUMP?
STOP IT!
FORGET ABOUT HIM ALREADY! IT'S OVER!
YOU CAN GET MAD AT ME, YELL AT ME, WHATEVER! I'LL TAKE IT FROM YOU --
LEAVE ME ALONE!! DO YOU THINK I CAN REALLY DO ALL THIS WITHOUT FEELING CRAZY RIGHT NOW?

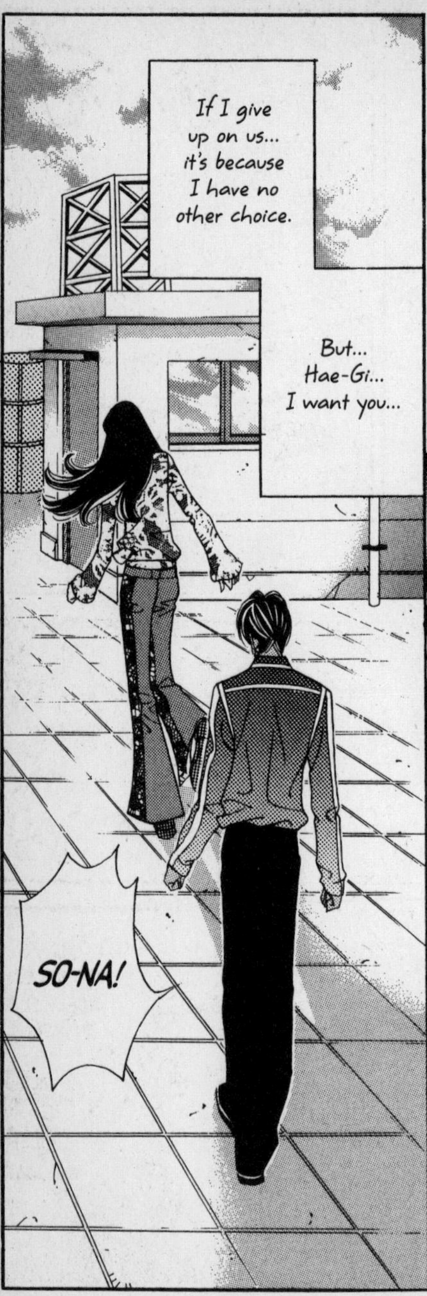
If I give up on us... it's because I have no other choice.
But... Hae-Gi... I want you...
SO-NA!
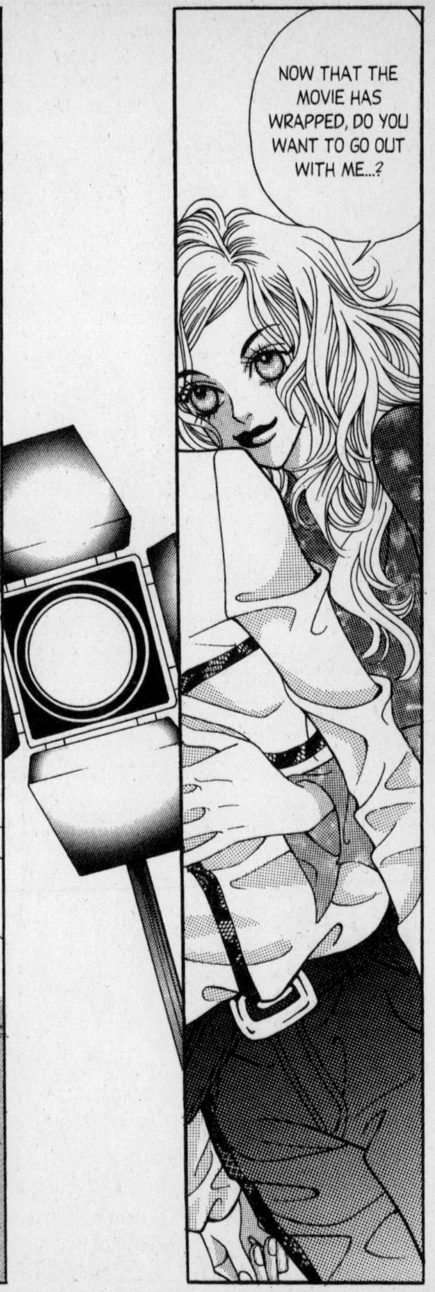
NOW THAT THE MOVIE HAS WRAPPED, DO YOU WANT TO GO OUT WITH ME...?

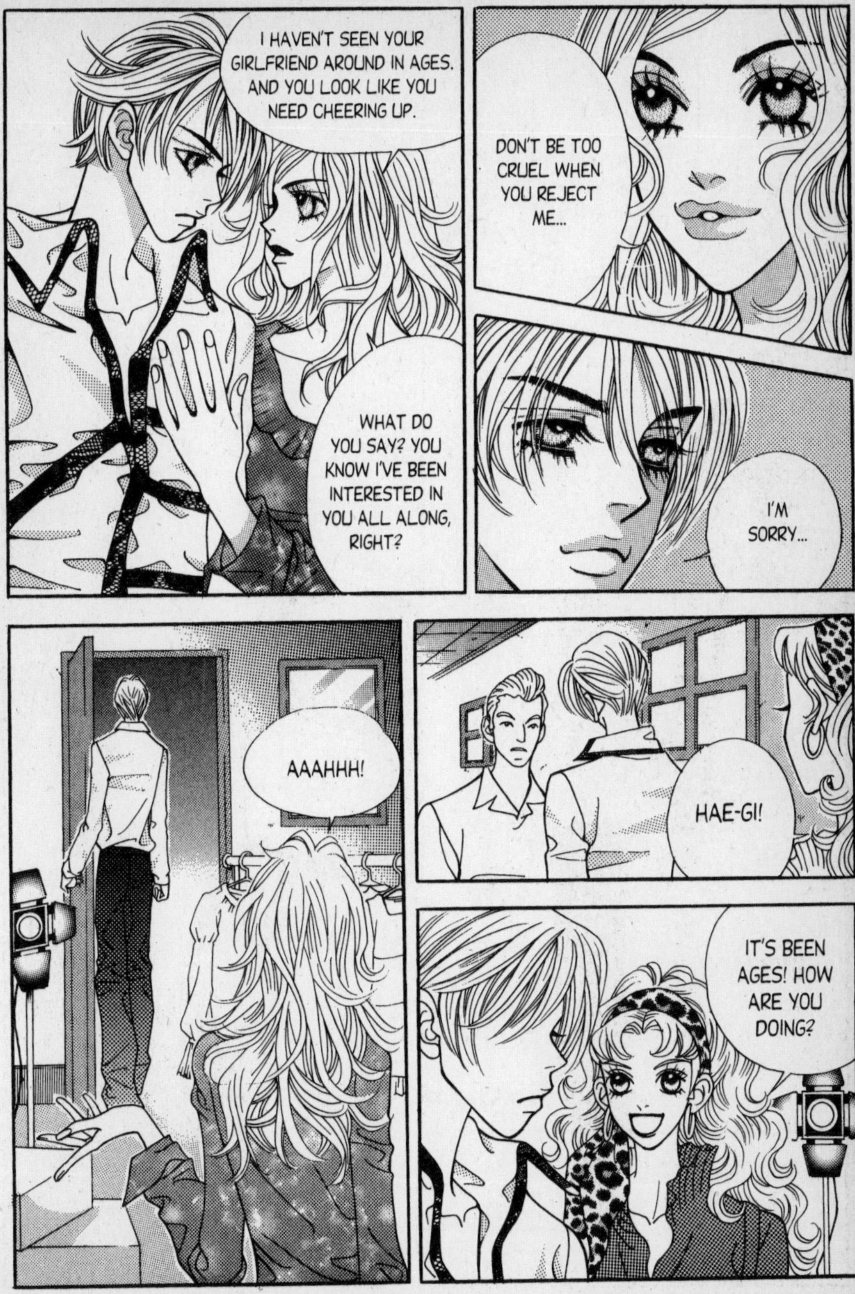
I HAVEN'T SEEN YOUR GIRLFRIEND AROUND IN AGES. AND YOU LOOK LIKE YOU NEED CHEERING UP.
WHAT DO YOU SAY? YOU KNOW I'VE BEEN INTERESTED IN YOU ALL ALONG, RIGHT?
DON'T BE TOO CRUEL WHEN YOU REJECT ME...
I'M SORRY...
AAAHHH!
HAE-GI!
IT'S BEEN AGES! HOW ARE YOU DOING?

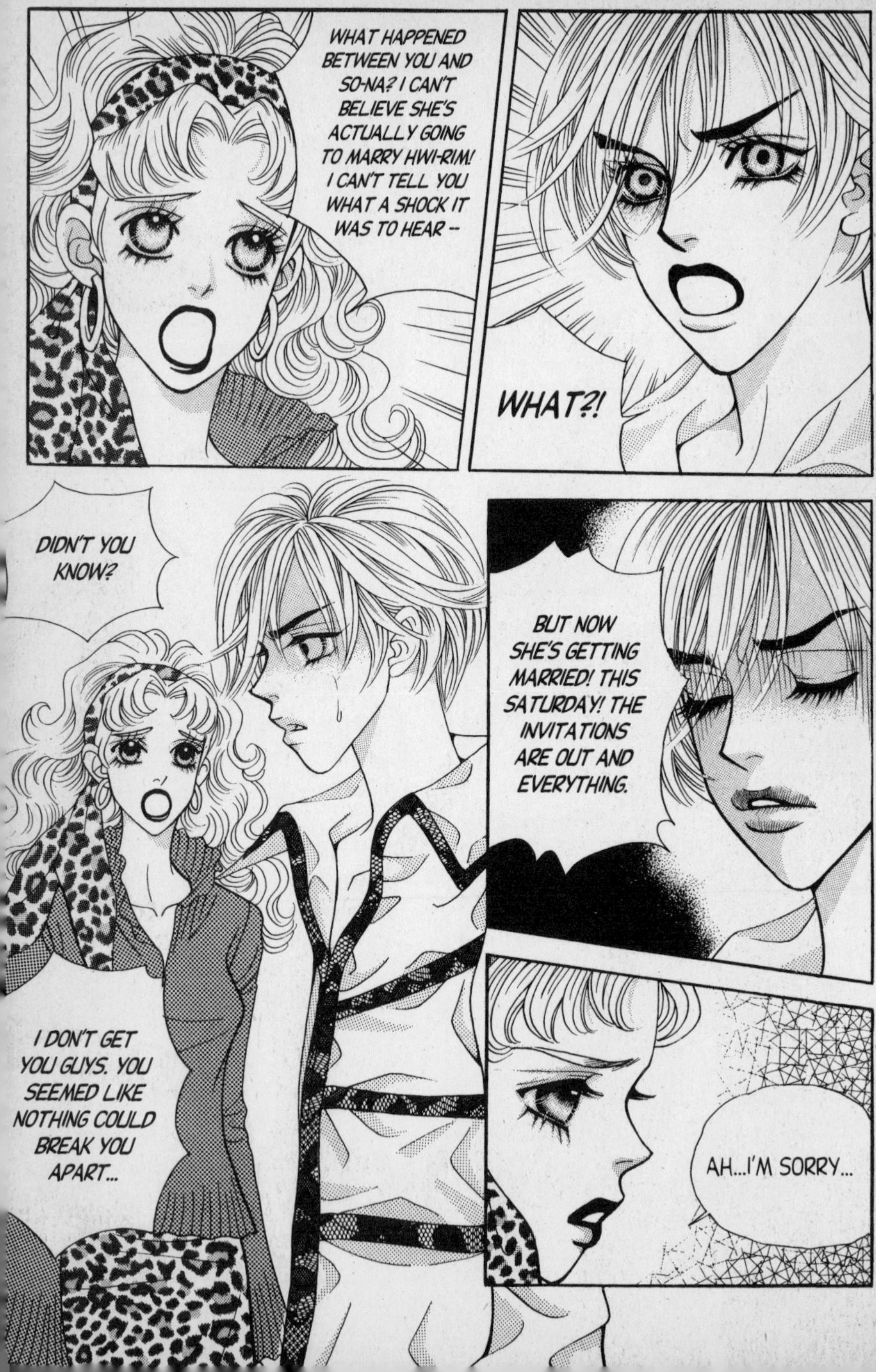
WHAT HAPPENED BETWEEN YOU AND SO-NA? I CAN'T BELIEVE SHE'S ACTUALLY GOING TO MARRY HWI-RIM! I CAN'T TELL YOU WHAT A SHOCK IT WAS TO HEAR --
WHAT?!
DIDN'T YOU KNOW?
I DON'T GET YOU GUYS. YOU SEEMED LIKE NOTHING COULD BREAK YOU APART...
BUT NOW SHE'S GETTING MARRIED! THIS SATURDAY! THE INVITATIONS ARE OUT AND EVERYTHING.
AH...I'M SORRY...

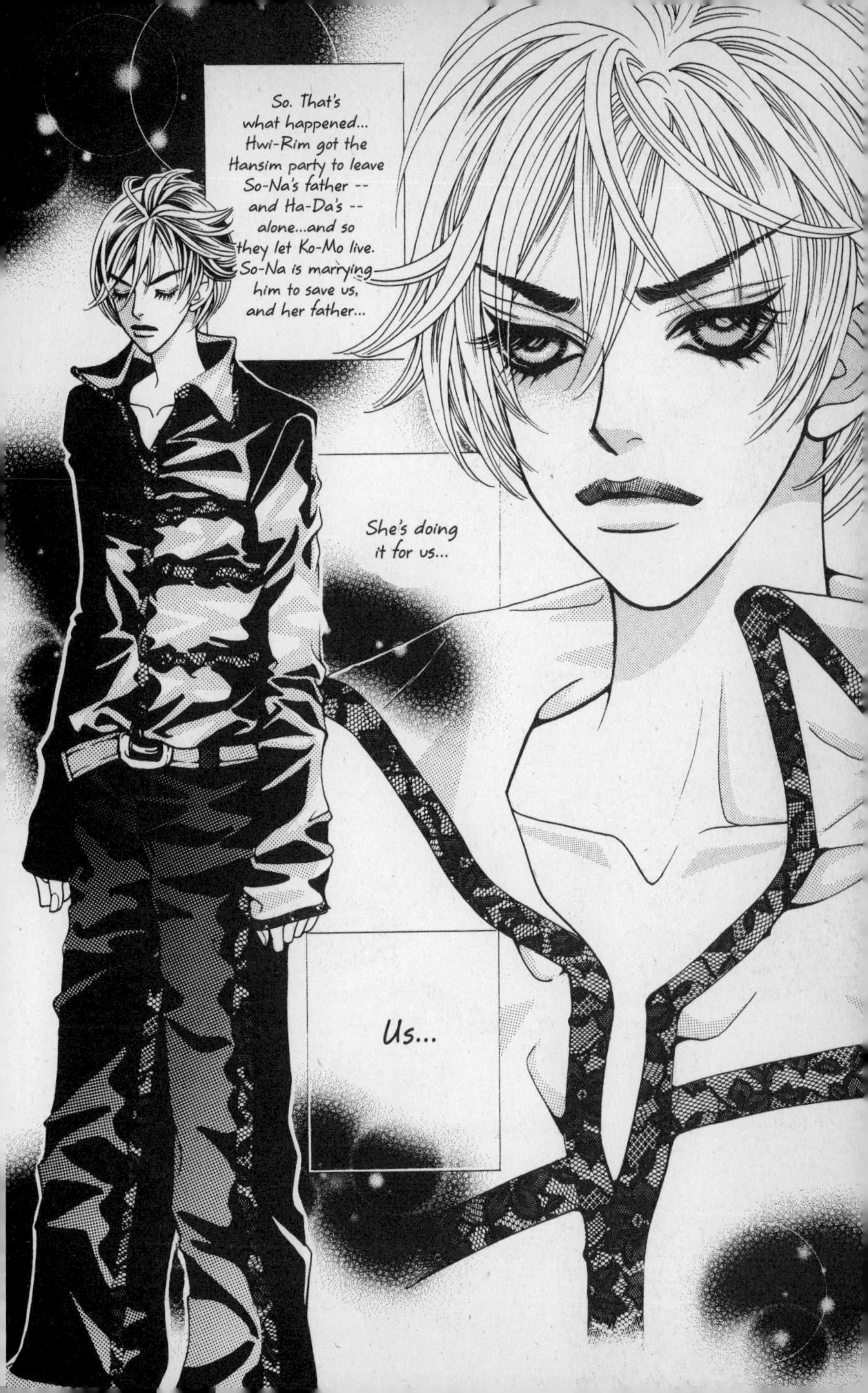
So. That's what happened... Hwi-Rim got the Hansim party to leave So-Na's father -- and Ha-Da's -- alone...and so they let Ko-Mo live. So-Na is marrying him to save us, and her father...
She's doing it for us...
Us...

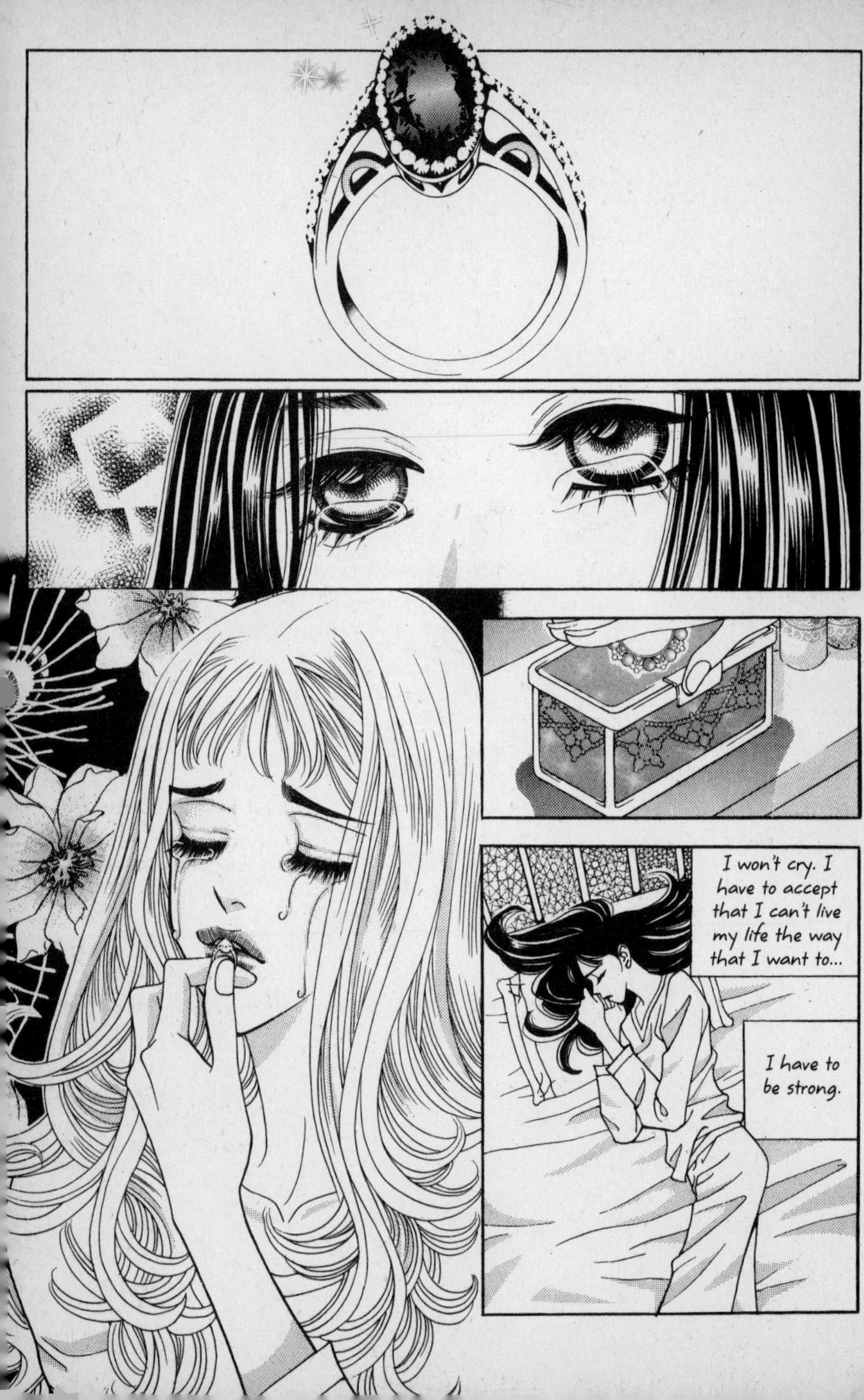
I won't cry. I have to accept that I can't live my life the way that I want to...
I have to be strong.

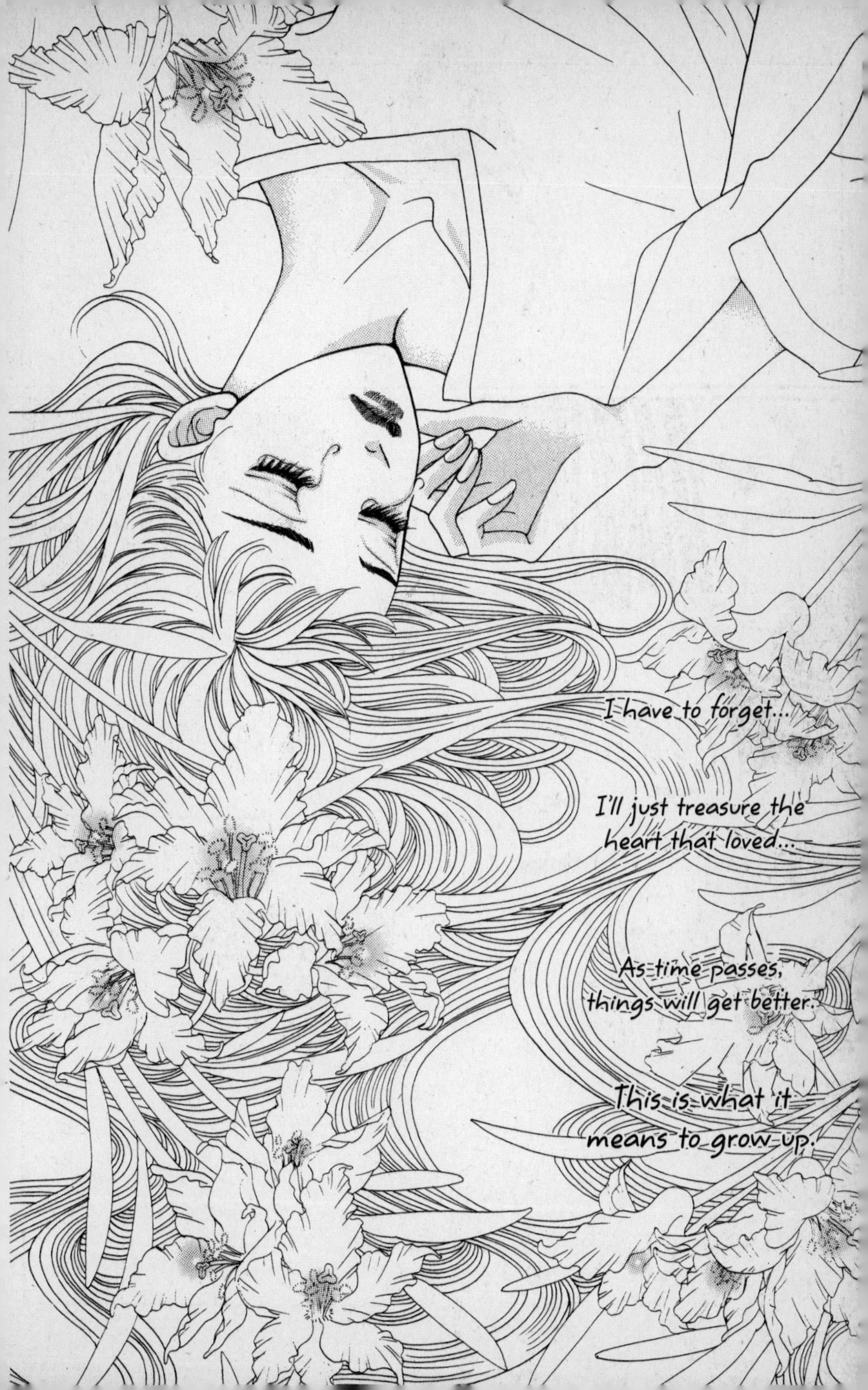
I have to forget...
I'll just treasure the heart that loved...
As time passes, things will get better.
This is what it means to grow up.

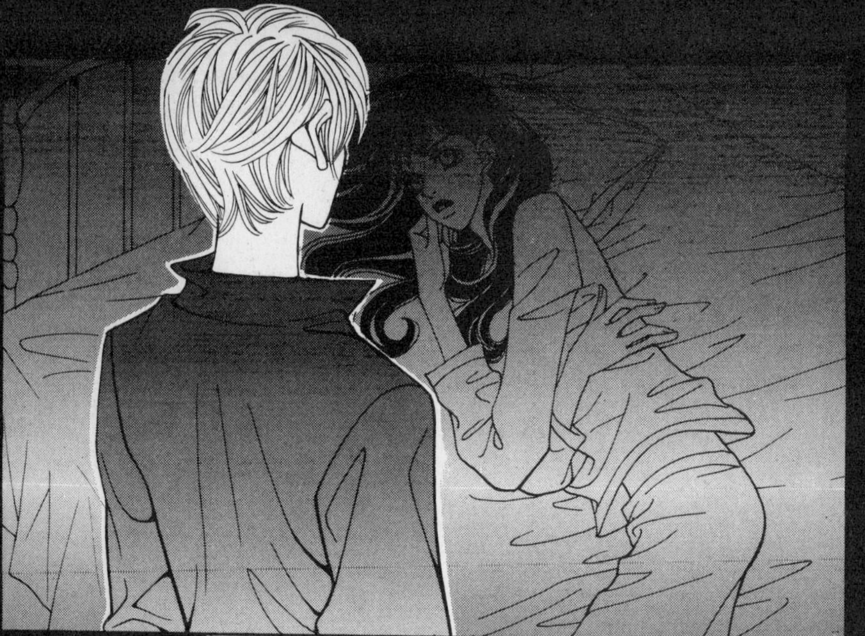
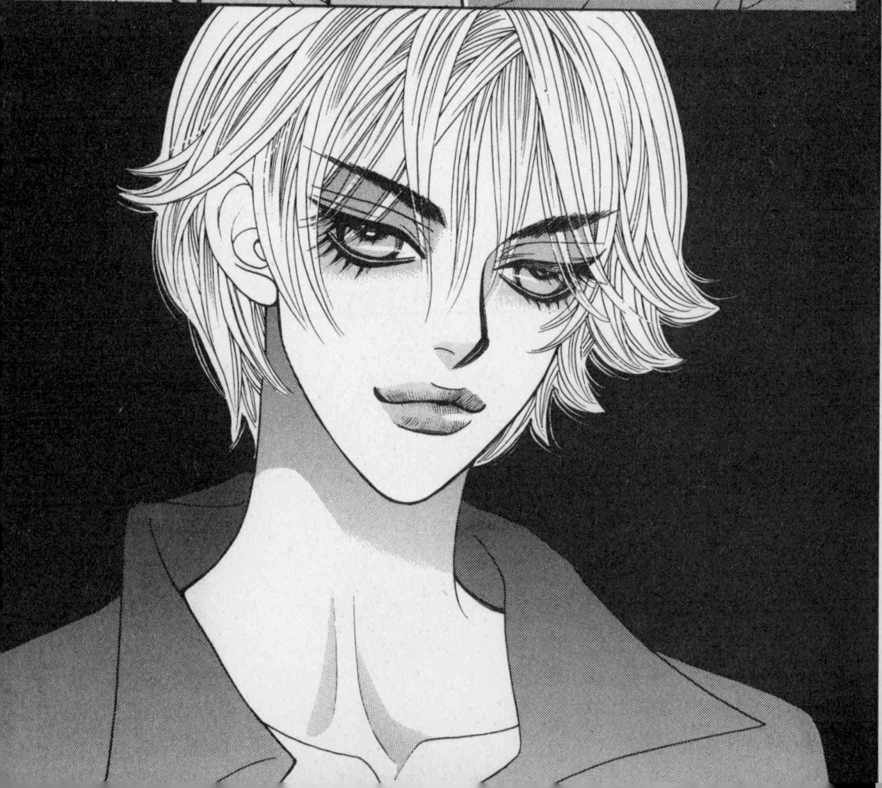

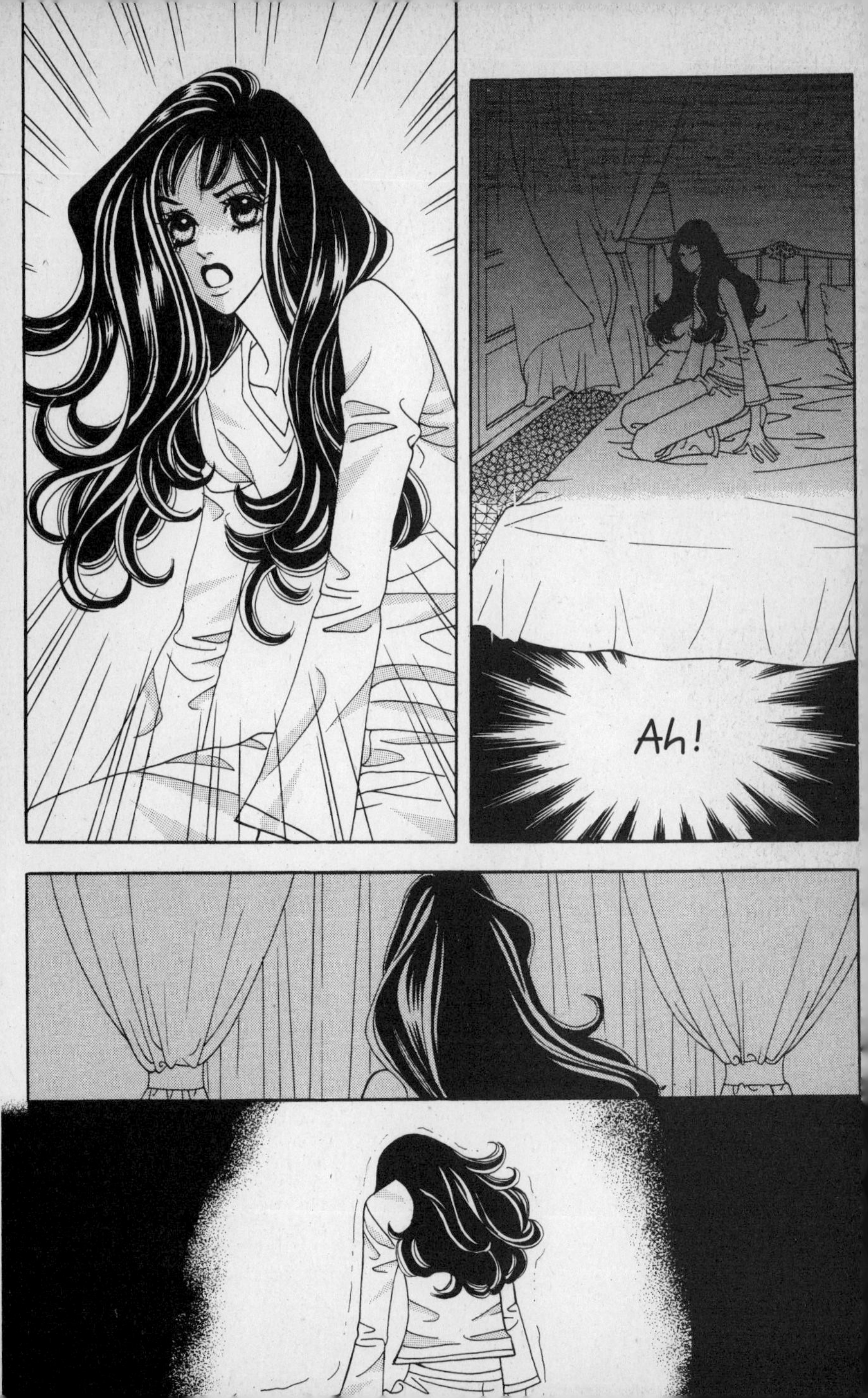
Ah!

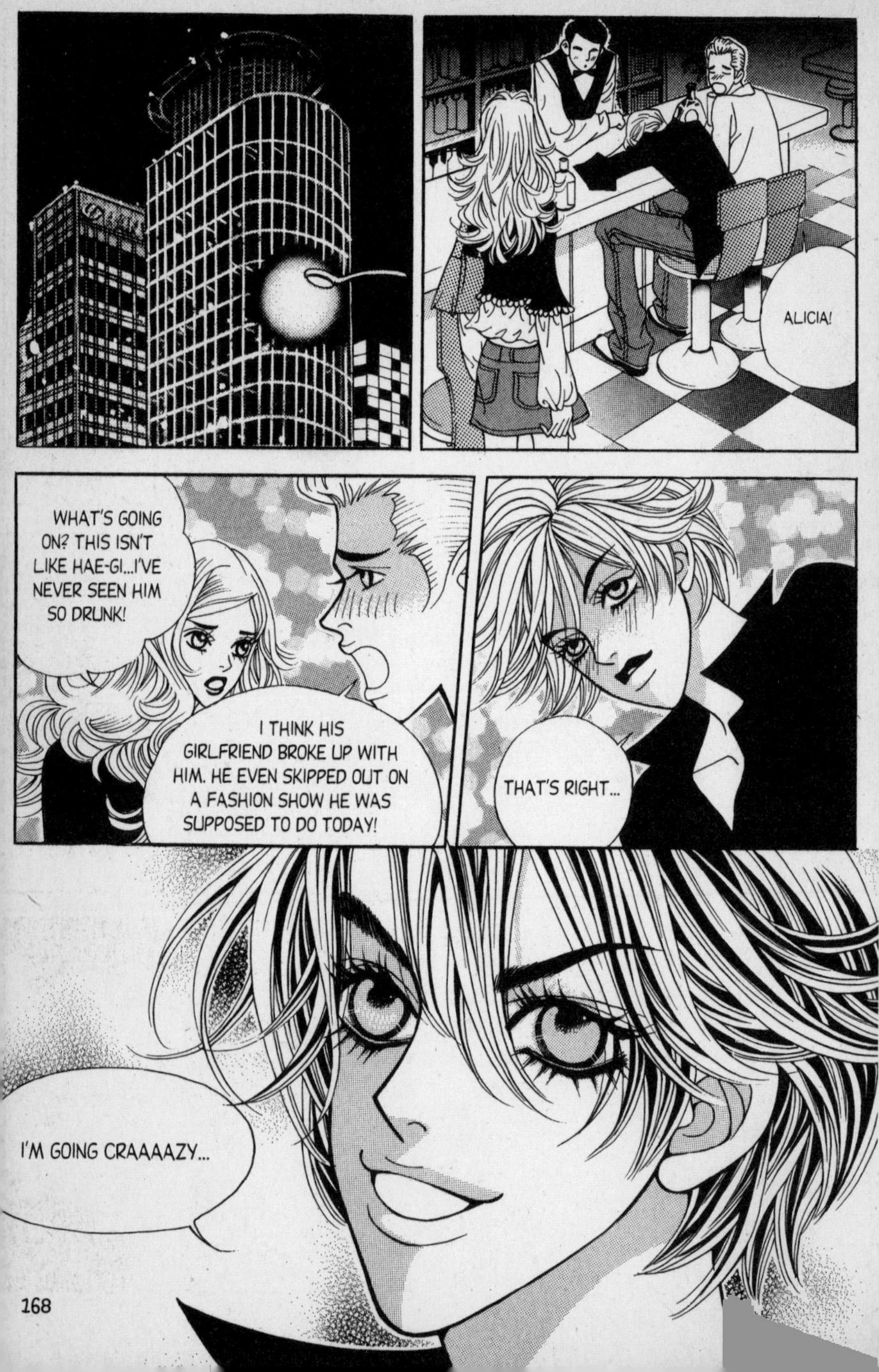
ALICIA!
WHAT'S GOING ON? THIS ISN'T LIKE HAE-GI...I'VE NEVER SEEN HIM SO DRUNK!
I THINK HIS GIRLFRIEND BROKE UP WITH HIM. HE EVEN SKIPPED OUT ON A FASHION SHOW HE WAS SUPPOSED TO DO TODAY!
THAT'S RIGHT...
I'M GOING CRAAAAZY...

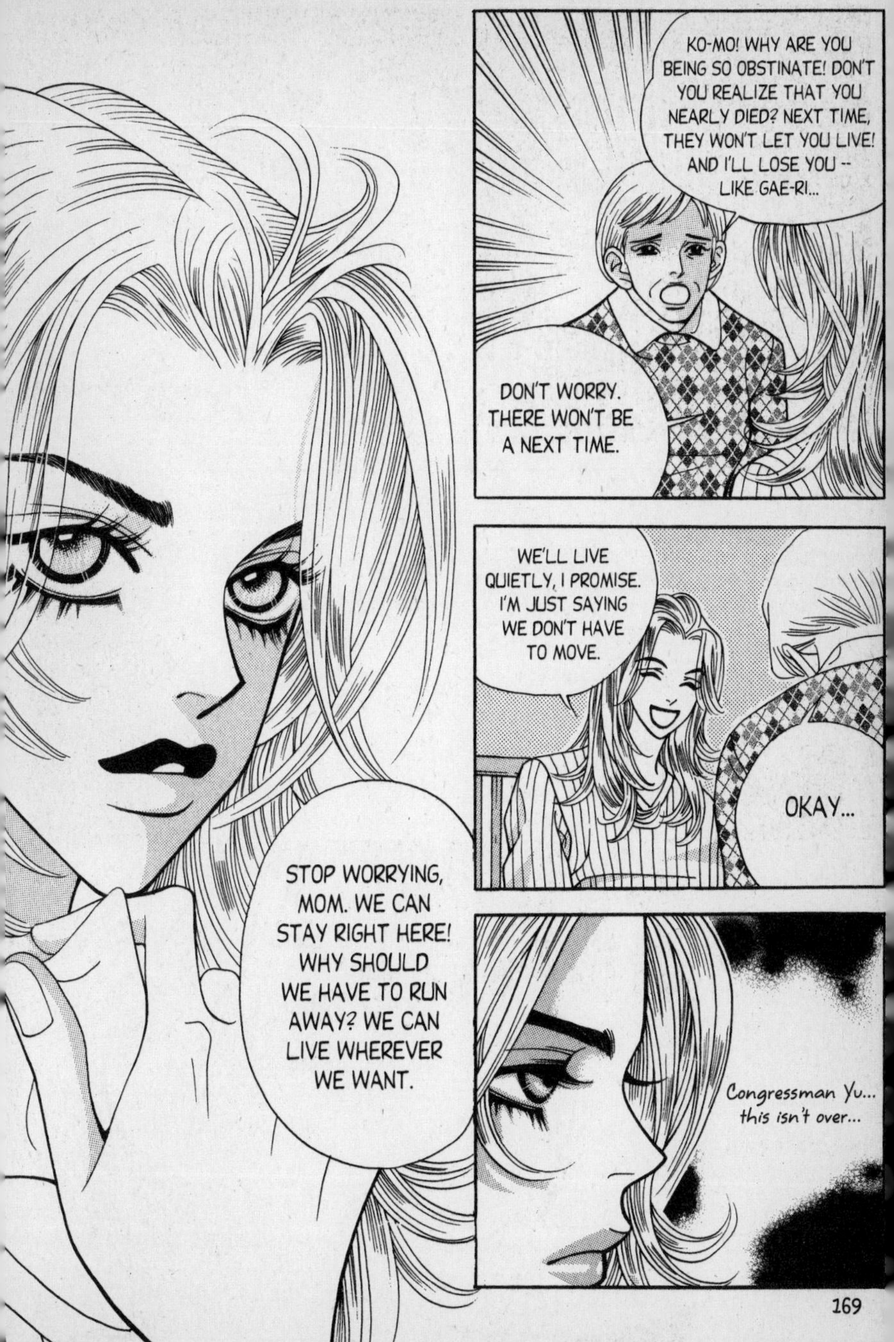
STOP WORRYING, MOM. WE CAN STAY RIGHT HERE! WHY SHOULD WE HAVE TO RUN AWAY? WE CAN LIVE WHEREVER WE WANT.
KO-MO! WHY ARE YOU BEING SO OBSTINATE! DON'T YOU REALIZE THAT YOU NEARLY DIED? NEXT TIME, THEY WON'T LET YOU LIVE! AND I'LL LOSE YOU -- LIKE GAE-RI...
DON'T WORRY. THERE WON'T BE A NEXT TIME.
WE'LL LIVE QUIETLY, I PROMISE. I'M JUST SAYING WE DON'T HAVE TO MOVE.
OKAY...
Congressman Yu... this isn't over...

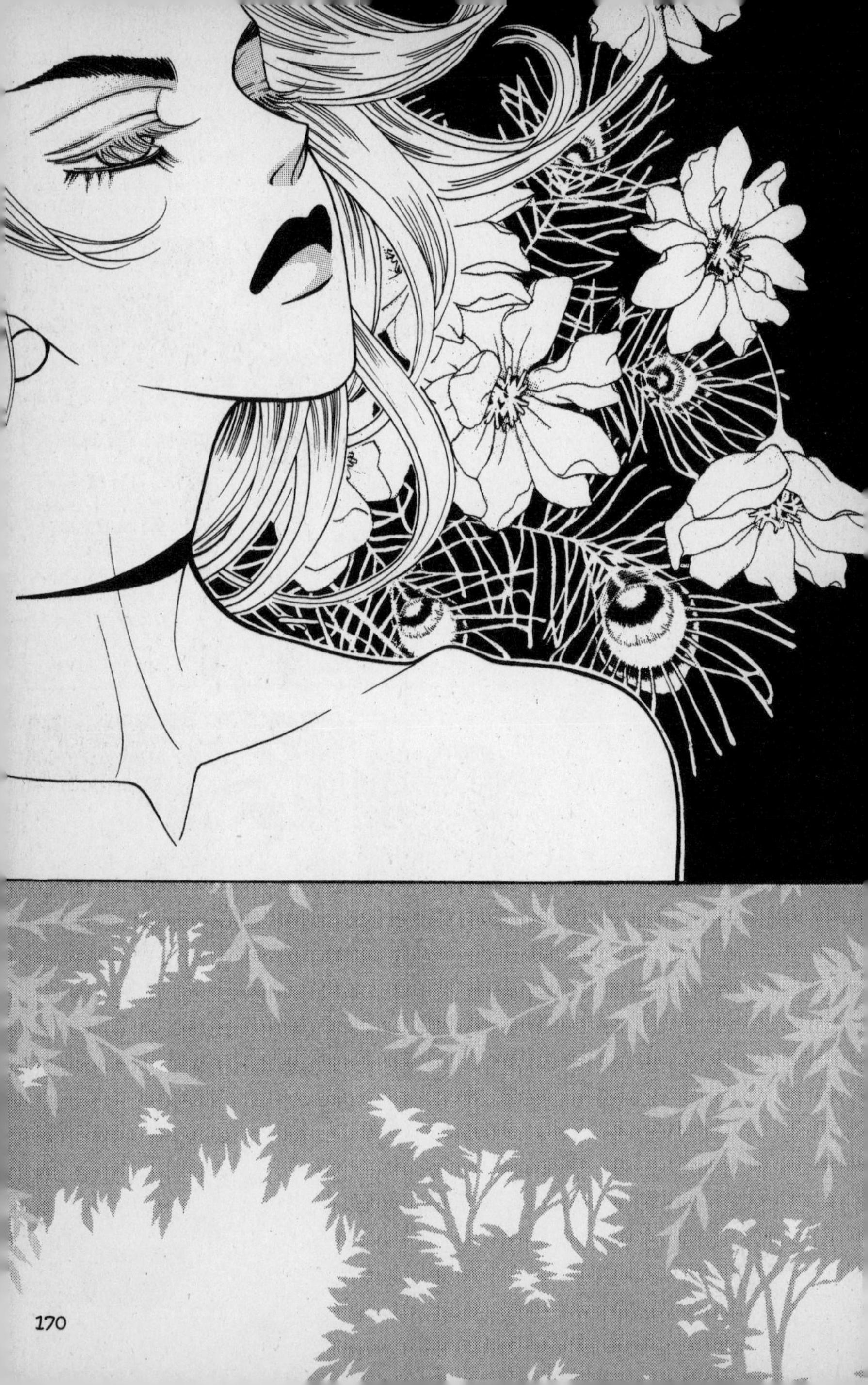

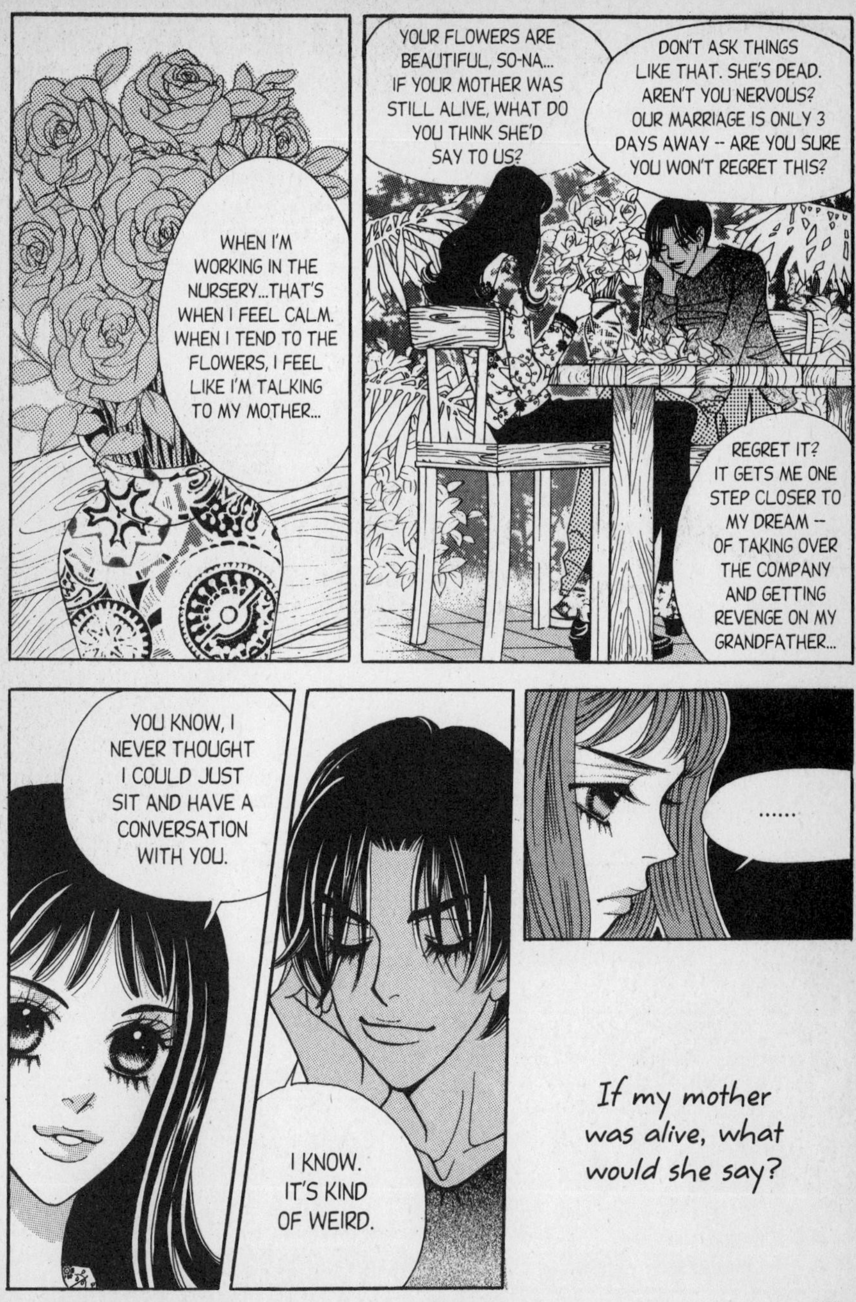
WHEN I'M WORKING IN THE NURSERY...THAT'S WHEN I FEEL CALM. WHEN I TEND TO THE FLOWERS, I FEEL LIKE I'M TALKING TO MY MOTHER...
YOUR FLOWERS ARE BEAUTIFUL, SO-NA... IF YOUR MOTHER WAS STILL ALIVE, WHAT DO YOU THINK SHE'D SAY TO US?
DON'T ASK THINGS LIKE THAT. SHE'S DEAD. AREN'T YOU NERVOUS? OUR MARRIAGE IS ONLY 3 DAYS AWAY -- ARE YOU SURE YOU WON'T REGRET THIS?
REGRET IT? IT GETS ME ONE STEP CLOSER TO MY DREAM -- OF TAKING OVER THE COMPANY AND GETTING REVENGE ON MY GRANDFATHER...
YOU KNOW, I NEVER THOUGHT I COULD JUST SIT AND HAVE A CONVERSATION WITH YOU.
I KNOW. IT'S KIND OF WEIRD.
......
If my mother was alive, what would she say?

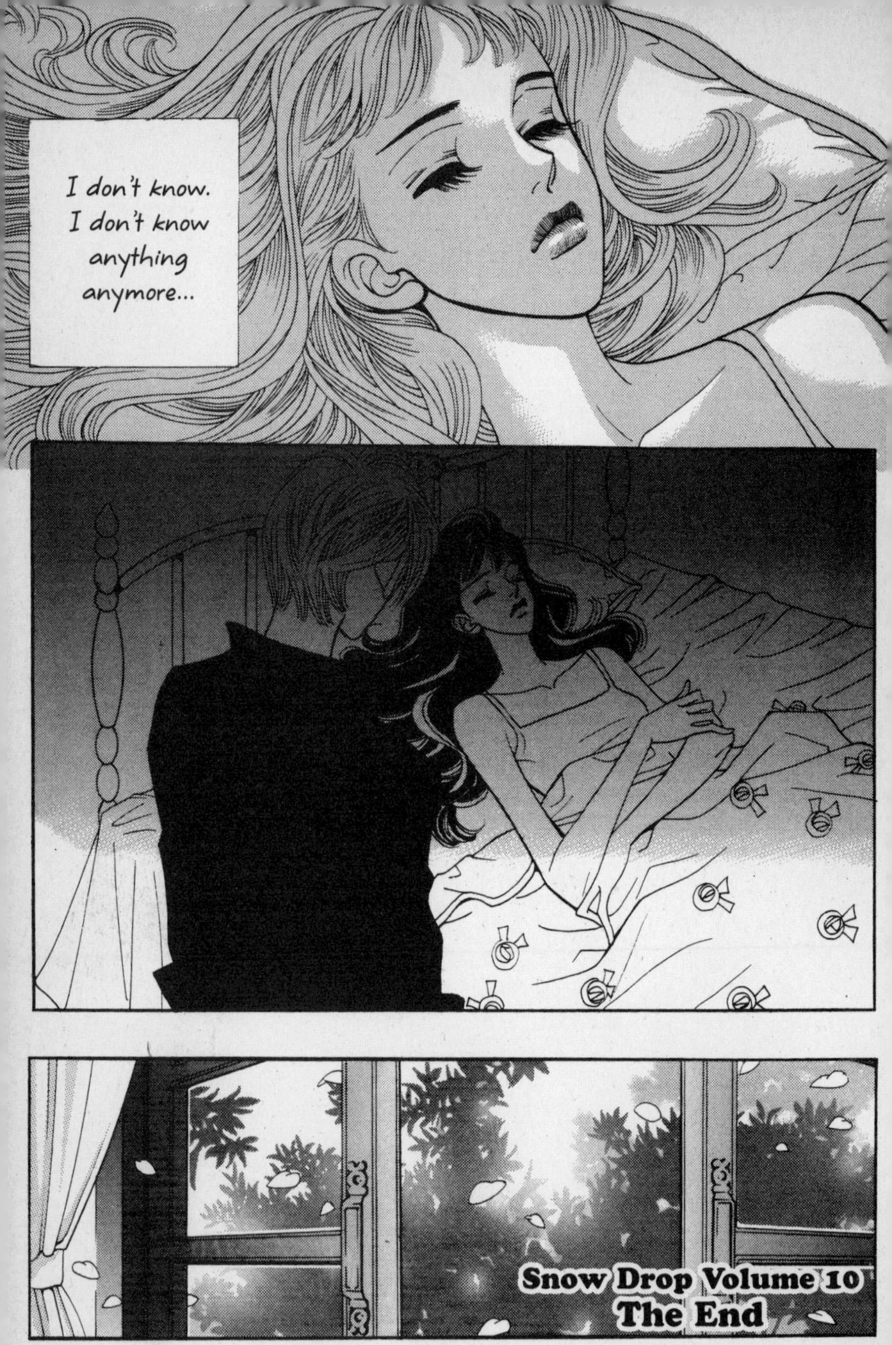
I don't know. I don't know anything anymore...
Snow Drop Volume 10
The End

Coming Soon

Snow Drop

Volume Eleven

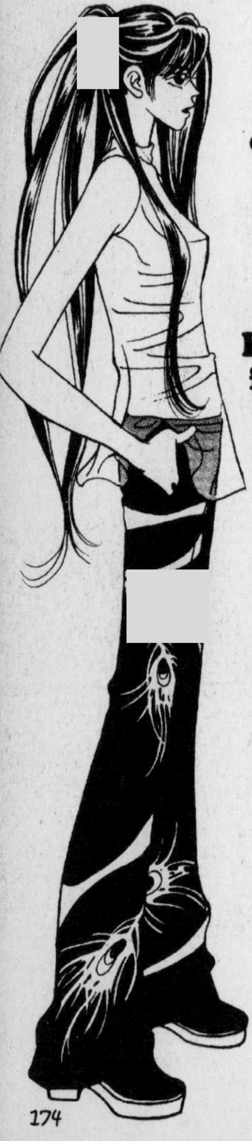

Hae-Gi and So-Na just cannot be apart and they decide to fight hard to keep their relationship together. However just as they redouble their resolve, a knife wielding Ko-Mo breaks into So-Na's father's room demanding an apology. Somehow, Ko-Mo's mother appears and falls to her knees pleading with him to stop. Although Ko-Mo-- who can't bear to see his mother on her knees-- removes his knife from So-Na's father's throat, two people none-the-less end up in the hospital.

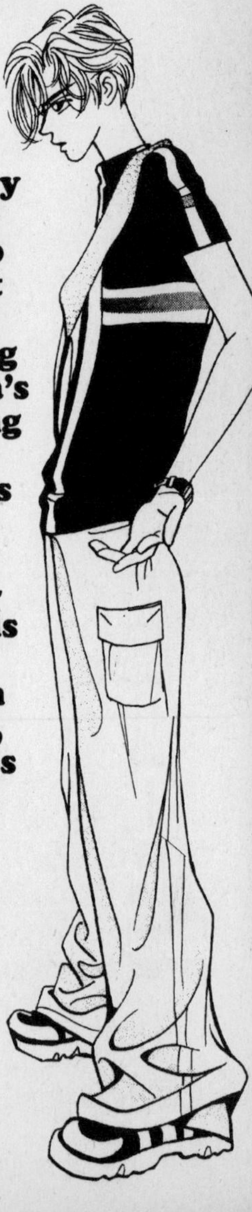

Drop in for
SNOW DROP Volume 11

OT
OLDER TEEN
AGE 16+

In the deep South, an ancient voodoo curse unleashes the War on Flesh—a hellish plague of voracious Ew Chott hornets that raises an army of the walking dead. This undead army spreads the plague by ripping the hearts out of living creatures to make room for a Black Heart hive, all in preparation for the most awesome incarnation of evil ever imagined… An unlikely group of five mis-matched individuals have to put their differences aside to try to destroy the onslaught of evil before it's too late.

VOODOO MAKES A MAN NASTY!

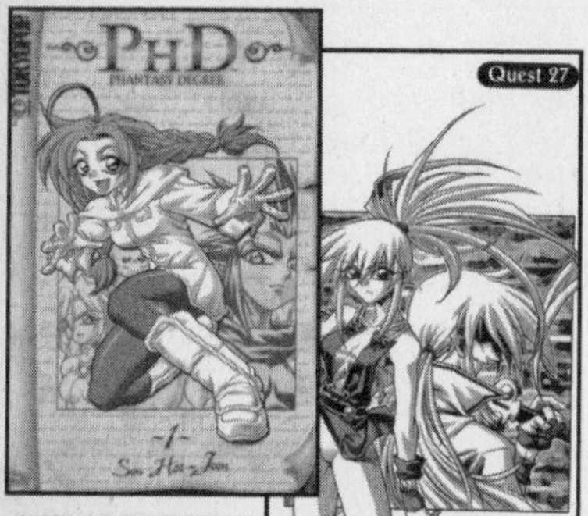
PhD
PHANTASY DEGREE
TOKYOPOP
Quest 27
~1~
Son Hee-Joon

CHECK OUT THE CREATOR'S *iD_eNTITY*

BY SON HEE-JOON

PhD: PHANTASY DEGREE

So you think you've got it rough at *your* school? Try attending classes at Demon School Hades! When sassy, young Sang makes her monster matriculation to this arcane academy, all hell breaks loose—literally! But what would you expect when the graduating class consists of a werewolf, a mummy and demons by the score? Son Hee-Joon's underworld adventure is pure escapist fun. Always packed with action and often silly in the best sense, *PhD* never takes itself too seriously or lets the reader stop to catch his breath.

~Bryce P. Coleman, Editor

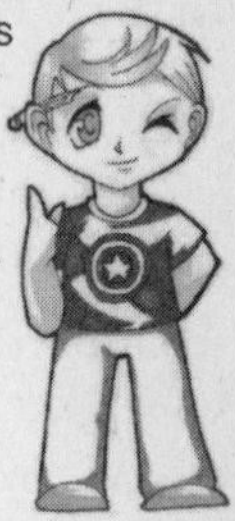

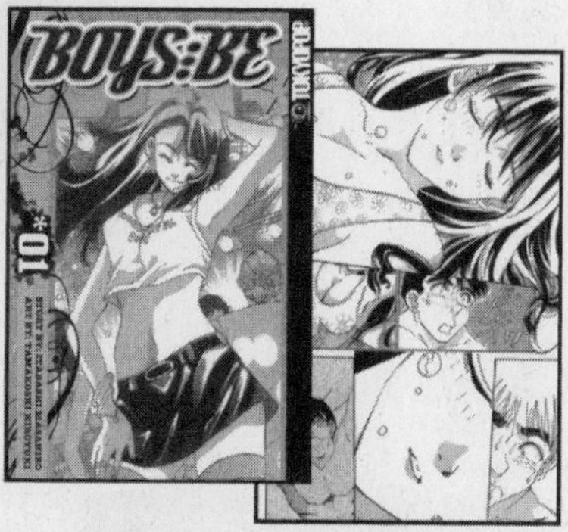
BOYS BE
TOKYOPOP
01

BY MASAHIRO ITABASHI & HIROYUKI TAMAKOSHI

BOYS BE...

Boys Be... is a series of short stories. But although the hero's name changes from tale to tale, he remains Everyboy—that dorky high school guy who'll do anything to score with the girl of his dreams. You know him. Perhaps you *are* him. He is a dirty mind with the soul of a poet, a stumblebum with a heart of sterling. We follow this guy on quest after quest to woo his lady loves. We savor his victory; we reel with his defeat...and the experience is touching, funny and above all human.

Still not convinced? I have two words for you: fan service.

~Carol Fox, Editor

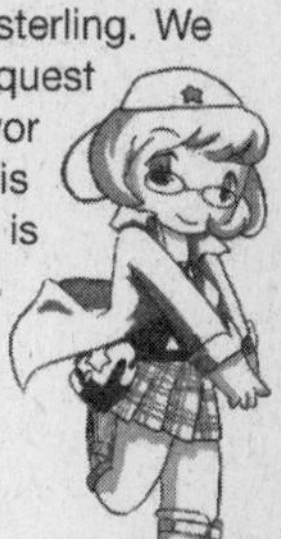

EDITORS' PICKS

TOKYOPOP MANGA SUPPLEMENT

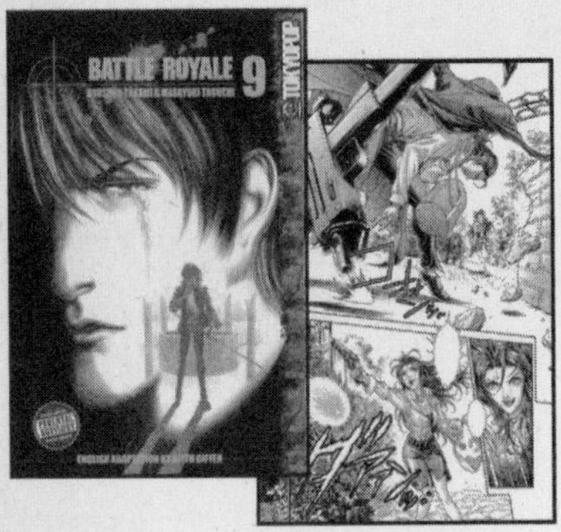
BATTLE ROYALE 9
TOKYOPOP

BY KOUSHUN TAKAMI & MASAYUKI TAGUCHI

BATTLE ROYALE

As far as cautionary tales go, you couldn't get any timelier than *Battle Royale*. Telling the bleak story of a class of middle school students who are forced to fight one another to the death on national television, Koushun Takami and Masayuki Taguchi have created a dark satire that's sickening, yet undeniably exciting as well. And if we have that reaction reading it, it becomes alarmingly clear how the students could be so easily swayed into *doing* it.

~Tim Beedle, Editor

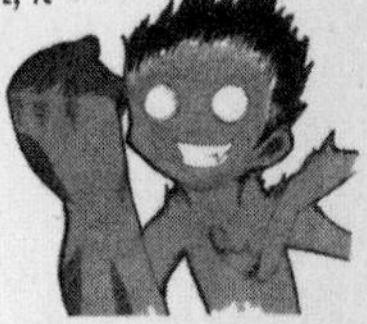

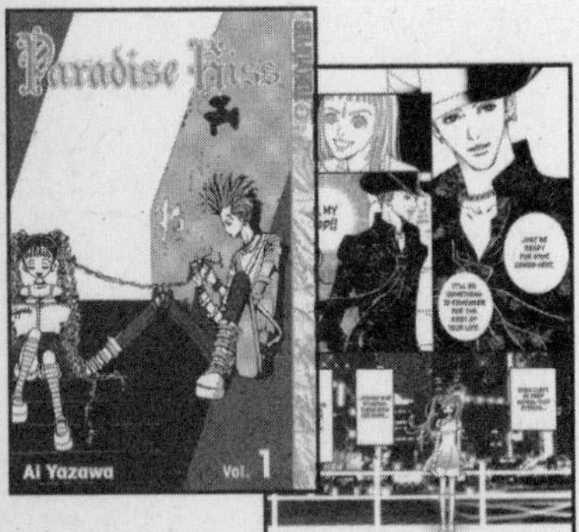
Paradise Kiss
Ai Yazawa
Vol. 1

BY AI YAZAWA

PARADISE KISS

The clothes! The romance! The clothes! The intrigue! And did I mention the clothes?! *Paradise Kiss* is the best fashion manga ever written, from one of the hottest shojo artists in Japan. Ai Yazawa is the coolest. Not only did she create the character designs for *Princess Ai*, which were amazing, but she also produced five fab volumes of *Paradise Kiss*, a manga series bursting with fashion and passion. Read it and be inspired.

~Julie Taylor, Sr. Editor

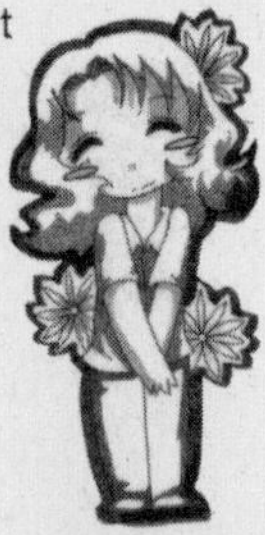

SHOWCASE TOKYOPOP MANGA SUPPLEMENT

RIZELMINE
BY YUKIRU SUGISAKI

Tomonori Iwaki is a hapless fifteen-year-old whose life is turned upside down when the government announces that he's a married man! His blushing bride is Rizel, apparently the adorable product of an experiment. She does her best to win her new man's heart in this wacky romantic comedy from the creator of *D•N•Angel*!

Inspiration for the hit anime!

© YUKIRU SUGISAKI / KADOKAWA SHOTEN.

HONEY MUSTARD
BY HO-KYUNG YEO

When Ara works up the nerve to ask out the guy she has a crush on, she ends up kissing the wrong boy! The juicy smooch is witnessed by the school's puritanical chaperone, who tells their strict families. With everyone in an uproar, the only way everyone will be appeased is if the two get married—and have kids!

© Ho-Kyung Yeo, HAKSAN PUBLISHING CO., LTD.

HEAT GUY J
BY CHIAKI OGISHIMA, KAZUKI AKANE, NOBUTERU YUKI & SATELIGHT

Daisuke Aurora and his android partner, Heat Guy J, work with a special division of peacekeepers to keep anything illegal off the streets. However, that doesn't sit too well with the new ruthless and well-armed mob leader. In the city that never sleeps, will Daisuke and Heat Guy J end up sleeping with the fishes?

The anime favorite as seen on MTV is now an action-packed manga!

© Satelight/Heatguy-J Project.

TOKYOPOP SHOP

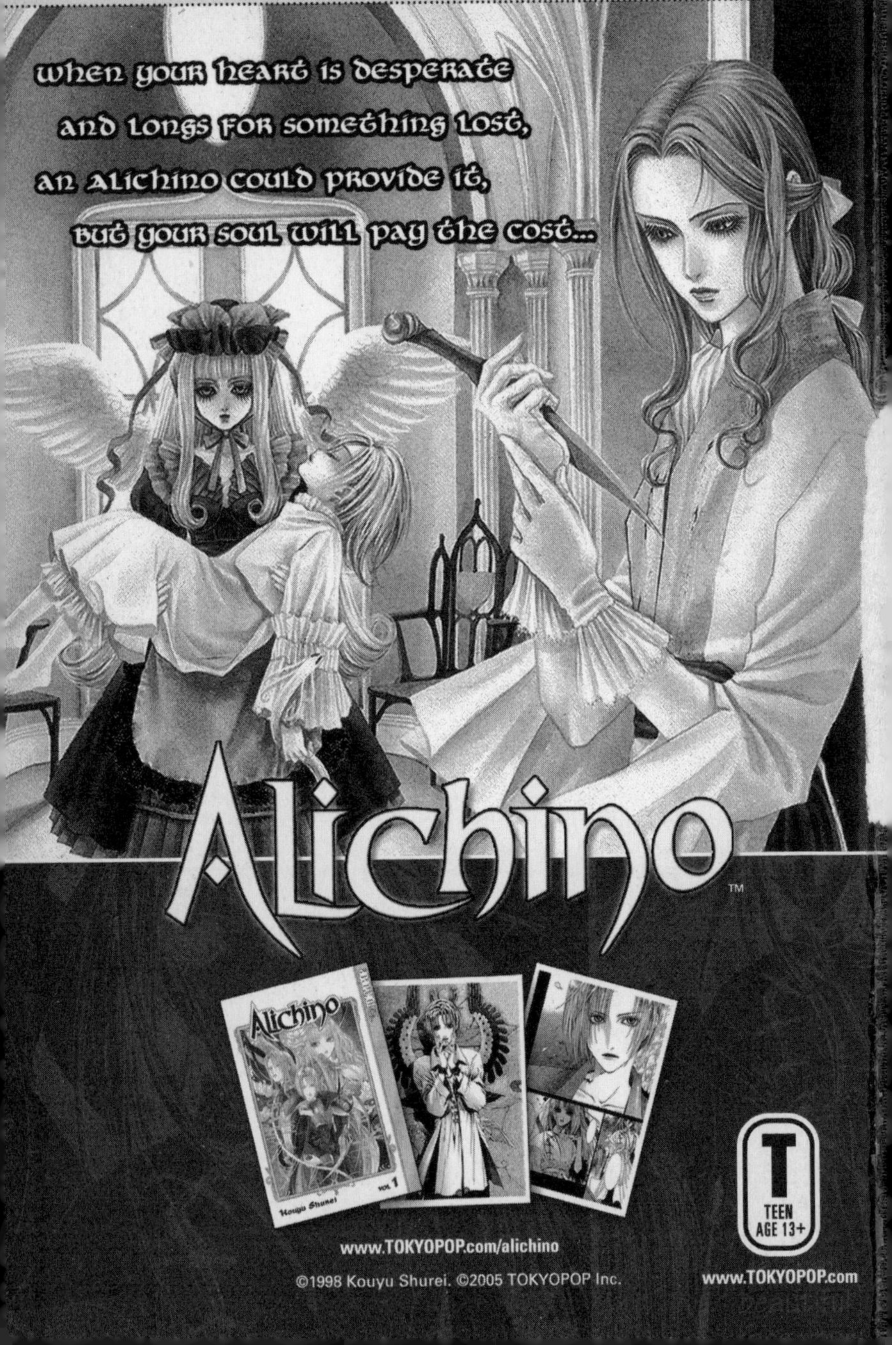

When your heart is desperate
and longs for something lost,
an Alichino could provide it,
but your soul will pay the cost...
Alichino™
Alichino
VOL 1
Kouyu Shurei
T
TEEN
AGE 13+
www.TOKYOPOP.com/alichino
©1998 Kouyu Shurei. ©2005 TOKYOPOP Inc.
www.TOKYOPOP.com